COMPUTERS IN SOCIETY

FOURTH EDITION

Editor

Kathryn Schellenberg
University of Guelph

Kathryn Schellenberg received her Ph.D. in sociology from the University of Utah and is presently assistant professor of sociology at the University of Guelph in Ontario, Canada. One of her areas of scholarly interest is the social impact of technology, especially computing, and she has taught several sociology courses dealing with this subject. Ms. Schellenberg has also conducted several studies on computer-related topics, and her current research centers on organizational and labor implications of very complex industrial automation systems.

Annual Editions
A Library of Information from the Public Press

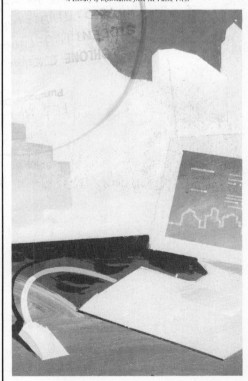

Cover illustration by Mike Eagle

The Dushkin Publishing Group, Inc.
Sluice Dock, Guilford, Connecticut 06437

The Annual Editions Series

Annual Editions is a series of over 55 volumes designed to provide the reader with convenient, low-cost access to a wide range of current, carefully selected articles from some of the most important magazines, newspapers, and journals published today. Annual Editions are updated on an annual basis through a continuous monitoring of over 300 periodical sources. All Annual Editions have a number of features designed to make them particularly useful, including topic guides, annotated tables of contents, unit overviews, and indexes. For the teacher using Annual Editions in the classroom, an Instructor's Resource Guide with test questions is available for each volume.

VOLUMES AVAILABLE

Africa
Aging
American Government
American History, Pre-Civil War
American History, Post-Civil War
Anthropology
Biological Anthropology
Biology
Business and Management
Business Ethics
Canadian Politics
China
Comparative Politics
Computers in Education
Computers in Business
Computers in Society
Criminal Justice
Drugs, Society, and Behavior
Early Childhood Education
Economics
Educating Exceptional Children
Education
Educational Psychology
Environment
Geography
Global Issues
Health
Human Development
Human Resources
Human Sexuality
International Business

Japan
Latin America
Life Management
Macroeconomics
Management
Marketing
Marriage and Family
Microeconomics
Middle East and the Islamic World
Money and Banking
Nutrition
Personal Growth and Behavior
Psychology
Public Administration
Race and Ethnic Relations
Social Problems
Sociology
Soviet Union and Eastern Europe
State and Local Government
Third World
Urban Society
Violence and Terrorism
Western Civilization,
   Pre-Reformation
Western Civilization,
   Post-Reformation
Western Europe
World History, Pre-Modern
World History, Modern
World Politics

Library of Congress Cataloging in Publication Data
Main entry under title: Computer Studies: Computers in Society. 4/E.
"An Annual Edition Publication."
   1. Computers and civilization—Periodicals. 2. Computers—Periodicals. I. Schellenberg, Kathryn, *comp.* II. Title: Computers in society.
ISBN 1-56134-070-7   303.4'834

Fourth Edition

Manufactured by The Banta Company, Harrisonburg, Virginia 22801

Editors/ Advisory Board

EDITOR

Kathryn Schellenberg
University of Guelph

ADVISORY BOARD

Virginia Anderson
University of North Dakota

Darryl Gibson
DePauw University

John Giglia
SUNY, Stony Brook

John Hansen
Central Michigan University

Allen Henry
Susquehanna University

Gene Kozminski
Aquinas College

Martin L. Levin
Emory University

Frank Naughton
Kean College of New Jersey

Christopher Roda
Thomas College

Kirby Throckmorton
University of Wisconsin
Stevens Point

Lawrence Turner, Jr.
Andrews University

Norman E. Wright
Brigham Young University

STAFF

Ian A. Nielsen, Publisher
Brenda S. Filley, Production Manager
Roberta Monaco, Editor
Addie Raucci, Administrative Editor
Cheryl Nicholas, Permissions Editor
Diane Barker, Editorial Assistant
Lisa Holmes-Doebrick, Administrative Coordinator
Charles Vitelli, Designer
Shawn Callahan, Graphics
Meredith Scheld, Graphics
Libra A. Cusack, Typesetting Supervisor
Juliana Arbo, Typesetter

To the Reader

In publishing ANNUAL EDITIONS we recognize the enormous role played by the magazines, newspapers, and journals of the *public press* in providing current, first-rate educational information in a broad spectrum of interest areas. Within the articles, the best scientists, practitioners, researchers, and commentators draw issues into new perspective as accepted theories and viewpoints are called into account by new events, recent discoveries change old facts, and fresh debate breaks out over important controversies. Many of the articles resulting from this enormous editorial effort are appropriate for students, researchers, and professionals seeking accurate, current material to help bridge the gap between principles and theories and the real world. These articles, however, become more useful for study when those of lasting value are carefully *collected, organized, indexed,* and *reproduced* in a *low-cost format*, which provides easy and permanent access when the material is needed. That is the role played by *Annual Editions*. Under the direction of each volume's *Editor*, who is an expert in the subject area, and with the guidance of an *Advisory Board*, we seek each year to provide in each *ANNUAL EDITION* a current, well-balanced, carefully selected collection of the best of the public press for your study and enjoyment. We think you'll find this volume useful, and we hope you'll take a moment to let us know what you think.

We can only guess at how the ever increasing power, diversity, and pervasiveness of computers and other information technologies might affect the patterns of our individual and social lives. However, it is hoped that *Computers in Society* will complement students' technical understanding of computers by acquainting them with the philosophical, economic, political, social, and psychological dimensions of the so-called computer revolution.

Contributors to the fourth edition come from a highly diverse range of backgrounds. Their collective writings highlight a wide spectrum of issues and views about how the information age will or ought to unfold. For the most part, their writing styles are very understandable and require no special training in "computerese"— the unintelligible technical jargon that can be a barrier to becoming informed on computer issues. A glossary is included, however, for the few terms that may be unfamiliar.

Because of its social focus, this book is organized to reflect the major dimensions of society rather than various aspects of computing. The major themes of the book are economy, community, and conflict. Many of these themes are also examined in an international context. The final section looks at some of the philosophical challenges posed by emerging technologies.

Each reading has been selected for its informational value, but "informative" does not, in this case, necessarily imply correctness or validity. In fact, some articles are included simply because they offer an opposing view to that argued by another. *Computers in Society* is meant to generate rather than answer questions on how computers will affect society. Hopefully, such queries will serve to clarify issues, broaden perspectives, provoke curiosity, and stimulate informed discussion of and participation in the computer age.

Readers can have input into the next edition by completing and returning the article rating form in the back of the book.

Kathryn Schellenberg

Kathryn Schellenberg
Editor

Contents

Introduction

Unit 1

The Changing Economy

Five articles examine issues related to developments in robotics, computer networking, the globalization of the economy, the rise of the service and information sectors, and the decline of North American manufacturing.

The concepts in bold italics are developed in the article. For further expansion please refer to the Topic Guide, the Index, and the Glossary.

Unit 2

Employment and the Workplace

Four articles examine the changing skill requirements of the work force, the electronic surveillance of workers, telecommuting, and the "do it yourself" trend.

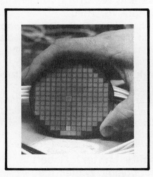

Unit 3

Social Interaction and Participation in the Information Age

Seven articles examine present and future implications of computing and other technologies for participation in social, economic, and political life.

The concepts in bold italics are developed in the article. For further expansion please refer to the Topic Guide, the Index, and the Glossary.

Unit
4

Ethical and Legal Issues

Seven articles look at various ethical and legal computing issues including information distortion, intellectual property rights, computer viruses, and the civil liberties of persons under investigation for alleged computer crimes.

The concepts in bold italics are developed in the article. For further expansion please refer to the Topic Guide, the Index, and the Glossary.

Unit 5

Individual Privacy in the Information Age

Six articles discuss threats to individual privacy, especially those posed by the existence of large electronic data bases. Some legal and technical means of protecting privacy are also reviewed.

The concepts in bold italics are developed in the article. For further expansion please refer to the Topic Guide, the Index, and the Glossary.

Unit
6

Computer System Reliability and Safety

Five articles examine potential dangers posed by electromagnetic fields and the implications of society's reliance on computer systems. Difficulties in producing reliable software are reviewed with emphasis on commercial, military, and medical applications. Recommendations for improving safety and reliability are also offered.

The concepts in bold italics are developed in the article. For further expansion please refer to the Topic Guide, the Index, and the Glossary.

Unit 7

Issues From the International Scene

Five articles examine issues related to computing in several nations, the technological and information gap between rich and poor nations, international competitiveness, and the global economy.

Unit 8

Philosophical Frontiers

Seven articles consider how new moral and philosophical challenges may arise at the cutting edge of technological achievements. The unit also examines a variety of ways computers might affect the way we perceive human nature.

The concepts in bold italics are developed in the article. For further expansion please refer to the Topic Guide, the Index, and the Glossary.

The concepts in bold italics are developed in the article. For further expansion please refer to the Topic Guide, the Index, and the Glossary.

Topic Guide

This topic guide suggests how the selections in this book relate to topics of traditional concern to students and professionals involved with computers in society. It can be very useful in locating articles that relate to each other for reading and research. The guide is arranged alphabetically according to topic. Articles may, of course, treat topics that do not appear in the topic guide. In turn, entries in the topic guide do not necessarily constitute a comprehensive listing of all the contents of each selection.

TOPIC AREA	TREATED IN:	TOPIC AREA	TREATED IN:
Intellectual Property	21. Software Patents 22. Programs to the People 25. Closing the Net	**National Security**	5. Does Corporate Nationality Matter?
International Relations	5. Does Corporate Nationality Matter? 6. Myth of a Post-Industrial Economy 37. Personal Computers and the World Software Market 38. Academic Computing: Los Andes Strategy 41. Tough Search for Talent	**Networks and Networking**	4. Taming the Wild Network Tiger 7. Tying One On 10. Telecommuters Bring the Office Home 25. Closing the Net 28. Prepare for E-Mail Attack 42. Why Transplants Don't Happen
		Privacy	26. Is Nothing Private? 27. Read This!!!! 31. Caller Identification
Interpersonal Relationships	12. Challenging the Myth of Disability 13. Hey You! Make Way for My Technology! 14. Doctor Is On 15. Virtual Reality 48. Love Among the Robots	**Robotic(s)**	3. Why Japan Loves Robots and We Don't 9. Invasion of the Service Robots
		Surveillance and Social Control	25. Closing the Net 26. Is Nothing Private?
Legal Issues	19. Photographs That Lie 20. Warning: Here Come the Software Police 23. Legally Speaking 24. Time Bomb 25. Closing the Net	**Software Reliability**	34. System on Overload 35. Programmed for Disaster
Manufacturing	3. Why Japan Loves Robots and We Don't 6. Myth of a Post-Industrial Economy	**Work and Employment**	5. Does Corporate Nationality Matter? 6. Myth of a Post-Industrial Economy 8. Skilling of America 10. Telecommuters Bring the Office Home 11. Do It Yourself 37. Personal Computers and the World Software Market 41. Tough Search for Talent
(The) Military	34. System on Overload 35. Programmed for Disaster 36. Robowar		

Introduction

Computer "revolution" is a widely used term these days. It implies that society is undergoing a radical transformation. This was the view of the late British computer expert, Christopher Evans of Britain. In his thought-provoking book, *The Micro Millenium*, Evans argued that the societal impacts of computers in general, and personal computers in particular, would rival the effects of the Industrial Revolution that:

> brought about immense shifts in all aspects of society, affecting the individual, his family, his neighbors, his domestic and working environment, his clothes, his food, his leisure time, his political and religious ideals, his education, his social attitudes, his life-span, even the manner of his birth and death. (1979:ix)

Moreover, Evans claimed the future is not one of our choosing. He stated that as we began to apply these powerful new tools to the tasks of bettering our lives, we set in motion a process that takes on an independent, unstoppable momentum. The best we may hope for is that we have enough time to anticipate and prepare for the future that will be thrust upon us.

There are those who disagree that a social revolution is underway. And even if there is a revolution, we, the people, will be pretty much in control of it. For example, in his book, *The Personal Computer Book*, poet Peter A. McWilliams argues that computers will no doubt have a dramatic impact on our lives and on society. But he also suggests that we are in command of our own fate when he states:

> For the most part, personal computers will prove their worth to the extent that they fit into your daily life, not to the degree that you adapt your life to be more in step with The Computer Age. (1984:15)

Contradictory predictions about the implications of computing are hardly surprising since people operate from many different premises about society and human nature. We need to keep this in mind when we try to make sense of competing claims about the future. This is not easy since many of us are not even aware of our own assumptions about social life, or how they might differ from other people's views. Most of us take certain things for granted—we believe them so strongly we simply assume other reasonable and intelligent people see things the same way.

This disagreement between Evans and McWilliams basically reflects the difference between how idealists and materialists look at the world. Those who feel that idealism and free will govern societies are uncomfortable with the kind of claims made by Evans—that cultural, political, and religious ideals can be influenced by technical innovation. They would argue that the ideals come first and are the foundation of society. Technical innovations are accepted or rejected according to whether they are in harmony with basic values. This assumption is implied in McWilliams's argument that computers are mere tools that people are free to use or avoid. Materialists on the other hand, insist that new technologies need not support any basic belief system. They maintain that if a technology can provide real material benefits such as greater wealth or longer life expectancy to society or to a powerful minority, it will be adopted. If some aspect of technology clashes with society's values and ideals, then the values, not the technology will be modified or abandoned. Clearly, Christopher Evans is in the materialist camp.

Social theorists and philosophers have debated for centuries over which of the competing social assumptions are valid. Like the rest of us, they continue to disagree about where the truth lies. For the past few centuries, there has been a growing tendency to look to "science" to settle these disputes. The first reading in this collection gives us some insight into how new scientific discoveries about physical nature shaped eighteenth-century views of social order and human nature. In "Science and the American Experiment," historian John Patrick Diggins describes the factionalism of post-revolution America and how Newton's laws of physics helped forge some ideological unity among the framers of the U.S. Constitution.

As Diggins' discussion also shows, scientific "truths" are subject to ongoing debate and revision. Moreover, science itself is, to the surprise of many people, very much shaped by social factors. A good example of this is modern Western medicine that is generally thought to be based on widely accepted scientific principles. However, as Lynn Payer illustrates in "Borderline Cases," medical practice in Western Europe and North America reflects differences in national cultures to a considerable degree.

Looking Ahead: Challenge Questions

Since medical practice varies from culture to culture, what kinds of problems (or benefits) could arise from the use of expert systems developed in other cultures?

If society has a choice about which technologies are developed and how they are used, then who should participate in making those choices? Should those with political power, wealth, or technical expertise assume the responsibilities of shaping our society? If everyone should have a say, how might we provide the opportunity for all to have their views and concerns taken into account?

SCIENCE AND THE AMERICAN EXPERIMENT

How Newton's Laws Shaped the Constitution

JOHN PATRICK DIGGINS

JOHN PATRICK DIGGINS, a professor of history at the University of California at Irvine, is the author of THE LOST SOUL OF AMERICAN POLITICS, *a study of the foundations of the constitutional system.*

IN THE WINTER OF 1786, only ten years after declaring independence from England and four years after concluding the war that underscored that declaration, America was falling apart. The single thing the thirteen former colonies seemed to have in common was a penchant for squabbling among themselves. Religious differences separated the Calvinists of New England from the Baptists of the South. The economic interests of northern merchants clashed with those of southern slave owners. Border disputes were common and periodically led to skirmishes. Atlantic states such as South Carolina envied their landlocked neighbors' proximity to the public lands of the Northwest Territories, and states such as New Jersey, with no seaports, were unhappy about paying import tariffs to New York and Philadelphia, whose harbors were well suited for shipping.

To make matters worse, the Articles of Confederation, ratified in 1781, had placed most of the nation's power with the states. Consequently, Congress was too weak to address broad domestic problems, the most troubling of which was a public debt of sixty million dollars, a legacy of the War of Independence. Small farmers, whose financial problems were especially acute, pressed state legislatures to issue paper money with which to pay their creditors. Though it undermined the value of hard currency, several states complied with the farmers' demands out of fear. And with good reason: when the Massachusetts legislature refused, armed bands forced a number of courts to halt foreclosures and imprisonment for debt. Though the rebels were soon subdued by state militia, their brief uprising, along with the other troubles brewing throughout the colonies, awakened leaders to the growing crisis: the confederation was on the verge of collapse.

At first, discussion about how to restore unity seemed destined to degenerate into bitter disputes, as well. A handful of former loyalists, who had opposed the war, and representatives of New England's upper classes called for a return to monarchy. Desperate and disgruntled, members of the military thought they could put the country back on course by installing themselves as its new rulers. But the most fundamental and far-reaching disagreement existed between the federalists, who desired a strong central government, and the antifederalists, who were reluctant to relinquish even a fraction of state autonomy. Nevertheless, the gravity of the situation was sufficient to persuade the various factions to set aside their differences; Congress and every state save Rhode Island accepted the federalists' invitation to a general convention to revise the Articles of Confederation.

The fifty-five individuals who gathered in Philadelphia in May of 1787 constituted the most outstanding group of American statesmen ever to have assembled in one room. Representing Virginia was George Washington, a hero of the war; James Madison, one of the greatest political intellects in the country's history; Edmund Randolph, the state's governor; and George Mason, author of Virginia's bill of rights. From Pennsylvania came Benjamin Franklin, spokesman for the colonies in their debate with Great Britain about self-government, and James Wilson, an exceptionally gifted lawyer. And the New York delegation included Alexander Hamilton, a talented champion of centralized government.

The group proved to be as bold as it was brilliant. Scarcely had the delegates cleared their throats when Randolph presented fifteen specific resolutions (almost certainly authored by Madison), whose scope greatly exceeded the charter of the convention: included was a proposal to create a national authority with sovereignty over the states; rather than fiddle with the Articles of Confederation, they would begin again, to frame a new constitution. And of what would this constitution consist?

Besides freeing the colonies of England's control, the War of Independence had sundered America's ties to the governmental traditions that had dominated England until the eighteenth century. The framers now aligned themselves with the intellectual movement that had recently swept across Europe—the Enlightenment; they rejected the political ideas of the past, turning elsewhere for models after which to pattern government. One of the most important of these models was nature itself, whose laws were viewed as templates for social laws. And the interpretation of nature considered most valid during the Enlightenment was that offered by such men as Isaac Newton, the English physicist. True, the U.S. Constitu-

This article is reprinted by permission of *The Sciences* and is from the November/December 1987 issue, pp. 29-31. Individual subscriptions are $18.00 per year. Write to The Sciences, 2 East 63rd Street, New York, NY 10021 or call 1-800-THE-NYAS.

tion represented the confluence of several intellectual, social, and political trends, but, of these, one of the most powerful and lasting was the growing popularity of science itself.

In turning toward science, the framers spurned two traditions that had shaped political thought before the Enlightenment. The first was Christianity, which defined man's nature in terms of a spiritual destiny that lay beyond history. Whether that destiny was fulfilled by prayer or work, government was considered a divinely ordained institution to be obeyed as much for salvation as for maintaining social order. The second tradition was classical republicanism, a political system with roots in ancient Greece and Rome, as well as in Renaissance Italy. In its purest form, a republican government is one in which power is exercised by elected representatives who are directly responsible to a body of citizens. Classical republicans sought to elevate people into patriots devoted to civic virtue and felt that this could be achieved best when government officials lived close enough to their constituents to exhort them to correct behavior and, in turn, to be accountable to them. Thus, it was presumed that republicanism worked only for small-scale governments, such as those that existed in sixteenth-century Florence, Milan, and Genoa.

To many of the scientifically oriented thinkers of the Enlightenment, these traditions, emphasizing as they did the repression of self-interest in the name of church and state, were unrealistic. The chief architect of this critique was the Scottish philosopher David Hume. Taking Newton's empiricism as his model, Hume held that there can be no knowledge of anything beyond experience. He conceived of philosophy in general, and of political thought in particular, as inductive, experimental sciences. Sound government must be based on the *science* of politics—on the direct observation of human behavior.

Such observation led Hume to conclude that human nature is uniform, that, even in the face of social and economic differences, invariant rules can be drawn from men's actions. The most important of these is that, since reason is a slave to the passions, political thinkers must be all the more scientific because they cannot expect the people to be so. Noting that, for centuries, the condition of the human race remained miserable under religious and classical authority, Hume argued that the aim of government should be not to exhort citizens to attain grace or virtue but to accept man as a pleasure-seeking creature. Rather than leading to political instability, man's pursuit of material gain will induce productive work habits and thereby contribute to the creation of wealth and progress, as long as government is designed to offset opposing passions. This picture of mankind accorded well with the world view of eighteenth-century science, which was based largely on Newton's three laws of motion, in particular, the third: for every action there is an equal and opposite reaction.

Both Hume's ideas about government and Newton's outlook on nature came together in early American political thought. Hamilton, Madison, and the other framers were particularly impressed with Hume's essay "That Politics Be Reduced to a Science." From Hume they learned that if government concerns itself with institu-

tions and political structures, rather than with manners and morals, a rich and powerful republic need not succumb to corruption. The clearest and most forceful articulation of this lesson is found in *A Defence of the Constitutions of Government of the United States of America*, composed in 1787 and 1788 by John Adams, later to become the second president, and in *The Federalist*, a series of eighty-five essays by Hamilton, Madison, and John Jay, then the secretary of foreign affairs, which appeared in New York newspapers, in support of the Constitution, between October of 1787 and August of 1788. It is no accident that these documents, brilliant expositions of the political theory that underlies American government, are studded with the language of natural science.

Adams wrote the *Defence* in response to French political thinkers who had criticized the American states for having governments whose branches were designed to reflect class divisions as a means of controlling them. Because postrevolutionary America had no monarchy, aristocracy, or peasantry, the French felt the country could dispense with its system of checks and balances and simply vest all authority in a single, national assembly.

Adams faulted the French for failing to realize that governmental abuse cannot be eradicated merely by entrusting power to an active citizenry. He argued that a strong executive branch was necessary to mediate between the rich and the poor, the powerful and the weak. Whereas the French believed that class differences could be abolished along with the executive branch, which remained for them a symbol of monarchal tyranny, Adams, like the skeptic Hume, was convinced that potentially explosive divisions of one kind or another would always exist in society and that democracy must be controlled to prevent the tyranny of any particular faction.

"All nations, from the beginning, have been agitated by the same passions," Adams observed. To him, there was only one solution to political power conceived as a force that expands until met by a counterforce: "Orders of men, watching and balancing each other, are the only security; power must be opposed to power, and interest to interest." Proof for the idea came from the classical mechanics of Newton (for every action, a reaction).

The laws of physics, as well as the maxims of geometry, were also used to support the political ideas in *The Federalist*. In number thirty-one, for example, Hamilton cited a variant of the laws of mechanics (the means should be proportionate to the end) to defend the constitutional clause that authorized the new government to make any laws necessary to carry out its objectives. (For example, the Constitution says that the government shall regulate commerce, but it fails to mention banking. Nonetheless, according to Hamilton, the government can create a banking system to regulate commerce.)

Elsewhere in *The Federalist*, Hamilton and Madison advanced the Newtonian principle that an effect cannot exist without a cause, to show why factions are inevitable. Since the differences that give rise to factionalism are "sown" into human nature, government should abandon any hope of abolishing the causes of factionalism and attend, instead, to the establishment of political structures that will counterbalance natural conflicts, thereby preventing them from erupting into civil strife. Extending this line of reasoning, both authors invoked the Euclidean theory that the whole is greater than the parts to arrive at one of the most astounding conclusions in modern political philosophy: a good and stable government can be constructed from defective human parts.

The framers also appealed to science to support their theories about the size of government. One of the main concerns of the antifederalists was that the Constitution would create an extended government designed to rule over a vast territory, a dangerous departure from the classical principle that republics must remain small for citizens to exercise control. Hamilton responded that the science of politics makes possible "the enlargement of the orbit of government." In this new, scientific scenario, liberty was to be preserved not by citizen participation—which, more often than not, yielded governments too parochial to be fair—but by fragmentation of power within a mosaic of countervailing devices and by a distancing of government from the people. To achieve these ends, the framers installed two key features in the Constitution: a separation of powers between the executive, legislative, and judicial branches of the federal government and a division of power between the federal and state governments.

That these features were linked so intimately to Newtonian theories of motion and force is only one of many signs that, in the late eighteenth century, the West was entering that period of history in which the scientific ethos would redefine all aspects of human endeavor. The Newtonian cosmology gave the framers confidence that the Constitution should accord with the ways of nature. If a government proportions its parts, Hamilton declared, its power will never constitute a threat to the security of its citizens. Balance and counterpoise bring stability and equilibrium. Liberty is preserved not by civic virtue but by the design of government itself, which, in turn, rests on the principles of physics and geometry. Unlike the systems of the past, the American government would be one of *mechanisms* rather than of men—"a machine that would go of itself," in the words of the nineteenth-century American poet James Russell Lowell.

Later generations were not uniformly overjoyed with a government conceived mechanistically. Woodrow Wilson, for one, believed that the Constitution had been so delicately balanced that it failed to allow for executive leadership. He felt that the framers had been mistaken in conceiving of politics as a branch of mechanics, because government "is a living thing." Thus, he called for a new constitution, one that would be open to adaptation, a government "accountable to Darwin, not to Newton." Yet, when one considers that the framers not only balanced power but countervailed the irrational interests and passions from which power springs, it could be said that they gave us a government that went beyond Darwin, one accountable to Freud as well as to Newton.

BORDERLINE CASES

How Medical Practice Reflects National Culture

LYNN PAYER

LYNN PAYER is a free-lance journalist specializing in medicine and health. Her most recent book is MEDICINE AND CULTURE, *published by Viking Penguin.*

MARIE R., a young woman from Madagascar, was perplexed. Hyperventilating and acutely anxious, tired and afflicted with muscle spasms, she visited a French physician who told her she suffered from spasmophilia, a uniquely French disease thought to be caused by magnesium deficiency. The physician prescribed magnesium and acupuncture and advised her that, because of the danger associated with the disease, she should return home to the care of her parents.

Yet when Marie R. ultimately moved to the United States, American physicians diagnosed her symptoms quite differently. As she soon learned, spasmophilia, a diagnosis that increased sevenfold in France between 1970 and 1980, is not recognized as a disease by American physicians. Instead Marie R. was told she suffered from an anxiety disorder; only after taking tranquilizers and undergoing psychotherapy did her condition improve. Now she seems cured, though she still wonders what she has been cured of.

Western medicine has traditionally been viewed as an international science, with clear norms applied consistently throughout western Europe and North America. But as Marie R.'s experience illustrates, the disparity among the diagnostic traditions of England, France, the United States and West Germany belies the supposed universality of the profession. In 1967 a study by the World Health Organization found that physicians from several countries diagnosed different causes of death even when presented with identical information from the same death certificates. Diagnoses of psychiatric patients vary significantly as well: until a few years ago a patient labeled schizophrenic in the U.S. would likely have been called manic-depressive or neurotic in England and delusional psychotic in France.

Medical treatments can vary as widely as the diagnoses themselves. Myriad homeopathic remedies that might be dismissed by most U.S. physicians as outside the realm of scientific medicine are actively prescribed in France and West Germany. Visits to the many spas in those countries are paid for by national health insurance plans; similar coverage by insurance agencies in the U.S. would be unthinkable. Even for specific classes of prescription drugs there are disparities of consumption. West Germans, for instance, consume roughly six times as much cardiac glycoside, or heart stimulant, per capita as do the French and the English, yet only about half as much antibiotic.

In one recent study an attempt was made to understand why certain coronary procedures, such as angiography—a computer-aided method of observing the heart—and bypass surgery, are done about six times as frequently in the U.S. as they are in England. Physicians from each country were asked to examine the case histories of a group of patients and then determine which patients would benefit from treatment. Once cost considerations were set aside, the English physicians were still two to three times as likely as their American counterparts to regard the procedures as inappropriate for certain patients. This result suggests that a major reason for the frequent use of the procedures here has less to do with cost than with the basic climate of medical opinion.

The diversity of diagnoses and treatments takes on added importance with the approach of 1992, the year in which the nations of the European economic community plan to dissolve all barriers to trade. Deciding which prescription drugs to allow for sale universally has proved particularly vexing. Intravenous nutrition solutions marketed in West Germany must contain a minimum level of nitrogen, to promote proper muscle development; in England, however, the same level is considered toxic to the kidneys. French regulators, following their country's historic preoccupation with the liver, tend to insist with vigor that new drugs be proved nontoxic to that organ.

Ultimately the fundamental differences in the practice

of medicine from country to country reflect divergent cultural outlooks on the world. Successful European economic unification will require a concerted attempt to understand the differences. At the same time, we Americans, whose medicine originated in Europe, might gain insight into our own traditions by asking the same question: Where does science end and culture begin?

WEST GERMAN MEDICINE is perhaps best characterized by its preoccupation with the heart. When examining a patient's electrocardiogram, for example, a West German physician is more likely than an American internist to find something wrong. In one study physicians following West German criteria found that 40 percent of patients had abnormal EKGs; in contrast, according to American criteria, only 5 percent had abnormal EKGs. In West Germany, patients who complain of fatigue are often diagnosed with *Herzinsuffizienz,* a label meaning roughly weak heart, but it has no true English equivalent; indeed, the condition would not be considered a disease in England, France or the United States. Herzinsuffizienz is currently the single most common ailment treated by West German general practitioners and one major reason cardiac glycosides are prescribed so frequently in that country.

In fact, for older patients, taking heart medicine is something of a status symbol—in much the same way that not taking medicine is a source of pride among the elderly in the U.S. Some West German physicians suggest that such excessive concern for the heart is a vestige of the romanticism espoused by the many great German literary figures who grappled with ailments of the heart. "It is the source of all things," wrote Johann Wolfgang von Goethe in *The Sorrows of Young Werther,* "all strength, all bliss, all misery." Even in modern-day West Germany, the heart is viewed as more than a mere mechanical device: it is a complex repository of the emotions. Perhaps this cultural entanglement helps explain why, when the country's first artificial heart was implanted, the recipient was not told for two days—allegedly so as not to disturb him.

The obsession with the heart—and the consequent widespread prescription of cardiac glycosides—makes the restrained use of antibiotics by West German physicians all the more striking. They decline to prescribe antibiotics not only for colds but also for ailments as severe as bronchitis. A list of the five drug groups most commonly prescribed for patients with bronchitis does not include a single class of antibiotics. Even if bacteria are discovered in inflamed tissue, antibiotics are not prescribed until the bacteria are judged to be causing the infection. As one West German specialist explained, "If a patient needs an antibiotic, he generally needs to be in the hospital."

At least a partial explanation for this tendency can be found in the work of the nineteenth-century medical scientist Rudolph Virchow, best known for his proposal that new cells arise only from the division of existing cells. Virchow was reluctant to accept the view of Louis Pasteur that germs cause disease, emphasizing instead the protective role of good circulation. In Virchow's view numerous diseases, ranging from dyspepsia to muscle spasms, could be attributed to insufficient blood flow to the tissues. In general, his legacy remains strong: if one is ill, it is a reflection of internal imbalances, not external invaders.

IN FRENCH MEDICINE the intellectual tradition has often been described as rationalist, dominated by the methodology of its greatest philosopher, René Descartes. With a single phrase, *cogito ergo sum,* Descartes managed logically to conjure forth the entire universe from the confines of his room. His endeavor is looked on with pride in France: every French schoolchild is exhorted to "think like Descartes."

Abroad, however, Cartesian thinking is not viewed so favorably, as it often manifests itself as elegant theory backed by scanty evidence. When investigators at the Pasteur Institute in Paris introduced a flu vaccine that had the supposed ability to anticipate future mutations of the flu virus, they did so without conducting any clinical trials. More recently, French medical workers held a press conference to announce their use of cyclosporin to treat AIDS—even though their findings were based on a mere week's use of the drug by just six patients. American journalists and investigators might have been less puzzled by the announcement had they understood that, in France, the evidence or outcome is not nearly as important as the intellectual sophistication of the approach.

Disease in France, as in West Germany, is typically regarded as a failure of the internal defenses rather than as an invasion from without. For the French, however, the internal entity of supreme importance is not the heart or the circulation but the *terrain*—roughly translated as constitution, or, more modernly, a kind of nonspecific immunity. Consequently, much of French medicine is an attempt to shore up the *terrain* with tonics, vitamins, drugs and spa treatments. One out of 200 medical visits in France results in the prescription of a three-week cure at one of the country's specialized spas. Even Pasteur, the father of modern microbiology, considered the *terrain* vital: "How many times does the constitution of the injured, his weakening, his morale . . . set up a barrier to the invasion of the infinitely tiny organisms that is insufficient."

The focus on the *terrain* explains in part why the French seem less concerned about germs than do Americans. They tolerate higher levels of bacteria in foods such as foie gras and do not think twice about kissing someone with a minor infection: such encounters are viewed as a kind of natural immunization. Attention to the *terrain* also accounts for the diagnostic popularity of spasmophilia, which now rivals problems with hearing in diagnostic frequency. One is labeled a spasmophile not necessarily because of specific symptoms but because one is judged to have some innate tendency toward those symptoms.

Although French medicine often attempts to treat the *terrain* as a whole, the liver is often singled out as the source of all ills. Just as West Germans tend to fixate on herzinsuffizienz, many French blame a "fragile liver" for their ailments, whether headache, cough, impotence, acne or dandruff. Ever since French hepatologists held a press conference fourteen years ago to absolve the liver of its responsibility for most diseases, the *crise de foie* has largely gone out of style as a diagnosis—though one still hears of the influence of bile ducts.

INTRODUCTION

Unlike their French and West German counterparts, physicians in England tend to focus on the external causes of disease and not at all on improving circulation or shoring up the *terrain*. Prescriptions for tonics, vitamins, spa treatments and the like are almost absent, and antibiotics play a proportionally greater role. The English list of the twenty most frequent prescriptions includes three classes of antibiotics; in West Germany, in contrast, the top-twenty list includes none.

English physicians are also known for their parsimony, and for that reason they are called (by the French) "the accountants of the medical world." They do less of virtually everything: They prescribe about half as many drugs as their French and West German counterparts; and, compared with U.S. physicians, they perform surgery half as often, take only half as many X rays and with each X ray use only half as much film. They recommend a daily allowance of vitamin C that is half the amount recommended elsewhere. Overall in England, one has to be sicker to be defined ill, let alone to receive treatment.

Even when blood pressure or cholesterol readings are taken, the thresholds for disease are higher. Whereas some physicians in the U.S. believe that a diastolic pressure higher than ninety should be treated, an English physician is unlikely to suggest treatment unless the reading is more than a hundred. And whereas some U.S. physicians prescribe drugs to reduce cholesterol when the level is as low as 225 milligrams per deciliter, in England similar treatment would not be considered unless the blood cholesterol level was higher than 300.

To a great extent, such parsimony is a result of the economics of English medicine. French, U.S. and West German physicians are paid on a fee-for-service basis and thus stand to gain financially by prescribing certain treatments or referring the patient to a specialist. English physicians, on the other hand, are paid either a flat salary or on a per-patient basis, an arrangement that discourages overtreatment. In fact, the ideal patient in England is the one who only rarely sees a physician—and thus reduces the physician's workload without reducing his salary.

But that arrangement only partly accounts for English parsimony. Following the empirical tradition of such philosophers as Francis Bacon, David Hume and John Locke, English medical investigators have always emphasized the careful gathering of data from randomized and controlled clinical trials. They are more likely than their colleagues elsewhere to include a placebo in a clinical trial, for example. When the U.S. trial for the Hypertension Detection and Follow-up Program was devised, American physicians were so certain mild hypertension should be treated, they considered it unethical not to treat some patients. A study of mild hypertension conducted by the Medical Research Council in England, however, included a placebo group, and the final results painted a less favorable picture of the treatment than did the American trial.

Almost across the board, the English tend to be more cautious before pronouncing a treatment effective. Most recently experts in England examined data regarding the use of the drug AZT by people testing positive for HIV (the virus associated with AIDS). These experts concluded that the clinical trials were too brief to justify administration of the drug, at least for the time being. Americans, faced with the same data, now call for treatment.

American medicine can be summed up in one word: aggressive. That tradition dates back at least to Benjamin Rush, an eighteenth-century physician and a signer of the Declaration of Independence. In Rush's view one of the main obstacles to the development of medicine was the "undue reliance upon the powers of nature in curing disease," a view he blamed on Hippocrates. Rush believed that the body held about twenty-five pints of blood—roughly double the actual quantity—and urged his disciples to bleed patients until four-fifths of the blood had been removed.

In essence, not much has changed. Surgery is more common and more extensive in the U.S. than it is elsewhere: the number of hysterectomies and of cesarean sections for every 100,000 women in the population is at least two times as high as are such rates in most European countries. The ratio of the rates for cardiac bypasses is even higher. Indeed, American physicians like the word *aggressive* so much that they apply it even to what amounts to a policy of retrenchment. In 1984, when blood pressure experts backed off an earlier recommendation for aggressive drug treatment of mild hypertension, they urged that nondrug therapies such as diet, exercise and behavior modification be "pursued aggressively."

To do something, anything, is regarded as imperative, even if studies have yet to show conclusively that a specific remedy will help the patient. As a result, Americans are quick to jump on the bandwagon, particularly with regard to new diagnostic tests and surgical techniques. (Novel drugs reach the market more slowly, since they must first be approved by the Food and Drug Administration.) Naturally, an aggressive course of action can sometimes save lives. But in many instances the cure is worse than the disease. Until recently, American cardiologists prescribed antiarrhythmia drugs to patients who exhibited certain signs of arrhythmia after suffering heart attacks. They were afraid that not to do so might be considered unethical and would leave them vulnerable to malpractice suits. But when the treatment was finally studied, patients who received two of the three drugs administered were dying at a higher rate than patients who received no treatment at all. Likewise, the electronic monitoring of fetal heart rates has never been shown to produce healthier babies; in fact, some critics charge that incorrect diagnosis of fetal distress, made more likely by the monitors, often leads to unnecessary cesarean sections.

Even when the benefits of a treatment are shown to exceed the risks within a particular group of patients, American physicians are more likely to extrapolate the favorable results to groups for which the benefit-to-risk ratio has not been defined. American physicians now administer AZT to people who are HIV-positive. But some physicians have taken the treatment a step further and are giving the drug to women who have been raped by assailants whose HIV status is unknown—to patients, in other words, whose risk of infection may be low. Whether the pressure for treatment originates with the patient or with the physician, the unspoken reasoning is the same: it is better to do something than it is to do nothing.

Unlike the French and the West Germans, Americans do not have a particular organ upon which they focus their ills—perhaps because they prefer to view themselves as naturally healthy. In reading the obituary column, for instance, one notices that no one ever dies of "natural" causes; death is always ascribed to some external force. Disease, likewise, is always caused by a foreign invader of some sort. As one French physician put it, "The only things Americans fear are germs and Communists." The germ mentality helps explain why antibiotic use in the U.S. is so high: one study found that American physicians prescribe about twice as much antibiotic as do Scottish physicians, and Americans regularly give antibiotics for ailments such as a child's earache for which Europeans would deem such treatment inappropriate. The obsession with germs also accounts for our puritanical attitudes toward cleanliness: our daily washing rituals, the great lengths to which we go to avoid people with minor infections, and our attempts to quarantine people with diseases known to be nontransmissible by casual contact alone.

Nor do Americans exhibit much patience for the continental notion of balance. Substances such as salt, fat and cholesterol are often viewed by U.S. physicians as unmitigated evils, even though they are essential to good health. Several studies, including a recent one by the National Heart, Blood and Lung Institute in Bethesda, Maryland, have shown that if death rates in men are plotted against cholesterol levels, the lowest death rates are associated with levels of 180; cholesterol levels higher or lower are associated with higher death rates. Low cholesterol levels have been linked to increased rates of cancer and even suicide—yet Americans tend to be proud when their levels are low.

THE ARRAY of viable medical traditions certainly suggests that medicine is not the international science many think it is. Indeed, it may never be. Medical research can indicate the likely consequences of a given course of action, but any decision about whether those consequences are desirable must first pass through the filter of cultural values. Such a circumstance is not necessarily bad. Many of the participants at a recent symposium in Stuttgart, West Germany, felt strongly that the diverse medical cultures of Europe should not be allowed to merge into a single one. Most medical professionals, however, ignore the role cultural values play in their decisions, with unfortunate consequences.

One result is that the medical literature is confusing. The lead paper in a 1988 issue of *The Lancet*, for example, superficially appeared to satisfy international standards of medical science. Its authors were German and Austrian; the journal was English; and the paper itself, which addressed the treatment of chronic heart failure, made reference to the functional classification of this disorder by the New York Heart Association. But on a closer look an American cardiologist found that many of the patients referred to in the paper would not, according to U.S. standards, be classified as having heart failure at all. Fewer than half of the patients' chest X rays showed enlargement of the heart, an almost universal finding in people with heart failure as diagnosed in the U.S. It would take a careful reader—or one attuned to German diagnostic traditions—to ferret out such misleading results.

The diverse ways different countries practice medicine present a kind of natural experiment. Yet because few people are aware of the experiment, no one is collecting the rich data the experiment could supply. What is the effect, for example, of the widespread prescription of magnesium for spasmophilia in France and for heart disease in West Germany? Likewise, soon after the hypertension drug Selacryn was introduced to U.S. markets, two dozen people died of liver complications attributed to the drug. Yet Selacryn had already been used for several years in France. Had similar cases gone unnoticed there and been attributed to the fragility of the French liver? Lacking an awareness of their differing values, medical experts of different nations may be missing out on an opportunity to advance their common science.

Finally, recognizing American biases may help us head off medical mistakes made when our own instincts lead us astray. As English medicine frequently illustrates, it is *not* always better to do something than it is to do nothing. And as the continental outlook reveals, a more balanced view of the relation between the individual and the disease might make us less fearful of our surroundings. If we put our own values in perspective, future decisions might be made less according to tradition and more according to what can benefit us most as physicians and patients.

The Changing Economy

That whole range of inventions we refer to as computers is having a major impact on the production, distribution, and consumption of goods and services in society. In other words, computers are transforming the economic system. Because the economy is tied to nearly every facet of social life, this transformation may have some very far-reaching consequences—such as those claimed of the Industrial Revolution (see Introduction).

To better understand why the economy is so important, consider a few of the social consequences of current economic arrangements in advanced societies. Our system of mass producing goods and services has given us a high standard of living. But it also means that most of us must live in or near a city and work in highly specialized occupations for large organizations over which we have little control. True self-reliance is rare. We depend on countless others to produce the basic goods and services needed to carry out daily life. In addition, our elaborate system of market exchange brings us into numerous brief and close encounters with complete strangers nearly every day. Such factors have helped to make the nuclear family's role in social and emotional fulfillment more important than it was in preindustrial societies.

We tend to take the social dimensions of our economic system for granted, but a significant change in even one part of its underlying structure could lead to unexpected side effects in other areas. For example, computers and telecommunications now make it technically possible for workers in many occupations to "telecommute" to work without physically leaving their homes. How will society be different if telecommuting becomes widespread?

In considering the impact of computers on the economy, there are two broad areas of interest. First, the production and sale of computer-related technologies and services employs millions of workers and contributes billions of dollars to the economy every year. Second, computing-related technologies have the potential to increase the productivity and efficiency of other economic sectors.

One of the secondary sectors is the mass production of manufactured goods. Relative to other sectors, the size of the manufacturing work force has been declining over the past few decades. A significant factor in this trend is that various forms of automation have enabled factories to produce more goods with fewer workers. According to some forecasts, the impact of robotics and other automated technologies on factory jobs and productivity will be similar to the impact of mechanization on farming. Just as a tiny fraction of the labor force is now able to feed the rest of the population, so, too, will a relatively few workers be able to produce society's needed manufactured goods.

However, automating the North American factory has not been easy. Despite the popular impression that robots are "taking over" they have actually been an embarrassing disappointment for many U.S. manufacturers. But in Japan, the experience with robots has been generally favorable. In "Why Japan Loves Robots and We Don't," Andrew Tanzer and Ruth Simon discuss economic, demographic, and cultural factors underlying the robot gap between the United States and Japan.

Currently, the majority of workers in advanced nations are employed in "services." Originally, service workers tended to perform domestic or personal services for the well-to-do. Today, the range of service occupations is extremely broad: examples include order takers at fast food restaurants, scuba diving instructors, fire fighters, 911 operators, and travel agents. The jobs of most service workers tend to center on various aspects of gathering, creating, analyzing, interpreting, and disseminating "information."

Accurate, current, information on the economy is extremely important. Try to imagine day-to-day survival without easy access to such ordinary information as schedules, prices, and telephone numbers. Business and government would screech to a halt without a relatively smooth and continuous flow of reliable information. In order to handle escalating information needs, corporate computers are being strung together into huge networks that "carry torrents of engineering, sales, marketing, and shipping data flowing this way and that." But, as explained in "Taming the Wild Network," these systems pose immense technical and management problems, that have in turn led to intense competition to find (and market) solutions.

The growing ability to quickly move information (and goods) around the world has contributed to the rise of a global economy. One feature of this new economy is firms that have operations spanning several different countries.

In many nations, globalization has raised concerns such as whether or not domestic workers can compete in international labor markets. In fact, one of the reasons why the manufacturing work force is declining in advanced nations is because many manufacturing operations have been relocated to less developed nations where labor costs are much lower. In "Does Corporate Nationality Matter?" Robert Reich addresses the issue of U.S. labor competitiveness and other concerns related to the global corporation.

Some analysts have suggested that all manufacturing will, and should, be controlled by offshore producers. Their rationale is that the most successful economies will be based on services (especially information) and high-tech industries. This view is challenged by Stephen Cohen and John Zysman in "The Myth of a Post-Industrial Economy." They contend that to allow manufacturing to disappear would "risk the wealth and power of the nation."

Automation of the office is addressed in "Tying One On." Alan Morantz describes how advances in computing and other information technologies are revolutionizing Canadian offices.

Looking Ahead: Challenge Questions

Do you think that as the computer age progresses, people will become more dependent on others for their basic needs, or more self-reliant?

Is the information explosion helping us become more informed as individuals? Are workers, parents, consumers, and voters more knowledgeable than in the past?

If you were an economic policy advisor to a foreign nation concerned about global corporations and a declining manufacturing sector, what advice would you offer? Would your recommendations be the same if you were advising your own country? Why or why not?

Why Japan loves robots and we don't

Always looking to the future, Japanese businesses are pinning
many of their industrial hopes on increasing use of factory robots.
So what if robots don't pay back their investment right away?
They are a great bet for improving manufacturing
quality and countering rising labor costs.

Andrew Tanzer and Ruth Simon

IN A FACTORY where Matsushita Electric makes Panasonic VCRS, a robot winds wire a little thinner than a human hair 16 times through a pinhole in the video head, and then solders it. There are 530 of these robots in the factory and they wind, and then wind some more, 24 hours a day. They do it five times faster and much more reliably than the 3,000 housewives who, until recently, did the same job with microscopes on a subcontract basis in Japan's countryside. The robots even inspect their own work.

A U.S. company can't get this technology—even if there were an American consumer electronics industry to take advantage of it. Matsushita invented and custom-made all 530 wire-winders to gain a competitive edge.

Robots were invented here, and the U.S. still leads in advanced research, from robotic brain surgeons to classified undersea naval search-and-destroy robots. But when it comes to using robots to solve practical problems—on the factory floor and in everyday life—Japan has no equal.

What may sound like science fiction to most Americans is taken for granted by ordinary folk in Japan. The Japanese are now accustomed to having robots do everything from make sushi to perform Chopin. Ichiro Kato, a roboticist at Waseda University, designed Wabot, a famous piano-playing, music-reading robot. Says Kato: "There will be one or more robots in every house in the 21st century."

Wabot's creator expects to see robots in people's homes doing dishes and washing floors. He envisions a humanoid robot with movable arms and a synthesized voice that will provide mobility and companionship to lonely old people. Kato, 64, says: "I'd like to live to see that day." Advances in artificial intelligence will put all this in the realm of the probable.

You probably haven't heard much about robots lately in the U.S., and for good reason. Robots have been an embarrassing disappointment for many American manufacturers. But in Japan companies of all sizes have embraced robots. The robots make it easier to quickly alter a production line to make several different product models. Japanese suppliers are in the forefront of these "flexible manufacturing systems," in which robots play a crucial role.

Now the technology is moving beyond the factory into hospitals, concert halls and restaurants.

In 1988 Japan employed two-thirds of all robots in use in the world, and last year it installed about $2.5 billion worth of new ones. Compare this with the U.S., which added only about $400 million worth of robots last year. "The total population of robots in the U.S. is around 37,000," says John O'Hara, president of the Robotic Industries Association. "The Japanese add that many robots in one year." To be sure, Japan has enough antiquated and small factories to leave its overall manufacturing productivity below that of the U.S. But robots will help narrow the lead. For example, U.S. carmakers are heavily robotized. However, the Japanese are installing new robots not simply to automate but also to make production lines more flexible. For example, Nissan's newer auto plants can produce hundreds of different variations on a given car model simply by reprogramming robots that paint auto bodies and install car seats, engines, batteries, windshields, tires and doors. In Japan, even small companies use robots in simple applications such as welding.

It is one more example of Japan's skill at grasping a new technology and putting it to work while others dither. It happened in consumer electronics, memory chip production and machine tools. Now it's happening in robotics.

As Japan's robot population grows explosively, the U.S. market for metal employees is inching up after falling sharply in the mid-1980s. In February Deere & Co. decided to can the robots it uses to paint tractor chassis and hire humans. The robots take too long to program for endless permutations of paint orders. Whirlpool's Clyde, Ohio washing machine plant has used articulated arms that resembled the human wrist, elbow and shoulder to remove washtubs from injection molding equipment. But the complex robots aren't up to running around-the-clock production. Whirlpool gave up on the idea of using robots for this job, opting for fixed automation—a technology the U.S. excels in.

"Robots give you a lot of flexibility, but there's also a lot of complication," says James Spicer, a director of engineering operations at Whirlpool. "To lift one cylinder at a time you don't have to duplicate the motion of a human arm."

So many other manufacturers have sent robots to the junkyard or slowed plans to add new ones that the U.S. robot industry is in shambles. Early robot producers like Westinghouse and General Electric abandoned robotics in the late Eighties because of disappointing sales. And one-time highfliers such as Unimation and GCA Industrial Systems have disappeared into bigger companies, while Prab and Automatix founder under heavy losses.

One of the few profitable U.S. robot companies is GMFanuc, a 50/50 joint venture between the carmaker and Fanuc, a leading Japanese robotmaker. The venture last year earned a few million dollars on sales of $165 million. Japanese producers aren't making any real money in robots, either. But many Japanese firms design and make robots for their own use to boost competitiveness and quality, so profits are not the issue. They don't buy robots based on a spreadsheet showing payback periods.

Now U.S. companies, having invented industrial robots and licensed the technology to Japan back in the 1960s, are in the awkward position of licensing back new Japanese technology. Cincinnati Milacron, number three in the U.S. robot business, aided Matsushita Electric's push into robotics by licensing it technology. Last year Milacron became a U.S. distributor for small welding robots produced by none other than Matsushita.

Why is Japan so robot-happy? It has to do with a lot more than economics. Japanese managers and government officials consider robots a key tool in combating a severe labor shortage at home. The alternatives would be moving the labor-intensive operations abroad or letting immigrants into Japan. The first alternative would deprive Japan of its manufacturing skills. "If you can fully automate manufacturing, there's no reason you have to go to Southeast Asia," argues Tadaaki Chigusa, a director of McKinsey & Co., Inc. (Japan). The second alternative, immigration, is unacceptable in the homogeneous, somewhat racist Japanese society.

While Chinese, Filipino or Korean laborers would not be very welcome in Japan, no such prejudice exists against robots. The Japanese seem to have been primed for robots with positive images in their popular culture as far back as the 1950s—much earlier than in the U.S. Japanese toymakers have churned out millions of toy robots, and the country's cartoons and comic books are filled with robot heroes. The prototype is Astro Boy, developed in Japan in 1953 and later exported to the U.S.

"Astro Boy is as well known in Japan as Mickey Mouse and Donald Duck are here," says Frederik Schodt, author of *Inside the Robot Kingdom* (Kodansha International, 1988), which argues the Japanese have been conditioned to feel comfortable with robots from a young age. "He's a very cute, friendly robot who's always fighting for peace."

Mostly, robots are portrayed favorably in Western popular culture nowadays, from *Star Wars'* R2-D2 to the futuristic Jetsons cartoon family. However, in Western tradition, robots have frequently been stereotyped as soulless humanoid machines or evil characters in works such as Fritz Lang's 1920s silent film *Metropolis* and the 1920 Czech play *R.U.R.* by Karel Capek, in which the word "robot" was coined to describe man-created monsters that turned on their masters, killing them

In Japan, friendly, peace-loving robots are seen as solving a growing blue-collar labor shortage. The number of Japanese high school graduates is stagnant, and fewer graduates are willing to get their hands dirty. "Young people would rather work at the Hotel Okura or McDonald's than in the factory," says Naohide Kumagai, associate director of Kawasaki Heavy Industry's robot division. Shirking factory work doesn't carry a heavy penalty: Last year's typical high school graduate had 2.5 job offers to choose from.

Robots are more than a mere substitute for human labor. They can do some things better than humans. "Robots are becoming indispensable because they provide a precision, quality and cleanliness man can't," says Toshitsugu Inoue, senior engineer in Matsushita's robot development department. Because robots work at a precise speed and don't make mistakes, inventories are easier to control.

As electronic components are miniaturized, robots are becoming essential for quality and high yields in the production of everything from very large scale integration chips (some of Japan's "clean rooms" are already unmanned) to watches and VCRs. The inverse is also true: Because Japanese manufacturers have robots, they can further miniaturize the product. The process is redefining the product. Many consumer electronic products are designed from scratch to be efficiently assembled by robots.

The Victor Co. of Japan (JVC) Ltd.'s Yokohama camcorder factory is bathed in an eerie silence. Automated guided vehicles quietly deliver pallets of components to 64 robots, which perform 150 assembly and inspection tasks. Two workers operate the robots, which assemble eight models on the same production line. Before the robots were installed in 1987, JVC needed 150 workers to do the same job. Just as important, JVC has redesigned the camcorder and its components, some almost microscopic, to be more efficiently assembled by robots. The robots also provide flexibility: They'll work around the clock—no overtime, sick leave or bonuses.

Japanese government industrial planners have since the 1970s provided a raft of incentives for robot research, development and use. The government allows accelerated depreciation for purchase of sophisticated robots and established its own leasing company to provide low-cost robots to the private sector. Japan's Ministry of International Trade & Industry provides small and medium-size companies with interest-free loans to buy robots. MITI is also pouring $150 million into developing hazardous-duty robots for use in nuclear power plants or fighting fires at oil refineries. This would be unthinkable in the U.S., because it smacks of industrial policy.

Politics and national differences aside, why has the U.S. lagged so far behind Japan in applying robots to manufacturing? "The companies selling robots plain lied about the capabilities of their equipment and the circumstances under which they could perform," says Roger Nagel, manager of automation technology for International Harvester (now Navistar Corp.) in the early 1980s and now a professor at Lehigh University. After struggling for two years to debug a robot brought in to load and unload stamped parts from a press, Nagel finally junked the robot. A Japanese customer would probably have worked more closely developing the robot with the supplier, incorporating ideas from the engineers and even from assembly workers on the customer's own factory floor.

One reason for the overblown expectations is that U.S. robot engineers often came from the field of artificial intelligence and had little if any experience on the factory floor. They were enamored of the idea of a mechanical human, an idea readily embraced by corporate executives who hoped to replace workers in "lights out" factories.

"I'm a guru when I get to Japan"

When American industrialist Joseph Engelberger arrived at Tokyo's Narita Airport in the spring of 1987, he was met by a limousine and whisked to the television studios of NHK, Japan's national broadcast network. There Engelberger, who built the first industrial robot in 1961, was interviewed on a popular national news program. The conversation followed what had become to Engelberger a familiar pattern. "Didn't the U.S. found the robot industry?" the interviewer asked. "Doesn't Japan dominate it today?"

"We all have a good laugh about it," says Engelberger, 64, who founded Unimation, the first robot-maker, and in 1968 licensed its technology to Japan's Kawasaki Heavy Industries. "I'm a guru when I get to Japan. I'm [considered] the founder of Japanese robotics."

He's no guru at home. Here, few people not related to Engelberger recall his last big network TV appearance, when he instructed his robot to open a can of Budweiser and pour it for Johnny Carson on the *Tonight Show* in 1966. "I had a hard time getting people in the U.S. to take me seriously," he says.

Engelberger's exploits may have been good for a few laughs at home, but they caught the Japanese government's attention. In 1967 it invited him to address 600 Japanese scientists and business executives. The session lasted five hours and led to an agreement with Kawasaki to license Unimation's technology.

Kawasaki remains a powerhouse in robotics, but Engelberger's Unimation has all but disappeared in the U.S. Its problems started almost immediately after its 1983 purchase by Westinghouse, which paid $107 million for Unimation with the hope of turning the $70 million company into a $1 billion business.

Unimation sold its first robot to General Motors in 1961 but was battered by GM's 1982 decision to start its own robot company in partnership with Japan's Fanuc. With Westinghouse putting little money into research and development, Unimation's sales and market share withered. The hydraulic robots it pioneered were soon supplanted by newer and more versatile electric robots. Unimation's West Coast researchers left en masse and formed Adept Technology, now a hot little maker of light assembly robots.

After years of heavy losses, Westinghouse sold Unimation's two main operations—the robotics unit to Staubli International A.G., a private Swiss outfit, and its factory automation unit to AEG, a unit of Daimler-Benz.

Engelberger left Unimation in 1984 but remains a robot evangelist. His new venture, Transitions Research Corp., is developing robots for the service industry in a low-slung building in Danbury, Conn., down the road from Unimation's former offices.

Engelberger isn't hurting personally. He received around $5 million when Westinghouse bought Unimation, enough to buy a 62-foot sailboat with some money left over to continue researching robotics on his own. But he wishes his countrymen would pay him at least a fraction of the attention the Japanese pay him.—R.S.

The result was overengineered robots that were costly and didn't work well on the shop floor.

"U.S. companies made robot hands that were so ungodly complex that in many cases they had no chance of standing up in a real industrial environment," says Dennis Wisnosky, former vice president of GCA Industrial Systems Group, once the number two U.S. robotmaker. The Japanese, by contrast, started with simpler robots such as spotwelders in car plants and then used their experience to build more complicated machines, such as robots that inspect the paint finish on car bodies with visual sensors.

In the U.S., robots have been slow to spread beyond automakers and their first-tier suppliers. A survey last year by Deloitte & Touche found less than 30% of U.S. manufacturers believed they had received significant benefits from new technology, down from more than 60% two years earlier.

It is a situation that should trouble those who recall the sad story of the U.S. numerically controlled machine tool industry. The technology was developed at the Massachusetts Institute of Technology in the 1950s and then exploited by the Japanese. "U.S. manufacturers didn't push the machine tool industry hard enough from a technology point of view," says George Chryssolouris, a professor of mechanical engineering at MIT. Japanese companies demanded more sophisticated machine tools so they could better compete in export markets. The result? When U.S. companies finally awakened to the need for sophisticated, high-quality tools, they were forced to turn to Japan.

One reason U.S. manufacturers aren't pushing robotmakers as hard as their Japanese counterparts is that companies here tend to be run by salesmen or accountants.

Here, manufacturing engineers get scant respect; in Japan they frequently run companies. The best known include Honda's Soichiro Honda and Sony's Akio Morita. By contrast, it's hard to name an American manufacturer who has made it to the top since the days of Henry Ford and Charles Kettering. While the Japanese revere manufacturers, Americans lionize entrepreneurs and inventors. That helps explain why a U.S. manufacturing engineer with a couple years' experience makes only $37,000 a year, compared with $44,000 for a software applications engineer. Why should a smart American kid tinker with robots and assembly lines when he or she can strike it rich writing a new personal computer software program or designing a hedging strategy for an investment firm?

The Japanese have been able to accept a slower payout. If they used the U.S. standard formula of about 30% return on capital investment—instead of the 20% return common in Japan—robot investments would be cut by half, says Edwin Mansfield, director of the University of Pennsylvania's Center for Economics & Technology. The Japanese prefer a simpler comparison. The average cost of an industrial robot is $40,000—about the same as the annual income, with bonus, of a skilled worker in a Nissan factory. But the cost of robots is dropping, while labor costs are rising. Investing now could save money ten years from now.

Will robots make a comeback in the U.S.? Yes, eventually. Companies that sacked robots for complex jobs are rehiring them for simpler tasks. Deere, for example, decided to kick robots off its spray-paint line, but now uses them to torque a series of about 20 identical cap screws on tractor transmissions, a boring, repetitive job with a high degree of human error. Instead of using robots as a quick

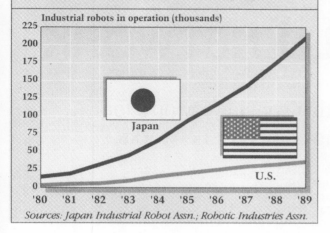

Andrew Christie/Forbes

The robot gap widens

Japan employs more robots than any other country, by far. Indeed, the U.S. has fewer robots installed than were added last year in Japan.

Industrial robots in operation (thousands)

Japan

U.S.

'80 '81 '82 '83 '84 '85 '86 '87 '88 '89

Sources: Japan Industrial Robot Assn.; Robotic Industries Assn.

fix, some companies are including them as part of a broad revamping of their entire manufacturing process. Electrolux Corp. designed a new upright vacuum cleaner to be more easily assembled by robots and employees in its new $40 million automated plant in Bristol, Va.

But it will be a long and slow road. The latest hot robot application in Japan is in construction. Komatsu Ltd. has developed a robot that installs panels of up to 1,100 pounds in the exterior walls of buildings, boosting labor productivity sixfold. Shimizu Corp. produces its own robots to spray fireproofing materials on steel structures, to position ceiling panels in buildings, to plaster floors and to lay concrete segments in tunnels.

Is the U.S. construction industry interested? Not a chance. "There's basically nothing going on," complains David Panos, assistant director of Carnegie Mellon University's Field Robotics Center, which is trying to ignite interest. "It's the same old story. They're focused on the short term. [The Japanese are focused on] the long term." Not to mention the outcry from powerful construction unions if jobs were threatened by robots.

Pioneered in the U.S., exploited in Japan. It's getting to be a too familiar story.

TAMING THE WILD NETWORK

The race is on to come up with a winning formula for managing business' sprawling computer networks

Mark S. Teflian remembers well the day United Airlines Inc. lost Seattle. It was a few years ago when suddenly all communications in and out of the company's Pacific Northwest ticketing offices went dead. Business there ground to a halt and angry callers lit up the switchboards. Several hours later, the telephone company told Teflian, now chief information officer of United's Covia computer and communications unit, what had gone wrong: It had hired someone near Seattle to put up a sign warning people to be extra careful when digging near a certain spot because a telephone cable lay close to the surface. The subcontractor accidentally rammed the warning sign's post through the very cable it was supposed to protect.

Teflian laughs about the incident now, but he has never forgotten the lesson it taught him and United: how indispensable—and vulnerable—communications networks can be. That cable, he discovered the hard way, was the only one in the area that could handle United's computer reservation traffic. Soon after, the airline installed a backup network based on earthling-proof satellites.

Despite the risks, businesses are stringing computers together at an astonishing rate. This year, U.S. companies will hook up 3.8 million personal computers in small office networks, raising the total by 48% over 1989. Many of those networks will tie into minicomputers and mainframes that also control thousands of terminals and printers in offices, banks, factories, and supermarkets. These networks now carry torrents of engineering, sales, marketing, and shipping data flowing this way and that, boosting productivity and improving competitiveness. As the zeitgeist of the on-line corporation takes hold, with companies everywhere trying to connect their multitudes of computers together, networks are fast becoming the modern corporation's vital infrastructure.

NERVOUS SYSTEMS. And not just at the obvious examples, such as a United Airlines or a Merrill Lynch & Co., which need globe-spanning access to computers and telephones for thousands of daily transactions. Networks are speeding communications and giving management up-to-the-second views of inventories, receivables, and market demand at businesses ranging from fast food to industrial chemicals to toy retailing. For many companies, networks have become essential means of production—their very nervous systems.

Nervous, indeed. As useful as they are, networks pose immense technical and management problems. The complexity of a single computer is hard enough to manage, but connect a dozen and the potential for trouble goes up exponentially. It gets even worse when they're in different cities—or countries. Says Kornel Terplan, a Munich-based consultant: "Many networks are so complex now that they just aren't manageable anymore."

With the costs of microcomputer power dropping, along with the cost of transmitting data over phone lines, it has become nearly routine in big companies to plop a PC on a desk and look for a network to link it to. It's easy to string wires and make the other physical and electronic connections to form enormous networks linking tens of thousands of machines. As a result, networks are growing like wildfire. But the techniques for controlling what goes on in them and ensuring their reliability trail badly. A simple local-area network linking a dozen PCs to a laser printer and a common file system is no big deal. But tie many such clusters together, warns Michael Howard, president of Infonetics Research Institute Inc. in San Jose, Calif., and "a lot of strange things happen." A computer glitch, for instance, can easily choke a network for electronic gobbledygook. Few companies have personnel who possess both the computer and telecommunications skills to put out such fires.

WAYWARD BACKHOES. And network failures are costly. Howard estimates that a typical large company loses $600,000 a year because of network problems. The more complex and far-ranging the network, the greater its vulnerability to such threats as wayward backhoes, software bugs, and determined assaults by hackers and computer viruses. CIGNA Insurance Co., which runs its own nationwide telephone and computer network, figures it can lose $25,000 an hour if one of its claims offices gets disconnected. At American Airlines Inc. last year, a problem at the Dallas computer center brought down the entire Sabre network for 13 hours—during which time flights had to be booked manually. Estimated cost: millions of dollars.

Not surprisingly, just about everybody in the computer and telecommunications business is hawking his own prescription for taming the wild network. It's big business—about $505 million a year for products and services, and headed for $1.8 billion by 1995, says Market Intelligence Research Co. It's also strategic. IBM, AT&T, Unisys, Digital Equipment, and Hewlett-Packard, among others, figure that in the 1990s, the supplier who helps a customer solve the networking problem—and in the process improves the bottom line—will gain enormous influence over what that customer buys. "If you control the nervous system"—the network—"you win the body," says William R. Johnson, Digital Equipment Corp.'s vice-president for telecommunications and networks.

The underlying assumption is that the supplier who sells the network-management scheme will gain the kind of "lock-in" that mainframe suppliers had 20 years ago when there was one, and only one, computer system in any company. As a result, "network management is one of the key strategic battlegrounds in the computer industry," says James Herman, a principal at Northeast Consulting Resources Inc.

LOOMING BATTLE. Indeed, the wide-open networking arena is creating new rivalries. In the 1980s, a widely anticipated epic battle between computer giant IBM and communications goliath American Telephone & Telegraph Co. never materialized. Absorbed by challenges to their core businesses, both companies scaled back forays into each other's turf. But in the 1990s, both intend to win in network management. Other competitors, such as General Motors Corp.'s Electronic Data Systems unit and Andersen Consulting, have jumped in by promising to "out-source" network management. For a fixed fee, they agree to run a corporation's network, and in some cases, its entire computer operations (page 21).

Getting someone to simply take the networking problem off your hands has a certain allure, but there's a trade-off: If the network is truly a crucial competitive tool, a company may not want what an outsider can supply—when all of its rivals can buy it, too. For example, a company such as Mrs. Field's Cookies Inc. has succeeded in large part because of its network. By spending the money to develop its own computer expertise, the chain of cookie shops has created an advanced network that lets managers in its Park City, Utah, headquarters find out immediately how well macadamia nut cookies are selling at a mall in Alabama. Philadelphia-based CIGNA Insurance spends nearly 3% of its revenues—almost $75 million a year—running its own network. Says Cliff Shorr, vice-president for communications management: "It give us higher reliability and lower transaction costs than our competitors."

The problem is that even in technologically savvy organizations, sprawling data networks look like a Rube Goldberg gizmo. Since no manufacturer makes all the individual parts, customers have shopped widely and now struggle to make it all work together. The 1984 breakup of AT&T and deregulation of the U. S. phone system spurred a huge wave of innovation in communications products and services. But it also led to networks with infinite combinations of modems, multiplexers, concentrators, protocol converters, private data lines, routers, brouters, bridges—to name just a few networking devices.

With some networks comprising as many as 100,000 devices, it's hard just keeping track of exactly what's in the network—and where. "Before [the AT&T] divestiture," says Philadelphia consultant Joseph M. Rozycki, "you took what you got [from AT&T]. Now, you're forced to be your own phone company."

FRANKENSTEIN. That would be headache enough. But the problem is compounded by the dozens of different brands of computers scattered throughout the offices, factories, and warehouses of large companies. Each has its own way of formatting and sending data. "The decentralized operations that were in such vogue in the early 1980s are now coming

GRAPHIC BY ROB DOYLE/BW

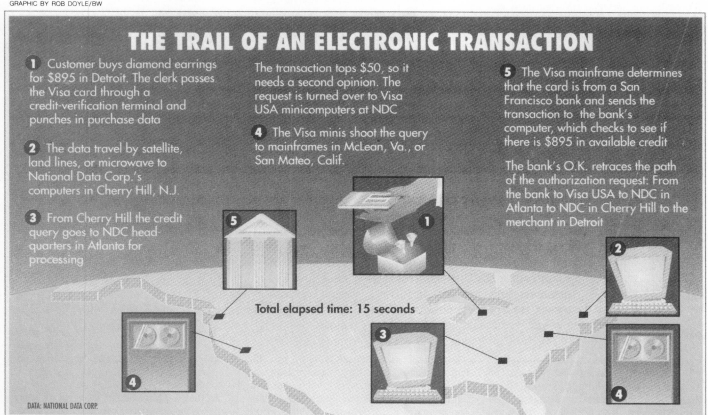

THE TRAIL OF AN ELECTRONIC TRANSACTION

1 Customer buys diamond earrings for $895 in Detroit. The clerk passes the Visa card through a credit-verification terminal and punches in purchase data

2 The data travel by satellite, land lines, or microwave to National Data Corp.'s computers in Cherry Hill, N.J.

3 From Cherry Hill the credit query goes to NDC headquarters in Atlanta for processing

The transaction tops $50, so it needs a second opinion. The request is turned over to Visa USA minicomputers at NDC

4 The Visa minis shoot the query to mainframes in McLean, Va., or San Mateo, Calif.

5 The Visa mainframe determines that the card is from a San Francisco bank and sends the transaction to the bank's computer, which checks to see if there is $895 in available credit

The bank's O.K. retraces the path of the authorization request: From the bank to Visa USA to NDC in Atlanta to NDC in Cherry Hill to the merchant in Detroit

Total elapsed time: 15 seconds

DATA: NATIONAL DATA CORP.

back to haunt us with these unlinkable systems," says Michael Morache, vice-president for marketing at Systematics Inc., a Little Rock-based systems integrator. Adds Mark Luczak, senior network specialist at Infotron Systems Corp., a maker of networking gear in Cherry Hill, N.J.: "We've unleashed a kind of Frankenstein."

Not that it's impossible to string a complex, worldwide network that works smoothly—it's just highly unusual. Texas Instruments Inc., the Dallas-based electronics giant, has a huge network that, among other things, helps engineers around the world collaborate. The net includes 23 mainframes, 2,000 mini-computers, 31,000 terminals, and 36,000 desktop computers.

But TI is one of the lucky ones. It carefully planned the expansion from just 200 terminals in Texas in the early 1970s to 50 sites in 18 countries today. Most companies haven't. Instead, they installed computers willy-nilly, and the problems of networking are catching them by surprise. "The necessity of managing networks just wasn't recognized in the early '80s," says Howard Frank, president of consultant Network Management Inc. "The network-management systems we see today are only trying to correct the problems of the past five years." Adds Northeast Consulting's Herman: "I don't think there's a single part of the industry where there's a bigger gap between the real need and what you can get today."

What network managers get a lot of is sensory overload. Each brand of equipment in a network usually reports to a separate control computer, using its own codes and protocols. With a screen to monitor each brand of network components, a network control room · may start to resemble a television showroom—or, as Ted Hanss, a networking project manager at the University of Michigan puts it, "the flight deck of the Starship Enterprise."

'BABOON-PROOF.' These dimly lit rooms may contain dozens of computer monitors, each displaying in graphics and lazily scrolling text the status of its respective network components. Each device on the network regularly checks in with an update on its status—up-and-running or experiencing difficulty. Usually, all is calm. But when trouble hits, it can look like the meltdown scene from *The China Syndrome*: Thousands of alarm signals may flood across those screens at once, making it tough to figure out what's wrong, let alone what to do about it.

What customers want, and what dozens of suppliers are rushing to develop, is an "integrated" network-management system. The idea is to collect all status re-

---

Commentary/by Peter Coy

THE PERILS OF PICKING THE WRONG STANDARD

To understand why computer standards are such a problem, consider the typewriter. The ungainly layout of the Qwerty keyboard was introduced in 1873 to slow down typists so they wouldn't jam the keys. That design imperative quickly disappeared, yet Qwerty has turned back all attempts—including one by its own inventor—to replace it with something faster. The productivity cost? Undoubtedly billions of dollars.

There are two morals to the Qwerty story. One is that picking a standard too soon can lock you into obsolete technology. The other is that even a mediocre standard is better than none. After all, Qwerty caught on so quickly because typists didn't want inconsistent keyboards—"interfaces," in today's jargon.

TIME PRESSURE. The tension between engineering perfection and timeliness shapes most of today's debates over computer standards, especially those involving management of computer networks. First, the engineering challenge is enormous. Imagine trying to manage all the traffic in Chicago while sitting in Toledo and watching a bank of TV screens. Imagine that every time George Bush comes to town, you have to reroute traffic by remote control. And now imagine that your computer from Company X can't fully control the monitoring cameras and traffic lights in Chicago built by Company Y because they use different standards. So much for that Presidential motorcade.

What makes network management so hard is that it has to build on lower-level networking technologies, which themselves are evolving. The International Organization for Standardization (ISO) in Geneva hammered out a broad, conceptual standard for network management, but customers demanded more. So, as soon as they saw a draft

of the ISO proposal, computer and phone companies formed the Network Management Forum to refine the concept for use in products that would let different network suppliers' systems communicate easily with each other.

The industry forum was criticized by some techno-thinkers for seeking a "quick and dirty" solution. Ironically, though, it wasn't quick enough. Hundreds of important customers got tired of waiting for the forum standard and adopted a different one that was less complete but had the great virtue of being available. This Simple Network Management Protocol, created for the 35-nation Internet research network, has caught on so quickly that some standards advocates now fear that it may eclipse the Network Management Forum's entry for years to come. They complain that the Internet format is out of sync with the ISO standard and is based on outdated technology. But it's available now. Shades of Qwerty.

CACOPHONY. The challenge, of course, is to bring out official standards before makeshift ones take root. It was easier in the old days, when technology emerged more slowly and from fewer sources. Broadly speaking, it was IBM in computers and American Telephone & Telegraph Co. in phones. Whatever they used became de facto standards.

Antitrust suits pushed IBM and AT&T to let other equipment connect to their mainframes and networks. That opened the way for new companies, lower costs, more choices. And cacophony. Now, it is up to the people who buy computers—and who benefit from the new choices—to force their suppliers to agree on workable standards for network management. A Qwerty-like expedient won't work in the Information Age.

---

ports and alarm signals, no matter what brand of equipment they come from, and present network operators with only the most useful and urgent information—on just one or two screens. Such a system might normally display color-coded overview maps of the network, but also would

let technicians zoom in on small details anywhere they wish. And artificial-intelligence software might filter incoming alarms, give detailed advice, and even act automatically to, say, reroute traffic around a dead switch. "Everyone would like a baboon-proof way of handling those

OUTSOURCING: MORE COMPANIES ARE LETTING GEORGE DO IT

Do you sometimes wish that your company's tangled network would just go away? Dozens of American corporations—GE, Avon, Eastman Kodak, H. J. Heinz, and Duracell among them—have made it happen. They have forged multiyear, multimillion-dollar alliances with computer makers, telephone companies, and high-technology consultants to take networks off their hands.

It's called outsourcing, and it makes good sense. It could cut annual data and telecommunications expenditures by as much as 30%—and it trims capital outlays. What's more, outsourcing can keep a company from getting stuck with obsolete equipment. For systems integrators, such as Andersen Consulting, Electronic Data Systems, and Perot Systems, it's a logical extension of existing businesses. For companies such as IBM, AT&T, and Digital Equipment, it's a hot growth opportunity when sales of mainframes, PBXs, and minicomputers are slow.

The concept is catching on. IBM has won four outsourcing deals worth about $700 million, and Electronic Data Systems Corp. has grabbed 10 for $7 billion. Of the 100 top information-technology buyers, 20% are expected to farm out parts of their networks in the next year, says market researcher Yankee Group. Outsourcing revenues will double from $5.9 billion last year to $12.8 billion in 1994, predicts Input, a computer consulting firm.

THE NEXT WAVE. Outsourcing is growing because corporations want to use technical resources for more strategic projects. A decade ago, companies such as American Airlines Inc. created their own networks to gain competitive advantages. Now, says Katherine M. Hudson, vice-president and director of corporate information systems at Eastman Kodak Co., networks are "critical to our business, but it's not critical that we operate them."

Kodak recently farmed out its network to IBM, DEC, and BusinessLand for an estimated $500 million over five years. That, analysts say, could trim Kodak's data-processing budget by a whopping 50%. Bank South Corp. expects similar returns. In 1989, it chose IBM to run its data network for 10 years. "Conservatively, we'll save $25 million," estimates James A. Dewberry, the bank's executive vice-president.

But there are limits. "You're asking too much of human nature to ask outsourcing to work completely," says David M. Edison, executive vice-president of outsourcing provider Westinghouse Communications Systems. Merrill Lynch & Co., for example, last fall announced with great fanfare plans for a $50 million, five-year contract with IBM and MCI Communications Corp. to manage its voice and data network. Within months—and without fanfare—Merrill backed out. IBM and MCI didn't have "the right mix of people to make it work," says DuWayne Peterson, Mer-

rill's executive vice-president for operations, systems, and telecommunications. IBM and MCI are still working with the brokerage on other networking projects, however.

BUYING IN. Merrill may have gotten caught up in outsourcing overkill. To win business, says Howard Anderson, president of Yankee Group, outsourcing companies are "talking big and offering financial incentives." EDS even purchases stakes in ailing companies in return for contracts. In September, it announced plans to pay about $25 million for 50% of Westwood Equities Corp. It expects to get $300 million in outsourcing work over 10 years.

The Bank South/IBM deal represents a good balance in outsourcing. IBM is building a new data center for the bank, which it will staff, run, and keep upgrading. It will also have the right to sell excess network capacity to other customers. But Bank South will hold on to "the core of our business," says Vice-President Dewberry: developing the software for business applications that run on the network.

Even with its shortcomings, outsourcing is likely to become a popular solution. Many companies need to pare costs and are hard pressed to find people to manage increasingly complex networks. For them, farming it out is the only way out.

By Jeffrey Rothfeder, with Peter Coy, in New York, Gary McWilliams in Boston, and bureau reports

---

[different] information feeds," says Tyrone Pike, president of New York network designer LANsystems Inc.

For now, the network-management game is being led by just a few large, influential players. AT&T has seized on it as a market where its unparalleled knowhow in managing communications circuits will finally give it an edge in computers. That's putting it on a collision course with IBM, which wants to establish its near-ubiquitous mainframes as the control hubs of corporate networks worldwide. DEC, the No. 2 force in computers, has also launched a comprehensive management scheme that it hopes will strengthen its already substantial role in many major networks.

Big Blue elevated network management to a strategic marketing issue mainly at DEC's prodding. In 1986, DEC was well ahead of IBM in connecting

computers of different sizes. To deflect attention from its relative weakness on that score, IBM renamed a group of its previously distinct networking programs "NetView" and began pitching their ability to manage its mainframe-based networks. That suddenly put DEC, with no mainframe to sell, on the defensive. Just like that, "IBM created an industry," says Steve Wendler, a former DEC employee now with market researcher Gartner Group in Stamford, Conn. "It masterfully outmarketed DEC by redrawing the battlefield."

Since then, IBM has pushed network management as a key role for its System/370 mainframe. With inexpensive, microprocessor-based machines taking on mainframe powers, the 370's traditional *raison d'etre*—large-scale processing—has been severely questioned lately. But IBM already has sold an esti-

mated 10,000 copies of NetView, a mainframe package that costs anywhere from $20,000 to $300,000, depending on the size of the network. NetView oversees the so-called logical aspect of networks—routing traffic around failed hardware and transferring massive blocks of data between machines. AT&T, on the other hand, leads in managing the physical aspects of networks—the actual wires and circuits connecting computers and telephones in one city to those in another. Now it sells Accumaster Integrator software for network management. It is also selling its services. For example, 20 AT&T technicians are working full time at Ford Motor Co. to keep its voice and data networks running smoothly. DEC remains well behind, but DEC's Enterprise Management Architecture, praised by many network technologists, could win substantial market share.

NEUTRALS. Other emerging players range from Nynex Corp. to Motorola Inc., through its Codex data communications unit. One notable independent is Systems Center Inc. in Reston, Va. The $77 million supplier of mainframe software acquired a package called NetMaster early this year. It's similar to NetView, but besides running on IBM mainframes, it runs on machines from Tandem and DEC, allowing those rivals to manage the world's 38,000 IBM mainframe-based networks. Says Systems Center Chairman and CEO Robert E. Cook: "We're the neutral player."

Neutrality is getting to be one of the hottest issues in network-management circles, at least among customers. As they're doing when shopping for computers, buyers are insisting on industry standards for networks. They fear computer makers will use proprietary networking software as a new lock-in. "Old habits die hard," says Colin Crook, Citicorp's chairman for corporate technology. A standard communications code used by controllers throughout the network would let every PC, modem, and data switch on the system report to one central computer.

Coming up with such a lingua franca is no easy matter (page 20). Since 1988, the Network Management Forum, led by the biggest computer and phone companies, has tried to create one. But while they hammer it out, some 25 suppliers are adopting Simple Network Management Protocol (SNMP), a less comprehensive standard but one that is easy to add

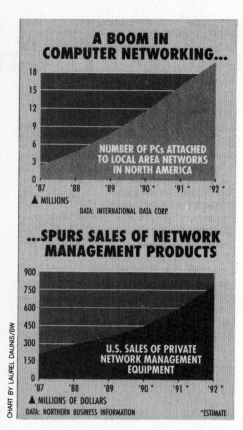

A BOOM IN COMPUTER NETWORKING...

NUMBER OF PCs ATTACHED TO LOCAL AREA NETWORKS IN NORTH AMERICA

▲ MILLIONS

DATA: INTERNATIONAL DATA CORP.

...SPURS SALES OF NETWORK MANAGEMENT PRODUCTS

U.S. SALES OF PRIVATE NETWORK MANAGEMENT EQUIPMENT

▲ MILLIONS OF DOLLARS

DATA: NORTHERN BUSINESS INFORMATION   *ESTIMATE

CHART BY LAUREL DAUNIS/BW

to existing products. Many observers believe, however, that eventually the Forum's Common Management Information Protocol is most likely to prevail.

With no dominant standard, suppliers are putting high-powered marketing efforts behind their own network-management schemes. "You're not going to make money on network management right now," says Dale Kutnick, president of consultant Meta Group in Westport, Conn. "It's more about account control and winning the next phase of equipment purchases." Many customers don't want to cede that kind of influence, notes Crook. Problem is, "most customers have been so disorganized until now that they haven't been able to exert pressure on this issue," he says.

That's changing, though. A group of corporations that includes GM, Ford, General Electric, Amoco, Eastman Kodak, Merck, and Du Pont has just formed the User Alliance for Open Systems—briefly known as the Houston 30, because of an August meeting there. With aggregate computer budgets in the billions, the group is demanding that suppliers move faster toward industry-standard gear—particularly for building and managing networks.

But even with standards, managing huge networks will remain a challenge for both customers and suppliers. For suppliers, they'll always be one of the largest and most complex "machines" ever devised—and a source of continuing competitive battles. And for the corporations that use them, they'll be an essential—albeit little understood—business tool.

By John W. Verity, Peter Coy, and Jeffrey Rothfeder in New York, with bureau reports

Does Corporate Nationality Matter?

*U.S. competitiveness
policy should
be based on
company behavior,
not ownership.*

ROBERT B. REICH

Robert B. Reich teaches political economy and management
at Harvard University's John F. Kennedy School of Government. He is the author of many books on government and
international trade, among them *The Next American Frontier*
and *Tales of a New America*. His latest book, which deals
with the themes in this article, is entitled *The Work of
Nations: Preparing Ourselves for 21st Century Capitalism*,
published by Alfred A. Knopf.

Charles Erwin ("Engine Charlie") Wilson, president
of General Motors when Eisenhower tapped him to
become secretary of defense in 1953, voiced a fundamental American belief at his confirmation hearing.
When asked whether he would be capable of making a
decision in the interest of the United States that was
averse to the interest of GM, he said that he could, but
that such a conflict would never arise: "I cannot
conceive of one because for years I have thought that
what was good for our country was good for General
Motors, and vice versa. The difference did not exist."

Such presumed connections are becoming at-
tenuated in the new global economy. U.S. "competitiveness" is no longer the same as the profitability,
productivity, or world market share of American-
owned corporations. A better definition of national
competitiveness is the capacity of a country's citizens
to maintain and enhance their standard of living, without going into debt to the rest of the world. This goal
depends less on the competitiveness of U.S. corporations than it does on the value that the American

workforce is able to add to the global economy. And
what is good for the American workforce is no longer
necessarily the same as what is good for the U.S.
corporation as it increasingly engages in international
competition.

The new global corporation

The U.S. multinational corporation has, of course,
been with us for many decades. But the new global
U.S. corporation marks a major step in its evolution. A
much larger proportion of its workforce is foreign;
and, increasingly, it does a great deal of its sophisticated work—including research, development, engineering, and complex fabrication—outside the
United States as well.

Fifty-five percent of IBM's world employees are
now foreign, and the percentage is growing. IBM
Japan boasts more than 18,000 Japanese employees
and annual sales of more than $6 billion, making it
one of Japan's major exporters of computers. Or consider Whirlpool. After cutting its American workforce
by 10 percent, shifting much of its production to
Mexico, and buying Dutch-owned Philips' appliance
business, Whirlpool now employs 43,000 people in 45
countries—most of them non-Americans. Or Seagate
Technology—a California-based world leader in hard-
disk drives—27,000 of whose 40,000 employees work
in Southeast Asia.

U.S. firms now employ 11 percent of the workforce of Northern Ireland. On the other side of the

From *Issues in Science and Technology*, Winter 1990-91, pp. 40-44. Copyright © 1991 by the National Academy of Sciences,
Washington, D.C.

world, 200 U.S. firms employ more than 100,000 Singaporeans to fabricate and assemble electronic components. Singapore's largest employer is General Electric. Taiwan counts AT&T, RCA, and Texas Instruments among its largest exporters.

Even America's major utilities are going global. Bell South, the largest provider of basic telephone services in the United States, now has operations in more than 20 countries—developing cellular telephone networks in Argentina and France, cable systems in France, management software in India, voice and data system designs in China, digital network technical services in Guatemala. Bell Atlantic just spent $1.5 billion to acquire New Zealand's Telecom, that nation's largest telephone company.

All told, more than 20 percent of the output of U.S. firms is now produced by foreign workers on foreign soil, and the percentage is rising quickly. At the present rate, overseas capital spending by U.S. corporations will have risen 14 percent in 1990, on top of 13 percent in 1989, and 13 percent the year before. That's compared to a rate of capital investment in the United States hovering at a bit over 6 percent a year. U.S. firms are now increasing investment at a faster pace in Western Europe alone than they are in the United States. They've accounted for over half of the flurry of acquisitions of European companies in the last six months and a hefty percentage of the new factories now going up.

Much of what the new global U.S. corporation produces abroad is exported back to the United States. In fact, approximately one-quarter of America's trade imbalance is attributable to U.S. firms that make or buy things abroad and then ship them back here. When offshore production is taken into account, U.S. firms are no less competitive than they were in the 1960s; they account for about the same share of global exports as they did 25 years ago—17 percent—even though exports from the United States have steadily declined.

Although it was once only undesirable low-wage, low-skill jobs that were moving offshore, U.S. firms are now hiring skilled workers abroad to do complex things. Texas Instruments maintains a software development facility in Bangalore, where 50 Indian programmers are linked by satellite with Texas Instruments' Dallas headquarters. Engineers in Singapore, meanwhile, are developing a new generation of laser printers for Hewlett-Packard and high-resolution video screens for Apple. In August, Hewlett-Packard announced that it was moving its world headquarters for the design and production of personal computers to Grenoble, France. The list of U.S. firms that have recently opened R&D labs in Japan reads like a "Who's Who" of corporate America: Eastman Kodak, W.R. Grace, DuPont, Merck, Procter & Gamble, Upjohn, and IBM, to name a few. And U.S. firms are scrambling to set up labs in Europe.

Here again, the aggregate figures suggest the trend: According to the National Science Foundation, U.S. firms increased their overseas spending on R&D by 33 percent between 1986 and 1988 (the last date for which such data are available), compared with a 6 percent increase in R&D in the United States. It is not clear how much of this trend is due to the promptings of foreign governments, but a large part of the reason is that U.S. firms can find highly qualified researchers abroad. For U.S. firms, one can no longer assume that highest "value added" occurs in the United States.

Meanwhile, of course, foreign companies have been stepping up their investments in the United States. Foreign firms now account for more than 13 percent of America's manufacturing assets and employ more than 8 percent of America's manufacturing workers—or about 3 million Americans. Even as some U.S. firms have reduced their American workforces, foreign firms have expanded theirs: Between 1987 and 1990, the Big Three U.S. automakers laid off 9,000 American autoworkers, while foreign firms hired more than 12,000. Since 1975, over 20,000 Americans have lost their jobs in U.S. firms that once manufactured televisions in the United States, but over 15,000 Americans have been hired by foreign firms to manufacture televisions in the United States.

Foreign firms are also stepping up their research, development, engineering, and complex production in the United States. During the 1980s, foreign firms invested about the same amount of money in the United States on R&D per manufacturing worker as did U.S. firms. European multinationals, like their U.S. counterparts, place R&D activities in all of the major markets in which they participate; they show little if any tendency to concentrate R&D at home.

Some nations' firms are, of course, more nationalistic than others, in that they tend to keep more of their high-value-added activities at home and are more reluctant to promote foreign nationals to high positions of authority. Japanese firms in particular display such characteristics—although even here it is difficult to generalize because certain Japanese firms, such as Sony, have made significant progress toward becoming truly global corporations.

The point of my argument is that a firm's nationality no longer determines its behavior. And it is behavior that matters.

The standard of living of Americans depends far more on what it is they can do than it does on the assets they own.

The real American interest

U.S. economic well-being rests on the ability of Americans to add value to the global economy, regardless of the nationality of the corporation they happen to be working for. American shareholders do, of course, benefit from the global successes of U.S. corporations to the extent that such successes are reflected in higher share prices and dividends. But American investors also benefit from the successes of non-U.S. firms in which they own shares. (Cross-border equity investing by Americans, British, Japanese, and Germans is increasing by about 20 percent a year.) Thus, in today's global economy, the total financial return to Americans from their equity investments increasingly depends on how much money Americans have invested in global portfolios comprising both American- and foreign-owned companies, and on the care and wisdom with which Americans have selected such portfolios. The profitability of "U.S." corporations is beside the point.

In any event, the standard of living of Americans (as well as the standard of living of other nations' citizens) depends far more on what it is that they can *do* than it does on the assets they own. And what they are able to do depends, in turn, on the education and training they receive. Global corporations that give the nation's citizens good jobs involving on-the-job technical training; experience in complex engineering, research, or development; or training in the sophisticated use and application of information, are thus of substantial value.

That American citizens "control" a certain global corporation as its top officers and directors is no guarantee that the corporation will provide Americans with such high-value jobs. The logic of global capitalism, in fact, requires that U.S. firms allocate their production across many nations, wherever they can earn the highest return for their shareholders. Not even the most patriotic of American executives is authorized by shareholders to forego profitable opportunities abroad for the sake of improving the skills and competitiveness of the American workforce.

In fact, the new logic of global capitalism requires that U.S. firms go to great lengths to show their foreign employees, suppliers, customers, and host governments that they are not playing favorites by biasing their location decisions in favor of the American workforce. They must be "good corporate citizens" wherever they do business, as must any other global corporation. IBM makes a substantial effort to be a Canadian corporation in Canada, a Japanese corporation in Japan, and a European corporation in Europe. (The same principle applies to Japanese firms. If they continue to display nationalistic tendencies, they will encounter increasing resistance from their foreign constituencies. Not the least, they will have difficulty hiring highly talented non-Japanese executives.)

Even when it comes to national security, the fact of U.S. corporate nationality is less relevant than the location of production. A foreign-owned firm operating in the United States that trains Americans to do complex tasks pertinent to designing or fabricating weapons, for example, is far more important to our future security than an American-owned firm that designs and fabricates weapons for the Pentagon in another nation. Moreover, unlike foreign assets held by U.S. firms that are subject to foreign political control and, occasionally, to expropriation, foreign-owned assets in the United States are secure against sudden changes in foreign governments' policies.

Policy implications

During the past few years, as U.S. policymakers have become increasingly worried about the country's declining competitiveness, a number of laws and policies have been invoked to stem the tide. But because they are premised on the incorrect notion that the competitiveness of the U.S. corporation is roughly equivalent to the competitiveness of the United States, these measures may end up jeopardizing the real standard of living of Americans instead of enhancing it. Consider these examples:

Publicly supported research and development. By law, U.S. national laboratories may license their inventions to private firms, but only to American-owned private firms. Similarly, participation in research consortia funded in part by the federal government is limited to American-owned firms. Such policies make little sense. The goal of publicly supported research and development should be to enhance the skills and

...s of American scientists, engineers, and tech-
...s. But there is no reason to suppose that U.S.
...s that receive federal research support will necessarily utilize their research in the United States; they
may just as easily apply it to engineering and development projects abroad. A more sensible policy, therefore, would require that any global firm that receives
government research assistance—regardless of nationality—undertake in the United States a certain
amount of the engineering and development that flow
from that research.

Trade policy. For the same reason, we should be
less interested in opening foreign markets to
American-owned firms than in opening those markets
to companies that employ Americans—even if the
companies happen to be foreign-owned. By this logic,
for example, it makes little sense for the U.S. Trade
Representative to expend scarce bargaining "chits"
trying to get Japan to open its market to retail firms
such as Toys-R-Us (most of whose inventory comes
from Southeast Asia and Latin America). By the same
token, a high priority should be to ensure that the
European Community not erect barriers to the impor-
tation of American-based entertainment—television
shows, videos, records, and so forth—even if the
Americans who produce such entertainment happen
to work for Sony.

Antitrust policy. The Justice Department is about
to relax antitrust policy to permit certain joint production agreements and has signaled that the relaxed
policy would apply only to American-owned firms;
the House of Representatives has already moved to
deny foreign-owned companies relaxed antitrust rules
on joint production ventures. But corporate nationality
has little bearing upon whether a joint production
agreement potentially enhances the competitiveness
of the American workforce by generating significant
economies of scale within the United States. A decision whether to allow such an agreement should
turn, rather, on whether participating firms could gain
such efficiencies on their own, simply by enlarging
their investment in the United States; whether such a
combination of companies would allow higher levels
of productivity within the United States; and whether
the combination would substantially diminish global
competition. National origin should have nothing to
do with it.

Foreign direct investment. Under the Exon-Florio
Amendment to the Omnibus Trade and Competitive-

ness Act of 1988, a high-level Committee on Foreign
Investments in the United States can block a foreign
acquisition of a U.S. firm. Other proposed legislation
would make it even more difficult for foreign firms to
acquire U.S. companies. These policies, too, make little sense. If a foreign owner is willing to invest the
capital to make the company globally competitive
and to provide high-quality jobs for Americans, the
United States benefits. Thus, it is not surprising that
America's governors spend a great deal of time and
energy promoting their states to foreign investors and
offer big subsidies to foreign companies to locate in
their states, even if they compete head-on with existing
American-owned businesses.

If there is reason to believe that a proposed acquisition of a U.S. firm by a foreign firm will give
the foreign firm—or a group of foreign firms—the capacity to monopolize an industry, U.S. antitrust laws
are sufficient to block the acquisition. Thus, to the extent that Japanese semiconductor firms are behaving
like a cartel and the purchase of a U.S. company such
as Perkin-Elmer (a supplier of production equipment)
would enhance their market power, the Justice Department or the FTC should prevent the acquisition. But
note that the decision does not turn on corporate
nationality *per se*, but on corporate behavior. Precisely
the same stricture should be applied to U.S. firms
operating in the same monopolistic manner.

Tax evasion. Responding to Internal Revenue Service figures showing that foreign-owned firms in the
U.S. in 1986 reported $550 billion in gross receipts but
showed $1.5 billion in tax losses, several members of
Congress have introduced bills to give the IRS new
powers to monitor U.S. units of foreign multinationals
and impose a capital gains tax on the sale of the holdings of some foreigners. But to the extent that global
firms have been evading U.S. taxes by transferring
profits to their foreign units, the problem is hardly
limited to foreign-owned firms. Using many of the
same techniques (many of which were devised by
American tax lawyers in the first place), global U.S.
corporations have for years been using "transfer pricing" to allocate their profits in ways that reduce their
income taxes. Here again, corporate nationality is irrelevant; if a federal response is warranted, it should
apply broadly to all global corporations.

Political activities. Bills are being readied to bar
U.S. subsidiaries of foreign corporations from forming
political action committees or hiring former federal
officials to lobby on their behalf. Although concerns

about foreign interference in the U.S. political process are understandable, we should nonetheless remind ourselves that—as in the other policy areas enumerated above—the underlying issue has less to do with corporate nationality than with corporate behavior. Where it is appropriate for U.S. corporations to have access to Washington policymakers, it is just as appropriate for foreign firms operating in the United States to have such access.

Restrictions on the political activities of such foreign companies necessarily reduce the access of Americans working within such companies to the U.S. political process; American employees of such firms as Pillsbury, First Boston, and Marine Midland Bank would thus be denied the sort of representation accorded to their compatriots who happen to work for American-owned firms. On the other hand, where such access is misused—with the result that the firm is helped but the nation's interests are jeopardized—the problem is the same whether it is caused by a foreign or a U.S. firm. In order to guard against such misuse, restrictions on political action committees and on the lobbying activities of former federal officials would seem appropriate regardless of the nationality of the firms that utilize them.

A national competitive strategy

Nothing I have said is inconsistent with a bold national strategy to improve U.S. competitiveness. Indeed, I have long advocated just such an initiative. At its heart would be public investments in education, training, and infrastructure designed to improve the capacities of Americans to identify and solve problems, and to link those capacities to the world economy. A skilled workforce, coupled with superb infrastructure, will attract global capital to create good jobs. Such a strategy would also feature agreements with global corporations to undertake high-value-added development and production in the U.S., and thus give Americans on-the-job training in the technologies of the future.

But however we design our industrial policy, the nationality of corporate ownership should not play a significant role. In today's global economy, most factors of production are highly mobile. Money, technology, and state-of-the-art factories and equipment move almost effortlessly across borders, so that corporations are becoming global entities that are only loosely linked to nations, if at all. The U.S. competitive future depends on the one factor of production that is rooted at home: our workforce.

Recommended reading

Norman Glickman and Douglas Woodward, *The New Competitors*. New York: Basic Books, 1989.

Edward Graham and Paul Krugman, *Foreign Direct Investment in the United States*. Washington, D.C.: Institute for International Economics, 1989.

De Anne Julius, *Global Companies and Public Policy*. London: Royal Institute of International Affairs, 1990.

Robert B. Reich, "Who is Us?" *Harvard Business Review*, January-February 1990.

The Myth of a
Post-Industrial Economy

The United States cannot afford to abandon its basic manufacturing industries. Relying on a shift to services or high technology is irresponsible analysis and perverse policy.

STEPHEN S. COHEN AND JOHN ZYSMAN

STEPHEN S. COHEN AND JOHN ZYSMAN are professors of planning and political science, respectively, at the University of California at Berkeley. They co-direct the Berkeley Roundtable in International Economy (BRIE).

MANUFACTURING matters mightily to the wealth and power of the United States and to our ability to sustain the open society we have come to take for granted. But this contention is a distinctly minority view in the United States today. In part this is due to the power of a central tenet of American economic thought: government policy should be indifferent to what makes up the gross national product.

This conventional view is supported by numerous authors in books, journal articles, op-ed pieces, and expert testimony. They point to the relentless decline in manufacturing employment—from 50 percent of all jobs in 1950 to 20 percent now—and the increase in service jobs, which now constitute about 70 percent of all employment. These figures underwrite the mainstream view that economic development is a never-ending shift from activities of the past up into newer, more profitable activities. The United States shifted from farming to industry. Now we are shifting from industry to services and high technology.

The lesson for government is clear: keep hands off. For example, in his latest Report to the Congress on Trade Agreements, President Reagan sets out the following framework for understanding a troubling trade imbalance. "The move from an industrial society toward a 'postindustrial' service economy has been one of the greatest changes to affect the developed world since the Industrial Revolution. The progression of an economy such as America's from agriculture to manufacturing to services is a natural change."

The New York Stock Exchange, in a recent report on trade, industrial change, and jobs, put it more pointedly: "A strong manufacturing sector is not a requisite for a prosperous economy."

Or, in the words of a *Forbes* editorial, "Instead of ringing in the decline of our economic power, a service-driven economy signals the most advanced stage of economic development. . . . Instead of following the Pied Piper of 'reindustrialization,' the U.S. should be concentrating its efforts on strengthening its services."

In this view, America's loss of market share and employment in industries such as textiles, steel, apparel, autos, consumer electronics, machine tools, random-access memories, computer peripherals, and circuit boards is neither surprising nor bad. It is not a sign of failure but part of the price of success. The United States should be shedding sunset industries and moving on to services and high tech, the sunrise sectors. Such a change is part of an ever-evolving international division of labor from which everyone benefits.

This view is soothing in its message, calm in tone, confident in style, and readily buttressed by traditional economic theory. We believe it is also quite possibly wrong. At the heart of our argument is a notion we call "direct linkage:" many service jobs are tightly tied to manufacturing. Lose manufacturing and you will lose—not develop—those high-wage services. Nor is the relationship between high tech and manufacturing, like that between services and manufacturing, a simple case of evolutionary succession. High tech is intimately tied to manufacturing, not a free-floating laboratory activity.

Our argument takes issue—fundamentally—with the widely articulated view that a service-based, "post-industrial" economy is the natural successor to an industry-based economy, the next step up a short but steep staircase consisting of "stages of development." Because the traditional view justifies economic policies that risk the wealth and power of the United States, it is, for all its conventionality, a terribly radical guide for policy. If the United States wants to stay on top—or even high up—we can't just shift out of manufacturing and into services.

Nor can we establish a long-term preserve around traditional blue-collar jobs and outmoded plants. If the United States is to remain a wealthy and powerful economy, American manufacturing must automate, not emigrate. Moreover, it must automate in ways that build flexibility through the imaginative use of skilled labor. In a world in which technology migrates rapidly and financial services are global, the skills of our workforce and the talents of our managers together will be our central resource.

Linkages and Wealth

Most celebrations of the shift from industry to services construct a parallel to the shift from agriculture to industry. According to that argument, the shift from low-productivity, low-paid farm labor to higher-productivity, hence higher-paid employment in industry is precisely what economic development is about. The same developmental movement, the same "creative destruction," is now being repeated in the shift out of industry and into services and high tech.

This view of economic history, although familiar and reassuring, is misleading. It confuses two separate transitions: a shift out of agricultural production and a shift *of labor* out of agriculture.

The first shift never occurred. U.S. agricultural production did not go offshore or shrivel up. To the embarrassment of those who view the cultivation of large quantities of soybeans, tomatoes, and corn as incompatible with a high-tech future, agriculture has sustained the highest long-term productivity of any sector of the economy. We automated agriculture; we did not send it offshore or shift out of it. As a result we developed massive quantities of high-value-added, high-paid jobs in related industries and services such as agricultural machinery and chemicals. These industries and services owe their development, scale, and survival to a broad and strong American agricultural sector.

Even the employment shift from agriculture merits a second look. The generally accepted figure for U.S. agricultural employment is about 3 million, or 3 percent of the workforce. But this figure arbitrarily excludes many categories of employment. Are crop dusters and large-animal veterinarians employed in agriculture? The 3 million figure is blind to such important economic realities. If we ask what would have happened to employment (and wealth) if the United States had shifted out of agriculture instead of moving labor off the farm, we encounter the notion of linkage: the relationship of agricultural production to employment in tractor repair, ketchup making, and grape crushing.

The more advanced a production process, the longer and more complicated the linkages. Primitive farmers scratch the ground with sticks. They need very little from outside. Their productivity is also very low. Modern farmers head a long, elaborate chain of specialists, most of whom don't often set foot on the farm, yet all of whom are vital to its successful operation and directly depend on it.

Such linkage is not a new notion. But conventional economics does not like linkages to be used as evidence of some special economic importance for particular sectors. Linkage has no place in a discussion of a subject like why manufacturing matters, critics say. Their objection is not that linkages are dubious or rare, or impossible to demonstrate. Rather, it is that they are ubiquitous. In economics, everything is linked to everything else.

The linkages admitted in traditional economics are all of the same special kind: they are loose couplings. Each is a simple market relationship between a buyer and a seller, and each involves a traded good. The United States can, in principle at least, make cars or textiles with imported machines. We do it every day, though at a steadily shrinking volume. These are the loosest linkages imaginable.

There are, however, tighter linkages, such as those between agricultural production and the food-processing industry, which employs about 1.7 million Americans. Here the linkages are tight and concrete. Move the tomato farm offshore and you close the ketchup plant or move it offshore also. It is technically possible but economically difficult to mill sugar cane in a country far from the sugar fields, or to process tomatoes far from the tomato patch, or to dry grapes into raisins far from the vineyard. An economy like ours is based on an enormous number of such tight bonds. It is not simply a system of loose linkages like those that dominate the models from which conventional economics produces its conventional prescriptions.

It is extremely implausible that the United States would sustain a major agricultural-chemicals industry if it were not the world's largest and most advanced market for those products. It is not likely that we would have developed the world's largest agricultural-machinery industry in the absence of the world's largest agricultural sector. Were the wheat fields to vanish from the United States, the machinery makers would shrink and so would their suppliers of parts, computers, trucking, and janitorial services.

The Department of Agriculture provides estimates of agriculture-dependent employment, but they outrageously overstate the case by tracing the food and fiber chain up through textile mills and food stores. Their 1982 estimate was 28.4 million jobs dependent on agriculture. Using rather conservative assumptions, we found that 3 to 6 million jobs—in addition to the 3 million traditionally classified as agricultural—can be considered part of this sector.

Manufacturing Linkages

If we turn from agriculture to industry—where direct employment is 21 million jobs—we find that even a remotely similar "linkage rate" would radically alter the place of manufacturing in the U.S. economy. The employment of another 40, 50, or even 60 million Americans, half to three-quarters of whom are counted as service workers, depends directly upon manufacturing production. If manufacturing goes, those service jobs will go with it.

If we lose control and mastery of manufacturing production, the problem is not simply that we will be unable to replace the jobs lost with service jobs, or simply that those service jobs will pay less, or that the scale and speed of adjustment will shock the society—and polity—in potentially dangerous ways. It is that the high-paying service jobs that are directly linked to manufacturing will, after a few short rounds of industrial innovation, whither away, only to sprout up offshore.

Many service jobs that follow manufacturing, such as wholesaling, retailing, and advertising, would not be directly affected if manufacturing were ceded to offshore producers. The same sales effort is involved in selling a Toyota as in selling a Buick.

The services that are directly linked to manufacturing are concentrated in that relatively narrow band of services that precedes it. Examples of such activities include design and engineering services; payroll, inventory, and accounting services; finance and insurance; repair and maintenance of plant and machinery; training and recruitment; testing services and labs; industrial waste disposal; and the accountants, designers, publicists, payroll, transportation, and communication firms who work for the engineering firms that design and service production equipment.

Two questions pose themselves. The first concerns the nature of the linkages. How can we go about determining how many jobs would vanish from the U.S. economy if manufacturing were lost? The second involves scale: do services to manufacturing constitute a scale of employment sufficient to justify a new set of concerns, a rethinking of theory, and a recasting of policy?

The President's Report on the Trade Agreements Program provides an approximate answer for the second question: "25 percent of U.S. GNP originates in services used as inputs by goods-producing industries—more than the value added to GNP by the manufacturing sector."

But charting how much of this service employment is tightly linked to manufacturing is difficult. It should be right at the top of the economics research agenda, so that it can get to the top of the policy debate. Unless it can be shown that the overwhelming bulk of those services are weakly linked to manufacturing, we must quickly reformulate the terms of that policy debate.

Some of those services that precede are so tightly linked to manufacturing that they are best understood as direct extensions of it. These would include truckers who specialize in shipping raw materials, components, and semi-finished goods. The U.S. textile industry, for example, is a major employer of trucking services. The category of services tightly linked to manufacturing is real, and it is peopled. But unfortunately we do not yet know how big it is.

Is Exporting Services an Answer?

If, indeed, many services are tied to manufacturing, can the United States significantly offset its trade deficit in merchandise by running a surplus in trade of services? Recent experience provides no reason for assuming—wishing is a better word—that the United States is better at exporting services than it is at exporting manufactured goods. The total volume of service trade is an order of magnitude less than trade in goods. Consequently, only a sudden multiplication of service exports could compensate for the present deterioration in traded goods.

There are a number of problems with counting on an expansion in American service exports. First, almost all the current trade surplus in services stems from interest on old loans abroad. These loans are not very bankable since Third World nations threaten to default. Indeed, our obligations to foreign countries now exceed theirs to us. The United States is a debtor nation.

Second, as with domestic services, large segments of trade in international services are directly tied to a strong and technologically advanced manufacturing sector.

Consider U.S. exports of engineering services. These top-of-the-line services are knowledge-intensive and employ highly paid professionals who in turn purchase significant amounts of other services, including telecommunications, data processing, computer programming, and legal advice. Competitive advantage in engineering services depends upon mastery and control of the latest production technology by U.S. producers. Not very long ago we exported such services in the steel industry. Then U.S. steel producers fell behind in the design and operation of production technologies and facilities. When leadership in production changed hands, the flow of services for this industry also reversed. Now we import those services from our former customers in Europe and Japan, and might soon obtain them from Korea and Brazil.

Third, it is not only engineering services that go through this development cycle. Financial services—a sector in which the United States is said to have a strong competitive advantage—are often cited as an area where export earnings could offset deficits in the merchandise account in a big way. Financial services are high in knowledge and technology, and are supposedly located within the most advanced economy: ours.

But the situation in banking services may be less rosy than we like to think. There is no compelling reason to assume a special advantage for U.S. banks compared with their competitors. Foreign banks are bigger, and they are growing faster than U.S. banks. A recent listing of the world's largest banks included 23 Japanese banks, 44 European banks, and only 18 U.S. banks.

U.S. banks are not even particularly succeeding in holding on to their home market. For example, foreign banks are doing as well in California as foreign auto producers. Six of the ten largest banks in California are now foreign owned, up from two of ten five years ago. Foreign banks now account for about 40 percent of the big commercial loans—the high end of the business—made in New York and San Francisco. Service trade is not an alternative to trade in goods.

The High-Tech Link

Some analysts, such as Robert Z. Lawrence of the Brookings Institution, take comfort in the fact that high-technology exports have grown in importance for the United States. They see that as a sign of a healthy, normal development process. But the supposed U.S. advantage in high-technology goods is also deeply misleading. It suggests less a distinctive international advantage than a deep incapacity to compete with our industrial partners even in more traditional sectors. A failure by American firms to remain competitive in manufacturing processes seems to underlie this weakness. Moreover, the U.S. position in high-technology trade is quite narrow and fragile.

In the early eighties the range of high-technology sectors from which a surplus was generated was actually quite narrow: aircraft, computers, and agricultural chemicals. The overall high-tech surplus disappeared by 1983, and in 1984 and 1985 high technology, too, ran a growing deficit. Moreover, a substantial portion of U.S. high-tech exports are military goods, which indicates more about the character of America's strategic ties than about its industrial competitiveness. At a minimum, military sales reflect such factors as foreign policy far more than simple commercial calculus.

Like the service industries, much of high tech is tightly linked to traditional manufacturing. Most high-tech products are producer goods, not consumer items, despite the popularity of home computers and burglar alarms. They are bought to be used in the products of other industries (such as microprocessors in cars) or in production processes (such as robots, computers, and lasers). If American producers of autos, machine tools, telephones, and trousers don't buy American-made silicon chips, who will?

A second tie to manufacturing is even tighter. If high tech is to sustain a scale of activity sufficient to matter, America must control the production of those high-tech products it invents and designs—and it must do so in a direct and hands-on way. Unless R&D is closely tied to manufacturing—and to the innovation required to maintain competitiveness—it will lose its cutting edge. For example, by abandoning the production of televisions, the U.S. electronics industry quickly lost the know-how to design, develop, refine, and competitively produce the VCR, the next generation of that product.

Defense: A Footnote

Until now, we have treated military needs in parenthesis, as they are treated in conventional economics. However, it is not easy to make exceptions for something as big as the U.S. military effort. Exceptions of that scale are never without consequences for the rest of the system.

A strong domestic manufacturing capability greatly reduces the costs of our defense effort. Diverse and leading-edge production of technologies such as semiconductors, computers, telecommunications, and machine tools makes the costs of advanced weaponry much lower than if we had to create an industrial structure exclusively for military use.

If U.S. commercial semiconductor manufacturers, say, fall behind foreign competitors, the military might not even be able to produce the components for its own use. Domestic capability in critical links in the production chain—for example, mask-making, clean rooms, and design and production tools for semiconductors—could quickly disappear.

Such an erosion of our ability to produce critical technologies would massively reduce our strategic independence and diplomatic options. Whatever the ups and downs of military spending and the changes in defense strategies, our basic security is built on the assumption that the United States will maintain a permanent lead in a broad range of advanced industrial technologies. Loss of leading-edge capacity in chip making would quickly translate into a loss of diplomatic and strategic bargaining chips.

This argument suggests that commercial development often drives military capability. It is the reverse of the common notion that military needs drive commercial development. If the United States had to support the full weight of a vast arsenal economy, we would become vis à vis Japan not so different from the arsenal Soviet economy vis à vis that of the United States.

Manufacturing and Wealth

Sometimes new notions capture the public fancy, resonate to some element of our experience, and color the way we see the world. The concept of a "post-industrial" society is such a notion. But it also obscures the precise nature of changes in the U.S. economy and what they mean.

Things have changed: production workers go home cleaner; more and more workers leave offices rather than assembly lines. And the organization of society has changed along with the technologies of product and production.

But the relationship of changes in technology and society to changes in the fundamentals of economics—the process of creating wealth—is less clear. There is not yet, nor is there likely to be in the near future, a post-industrial economy. The division of labor has become infinitely more elaborate and the production process far less direct—involving ever more specialized services as well as goods and materials located far from the traditional scene of production. However, the key generator of wealth for this vastly expanded division of labor remains production. The United States is shifting not out of industry into services but from one kind of industrial economy to another.

Insisting that a shift to services or high technology is "natural" is irresponsible analysis and perverse policy. The competitiveness of the U.S. economy—the ability to maintain high and rising wages—is not likely to be enhanced by abandoning production to others. Instead of ceding production, public policy should actively aim to convert low-productivity, low-wage, low-skill production processes into high-technology, high-skill, high-wage activities—whether they are included in the manufacturing unit itself or counted largely as service firms.

America's declining competitiveness is troubling precisely because emerging fundamental changes in production technologies and the extent and forms of international competition are likely to prove enduring. The international hierarchy of wealth and power is being reshuffled, and it is happening fast and now.

Canadian companies are adopting networking technology with a vengeance

TYING ONE ON

Alan Morantz

DONALD LESLIE HAS ENGINEERED COMPUTER nirvana, or a reasonable facsimile. A partner and the national director of information management for accounting firm Clarkson Gordon, Leslie has overseen a massive purchase of 1,300 Apple Macintosh computers. Each one talks to the next to create an electronic community spanning 11 floors in two buildings in downtown Toronto. He is also developing a new kind of software that will encourage people to work together on projects and prod them to action. And when his firm moves into its own tower in two years, Leslie will likely oversee the installation of state-of-the-art telephone cable that carries not only voice, but data and images as well. If all this were not enough to grant him membership to the computer-networking hall of fame, he has even incorporated the technology in his own home. "My two sons have Macintoshes," says Leslie, "and I'm going to network them into my laser printer at home, so that'll keep them from bugging me. They'll access the printer from their bedroom."

Presumably, Donald Leslie's household, like his workplace, is operating more efficiently these days. Leslie is part of a wave of businesspeople who have tapped into a vital force shaping business large and small: The era for personal computers has truly arrived. Canadian companies are now adopting networking technology with a vengeance.

BRANCHING OUT

Networking technology is linking the once-lowly desktop computer with the company's mainframe and with other personal computers, establishing small work groups that are tied together electronically. The current trend by big corporate users is to link all of these small local area networks (LANs) within offices and among branch operations with the help of "bridges," "routers" and "gateways." The power of integration is sweeping through all aspects of information technology: apples and oranges of hardware working together; software now prodding people to work more closely with one another; office machines taking on wholly new functions. "What everyone is looking for now is the glue," says Jan Duffy, a partner in the information technology division of Peat Marwick Consulting Group in Toronto. "Once you get the critical mass of computers, you realize how much more valuable the networking technology is to you. We have been searching for this integration for the last two or three years; however, we haven't been demanding it as much as we are this year."

While computer networks using minicomputers (also called "dumb" terminals because they must rely on a microcomputer for instructions) have been around for years, the new networks are based on microcomputers that put the raw processing power on workers' desks. As companies open themselves to the world of microcomputer networking, they are facing a new set of management issues that, if avoided or dealt with sloppily, can undermine the technological payoff that they're seeking. The stakes for the individual are no less significant: The networking of microcomputers can either give workers a broader role in decision making or expose them to such rigid monitoring of work as to evoke the spec-

Originally published in *enRoute*, June 1989, pp. 4, 7-8, 11-12, 15-16, 20, 23-24, 26, 30, 33-34. Copyright © 1989 by Alan Morantz. Reprinted by permission of the author.

tre of Big Brother. "The period we're going through now is more revolutionary than evolutionary," says consultant Harvey Gellman of Gellman, Hayward & Partners of Toronto.

Gellman has been in the computer industry since 1955. "Noncomputer people are using micros and that is eroding the power base of the central systems organization. People believe that the hierarchical organization is still going to exist. But it seems to me future organizations will be networks of relationships, and the whole pyramid will flatten out."

2-4-6-8, WHY SHOULD WE INTEGRATE?

There are several components to a local area network. Typically, it requires a software program, such as Novell NetWare, Banyan Vines or Microsoft LanManager, to allow the machines to communicate with one another; a network "card" installed in a central microcomputer (usually called a "server") enables it to operate as the quarterback; and a cable, of which there are about 35 varieties, is the physical connection. The network should be invisible to the user, who may work on usual applications but will now have access to coworkers' files and perhaps the corporate database.

Evans Research Corporation in Toronto estimates that Canadian sales of LAN equipment for microcomputers grew by 31 percent last year, while Dataquest Inc. estimates 19 percent of business personal computers in the United States are already hooked into LANs. According to a survey of corporate buying plans for the coming year by consultants at Peat Marwick for MicroAge Computer Stores, "the most dramatic expenditures will be in the area of LANs, which may signify the movement from task automation (geared to improve individual productivity) to process automation (geared toward group computing). This is not surprising at a time when connectivity and sharing information are considered to be of critical importance."

The switch to process automation recognizes that people within an organization rarely work in isolation. For example, projects and reports now move from department to department to be worked on by many specialists at the same time. The network therefore becomes the messenger that facilitates this new working arrangement. Jan Duffy, who coauthored the Peat Marwick study, says that the returns of computer investment come when an organization realizes that it jibes with corporate objectives.

ON THE FAST TRACK

Increasingly, with the help of networks, the personal computer is, in some cases, supplanting the powerful mainframe. The Canadian information technology industry grew by 6.7 percent in 1988, according to International Data Corporation (Canada) Ltd. (IDC), and that revenue growth is being fuelled by the single-user systems market, the fastest growing hardware segment in 1988. The value of this market reached almost $2 billion, a growth of more than 19 percent from 1987. By contrast, the mainframe market dropped by almost one percent, to $1.2 billion. IDC says that by 1992, single-user systems will claim about 50 percent of the market.

Comcheq Services Limited of Winnipeg provides a dramatic example of how powerful personal computers have become in the networking era. The company, which provides an automated payroll service to about 6,000 Canadian companies, had been leasing time on a Control Data mainframe at its head office. Each day, someone in each of the company's branch offices would key in payroll data and transmit the information to the mainframe in Winnipeg for processing, with the reports being transmitted back. Until last year. "Ten 386 microcomputers [those sporting the powerful Intel 80386 microprocessor] replaced our mainframe," says John Loewen, Comcheq president and general manager. "The obvious reason is cost; they're a tenth of the cost." Now each branch does its own processing on a 386 personal computer, and the computer network, using Waterloo Port, which was developed by Waterloo Microsystems. "Between computer fees for the mainframe rental and communications costs, we figure we will save between $800,000 and $1 million per year. People feel in better control of their operation."

With the price of networks and personal computers coming down, small businesses are eyeing the same benefits. "I think in some ways smaller businesses have an advantage in networking," says Dwight Wainman, a partner in Wainman and Kydd Chartered Accountants of Toronto and a consultant to smaller firms. "They can integrate faster because networking is getting cheaper, and they are not stuck with the hang-ups of centralized control in large companies." Wainman practises what he preaches. His own medium-sized firm of 40 employees installed its first of two networks four years ago to link his IBM personal computers. The machines now share two laser printers and computerized audit files. Six Macintoshes are also integrated.

Company-wide networks also affect how people work. With the decline of a paper-based system, for example, the role of support staff can be altered overnight, and with company-wide electronic mail-networking's number one application, where all internal and external messages are recorded on a computer—the supervisor and supervised are brought closer. Wainman's accounting firm, which has several LANs, employs only four support staff.

"People have to understand that the way they work changes drastically with networks," says Michael Corlett, manager of computer services of McKim Advertising in Toronto. "A big reorganization has to take place, especially in the relationship between work groups. Let's say there are three departmental and project relationships. Instead of having to go through a chain of command to get things done, you're in direct communication with everyone else. You check your [electronic] mail on your computer screen, and there is no more going through a secretary. You can probably get 20 to 40 percent of your people back into the job rather than doing support stuff."

GROUP THERAPY

Perhaps the most dramatic changes in how people work with one another will be brought about as the new wave of software, called "groupware," is introduced this year. A natural outgrowth of LANs, groupware is roughly defined as "computer-supported cooperative work"—it actually integrates work activities. These products coordinate the daily tasks of administration, enabling work groups to have discussions, coordinate calendars, be reminded of deadlines, track projects and follow up on details. Groupware will "make possible a new level of integration, not just of computer networks or standards, but of what people do," claims Terry Winograd, an associate professor at Stanford University in California. At its best, groupware offers a structure within which business decisions can be reached quickly and with the greatest amount of input.

Although groupware is still in its early development, the few programs now commercially available indicate some of the possibilities of the technology. MarkUp and For Comment, for example, are geared to document editing and reviewing, which is a highly collaborative process. These programs are the electronic equivalent of marking a transparent overlay on an original document. They allow a number of people to comment on a report, seeing and adding to each other's remarks without altering the original version.

Another groupware program, the Coordinator, allows members of an electronic work group to send message requests and helps those on the receiving end to respond by either accepting or rejecting the request or by proposing alternatives—an approach Coordinator's manufacturer calls "conversation management." The program keeps track of electronic dialogue. It prods people into taking action and includes a calendar to record commitments.

Corlett is looking seriously at establishing a pilot project at McKim Advertising by using the Coordinator and other assorted software. But he is not convinced groupware will fly in the business world. "I like the theory and philosophy behind it," he says. "But I've got some serious doubts. People won't be disciplined that way. They'll go around it, especially when you're paying them a lot of money to be undisciplined and creative."

One way to avoid sabotage is to develop groupware that suits the needs of the employees. Clarkson Gordon is at the early stages of designing a groupware program in-house, allowing a number of auditors to work on audit files at the same time.

BEWARE BIG BROTHER

Groupware will require a careful management hand to overcome workers' fears of invasion of privacy and of bosses meddling in day-to-day operations. These fears are not unjustified. LANs are capable of performing "audit trails," which allow a supervisor to keep tabs on employees. "The control is ultimate," says David Blancard, marketing manager for Novell Canada Ltd., a major LAN supplier. "You can stipulate that a secretary can do word processing on a particular machine only during certain hours; otherwise, access is denied. Our product maintains an audit trail that reports what the users did during their sessions on the computer. You can determine which file was opened, what was done to it, whether any attempts were made to alter it and how long the user was working on the file."

Managers are not necessarily anxious to employ these monitoring features. After all, they conjure up images of an "information factory," in which workers' performance is scientifically measured and clinically analyzed. Duncan Sutherland, Jr., a U.S. technology consultant and author of *Officing: Bringing Amenity and Intelligence to Knowledge Work,* says offices that are truly operating at peak performance are those that are people-oriented not technology-oriented. He says that offices should not be viewed in the same way as factories or farms are. Sutherland writes, "The purpose of the office is not to produce 'information' but to acquire new knowledge that can help the organization accomplish its physical goals. The office is an expansion of the

AND NOW, A LINE ON FAX
Putting a fax board in your PC can get you on the fax line

Neil Levine's personal computer leads a double life. By day it is a faithful office servant, processing letters, crunching numbers. By night it is a facsimile machine.

Levine has turned this trick by installing a $500 fax "board"—a 4" by 5" electronic circuit board—in a slot inside his computer. The computer now transmits and receives files to and from any fax machine. As vice president of Zynpak Packaging Products Inc. of Toronto, Levine has all his invoices stored in his computer. Each night at 8, the personal computer is programmed to transmit the day's invoices to his customers' fax machines. "The fax board is indispensable," he says. "I do about 500 to 600 invoices a month, 400 of those faxed out, so I save a lot in postage and envelope costs."

Levine also has an inexpensive desktop fax in his office, which he often uses for incoming fax messages. If he receives a message on this machine that he would like to store in his computer, he simply faxes the piece of paper across the room to his PC.

Levine, in a basic way, is following the rules of office technology integration, which sees the personal computer swallowing up the role of other office products. To make the fax-computer connection, you can either buy a top-level facsimile that can be linked to the computer or install a fax board and related software in the computer itself. The interest now seems to be particularly high for fax boards. "Four years ago, only 1,000 fax boards were bought in the United States," says Brian Mintz, vice president of Gentek Marketing Inc. in Concord, Ont. "But this year, we expect to sell at least 120,000."

Gentek distributes two types of fax boards of varying speeds, selling for $695 and $1,295. Generally, the less expensive fax boards are slower and interrupt work on the computer when a message comes in. Mintz says the board and software are easily installed and a dedicated fax line is not required.

Fax boards come with software that converts computer text into a language the fax can understand. You can choose to read the fax message on your computer screen, save it in the machine's memory or auto-matically print out a hard copy. The board lets you send documents to multiple fax locations without duplication of effort, at preprogrammed times. Thousands of telephone numbers can be stored in the computer's memory to be used by the fax. The beauty, for a large company, is that this is private communication, allowing you to bypass the central fax and a hundred prying eyes. For the smaller firm, these boards are an economical alternative to desktop faxes.

Fax board prices appear to be dropping as the level of interest grows. The best fax boards are those that transmit messages quickly (9600 baud rate) and operate without disrupting other work on the computer. There are a variety of fax boards on the market, with prices that range from $400 to $1,300, depending on the speed of transmission. Desktop fax machines sell for between $1,500 and $15,000, with the more expensive models—those that cost more than $6,000— offering larger memory and the ability to send documents directly from the personal computer.

There are several limitations to fax boards. If you want to transmit a document that is not in the computer's memory, you may need a scanner to read it and load it into the computer in a form the computer will understand. These scanners cost anywhere from $700 to $7,000. For incoming fax messages that you want to edit on a word-processing package, you'll need a software program that converts the fax image into computer text. These optical character-recognition programs are not known for their accuracy, because fax images can get distorted during transmission. But two California companies, Calera Recognition Systems Inc. and Caere Corporation, are now marketing products which, they claim, offer 99-percent accuracy for less than $3,000.

Because fax boards need a variety of support machines to function properly, desktop fax manufacturers are not yet feeling threatened. Jeff Speak, manager of the telecommunications division of Crowntek Business Centres in Markham, Ont., says, "The technology is here, but the reality is that there will always be paper. We see fax boards as an enhancement."

mind, not the body." Getting caught up in measuring and monitoring office workers' performance via computers, he says, will only undermine the creativity and flexibility that companies need.

POWER TOOLS

To enable personal computers to operate in this integrated environment, computer manufacturers and software developers are racing to develop powerful new products. Microcomputers now on the market for less than $10,000, including some laptops, can handle complex tasks once reserved for machines 20 times more expensive. This new computer generation has replaced complicated and esoteric commands with user-friendly graphic icons such as a trash can to erase data and a paintbrush to draw lines and circles. This path, which drastically reduces training needs, was commercially pioneered by Apple with the Macintosh in 1984.

WORKING WITH A NET

Computer manufacturers are also realizing that

success in the networking age depends on compatibility with their rivals' equipment. Digital Equipment, for example, entered joint technology agreements with Apple, Compaq and Tandy—a remarkable feat in an industry with strong proprietary instincts. Observers are also hoping that efforts to establish Unix as a standard operating system will soon bear fruit. (The operating system dictates how the computer processes software.) Unix works on a wide variety of computers, which makes it ideal for networking, whereas Microsoft's outdated Disk Operating System (DOS)—the operating system of the non-Apple microcomputer world—works only on microprocessors designed by Intel Corp.

IBM's new generation of personal computers—Personal Systems/2, combined with the new operating system it designed with Microsoft, called Operating Systems/2—was built with networking in mind. When it was introduced in 1988, OS/2 was heralded as the natural successor to DOS. "DOS is like the Volkswagen Beetle," says Alan York, president of QS Systemsmiths Management Associates of Burnaby, B.C. "It's limited by its original design. DOS was never intended to be used the way it's used today."

Personal computers using OS/2 network easily with IBM mainframes and minicomputers, running the same software. Unlike DOS, OS/2 promises to be easier to use because the operator interacts with the computer via pictorial commands. Also, several applications can run simultaneously—say, word processing and spreadsheets—leading to much more effective utilization. But corporations are reluctant to get on the OS/2 bandwagon because of the cost, and, as yet, there are few software programs operating on OS/2 to get excited about. Many observers say it will not be until later this year that there will be enough software developed to judge the value of OS/2. But Dave Thomas, brand manager for personal systems at IBM Canada Ltd., expects that by 1990, OS/2 sales will equal those of DOS.

OS/2 has other detractors who wished IBM had spent its time developing better network software. Even with the growth of corporate networks, documents prepared by one machine cannot be read or manipulated by another, causing a bottleneck. Peat Marwick's study for MicroAge Computer Stores indicated that a surprisingly high 26 percent of information is manually rekeyed from reports generated by existing corporate computer systems, and he figures that the reason is the lack of compatible application software. "Over the next 18 months I expect to see better network software," says Michael Finkelman, supervisor of microcomputing technology at C-I-L Inc. "In a sense, OS/2 has hurt network software because the designers had to concentrate on that. We would have been far better served if they had worked toward building network and work-group applications." Malcolm MacTaggart, general manager of Microsoft Canada Inc., says it takes three years for technology to be accepted.

LANs-ING ON YOUR FEET

But corporate networking raises many more management issues than it answers. Linking personal computers exposes companies to a number of risks, among them breaches of security and software "viruses," rogue programs that can debilitate entire computer systems. And, in many cases, the perceived benefits of a network may not be worth the cost. Dylex Limited, a Toronto holding company of fashion retailers, is installing its first network for 20 personal computers this year after considerable soul-searching. "My vice president has been pushing me for four years to get into this, figuring we were missing out on something," says Peter de Jager, manager of the information centre. "But if you're not sharing data, it can be an expensive solution."

LANs vary widely in price. A software-only LAN that uses standard serial cable but offers limited performance can be bought for less than $150 for each microcomputer that is linked. David Blancard of Novell Canada says an average LAN connecting 10 to 12 microcomputers costs between $800 and $1,000 per machine, not including any additional linkages to such things as the company mainframe.

RIGHT ON TARGET

A clearheaded approach to information management starts from the top. Some senior managers would be shocked to discover the true cost of aimlessly getting into computers. Studies show that while personal computers are getting relatively inexpensive and are viewed almost as commodities, the actual cost per workstation may be as high $20,000 including training and support. This fact may finally bring management information systems (MIS) departments into the mainstream of the corporation, broadening their role "from builder of information systems to architect and planner for corporate-wide information systems," as James Yeates, president of ComputerLand, describes it.

This transformation will happen at different rates and must start at the top. But often the transition is not smooth. "With few exceptions, our senior management is somewhat less than enthusiastic about the advent of the computer," says Corlett of McKim

LAPPING IT UP
Powerful new laptops now tie into the office network

One of the great ironies of the computer world is that laptops—once thought to be, at best, mere extensions of desktop models and, at worst, toys—are starting to supplant their bigger cousins. Executives and salespeople in almost all industries are willing and even eager to extend their office to their car and home. And with the new generation of laptops, businesspeople can work on data bases and spreadsheets for powerful number crunching on the road and in the air. With a cellular telephone, a modem or a facsimile "board" built into the laptop, some businesspeople may never need step into the office again.

A pilot project set up by Air Canada is a case in point. Last fall the airline began offering Toshiba laptops at no charge to first- and executive-class passengers on flights between Vancouver and Toronto. The laptops, loaded with popular word-processing and spreadsheet programs, were "enthusiastically received," says Air Canada's public affairs director, Norm Garwood. The pilot project, the results of which are now being studied by the airline, has also underscored the need for precau-

tions: Computer disks need to be protected from airport-security equipment and from magnets on fold-out trays.

The breakthrough for laptops, or "clamshells" as they're called, is coming about because of improved processing power and memory, and their ability to link up with existing corporate networks. They have even become a status symbol.

"There's a lot of demand for laptops that can network," says Julia Tipton, product manager for microcomputers for Toshiba of Canada Limited. "Because we've gone in the direction of networking in our product development, we've broken the barriers and people are accepting them as desktop replacements. Everyone has to take work home occasionally." Adds Tom Ward, marketing manager for NEC Canada Inc., "Our larger customers want the option of connectivity."

The laptop manufacturers are happy to oblige, judging from recent product announcements from Toshiba, Compaq, NEC and Zenith. Consequently, the laptop market has become segmented. Laptops now range in weight from NEC's UltraLite, weighing 2 kg (4.4 lb), to To-

shiba's T5200, at about 9 kg (19 lb). Laptops also range in price from $1,000 for a simple model without a hard disk drive to $17,000 for Toshiba's top-of-the-line model.

Dwight Wainman, a partner at Wainman and Kydd Chartered Accountants in Toronto, uses a Toshiba 5100 when he is at a client's office and feels that he has plenty of power to crunch numbers. When he returns to the office, he simply plugs his laptop into his Novell network and continues working. "The portables are expensive," he says, "but they're worth it. We're still waiting for them to drop in price."

Just how far laptops have come in bridging portability and desktop power can be seen in the shrewd design of NEC's ProSpeed 386. The company calls this product a "modular workstation" that has two components. One is the standard laptop computer itself, which has a powerful 80386 processor and weighs less than 8 kg (18 lb). The innovation is in what NEC calls its Docking Station. An operator simply slides the laptop into the Docking Station that's on top of the desktop computer. The laptop list price in Canada is

$11,799, and the Docking Station sells for $1,599.

Similar thinking went into the design of the Compaq SLT/286, which is less powerful but also less bulky than the NEC. You can fit this computer on an airline tray with room to spare, and it weighs in at about 6 kg (14 lb). When the SLT/286 is used in your office, it can snap into the top of an optional Desktop Expansion Base that plugs the computer into the company's network. The computer sells for $7,999 or $8,899, depending on the size of the hard disk.

Widespread use of laptops is still hindered by concerns about screen resolution, keyboard design (many lack numeric keypads and have crowded keys, for example) and inadequate battery life of about two hours on the more demanding laptops. Manufacturers are working on eliminating these shortcomings. They are building systems that temporarily shut down components when not in use, thereby conserving battery life. What's more, laptops are starting to offer crisp black-on-white resolution with the option of adding color monitors.

Advertising. He has the unenviable task of managing technology in a company whose business is creativity and serendipity. "People like me are regarded as a necessity, rather than a corporate asset. There are no signs of that changing in the future."

One company that seems to be managing the process well is Canadian National Railways in Montreal. CN, which owns between 4,000 and 5,000 microcomputers, established a strategic-products advisory committee made up of members of the information-systems department and key computer users within the company. Says Ronan McGrath,

controller and vice president of accounting, "We've come to the conclusion that you've got to supply choices [of computers] to end users, while maintaining connectivity. We have highly computer-literate staff who, managed well, can be a huge advantage."

CN's information-services department provides free training at night to all employees, and when the company develops new software applications, training is included in the budget. "Computers have provided a high speed of access to information and flexibility in data manipulation throughout the company," says McGrath. "It's a culture change."

TEL-IT LIKE IT IS

Unlike their computer-manufacturing counterparts, telecommunications vendors have always been a chummy lot. The fact that you can make a telephone call to China with a reasonable chance of getting through is a good example of the universality of standards. But telecommunications has developed its own important version of integration that will have a major impact on office technology. It is called ISDN, or Integrated Services Digital Network. When in place in Canada, this digital network will allow the transmission of voice, data and images on a single line. As a result, ISDN will make modems (which only transmit data) obsolete and thereby streamline corporate telecommunications. For example, computers, printers, utility meters, alarm systems and televisions can be plugged into the same jack as your telephone. Just as easily as you can make a telephone call now, you will be able to make a computer call anywhere around the world instantly. Says Steve Jones, director for ISDN of Northern Telecom Canada, Ltd., "With ISDN, the phone jack will be for communications what the electronic outlet is for power." ISDNs can also act as gateways linking LANs across the country.

ISDNs are already in service in the United States, Japan and western Europe. In Canada, trials have been going on since 1987. This September, The New Brunswick Telephone Company will be the first to offer ISDN commercially. A survey by Angus Tele-Management Group showed that 65 percent of companies with an average of 2,000 employees plan to start using ISDN within four years. The survey also found that nearly half the respondents said they were dissatisfied with the suppliers' lack of knowledge of the technology. "We believe there will be a fair demand from large companies," says Lis Angus, executive vice president of Angus TeleManagement Group in Pickering, Ont. "Our survey showed that a hefty 20 percent would like to start using it in pilot projects within the next year."

OFFICE MACHINATIONS

The move toward integration is also changing office machinery. There are now products that combine a variety of functions, save money and conserve space. Software vendors such as Microsoft and Lotus now offer packages that integrate several popular applications—including word processing, spreadsheets, database management and communications—so that users can incorporate, for example, a spreadsheet into a document.

Fax machines will also be better integrated in offices. Panasonic last year introduced a compact fax that also acts as answering machine, speakerphone and copier. This 5-kg (12-lb) "electronic messaging system," which retails for $2,395, was presold four months in advance, reports Beth Martin, Panasonic's marketing manager of data products. NEC and MITA Copystar Canada Ltd. have since come out with competing products. "Small businesses are very interested," says Martin. "It's popular with smaller franchise stores where they don't have a lot of telephone lines, but they want convenience. Fax machines are also being linked up with computers (see box on page 36).

HALCYON DAYS

These are interesting days for computer users and makers alike. Manufacturers are facing sophisticated and demanding customers who are exhibiting a lot less brand loyalty than the early, halcyon days of personal computing. But this is an industry that pushes new hardware the way Paris pushes hemlines. Says Microsoft's MacTaggart, "One of the things I don't like about our industry is that it has had this mentality of telling people, 'Aren't we brilliant because we developed this technology?' rather than saying, 'Technology is not what's important. What's important is what you can do with it.'"

Employment and the Workplace

Whether we work and the kind of work we do influence our standard of living, our social status, our self-image, and even our sense of spiritual or moral worth. As societies move through stages of technological change, the nature of work is correspondingly altered. In this process, new jobs are created, while others become obsolete and disappear. Economic and emotional hardship for displaced workers then occurs. Still, there is always some concern that the number of new jobs may be fewer than the number lost. During the Industrial Revolution, for example, many people worried that mass unemployment and impoverishment would result as machines displaced human labor.

While it is true that industrialization made many jobs obsolete, it did lead to the creation of far more jobs than were eliminated. According to U.S. census records, there were only 323 different occupations in 1850. Now there are more than 20,000 job specialties. Furthermore, social reforms eased competition for jobs and gave workers more time for personal and educational pursuits. These include a shortened work week, annual vacation time, paid retirement, and prolonged schooling for the young. Rather than causing impoverishment, these reforms have enabled wages and living standards to rise immeasurably.

The contemporary work scene is not without problems, however. Many of today's jobs require little skill and offer low wages. Some are dangerous. Too many people are unable to find work at all. And as computing technologies enter the workplace at an accelerating pace, many of the same concerns expressed during the Industrial Revolution are again being raised.

One of the most pervasive worries is that new technologies will eliminate a significant portion of the jobs that currently exist. Automation and off-shore production have already cost thousands of manufacturing jobs, and the same forces are starting to threaten some clerical jobs as well. There is further fear that existing jobs will be de-skilled and the majority of newly created jobs will be in low-skill, low-pay areas. Optimists, on the other hand, predict that average jobs in the future will be more skilled, more satisfying, and better paying than now. It is still too early to decide which of these predictions is correct, but recent developments give us cause for both concern and optimism.

A Canadian study by Graham S. Lowe (1991) found that white-collar workers tended to report that computers and automation had led to increased job skills and had made their work more interesting. However, there is no question that computers do make a lot of jobs easier (and duller). Supermarket cashiers, for instance, need only a fraction of the skills that were needed before bar code scanners became common. As these examples show, deskilling and upgrading are both possible, but they may not be equally probable. In order for jobs and workers to become more skilled (and for displaced workers to move into new higher-skilled jobs) there must be a widespread system for retraining those whose skills become obsolete. In "The Skilling of America," Jack Gordon argues that in order for corporations to remain competitive in the new global, high-tech economy, they should be upgrading jobs and training workers to fill them. He claims, however, that most businesses are "looking for ways to cut wages instead for ways to skill up jobs," a strategy that could put the United States on the road to resembling a Third World country.

A large portion of the labor force is employed in the service sector, and the range of service jobs is extremely broad. In "Invasion of the Service Robots," Gene Bulinsky outlines how computer-controlled robots are moving into service jobs as diverse as performing maintenance duties in nuclear plants, or assisting the handicapped.

Working at home via computer and telecommunications is another controversial practice. So far, it is an option for only a few workers, but it could become widespread in the future. In "Telecommuters Bring the Office Home," Stuart Newman explains that there are advantages and disadvantages of telework. For some, it has proved to be a terrific opportunity, and for others, a failed experiment.

In the final article in this section, Brian Hayes takes a philosophical look at the "Do It Yourself" movement. Technology is making it easier to bypass some of the steps (and jobs) in a complicated sequence of tasks. Current trends, says Hayes, appear to be "bad news" for several occupations. Nevertheless, he notes several reasons to be optimistic about the "do-it-yourself phenomenon."

Looking Ahead: Challenge Questions

Highly trained professionals such as physicians and lawyers sell their scarce, valuable, and expert knowledge. We now see that some of this expert knowledge is being packaged in easy to operate "do-it-yourself" computer programs. What are some of the positive and negative implications of consumers bypassing professionals on legal and medical matters?

In the "Skilling of America," Jack Gordon describes some successful training programs offered by IBM and AT&T, two of the largest, wealthiest corporations in the world. Are the kinds of programs described by Gordon realistic for most organizations (that typically have between a few dozen and a few hundred employees)? What kinds of training strategies could "typical" firms adopt?

Unit 2

THE SKILLING OF AMERICA

Do we want to skill up or dumb down jobs? It's time to decide. And blowing smoke at the issue won't help.

Jack Gordon

Jack Gordon is editor of TRAINING.

OUR STORY SO FAR. . . .

Hunter-gatherers invented agriculture and stopped roaming around all the time. Cities resulted. These were populated in part by tradespeople, artsy-craftsy types who took clay and metal and leather and cotton, turned them into pots and tools and sandals and textiles, and sold them. Then the Industrial Age showed up. People went to work in factories, where big machines made tools and textiles and newfangled gadgets more economically than artsy-craftsy types could.

In America, many of the people available to work in factories were illiterate immigrants. The big machines were alien and baffling to them. Things looked bad. Then Frederick W. Taylor taught factory owners how to design jobs that were extremely easy to learn. The way to do this was to study the production steps the machines could not perform by themselves, and break them down into simple subtasks. Each subtask became a job; each tiny piece of the original production process that an artsy-craftsy type used to perform all by himself—each decontextualized particle of that erstwhile trade—turned into something for a person to do all day, every day. An illiterate immigrant could learn to do such a job very quickly. So could an extremely stupid person. Stupidity was a blessing, in fact, because if you had any brains or imagination at all, one of these jobs would quickly bore you right out of your skull. The only thinking to be done was done by managers, college-degreed professionals and some skilled technicians like machinists and tool-and-die makers. Taylor still catches a lot of guff for this, even though he wasn't really such a bad guy.

Then more and more people started to work in offices instead of factories. Any fool could see that the Information Age would be along shortly, but a lot of office work nevertheless was designed very much like factory work: Each person did one little fragment of some larger task, like "claims processing," then passed the work on to somebody else, who did another fragment, and so on. The difference was that the work being passed around involved pieces of paper instead of hunks of metal.

Then computers and industrial robots arrived. Right behind them came the New Global Economy and lots of shouting about the competitive need for everybody to produce higher-quality goods and services. Some of the college-degreed professionals got very excited. They talked and talked about all the new skills workers would have to learn, and how much smarter workers would have to get in order use the computers and robots, and make better products and perform better services. Most of the time, though, companies went right on designing jobs the same old way: Figure out what stuff the machine needs a human to help it do, break that stuff into parts ("data entry"), and turn the parts into jobs. Plenty of dull jobs in offices and factories got even duller. And the pay got worse. Sometimes the computers and robots just plain took over jobs that people used to do. In came the machines, out went the people.

This didn't occur everywhere. A few companies wanted to see what would happen if they tried to reverse the fragmenting and de-skilling trend that began back in the Industrial Age. They experimented with turning job fragments back into something resembling whole jobs. They started asking workers to think, and sometimes to decide for themselves how to make products and perform services. They did this even though it made the jobs harder to learn, and thus tended to drive up wages. It drove up wages because now the company couldn't just hire any extremely stupid person who happened to walk by, and teach him the job in about an hour, and pay him peanuts. Instead, the company had to do quite a lot of training.

Here's why these few companies were going to all this trouble: They figured that in the long run, they'd make more money and be more likely to survive in the New Global Economy.

The college-degreed professionals proclaimed that these few companies were obviously the leaders, and all the other companies were bound to start following them any minute. And that's more or less where we are today: waiting to see.

For years fashion has dictated that we speak of the average job of tomorrow as demanding a smarter, more highly skilled worker than does the average job today. The notion has become so commonplace that it often is advanced not as a prediction or even as a probability but as a self-evident fact.

The reasoning: Technological gadgets are taking over more and more of the repetitive, the routine and the manual tasks that once constituted a significant amount of human work. That leaves humans with the unusual, the creative and the conceptual. Spurred by the ferocity of global competition, lashed by the universal imperative to improve the quality of goods and services, business is reorganizing itself on a grand scale. And it is doing so in such a way that the work available for people to perform is growing inexorably more complex.

Think of it as an equation: $AT = ID$.

Advancing technology equates to greater intellectual demands upon the worker. Look at those (formerly) humble factory workers at model companies like Motorola and Corning and Johnsonville Foods. Many of them now tinker with computers and interpret statistical charts. Many of them are organized into teams that perform all sorts of tasks (production scheduling, hiring) once reserved for managers and staff specialists. There's the future of the average worker for you. No doubt about it.

Unfortunately, this is balderdash. True, our future as a prosperous nation may very well depend upon the skilled-up workplace becoming the norm instead of the exception, but there is nothing inevitable about it.

That point was made forcefully last year by the Commission on the Skills of the American Workforce, sponsored by the National Center on Education and the Economy. In a report called *America's Choice: High Skills or Low Wages,* the commission announced its finding that the vast majority of U.S. businesses are not following in the footsteps of the so-called model companies and apparently do not intend to.

Indeed, the commission claimed that the much-ballyhooed "skills gap" in the American work force does not really exist—not in relation to the jobs employers currently want noncollege graduates to perform. Yes, the commission said, most employers do complain about job candidates with low "skills." But when you pin these employers down, in eight out of 10 cases the "skills" they're complaining about have nothing to do with literacy or mathematics or critical-thinking abilities or any sort of technical expertise. Instead, the skills in question boil down to "a good work ethic and appropriate social behavior: 'reliable,' 'a good attitude,' 'a pleasant appearance,' 'a good personality. . . .' "

In other words, what most employers want is workers who will show up on time, smile at the customers, keep the profanity and intramural bickering down to a dull roar, defer to their managers and do what they're told. The complaint about noncollege graduates is that they are uncouth ignoramuses; the desire is for couth ignoramuses instead.

By "noncollege graduates," incidentally, the commission is referring to people it says will perform more than 70 percent of all American jobs in the year 2000.

Furthermore, the commission claims, 95 percent of employers do not expect their skill needs to change significantly in the foreseeable future. They see no reason why the jobs they'll have to offer tomorrow would call for better-educated, more highly skilled workers than the jobs they have to offer today. The exceptional 5 percent are mostly large companies in manufacturing, communications or financial services.

America's choice? The business world is making it right now, the commission says, and the bulk of companies are choosing poorly. They are looking for ways to cut wages instead of for ways to skill up jobs, thus making jobs more productive, thus making the people perform the jobs worth more money.

I must be said that this report seems to have made no significant dent in the national rhetoric, which continues to insist that jobs are growing inexorably more complex and demanding. The 95 percent figure, in particular, draws skepticism from many quarters (see box). But if that figure is even in the right ballpark, it follows that a great deal of the corporate world's howling about the sorry state of the public education system is, to put it mildly, insincere.

Exactly so, concluded professor Robert B. Reich of Harvard's John F. Kennedy School of Government in a *Business Month* article last November: "Forget all the PR about corporate 'partnerships' with local schools. Whatever American corporations are giving through the front door, they're taking away much more through the back." He refers to common corporate practices such as inviting municipalities to engage in bidding wars to attract new plants or to keep old plants from closing. For "bidding wars," read: Which city will offer the biggest tax breaks in order to attract or save some jobs? According to Reich, the corporate share of local property tax revenues, which pay for local schools, dropped from 45 percent nationally in 1957 to 16 percent in 1989.

"The inescapable conclusion," Reich wrote, "is that American Business isn't really worried about the future of the work force. Why? Because American corporations increasingly are finding the workers they need outside the United States, often at a fraction of the price."

This is one form of the "low-wages" option described in *America's Choice.* A key feature of the global economy is that one can now transfer data, information and money all over the planet at lightening speed. This makes it much easier to move jobs to places like Mexico and Thailand, where people will work for less money than Americans can live on.

Another way to make the "low-wages" choice is to use technology to de-skill work even further—to finish the job the Industrial Revolution started. "This plant was so modern, so glorified and so built-up that all they needed were monkeys to push buttons. And that's what we hired," said a supervisor in a high-tech printing plant, quoted last year in *Technical & Skills Training* magazine. If you can hire monkeys to push buttons in high-tech factories or "electronic sweatshops," of course, you get to pay them peanuts.

Economic indicators lend credence to the commission's assertion that the bulk of American companies are choosing the low-wages option. *Business Week* reports that median family income (in inflation-adjusted dollars) has been stagnant since 1973. Worse yet, "real wages" in the United States have dropped by 6 percent since 1980, except in certain industries that export significant amounts of their goods and services. (Among these are aircraft, computers, entertainment, chemicals and, ironically, higher education, which "exports" its product by training foreign students in subjects such as math and engineering, then sending them home.)

The low-wages choice dooms most Americans to a slow but sure trip toward impoverishment, the report concludes. If we keep traveling down this road, we'll eventually start to resemble a Third World country. We will have atomic weapons, of course, but then so does India.

And it's all so hideously pointless, moans the commission. The Japanese aren't beating our pants off in automobiles and electronics and so on by paying their workers lower wages. The way to compete in the global economy is not to design jobs that monkeys can do and pay them peanuts. The way to compete is by creating "high-performance organizations" that operate with well-educated, highly trained and—yes—well-paid workers.

"High-performance organization" is about as good a label for this idea as any other. Reich calls it creating jobs that "add value in the world economy." Tom Peters calls it "train, train, train until you die!" Johnsonville Foods CEO Ralph Stayer calls it "intellectual capitalism." Former Labor Secretary Elizabeth Dole formed task forces and issued calls for national training programs that would provide workers with "portable" skills that would keep them employable if their current jobs vanished. Late last year, that American Society for Training and Development went so far as to hang a price tag on it all, announcing the American employers need to do an additional $15 billion worth of training every year—$15 billion more than they're doing now, that is.

And yet somehow, in the face of all this, the vast majority of companies evi-

DID *WORKFORCE 2000* GET IT WRONG?

The Commission on the Skills of the American Workforce is not some ragtag collection of bureaucrats. Its members include two former secretaries of the U.S. Department of Labor; the CEOs of companies including Eastman Kodak, Corning Inc. and Apple Computer; a pair of university presidents; a former governor; union bigwigs including the president of the United Auto Workers; and the head of the National Urban League.

When a group with these credentials issues a report insisting that the conventional wisdom about the job market in this country is dead wrong, one would expect purveyors of that conventional wisdom to sit up and take notice. Last year, in *America's Choice: High Skills or Low Wages,* the commission flatly contradicted the prevailing belief that American jobs, as a whole, are growing increasingly complex, and that it will take workers with more education and higher-level skills to perform them (see main story). Yet to all appearances, the conventional wisdom has emerged virtually unscathed. Why?

One reason may be the widespread credulity attached to the findings of *Workforce 2000,* the 1987 demographic study commissioned by the U.S. Department of Labor and conducted by the Hudson Institute of Indianapolis. According to *Workforce 2000,* tomorrow's average job will demand a more skilled worker than today's, and that's that.

In 1987, William J. Maroni, now a consultant with SJS Inc. of Providence, RI, worked for the Labor Department and was connected to the *Workforce 2000* study. He later served as a field researcher for the Commission on the Skills of the American Workforce.

That field research convinced Maroni that "we oversold those few conclusions in *Workforce 2000* [which said] jobs were being skilled up." He points out that the Hudson Institute did no "primary research" for that study; it used data from the Bureau of Labor Statistics to make its projections. When the commission's research teams went into actual companies to conduct in-depth interviews and study real jobs, Maroni says, it became clear that BLS skill classifications can be misleading.

"At Ford [Motor Co.], for instance, we talked to a middle-aged guy who was using a computer on the factory floor. He was so proud of being computer literate—never expected to learn about computers at his age, and so on." Maroni's team seemed to be bearing personal witness to a chapter of the inspiring story that has become a classic in the folklore of "model companies": downtrodden factory worker becomes Master of Technology and achieves self-actualization in the Computer Age.

Alas for pleasant illusions, Maroni and his mates made the mistake of hanging around for several hours to watch this man do his job. It became evident that he knew nothing except "which buttons to push" when certain information appeared on his screen. "He had no computer skills that he couldn't have learned in about two days," Maroni says. Yet BLS would classify that as a highly skilled job because a computer is attached to it.

"We promoted *Workforce 2000* so well that now we've got a lot of confusion out there about what a 'skilled up' job is," Maroni concludes.

Another reason why *America's Choice* might fail to shake the prevailing faith in the notion that jobs are being skilled up is that the report lacks a statistical vigor. The commission insists that its field research provided a deep and disturbing understanding of the true direction in which the country is moving, but the companies it studied do not constitute a representative sample of all U.S. employers. Although the report attaches numbers to some findings (e.g., 95 percent of all American employers do not expect to need more highly skilled workers in the foreseeable future than they do right now), the commission doesn't claim that those numbers are statistically precise.

Finally, the recommendations in *America's Choice* might suggest that the commission itself doesn't really believe its own findings. In one breath, the authors announce their conclusion that only 5 percent of employers give a tinker's damn whether the job candidates they see tomorrow are any better educated than the ones they see today. In the next breath, they propose a sweeping agenda of school reform and government-sponsored vocational training programs intended to ensure that henceforth, every young American who goes looking for a job will be a proud representative of the best-educated and most highly trained work force in the world. The reader is left to wonder why 95 percent of these paragons won't simply be impoverished and numbed by the mindless, low-paying jobs they get.

According to Maroni, the explanation is that the commission expects the tide of history to change the minds of employers who are attempting to compete in the global economy on the basis of low wages rather than high skills. It expects history to get a helping hand in the form of continued proselytizing by model companies, especially winners of the Malcolm Baldrige National Quality Award. A well-educated work force would exert pressure of its own on companies to skill up jobs, Maroni says. And the government, by means of a national training tax and other measures, can nudge the process along as well. —J.G.

---

dently are going right on choosing the low-wages option.

Why don't they get the message? It can't be because they haven't heard it; the message has been shouted from every bully pulpit in the country. The problem must be that they don't believe it. Or maybe it all sounds fine as far as it goes, but they don't see how it applies to them. Maybe they don't know what to *do* with it.

And maybe this is because the message so often comes shrouded in large, billowing clouds of mysto smoke.

Mysto . . .as in "high-performance organization" and "value-added work" and "intellectual capitalism" and "portable skills."

Mysto . . .as in prescribing "training" in such relentlessly generic terms and on such a macro-level that it comes to sound like one big homogeneous bucket of magic dust, or an all-purpose vitamin compound cooked up by Dr. Feelgood at his Knowledge Lab in Learningland. Unfortunately for this line of talk, employers have *seen* "training." Many have paid repeatedly over the years for whoppingly expensive examples of "training" that didn't do much of anything for anybody.

Mysto . . .as in, when somebody does answer the question, "Train them to do *what*?" a great deal of the talk about value-added jobs and intellectual capital turns out to be merely code for the basic-skills issue: Teach them eighth-grade math and reading, if you must, but more importantly, teach them customer service skills (smile), interpersonal communication skills (develop a pleasant personality and keep the profanity down to a dull roar), teamwork (also the intramural bickering), and listening skills (pay attention and do what you're told.)*

Maybe what's needed is a little less macro-level evangelizing from bully pulpits and a little more concrete explaining of how some of this stuff is supposed to work. For example, let's take three aspects of the national discussion about skilling up the work force—creating whole jobs, "train, train, train," and "portable skills"—and see if we can talk about them minus the mysto.

WHOLE JOBS

"There are three things we know for sure," says consultant Marvin Weisbord of Block, Petrella & Weisbord of Plainfield, NJ. "One, there are no technological exemptions from human decision making yet. That's a fantasy. . . .

"Two, it's a losing proposition, and uneconomic, to try to make people extensions of machines—to have a keyboard operator entering 150 transactions an hour. That's not a fit job for humans." Attempts to use computers this way explain why many a large company has a technological skeleton in its closet—"the $30 million mistake they don't want the stockholders to know about. And it's always because of what these systems left for people to do. . . .

"Three, it's not possible to automate every job, because robots won't buy goods and services from each other. We can't automate everybody out of work and expect to make money. Long term, how can rich people stay rich in a world where nobody can buy anything?"

Companies exporting jobs offshore in search of cheaper workers are making the incorrect assumption that labor costs are the biggest part of their overhead, Weisbord says. "It's not hourly people you need fewer of, it's managers, supervisors and staff people." It is only the fragmentation of work at the bottom of the organization that creates the need for large numbers of managers and staff specialists. "Dumb jobs

lead to huge overhead: You need middle managers and staff specialization to make up for people doing bad work and not caring."

If the key to "skilling up" jobs is to "de-fragment" the work at the bottom of the organization, how does one go about that? Robert Janson, president of Roy Walters & Associates, a Mahwah, NJ, consulting firm, is a specialist in the subject.

You begin with your customers, Janson says. "How do you want customer transactions to work? How do you want to deal with your customers? You design jobs around that."

For instance, many companies find that their customers want "one-stop service." That is, when the customer contacts the company for some reason, she wants to deal with one person who can answer questions, solve problems and get things done. She doesn't want to be bounced around from department to department, from worker to supervisor, etc. (General Electric's GE Answer Center is a prime example of how the skills required to support this strategy can snowball. Customers who call GE's 800 number speak to an employee who now must have a college degree, sales experience and at least six weeks of intensive training on the technical workings of GE products.)

The same principle applies internally, Janson says. For instance, field reps who require information or support from corporate headquarters want to deal with one person or one team that can give them what they need. Technology now allows you to redesign jobs in order to create such people.

To do so, you need to look at the various tasks that make up some process—the fragmented jobs that carry the work from start to finish—and recombine them into whole jobs. In his training materials, Janson uses the reorganization of a major bank's letter-of-credit division as an example.

A letter of credit is "a service provided to finance business transactions between separate concerns working through financial intermediaries." Usually, the separate concerns are in different countries: A construction company in Argentina wants to buy some bulldozers from an American company; an Argentine bank arranges for an American bank to issue a letter of credit, which pays for the deal.

In Janson's example, the paperwork for 450 letters of credit wends its way through this division every day. The division is organized into three clerical departments: issues, amendments and payments. Then there's the accounting department, which records both credits and payments; the customer service

unit, which handles inquiries and complaints; and the main files unit, where records of everything are kept.

It typically takes two weeks for this division to issue a letter of credit. During that time, more than a dozen people do *something* with the batch of forms and papers that each case represents. As customer's application for a letter of credit arrives in the mail room and is sent to a clerk called a pre-processor. The pre-processor sends it to the issues department, where it is received by a log clerk, who assigns it an identification number and then gives it to a typist. The typist fills out an "offering ticket," one copy of which wends its way into a different thicket of the bureaucratic forest for checks and approvals, then straggles back to the main file. By that time, the main file has traveled up to a different floor of the building for verification of the customer's signature, then back down to a preparer, who gives it to a checker, who gives it to a credit typist, who gives it to a fanfold checker. From there the file is passed on to another preparer, a break-out checker, a manager, another checker and a credit-package preparer.

That's just the issues department. In the payment department, five people will handle this wad of paper. And God help the application that a customer wants to alter in some way (as many do), because that means a side trip to the joyless hellhole of the amendment department, where seven different people will fanfold, spindle and mutilate the poor thing.

In short, the letter of credit division is organized into three assembly lines, and everyone who works there performs a single, isolated piece of a production process, over and over again. Our job is to figure out how in the world we might reorganize this place to make it more efficient and competitive in the global economy.

Cutting-edge stuff, eh? Well, yes and no. Janson's 1979 case study is based on a reorganization that took place at Citibank in New York almost 20 years ago. What the bank did was to pare and combine all of those functions into a single job. As of the mid-'70s, the new system worked like this: A letter of credit application arrives and is given to an "account representative" (a former clerk, now retrained) assigned to the appropriate region: Middle East, South America, etc. The account rep sits at a workstation linked to a minicomputer. The computer contains all the necessary information on the customer's credit history and so forth. The account rep handles all the issuing and amending functions, as well as payment processing and accounting. The rep is also

---

*Save the stamp. I know that plenty of the training that goes on under these headings is not just designed to turn uncouth ignoramuses into couth ones. But plenty of it is, too.

the customer service agent for this account.

In case you lost track, that's three assembly lines and two auxiliary functions combined into one job, using the computer technology available in the 1970s. (True, some auditing oversight has been whitewashed out of this picture, Janson says, but the reorganization left behind no such thing as a person who was strictly a "checker.") Five years after the reorganization, revenues had nearly quadrupled while operating expenses had remained flat. The division was running with less than half as many workers; displaced clerks were retrained for other assignments in the bank.

What can we say about all this? Obviously we can agree that these clerks were "skilled up." Their fragment jobs were turned into whole jobs. Efficiency, productivity and competitiveness improved. The clerks undoubtedly care more about their jobs. Their working lives are almost certainly more interesting and enjoyable. We could crank up the mysto machine and rhapsodize about value-added intellectual capital and all, and we'd be perfectly justified. But we could also point out that nobody here had to be magically transformed into a nuclear physicist. What happened was this: The computer allowed a big bank to design a job the way it probably would have done in the first place had it been a small bank that handled only one or two of these types of transactions each day.

TRAIN, TRAIN, TRAIN

Take two companies, each doing a great deal of training. One is using training, successfully, as a strategic tool to improve its competitive position; it probably will continue to do so. The other is "slopping training on with a bucket," as the old phrase has it; it will probably stop doing so in a recession, or as soon as it becomes clear that business results—quality, service, sales, market share—are not improving.

How would we know which organization was which?

If we're seeking a company with an impressive track record in using training strategically, the exemplar is IBM. "We look at ourselves as a learning organization," says Ken Lay, the corporation's director of education-external programs. New buzzword, old concept: IBM has been a "learning organization" for several decades. When Lay says, "The key to business is education," he's quoting founder Tom Watson, who made that statement in 1933.

Almost nothing you hear anybody say about the "new" need for lifelong, continual learning and education is new to IBM.

IBM currently spends about $1.5 billion a year on training for its 374,000 employees worldwide; that's not counting the salaries paid to people while they're being trained. The company employs 7,000 training specialists. The average employee get 15 days of formal training every year, about 65 percent of it in a classroom and the rest via computer or interactive video. It doesn't seem to occur to the people who run this company that any employee at any level could possibly perform his job competently without being trained.

Yet for all this emphasis on employee education, the notion of training as a homogeneous wonder-substance is utterly alien to IBM. "You can't just have training for training's sake," Lay says. (He doesn't add, "for crying out loud," but it's there in his tone.) "You need the right education for the right person at the right time. You might call it 'just-in-time education.'"

How does the company go about ensuring just-in-time education? Largely by attending to the basics that have been preached for years (by people like Bob Mager, Thomas Gilbert, Joe Harless, Dugan Laird) under the heading, "How to design and conduct effective training in the working world."

Jobs at IBM are classified according to five major functions: marketing, service, information and office systems, technical and finance. Ninety percent of all jobs are further broken down into 85 major "job areas," Lay says. Three years ago the company finished a full-scale needs analysis to determine what people in each of those 85 areas ought to know and be able to do. From the findings came the latest edition of IBM's corporate training curriculum.

According to Lay, all training is designed and conducted using the classic instructional systems design (ISD) approach, about which there is nothing mysto whatsoever. Measurements of a course's effectiveness are built into its design, following Donald Kirkpatrick's familiar four-level evaluation model: Level 1, do the trainees say the course is well-designed and helpful? Level 2, did they master the material they were taught? Level 3, did they apply the skills they learned once they returned to the job? Level 4, has a business goal been met (Are sales increasing? Are customers more satisfied with the service they receive?) as a result of the fact that people *are* applying these new skills on the job?

In some cases, particularly with "soft skills" training, it's unrealistic to try to carry a rigorous evaluation all the way to Level 4, Lay admits. But for the most

part, he says, "If we see no business results, we kill the course."

Although the company offers some generic courses that cut across different job functions (time management, effective business writing, many management-training courses), the vast majority of its programs are tied directly to specific jobs. And only a minuscule fraction of all training is remedial. "Through our recruitment and hiring programs, we're able to get highly skilled people," Lay says. "The analogy is, you're starting with someone who has set a record in the 100-yard dash, and you're trying to improve on that."

If IBMers are so wonderful to begin with, why all the training? "In a market-driven company, you're constantly trying to raise your level of performance," Lay says. "You have to be obsessed with customer satisfaction. Our focus is on continual improvement. And that comes from the fact that our jobs change all the time."

Customer satisfaction, continual improvement, the accelerating pace of change—the phrases have become clichés, yet at IBM they are translated into very specific learning challenges. Obviously, many employees are forever having to learn about new products the company introduces—computer technology never sleeps—but it's more than that.

Take marketing, for instance. In days gone by, an IBM sales representative sold products to many different types of companies. Now the marketing function has been reorganized so that salespeople specialize by industry: A rep will sell computer systems only to banks or only to health-care organizations or to universities or to the securities industry. If you're going to do an effective job of selling a computer system to a company, Lay says, "you have to be able to help the customer focus on the processes" that the system will handle. To do that, you have to understand something about the customer's business. Thus, "Introduction to the Securities Industry" becomes a basic training course for an IBM sales rep.

Lay himself began his IBM career as a computer programmer. Then he went into marketing, where he spent his first year shuttling back and forth from training programs to the job. Then he switched to corporate education. That involved traveling to various IBM facilities, learning from specialists in instructional design, computer-based training, classroom instruction, evaluation and so on.

This brings up another heralded but often hazily described benefit of training for which IBM serves as a concrete illustration: the notion that the promise of extensive educational programs will help a company attract and keep good people. When TRAINING asked Lay for examples of in-house educational programs that would provide workers with "transferable" skills that would make them attractive to other employers if they left IBM, he couldn't relate to the question; unless they're accepting early retirement offers, people don't *leave* IBM. The worldwide attrition rate is 3 percent. Leave? Why? Because you're sick of finance and you want to go into sales? Well, hey. . . .

PORTABLE SKILLS

There is a desperate need, the macro-level talk insists, for a national system of training designed to "reskill" workers. Why? Because we live in a world where jobs are changing, mutating and vanishing faster than you can say, "So long, lithographers," In this utterly unpredictable, rapidly changing world (We're in *permanent white water!* We're in a state of *raging chaos!*), the worker's skills will soon become obsolete, if they aren't already, which is why he needs this retraining. Meanwhile, we'll all pretend not to notice that if things are *that* chaotic, any new skills we teach this guy may just as easily be obsolete by the time he graduates.

Ah, irony.

Yes, but suppose there were a system of training designed to keep workers employable in a fast-changing job market: What might one of those look like?

AT&T's Alliance for Employee Growth and Development Inc. was created in 1986 as part of the company's contract agreements with the Communication Workers of America and the International Brotherhood of Electrical Workers. Its charter is to provide training to AT&T's union workers that will keep them employable, either inside or outside the company. Its services are available to union members currently employed at AT&T and to those who have been laid off. Displaced workers remain eligible for up to two years.

To date, more than 50,000 people, one-third of them layoff victims, have completed at least one course sponsored by the Alliance. As for the other two-thirds, "People at AT&T all consider themselves at risk," says Don Treinen of the communication workers union, who serves as the Alliance's co-executive director. The company's work force has shrunk by 100,000 people since 1984, albeit partly due to the court-ordered breakup of the Bell System.

A worker wishing to use the Alliance's services must first go through 15 to 20 hours of career-planning sessions. These include skill inventories, aptitude tests and discussions with counselors. Through a network of 360 working committees at AT&T sites in 48 states, the Alliance also conducts marketplace surveys and compiles data from the U.S. Bureau of Labor Statistics and other sources, showing what kinds of jobs are available, inside and outside AT&T, and in various regions of the country. The committees also keep tabs on various training resources in their areas—programs available from universities, community colleges, private training vendors, public agencies and so on. Only when the worker settles upon a realistic career plan will the Alliance pay for any training.

"There must be a demand in the marketplace" for the type of job the worker is after, Treinen says, and the worker's aptitude for the job must be supported by the results of the planning sessions. "We won't train you for a job that's not there or for a job you're highly unlikely to get."

Provided the career plan is viable, however, the training options are wide open. The Alliance will pay for training in "anything AT&T doesn't," says Treinen. That is, if the company wants its union workers to learn something, the company does the training. If the worker wants to learn something that will qualify him for a different job at AT&T or elsewhere, the Alliance takes over—and the training occurs on the worker's own time. When some new technology is introduced on the job at AT&T, for instance, "it might mean they'll now need 10 workers instead of 100," Treinen says. "So 10 people will get training from AT&T in the new technology. We'll see the other 90."

The Alliance operates on an annual budget of $15 million, of which $2.5 million is earmarked for college tuition payments. The Alliance picks up the educational expenses for people who want to be teachers, counselors, nurses, software engineers—whatever. It has sent people to vocational-training courses covering everything from secretarial skills to underwater welding (including scuba diving). The Alliance also coordinates and pays for a great deal of computer training, most of which involves basic keyboarding and introductions to various software packages. Once you have "a grounding" in a few different types of computer software, Treinen says, potential employers are much more willing to teach you the specific applications they use.

Even with the emphasis on specific career planning, many Alliance-sponsored courses fall under the generic heading of basic skills. These are defined broadly to include not just academic skills but subjects such as problem solving, time management, teamwork, social skills and leadership (as in, how to take the lead when your work team is involved with some project in which you happen to have the most expertise). Of the 50,000 union members who have completed an Alliance-sponsored course, more than half have taken one or more of these kinds of courses.

When retraining can qualify a displaced worker for a new job within AT&T, the company makes out like a bandit. The Alliance spends an average of $2,000 on training for each displaced worker. The average cost to AT&T to lay off a worker, calculated in 1989, was $24,500: Layoffs are expensive, Treinen says, when you add up things like unemployment compensation, extended medical payments (the company is self-insured) and severance pay, especially since most displaced workers at AT&T have many years of service with the company and their severance packages amount to significant chunks of money. "So every time we place somebody internally at AT&T," he says, "it saves the company about $22,000."

JUST DO IT

None of these examples are meant to represent the one true path to the enlightened redesign of jobs, the delivery of continuous education to employees or the construction of a mechanism for retraining displaced workers. But they do demonstrate that all of these things can be done—are *being* done—in practical ways by practical people acting for practical business reasons.

It is axiomatic that we quickly forget most things we learn if we have no reason, need or opportunity to practice them. This principle does not vanish because a company decides to call itself a learning organization or a total quality manufacturer, or because its employees are "knowledge workers," or because the "pace of change" is accelerating.

Redesigning jobs, training and retraining may well be the most important economic challenges facing this country for the next decade at least. But they have to be linked. Training has to support jobs that are really changing. Retraining has to prepare people for work that really exists. Otherwise, we're spinning our wheels. And the bulk of employers will listen to the rhetoric, match it against the training they see with their own eyes, and go right on wondering what all the shouting is about.

INVASION OF THE SERVICE ROBOTS

Like human workers, robots are moving into services—especially jobs people find dangerous or boring. Their boosters see a much bigger market than in manufacturing.

Gene Bylinsky

FOR A LONG TIME robots have been stuck on the factory floor, toiling away at such repetitive, brute-force chores as welding car bodies and lifting heavy steel bars. Now they're breaking loose. Like their human colleagues, they are moving increasingly from manufacturing into services. For several years service robots have been at work in nuclear plants, where people risk exposure to radiation, and under the sea, where human divers require cumbersome and costly life-support systems. Today the protean machines are embarking on a multitude of new activities: taking care of the handicapped and elderly, picking oranges, cleaning office buildings and hotel rooms, guarding commercial buildings, even helping cops and brain surgeons. Doctors at California's Long Beach Memorial Hospital have performed more than 20 delicate brain operations with the help of a robot arm that drills into the skull with great precision. In Dallas a year and a half ago, police used a robot to bluff a suspect barricaded in an apartment into surrendering. When the robot broke a window with its scary mechanical arm, the man came running out the front door shouting, "What the hell was *that?*"

In U.S. laboratories, more than 1,200 robots perform such intricate tasks as weighing, measuring, and mixing minute quantities of chemicals, medications, and even DNA. The Navy is starting to deploy undersea robots with lobsterlike claws that snip the mooring cables of stationary mines, such as those currently threatening ships in the Persian Gulf. Other fields wide open for service robots include building and maintaining offshore oil rigs, working on construction sites, tending hospital patients, assembling space stations, pumping gasoline, preparing fast food, fighting fires, and inspecting high-tension electric wires.

REPORTER ASSOCIATE *Alicia Hills Moore*

"We're seeing the birth of a big, new industry," says Joseph F. Engelberger, 62, the father of industrial robotics and the principal driving force behind service robots. "Now that robots can be mobile and are starting to be able to see and feel, service jobs will eclipse the entire manufacturing scene for robotics." He envisions service robots soaring to $2 billion in annual sales in the U.S. by 1995, up from about $120 million today, mostly in undersea applications. (Like many such estimates in high technology, that $2-billion figure may well be optimistic.) By contrast, the U.S. market for industrial robots is expected to reach $370 million this year and $1 billion in the mid-1990s.

As with almost any new technology, the major innovators aren't the big, established companies—in this case industrial-robot makers GM Fanuc Robotics, IBM, and Cincinnati Milacron—but small companies such as Engelberger's Transitions Research Corp. (TRC) of Bethel, Connecticut. (About the only exception is Westinghouse, which provides service robots for nuclear utilities.) In the late 1950s Engelberger ignited the industrial robotics revolution by starting Unimation Inc., the first robot company.

TRC, a three-year-old privately held company with annual sales of about $1.5 million, is Engelberger's entry in the service-robot sweepstakes. The last time around, the Japanese in effect stole Engelberger's baby, the industrial robot. Because he could not afford to patent his robot in Japan, they ran away with it by copying and mass-producing the machines. Japanese robot makers such as Fanuc and Matsushita now control the world industrial-robot market. To keep the nascent service-robot industry from slipping into Japanese hands too, Engelberger has assembled an impressive lineup of big corporate backers for his projects, including Du Pont, 3M, Johnson Wax, Electrolux AB, Maytag, and Emhart, a Connecticut conglomerate that

had $2 billion in sales last year. While Japan isn't exactly asleep, as of now it is behind in the underlying technologies.

A VISITOR TO TRC can be greeted by a squat three-foot-tall robot, a test-bed for an automatic vacuum cleaner, rolling by Engelberger's office with its electronic innards exposed. Research on the vacuum cleaner is sponsored by Electrolux, the big Swedish consumer electronics concern. Designed to clean malls, supermarkets, factories, and airports without human assistance, it will sell for about $20,000 when it goes on the market next year. According to TRC, outside surveys show that a business with 35,000 square feet—the size of a small shopping mall—to clean could use the machine economically.

Other Engelberger robots include Help-Mate, a nurse's aide that will deliver meal trays to bedridden hospital patients. Along the way, the wheeled robot will take elevators and negotiate hallways by itself, doubtless startling unwary visitors. HelpMate will be tested starting next January at the Danbury, Connecticut, hospital; Engelberger plans to put it into mass production in 1989. It will sell for about $25,000 and will pay for itself in 2½ years if it is used 24 hours a day, according to TRC-sponsored studies.

Engelberger's "ultimate robot," as he calls it, will be a $50,000 household helper—assuming he can raise about $20 million to develop it. He sees this robot as a high-tech butler that would prepare meals, clean the house, cut the grass, clear the driveway of snow, and even fix household appliances such as refrigerators and washing machines. "You'll get value and return on investment compared with hiring a practical nurse at $9 an hour to help your old mother get around the house, as I do now, for example," Engelberger says. One snag: He hasn't yet figured out how to teach it to make the beds.

From *Fortune*, September 14, 1987, pp. 81–82, 84–86, 88. © 1987 Time Inc. All rights reserved.

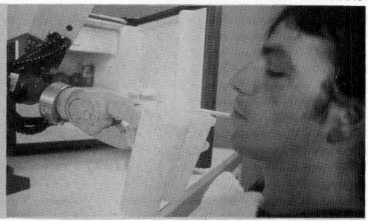

Robots That Help Quadriplegics

In Palo Alto, at the Veterans Administration Medical Center, a paralyzed patient gives orders to a voice-controlled $50,000 robot. Using a versatile hand (below), it gives him a drink, brushes his teeth, and shaves him. The system will soon be available for home testing.

Not everyone agrees that an all-purpose household robot will work. David Nitzan, director of the robotics lab at SRI International, thinks that it would make more sense technically to concentrate on single applications—a bathroom-cleaning robot, for example. But no one disputes that service robots are expanding. Among other things, Nitzan and his group are working on the vision system for a robot that would automatically sort packages for the U.S. Postal Service.

Why the service robot surge? For one thing, progress in core technologies—vision, mobility, controls—has been rapid. "It's a golden time," says William Whittaker, a senior scientist at the Carnegie Mellon University Robotics Institute in Pittsburgh, a leading developer of service robots. "A couple of years ago my feeling was that there was very little insight into either what to do or how to do it. But now those contributing or enabling technologies are there for the most part. There's the magnitude of the market, the potential and the inevitability of the technologies. It's as foregone as computing was 20 years ago. It has the same feel to it."

There are demographic pressures as well. Many service-robot suppliers see the rapidly aging U.S. population as a huge, new market. People over 85 now make up the fastest-growing segment of the elderly in the U.S., and 200,000 older Americans a year break their hips. Says Karen G. Engelhardt, director of the Health and Human Sevices Robotics Laboratory at Carnegie Mellon: "Never before have we seen a technology with such promise and potential to help this large and growing population in ways they never could be helped before."

BECAUSE SERVICE ROBOTS are often able to make repairs under hazardous conditions faster than people can, for example, they may deliver the increased productivity that has generally eluded the service sector. Shortages of service workers such as nurses are another force driving the advent of service robots. So are corporate policies and regulatory pressures against placing workers in dangerous settings. Since 1971, for instance, 54 deep-sea divers have been lost in North Sea offshore oil and gas operations. The shift toward robot submersibles has turned a lot of divers into shipboard robot operators—a much safer occupation. In nuclear plants, robots toil for hours at a time in highly radioactive areas in place of hundreds of employees, called jumpers or glowboys, who worked in short relays so as to minimize their exposure. In space, robots can significantly speed assembly of big structures like NASA's projected space station for the 1990s.

In those three settings—in nuclear plants, under the sea, and in space—cost savings are a big factor as well. Supporting deep-sea divers and astronauts working outside their spacecraft can cost up to $100,000 an hour. When a nuclear plant shuts down, replacing the lost electricity can cost a utility an estimated $500,000 a day; robots have already helped shorten those shutdowns.

The military, whose primary concern isn't economics, sees in the new robots a way to maintain high-tech superiority over more numerous enemy armies on a battlefield. The Pentagon is spending hundreds of millions of dollars a year to develop small unmanned tanks, intelligent robotic undersea vehicles, and flying spy robots that fill the gap between airplanes and satellites. Robert Finkelstein, president of Robotic Technology Inc. of Potomac, Maryland, who works closely with the Pentagon, says research and development outlays for robot systems will soar to $3 billion a year by 1995.

Both robot builders and users now recognize that the new robots can do a lot of things humans can't. Anthropomorphism—having robots imitate human activities—has fascinated robot buffs ever since the Czech playwright Karel Capek introduced the word "robot" into the lexicon. In his popular 1921 play *R.U.R.*, for Rossum's Universal Robots, Capek made robots look like mechanical counterparts of man. He derived the word from the Czech *robota*, which means work—including forced labor.

Anthropomorphism is appealing, but many robot builders think it is usually a wrong track in robotics because it fails to take advantage of some remarkable man-made devices and technologies. Although highly dextrous, the human arm and wrist, for instance, cannot twist completely around. A robot hand can. "We can try all we want to imitate mammals," says TRC's Engelberger, "but no animal has a built-in ball bearing." A robot arm that rotates in all possible directions, for example, is more useful than an imitation human arm that is limited by its joints.

In a remarkable demonstration of robotic agility, a nuclear-plant robot built by Odetics Inc. of Anaheim, California, not only walks on six legs but also can extend itself from a height of five feet to a total of 14 feet, becoming a kind of a mechanical giraffe. It can hang

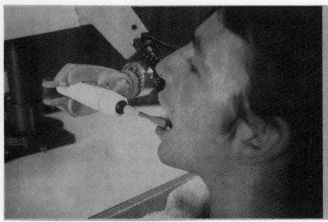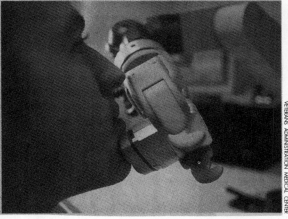

VETERANS ADMINISTRATION MEDICAL CENTER

from ledges inside nuclear plants, working upside down. By automatically changing the gripper in its hand it can do a variety of tasks, from changing light bulbs—a huge job in a nuclear plant—to lifting objects that weigh up to 300 pounds. Similarly, surveillance robots can do things a human guard cannot. Thanks to microwave vision, they can see through nonmetallic walls and in the dark can spot an intruder as far as 130 feet away.

Most robots in use today in space, under the sea, and in nuclear plants are operated from a distance by human workers as extensions of themselves. More often than not, the robots are tethered by a cable to the control station; the cable transmits electric power and serves as a communication link to the robot. Robot builders call this telerobotics, or teleoperation—an extension of human sensing and manipulating capability.

WHILE TELEOPERATION obviously keeps people out of hazardous environments, it has drawbacks. Operators can have trouble controlling remote robots and monitoring exactly what they're doing—for instance, when they're working undersea in murky waters. For greater versatility, a robot should work on its own, with minimal human supervision. Says Robotic Technology's Finkelstein: "The essence now is intelligent control systems. The technology for teleoperations is here now. The technology for automatic operations is being developed. If you have a tank as smart as an ant that knows how to tell an enemy from a friend, that could revolutionize warfare."

Currently, the U.S. Army is developing a walking truck to traverse roadless terrain, a contraption with fat, bent legs and a wriggling body that make it look like an immense, unearthly insect. The growing military applications of robots promise civilian fallout that could pay off for companies big and small. For example, military work on robots that navigate by themselves could be applied to trucks, automobiles, and factory vehicles.

Early designs for NASA's space station assembly robot, called Flight Telerobotic Servicer (FTS), resemble a refrigerator with a flat head and four arms. FTS will be a hybrid

between a telerobot and a fully autonomous machine. An astronaut can run it in two ways. In the teleoperated mode, the physical motions of an astronaut's hand will be reproduced by the robot's mechanical arms, which multiply the astronaut's force. The astronaut will work in shirtsleeves inside the space station; the robot will be outside.

Alternatively, the robot could operate "teleautonomously." The astronaut would transmit complex commands for it to interpret and execute. The astronaut, for instance, could command the robot to repair a nearby spacecraft. The robot would dock with the satellite and do its job without any further commands from its operator, who would watch the robot on his TV screen and intervene if needed. Six NASA contractors—Westinghouse, Grumman, Fairchild, Lockheed, Martin Marietta, and United Technologies—have just submitted preliminary design plans for the FTS robot.

Giulio Varsi, manager of automation and robotics for NASA's space station office, talks enthusiastically about developing space robots that "learn as they go along"—intelligent automatons with sufficient vision and a fine sense of touch that can modify their actions as circumstances change. Such technologies would help improve earth-based service robots. The initial FTS robot will cost about $200 million, in part because of its highly complex software, but subsequent versions could probably be produced for about $10 million apiece, Varsi says.

THE MOST SURPRISING demonstration of robot autonomy so far will take place as early as October at New Hampshire's Lake Winnipesaukee. In a game of wits, government and University of New Hampshire researchers will pit two untethered undersea robot craft working together against men in boats, who will try to detect the robots with sonar and other instruments. For their part the robots will work in tandem, using microprocessors guided by artificial intelligence software. The robot craft will attempt to elude their human pursuers by sacrificing one robot and having the other escape with TV pictures and other data it has gathered.

The key to making robots smarter lies in computer power that can enhance their intelligence, which is so far rather dim. Carnegie Mellon's Whittaker says that some of the service robots his institute has built have only reached the "intelligence of a worm." Robots as brainy as the pair in *Star Wars*, the timid android C3PO and its barrel-shaped electronic sidekick, R2D2, are at least 50 years away.

One reason: Progress toward giving robots humanlike sight and hands has been excruciatingly slow. In the case of sight, digital computers have trouble recognizing patterns that people spot almost intuitively. After about a decade of work, researchers at Stanford University who are trying to impart vision to robots have just scored what they consider an impressive victory. Their vision system can recognize about two dozen different objects—airplanes of varying shapes, for example—as belonging to a single class. A University of Utah–MIT project in progress for seven years has yet to produce a fully workable hand, although researchers have constructed a computerized prototype with tendonlike wires and four fingers run by 32 miniature motors.

Both research teams have come to appreciate the awesome complexity of human senses and information processing. Says Stanford researcher Thomas O. Binford: "The retina of one eye has roughly 100 million specialized vision cells and four layers of neurons, all capable of doing about ten billion calculations a second." All told, about 60% of the brain's cortex, the so-called thinking cap on top of the brain, is involved in handling visual information—a computational task that it would take 100,000 Cray supercomputers to handle, Binford estimates.

If researchers can get robots to see clearly and to understand where they are—another classic problem—that would make possible seeing-eye robots, among other things. The elusiveness of perfection does not deter the practical types, however. "University researchers sometimes unnecessarily complicate things," says Engelberger. "We take bits and pieces of available technology—ultrasound, infrared, TV cameras—and we tell our robots beforehand where to go."

ENGELBERGER PLANS to get around the "Where am I?" problem in his cleaning robot by using what he calls the Hansel and Gretel concept. In a typical operation, the robot begins by circling the perimeter of a room, bouncing sonar off the walls to locate itself. As the robot goes along, the Hansel and Gretel scheme comes into play. Those fairy tale tots marked their path in the forest by leaving a trail of bread crumbs to guide them back out. Birds ate the crumbs, of course, or there wouldn't have been a story. Each time Engelberger's cleaner makes a circuit, it will drop tiny pieces of fluorescent paper— "bread crumb equivalents," Engelberger calls them—to one side, creating a parallel, inner circle that it will follow the next time around. It's much like mowing a lawn in a continuous spiral from the outside in. As the robot follows the path, its scrubbing brushes will clean up the old trail just as Hansel and Gretel's birds did. This or similar approaches are a lot easier than trying to build up a comprehensive picture of the world inside a robot's brain.

As for hands: Many of today's robots can automatically change their "end effectors," tools that take the place of fingers to perform different jobs. Odetics, the Anaheim company that builds the walking robot, has just developed a hand that can grip a wider variety of objects and shapes—from a pencil to a railroad tie—than other models. It has two thumbs and one finger; the thumbs can rotate to grasp a payload, just as human thumbs can. Unlike a human hand or the University of Utah–MIT design, the Odetics hand requires no "tendons" in the arm or wrist to provide the power to move.

AT CARNEGIE MELLON'S Robotics Institute, Bill Whittaker sees the next important advances in service robots coming not in the basic technologies that make the robots possible but in combining them into working robots. Putting that view into practice, his institute has been turning out an impressive flock of robots. One has been used to decontaminate radioactive parts of the disabled Three Mile Island reactor. Another, a hulking brute of a machine about the size of a compact car, has four wheels and four stiff legs to walk with if its steering or the motors that drive its wheels fail. It can work with a hook, a crowbar, a shovel, a saw, a water-jet cutter, and other tools it carries.

Stanford University robot researchers have helped bring to fruition an impressive robot system that takes care of at least 13 needs of quadriplegics, from preparing canned soup and serving it to brushing their teeth afterward. During a recent demonstration of its remarkable skills at the Palo Alto Veterans Administration Medical Center, the robot greeted visitors with a brisk "Hi, Earthlings!" and proceeded to put on an impressive show. Because the research has been financed with federal funds, the system is available to any company that wants to build and sell it. Stanford and VA researchers figure it can be built for about $50,000.

What's coming will be even more surprising: smarter and even more mobile service robots that will be directed by a few simple words or even the gesture of a hand. Says the ever visionary Engelberger: "The list of service applications will grow because some of the more stultifying, demeaning, and downright dangerous human activities are in the service jobs. Robotizing those jobs is both possible and economically justifiable. This is not just an extrapolation of industrial robotics but literally a new slave class— mobile, sensate, service robots." Ready when you are, R2D2.

Telecommuters Bring The Office Home

Stuart Newman

Stuart Newman is a New York City based freelance writer and a business analyst for Chase Consulting Services, an internal group of the Chase Manhattan Bank.

A lot of people have decided to stop going to work. Not working, mind you, just going there. Fed up with the hassles of commuting and inflexible workplace schedules, many employees are avoiding the office entirely. Instead, they're telecommuting: working at home with the aid of computers, modems and facsimile machines.

Jack Nilles, president of JALA Associates, a Los Angeles-based technology management consulting firm, coined the term *telecommuting* in 1973. Since then it has come to mean many things to many people. Nilles defines it as an arrangement in which employees use a computer—or some form of telecommunications equipment—to work at home or in a satellite office close to home. He estimates the current telecommuting population to be roughly one million.

So who are these homebodies anyway? Ideally, they're employees whose jobs require them to handle a flow of information. Some examples are programmers, engineers, speech writers and business analysts. And while the type of job must translate well to a home environment, so too must the personality of the employee. A telecommuter must be capable of handling autonomy. Experienced workers make the best candidates.

"Usually telecommuters are people who have been on the job long enough to solve their own problems," says Gil Gordon of Gil Gordon Associates, a New Jersey based management consulting firm. "They must be confident and intelligent enough to function inde-

pendently." However, not all hiring situations are alike. And, in some cases, companies do recruit people at the onset with the intention of making them telecommuters.

EXPANDING THE HIRING POOL

By carefully selecting participants and planning prudently, many organizations have found telecommuting to be a boon to their operation. The geographic boundaries of a company's hiring pool widen since prospective employees need not live in the immediate vicinity of the worksite. A New York based company, for example, can extend its recruiting efforts far beyond the tri-state area. A telecommuter in the Midwest can tie into the home office as easily as an East Coast-based telecommuter.

Recruiting is also strengthened by the intrinsic lure of flexibility that accompanies work-at-home arrangements. Households are often run by dual wage earners who have less time for domestic responsibility. This factor, therefore, makes the prospect of working at home more attractive to job candidates.

In addition to becoming a stronger draw to applicants, work-at-home programs often result in increased output from staff. H. Lee Geist of Gulf Stream, Florida telecommuted from 1983 to 1987 during his ten-year stint as a speech writer for Borg-Warner. According to Geist, being less distracted meant being more productive. Furthermore, telecommuting enabled him to respond to family illness by moving from his home in Chicago to the warmer climate of the Sun-Belt.

Geist's experience is typical. For example, the Travelers Insurance Company, which has a telecommuting staff of 80, cites productivity increases of 20 percent. The human resources depart-

ment determines this figure by examining the number of lines of code generated by programmers. Company officials tout the program as a clear success, pointing to the number of people who have remained in it since its inception—28 out of 35.

In addition, the program has helped the company attract and retain key personnel. "We felt there weren't a lot of quality employees who could operate without a certain degree of flexibility," says Diane Bengston, assistant director of the Traveler's two-year commuting program. "Recruitment was a prime reason for offering work-at-home [arrangements] to employees."

That flexibility allows employees to arrange their daily schedules with greater ease. For example, shuttling children to and from daycare centers is less of a burden for working parents. But as a substitute for daycare itself, work-at-home arrangements have proven far less successful. "It's a myth to assume that a person can pursue work involving any level of concentration and take care of preschool children at the same time," says Kathleen Christensen, director of City University of New York's National Project on Home-Based Work, a research program that studies the effects of working at home on women and their families.

In fact, one of the pitfalls of telecommuting is that home workers can get roped into excessive household duties. "The assumption is that just because someone is home, he or she will do all the laundry, cook the dinner and take care of the kids," adds Gordon, "And if that individual doesn't learn to say 'no,' then there is a problem."

Some telecommuters may also feel very isolated working at home. While the prospect of working at home may appeal to a large segment of the population, it is a smaller group that can

From *Management Review*, December 1989, pp. 40-43. Copyright © 1989 by Stuart Newman.

actually deal with the four walls once they get there. Many people thrive on social contact. And for them telecommuting is often disastrous.

In addition, the promotability of home-based workers is an issue both the employer and the employee must consider. "Your career may be plateaued while you're telecommuting," explains Doug Willet, a second vice president of human resources and data processing at the Travelers. "It's difficult to move up when you're not visible in the home office." "It's not that you can't get a promotion because you're a telecommuter," adds Alice Simon, a Travelers spokesperson. "But generally promotions mean management responsibilities—which are difficult to perform remotely."

MANAGING TELECOMMUTERS

Although isolation can be a problem, there are a number of ways to prevent employees from feeling cut-off. One is to set a core time when workers must be in the home office. This provides them with the opportunity to interact with their co-workers. "It's easy to become paranoid when you're out of touch with the workplace," says Tom Miller, vice president and director of home office research at Link Resources, a New York-based market-research firm that has conducted a number of telecommuting surveys. "I think being in the office at least once or twice a week is healthy."

But while mandatory core time may be necessary for some, others do fine without it. Hedi Hesse, a systems analyst for Pacific Bell, has telecommuted since 1985. Although isolation was initially a problem for her, she soon adjusted. Hesse is currently under no requirements to be in the home office. "I had to learn to make the best use of the phone," she says. "It's really honed my organizational and planning skills because instead of leaving things to chance, I now simply call people."

Telecommuting also helped Hesse achieve goals that she otherwise would not have reached. "I wanted to go back to college. It was impossible for me to leave the office during the day, and the school didn't have classes at night. Frankly, I was ready to leave the telephone company until telecommuting made it possible for me to do a flextime schedule."

The list of benefits to employees does not end here. One obvious kickback for home workers is the elimination of the commute itself. "Just the trip back and forth, sitting in traffic for forty-five minutes to an hour, puts stress on you," says Cheryl Schatzman, a systems analyst and former telecommuter for the Hartford Insurance Company. "When I worked at home, my stress level was a lot lower than what it would have been had I driven to the office every day." Employers, in turn, save on office space with less employees operating under one roof.

Despite the advantages, management must consider several factors before adopting a telecommuting program. High on the list of *don'ts* is altering the employees' compensation package in any way. Not only can this lead to worker resentment, it can and has led to litigation.

Telecommuters of the California Western States Life Insurance Company took the company to court in December 1985. In their package, Cal-Western had included a change of payment mode from straight salary to a pay-by-the-piece basis without benefits. Eight workers soon became disgruntled and sued the company for more than a million dollars. They claimed that Cal-Western had used the arrangement as a deception to deny them due compensation. Ultimately, the company did give the workers a cash settlement for an undisclosed amount. "You can't just change work location, keep every other aspect of the job the same and then call these people independent contractors," Gordon says.

The misuse of telecommuting arrangements is a prime concern of the AFL-CIO, which passed a resolution calling for a ban on computer homework in 1983. Union officials fear a return to the cottage industries of the '20s and '30s, according to Dennis Chamot, associate director of the AFL-CIO's department for professional employees. During this period, the low wages and poor conditions of home workers eventually prompted the passing of the Fair Labor Standards Act of 1938.

Chamot recognizes that, in light of the support for work-at-home arrangements, it is unlikely that such a ban will ever become law. However, companies can avoid legal battles by making all work-at-home programs available on a volunteer basis, he advises.

Nilles, who has helped companies set up telecommuting programs, also emphasizes the importance of volunteerism. "Our rule is: If either the supervisor or the telecommuter doesn't want to participate, they shouldn't," he says.

DON'T JUMP RIGHT IN

In addition, he recommends that a formal planning process precede all work-at-home programs. "You have to do some planning. A manager can't just say, 'OK, next Monday you guys start working at home.'

The California State Telecommuting Pilot, a program of 200 government employees, enrolls potential telecommuters and their managers in training workshops before any home work begins. Managers attend the first session, where they are encouraged to discuss their concerns about the program. A second session is held for telecommuters; issues such as childcare arrangements and delineation of home work space are discussed.

The third, and final, session is the most intensive stage of the workshop. Here, the two groups meet together and draw up formal guidelines to be followed during actual telecommuting.

David Fleming, program manager of the California Pilot, looks at three areas of an employee's profile before enrolling that person in the program. First, he examines the job itself, separating tasks into those that are telecommutable and those that are not. Next, he decides if the employee's personality is a fit for telecommuting.

The final factor he considers is the relationship between the manager and the subordinate. "If it's not good, you're starting out on the wrong foot," Fleming says. "Telecommuting is based on mutual trust."

The Travelers also precedes telecommuting with formal training. Participants address issues such as time management, setting objectives, organization and measuring performance (for managers). Travelers' Willet believes that preparation has been essential to his group's success. "We look at things we think the telecommuters ought to know about and spend a lot of time creating the right environment."

In addition, Travelers conducts extensive studies of telecommuters' equipment needs and provides all necessary hardware to keep them up and running. "If you're going to support telecommuters, you must commit to the technical tools that will make your program successful," adds Link Resources' Miller, who is also a telecommuter.

One notable technology for this purpose is voice mail, a company-wide answering system that connects individual employees' voice-mail boxes. Since telecommuters can access the system from home—dialing in to receive or leave messages—it brings them back into the information loop. And using voice mail is as easy as placing a phone call.

The evolution of technology in the workplace—the computer and the facsimile machine, in particular—has helped telecommuting become a viable work option. "There has been an increasing recognition, first on the part of the employees, and then on the employers, that the home is a valid place to work," Miller says.

And the use of telecommuting could rise further as the availability of service-oriented jobs escalates. Occupations that handle physical materials—factory and warehouse work, for example—are being over-shadowed by those that handle information. This, coupled with the ability of computers to transfer that information, has made work-at-home arrangements an increasing possibility for today's worker.

Telecommuting has brought a wealth of opportunities to many people. For one thing, it allows them to be closer to their families. "One reason people dog it out at home is that they find the quality of their lives improving," says Dorothy Denton, executive director of the American Home Business Association, a Connecticut-based consulting firm. "It doesn't mean they spend all the time with their children. But just having one or more parent in the home seems to bring the family together," she explains.

Telecommuting is a relatively new phenomenon. It has yet to prove its permanence or reveal all its handicaps. The sphere of influence—improvements in home life and such—is not yet entirely known. Its success depends on many factors, some predictable, some not. And its lure is not universal. For some, it has been nothing more than a failed experiment. For others, it is an invaluable means of fulfilling personal objectives.

There are, of course, still some surprises in store. "Ten or twelve years ago," Nilles says, "I thought that productivity increases would be the major incentive for work-at-home programs. But as it turns out, more often than not, it isn't number one." The two most-quoted reasons for telecommuting? "Companies are running out of office space or they want to attract and retain some specially talented people," he says. "And telecommuting as a management tool can make that happen."

Do It Yourself

Brian Hayes

BRIAN HAYES *is the editor of* AMERICAN SCIENTIST.

They say we live in a service economy, that today the main business of business is not making things but tending to people's needs. We do for one another—you flip my hamburgers and I baby-sit your kids—and by some magic, wealth is created out of the transaction. Three-fourths of all jobs in the United States are service-sector jobs. And yet, to a remarkable degree we inhabit a self-service world.

Within living memory, people who were no more than respectably rich needed servants to help them dress in the morning and bathe in the evening. Now most families wash their own clothes, cook their own meals, clean their own house, drive their own car, mow their own lawn, shine their own shoes. The self-service elevator is all but universal. The telephone company has persuaded us to dial our own calls and now expects us to install our own telephones. In the past decade we have learned to pump our own gas. When we move the household, some of us rent a truck and haul our own furniture. We go to an automatic teller machine to do our own banking. There is even do-it-yourself surgery: after a minor operation not long ago, I was sent home with instructions on how to remove my own sutures.

The new emphasis on doing it yourself has brought with it tremendous social and technological change. Consider the supermarket, an institution founded on the idea of self-service shopping. The supermarket was made possible by changes in the packaging of goods, and it has given rise to further changes in both packaging and marketing, not to mention eating habits. Do-it-yourself laundry has a similar history. It was not enough to develop the automatic washing machine. A precondition for the success of that device was a detergent that would clean with a mere swishing in water rather than heavy-duty rubbing. And the advantages of the washing machine were not fully realized until the textiles industry developed fabrics that respond well to such treatment, thereby eliminating the need for the ironing board as well as the washboard.

The automobile provides another example. Do-it-yourself transportation is favored so strongly in most American cities that alternative means of getting around can barely survive. The result of the attachment to the automobile has been a thoroughgoing transformation of the landscape, the atmosphere, the world economy and the urban way of life. Nations are ready to go to war for the right to sit in a rush-hour traffic jam.

Not all the changes brought on by the do-it-yourself movement are entirely for the best. Supermarket packaging is overflowing our garbage dumps; phosphate-rich detergents are suffocating our lakes; the automobile is suffocating *us*. Nevertheless, the social effects of the do-it-yourself movement seem primarily beneficial. They reinforce the more democratic and egalitarian tendencies in American society. In my own life, at least, the new order is welcome. I believe self-reliance is a virtue. I am made uncomfortable by the close attention of personal servants. I will drive an extra mile to find a gas station with a self-service pump. I certainly want no one else to draw my bath for me in the evening.

I would also like to believe that the self-service economy would be welcomed as an emancipation by those who toiled at pumping gas, shining shoes or pressing linen at steam-driven mangles. But of course the change in their lives has been a change for the better only if they have been put to better work; too often they have merely been put out of work.

The most dramatic social changes—but also the most ambiguous—are the ones that affect the roles of women. When the middle-class family gave up household servants in the 1930s, 1940s and 1950s, the work of those servants was taken on by the wife, who became cook, butler, valet, chauffeur. Indeed, wives are the heroes and pioneers of the do-it-yourself revolution. For some years—for a generation or two—a life of doing it yourself at home was the only choice available to many women. Lately that way of life has changed, as women have been welcomed back into the work force or have been compelled by economic necessity to rejoin it. One might therefore suppose that even men would now be learning to do for themselves. Perhaps some of us are.

Most of the developments mentioned above focus on the home and private life. There is a similar movement toward self-reliance under way in the workplace. In decades past the middle-class man of affairs—the one whose household included a cook, a gardener and a charwoman—was surrounded at the office by an equally elaborate support staff. In Dickens and Melville we read of copyists and clerks and office boys—all male. With the invention of the typewriter and carbon paper, copyists were eliminated, and subsequently women were admitted to office work as typists, stenographers and secretaries. Then came the photocopying machine and another shuffling of personnel; the typing pool was abolished. Now further changes are in progress or in prospect, driven this time by the availability of cheap computing power.

One case in which the issues are particularly clear is electronic mail (known to

This article is reprinted by permission of *The Sciences* and is from the March/April 1991 issue, pp. 13-15. Individual subscriptions are $18.00 per year. Write to The Sciences, 2 East 63rd Street, New York, NY 10021 or call 1-800-THE-NYAS.

those who use it as e-mail). In my work I carry on a fair amount of correspondence, most of it on paper but a growing proportion flowing over the electronic networks. Most people who write to me on paper employ secretarial help to produce their letters. Electronic mail, in contrast, is strictly a do-it-yourself operation. As far as I know, I have never received an e-mail message that did not come directly from the hand of the sender. My own habits reflect the same pattern: when letters must be sent on paper, I often dictate them, but e-mail messages I always write and dispatch on my own.

An important reason for the difference is the greater convenience of electronic mail, even when each kind of missive is prepared with the aid of a computer and word-processing software. With e-mail there is no need to feed letterhead stock through the printer and follow it with an envelope; once you have written the message, a single keystroke sends it on its way. Furthermore, standards of formality are more relaxed on the electronic network; no one bothers about typographical errors, and there is no such thing as a second draft. The tone is conversational, which is to be expected in a medium in which messages are delivered in seconds or minutes rather than in days. Perhaps most important, the sociology of network communications is quite different from that of the U.S. mail. The idea of e-mail was born on the ARPANET, the national computer network set up by the Department of Defense twenty years ago. The early users of that system belonged to the research community, and most of them were computer enthusiasts. They would no more ask a secretary to sit at their terminal and read their e-mail than a sports car enthusiast would hire a chauffeur to drive her Ferrari. (Of course some people in the academic world do not have a secretary—or a Ferrari.)

Another area in which the do-it-yourself movement has had a remarkable influence is engineering. A few years ago a mechanical engineer required the support of a cadre of subordinate designers, draftsmen and detailers, who spent most of their time preparing drawings. Today an engineer working alone can readily produce finished drawings and specifications entirely without (human) assistance. This feat is made practical by computer-aided design, or CAD, in which three-dimensional shapes are sketched and refined on a computer screen, while a corresponding data base records the evolving properties and relations among the represented objects. In some cases the output of the CAD program can directly control a computer-driven machine tool, so that the engineer not only designs the object but even manufactures it single-handedly.

In electronic engineering, computer assistance is all but mandatory. The designer of an integrated circuit works with a CAD program to define the structures that will be built up in various layers of metal, semiconductor and insulator on the surface of a silicon chip. Another program verifies that the design obeys all the geometric rules established for a given semiconductor technology, and still another program simulates the operation of the circuit. When the design is complete, the data files can be transmitted (over the same networks that carry e-mail) to a "silicon foundry," where the chip is fabricated. Again a single individual has been given control of an entire manufacturing process.

What prompts these reflections on doing it yourself is a recent personal experience that has given me a sense of liberation similar to what I imagine an engineer might feel on turning an idea directly into hardware. Part of my work is to devise illustrations—drawings, diagrams, graphs and the like—for magazine publication. For many years I have done this by collaborating with an artist, who would attempt to draw what I dreamed up. The process would start with my sketch, however crude, which would serve as an aid in communicating with the artist. Then the artist would show me a more refined sketch, which I would revise; after two or three iterations of this process we would converge on a finished illustration. The multiple cycles of revision were needed not because the artist failed to follow my instructions but because I never seemed to know what I wanted to see until I had seen it.

Now I have discovered, to my surprise, that with the help of certain computer software I can prepare many routine illustrations on my own. The computer has not made an artist of me, but it offers so much assistance with the elementary, mechanical aspects of drawing—making round circles, ruling straight lines—that someone without much aptitude or training can fake it quite successfully. As a drawing tool the computer is not so much a better pencil as a better eraser. It allows you to see immediately where you have gone wrong and to revise endlessly without rubbing a hole through the paper. It also solves the "Plan Ahea" problem: if an illustration drawn on paper does not fit its allotted space, the artist may well have to start all over; working on a computer, however, one merely tugs at a corner of the drawing to rescale it.

Computer programs for drawing and illustration make up part of the technology called desktop publishing. Getting a bit of prose printed was once a collaborative effort of at least eight people. A writer wrote it; an editor edited it; a compositor set it in type; a proofreader checked the compositor's work; a designer laid out the pages; a printer or a paste-up artist put the type into the pages; a lithographer or a stereotyper created printing plates; a pressman (or a press crew) ran off the copies. Most of this work can now be done by one person, sitting at one machine. Writing, editing, setting type, proofreading, designing and putting type into pages all are tasks for the solitary desktop publisher; only platemaking and printing still require investments of craft and capital that are beyond the means of the individual.

In music too, as in the graphic arts, there is the promise of a new autonomy. The computer will not turn you into a musician or a composer, but it will remove some of the emphasis on performance skills. With a computer program called a sequencer you can piece together a melodic invention note by note, as slowly as you please, and the machine will then play the composition at its proper tempo. You can keep trying different notes until you finally stumble on the right one. Moreover, you become conductor as well as composer, and you can hear your work in its fully orchestrated form without hiring Carnegie Hall. A one-man band indeed.

Even in areas as cool and forbidding as statistics and mathematics the computer has introduced a new spirit of self-sufficiency. There was a time when a biologist with experimental results to analyze might have asked the advice of a statistician and would surely have enlisted the help of a graduate student to perform the numerical work. Computer programs have now taken the drudgery out of the more routine mathematical tasks—fitting a curve to data, say, or estimating statistical significance. What is more remarkable is that there is mechanized help available even for higher mathematics: with a program for symbolic manipulation I can solve equations beyond my capacity with paper and pencil. I feel sheepish in saying it, but I can come up with answers to problems I do not understand.

What about do-it-yourself computing? A long-standing dream of computer science is to dispense with the profession of programming and enable those who use computers to create their own software. A lot of that is going on: much excellent software is being written by people whose training is not in computing. So far, however, people have been adapting to the needs of the machine, not the other way around. Physicists learn to speak FORTRAN; astronomers control their telescopes with programs they write in

FORTH; businesspeople master the intricacies of linear programming and other algorithms for optimization. The software that will make computing easy for everyone does not yet exist, but it may not be an altogether vain notion.

I have said that I welcome the social effects of self-reliance in personal life, but what about the consequences of such changes in the workplace? The various trends described above would appear to be bad news for secretaries, draftsmen, illustrators and proofreaders, among others. The compositors who once operated stately Linotype machines have already been displaced. The jobs of programmers may one day be in jeopardy, and for that matter editors are not totally secure.

On the other hand, one ought to keep in mind that telling a machine what to do will always be more difficult than telling a person what to do. It seems unlikely, therefore, that captains of industry will ever give up their trains of aides and assistants. As a matter of fact, the social milieu of most large corporations seems set up to reward dependency and to discourage self-reliance. After all, it is a milieu dominated by people whose very function is not to do it themselves but to tell someone else to do it. The way to get ahead in that world is to manage people, not to operate machines. As long as the boss claims she cannot type, the secretary will not disappear; but with any luck, he might get to do more interesting work.

There are other reasons for having misgivings about the do-it-yourself movement. In the arts and the sciences the changes under discussion here amount to a triumph of amateurism. Computer-based tools may compensate to some extent for the amateur's lack of skill, but they cannot make up for a failure of taste or judgment. Professional artists and designers cringe at some of the products of desktop publishing, which tend to show the exuberant recklessness of a child's first adventure with a can of spray paint. Even when the worst offenses are avoided, it often seems that something is missing. A living and breathing artist will listen to your plans and then respond, "I have a better idea." Computer programs do not volunteer.

In the end the main effect of the computer on aesthetic sensibilities may be to increase our appreciation of those arts and crafts that continue to resist mechanization. I have learned to produce meticulous diagrams of carefully plotted geometry, but what I admire most is the sure brush stroke of the watercolorist, who works in a medium that supplies no erasers, in which it has to be done right the first time.

Finally, I must admit to a doubt about the healthfulness of all this autonomy and self-sufficiency. Doing it yourself offers important psychological rewards and gratifications, but as a way of life it can surely be taken too far. Ultimately we are left with a vision out of science fiction: the isolated mastermind, seated at a vast control panel full of dials and knobs, pushing a button to synthesize a string quartet or publish a book or start up an assembly line. It is a vision of power and control, but rather lacking in human warmth.

Social Interaction and Participation in the Information Age

The economic system provides members of a society with the means of earning an income and acquiring the goods and services they need. As important as these functions are, a thriving society also needs a feeling of community or identity among its members. This point was stressed by the French social scientist Emile Durkheim (1858–1917). He criticized those who implied that economic factors alone could tie society together, and he argues that unless people had shared beliefs, values, and expectations, economic exchange would be difficult to maintain. Economic interests alone, argued Durkheim, make people friends one day and enemies the next. In order for economic exchange to work, the parties must agree in advance on the terms of trade. Each must trust the other's integrity to fulfill his or her obligations—deliver the goods, perform the work, pay the agreed price.

In traditional societies, strong kinship ties and a shared religion provide the foundation for group identity and common values. People also have common life experiences. They work at the same occupations (farming, hunting, fishing) and face the same challenges of existence. Social norms and expectations are dictated by tradition. Because of strong group ties and shared beliefs, members have a "collective conscience."

In modern societies, the sense of community and belonging can break down. Though mass production results in the outward appearance of a homogeneous culture, other forces foster differences between people. Rather than a single unifying set of sacred values and beliefs, there are countless competing moral and philosophical perspectives. Families are smaller and have weaker ties with extended kinship groups. People work in very diverse occupations. Differences in work and social position make it difficult for people to identify with each other's needs and interests. Traditional standards of behavior no longer apply. Individuals are often anonymous to each other as they go about their daily affairs. People may feel insignificant, powerless, and alienated.

Under these conditions, social cohesion can easily be splintered by factionalism. Group solidarity can be eroded by self-interested individualism. In his day, Durkheim argued that the problems of rising crime, divorce, and suicide were symptoms of isolation and social disintegration. He was concerned with finding ways to reduce the alienation of modern life and reunite society with itself. He hoped that ultimately, a new form of social stability would emerge, one based on the rule of law and contracts. However, the continuing debates and clashes over such issues as abortion, sex education, surrogate parenting, women's rights, and gun control underscore the fact that it is very difficult to formulate laws and contracts that all the people will uphold.

In this section, articles examine how computers are affecting various aspects of social participation and community. The first focuses on disabled people. Besides the physical or mental challenges of coping in a modern world, people who are disabled are often relegated to marginal economic and social status. In "Challenging the Myth of Disability," Alan Brightman, the manager of Special Education and Rehabilitation at Apple Computer, Inc., discusses the experience of disability and Apple's goal of using computer technology to help change the "quality of life of the disabled person and how disability is perceived by the rest of society." He also encourages the rest of us to get involved, and thus "build a bridge to a new community."

People who are disabled are not the only ones who can benefit socially from new technologies. If the forces of modern life separate us from family and friends, telephones, cars, and airplanes are among the many technologies that can help us maintain close ties even across vast geographic distances. We even have laws and etiquette norms that dictate legal and proper social behavior with respect to these technologies. According to David Lyon in "Hey You! Make Way for My Technology!" telephones, cars, and personal computers are now impairing good human relationships and common courtesy. Lyon humorously argues new consumer technologies are partly to blame for a rise in rudeness and a decline in civilization as we know it.

Sometimes, the stresses of life cause people to seek help from professional therapists or counselors. In "The Doctor Is On," Lisa Davis discusses the development of a few new computer programs for psychotherapy. She identifies positive features of these programs but also highlights some important limitations on the value of replacing a human touch with computerized compassion.

The new field of "Virtual Reality" described by Robert

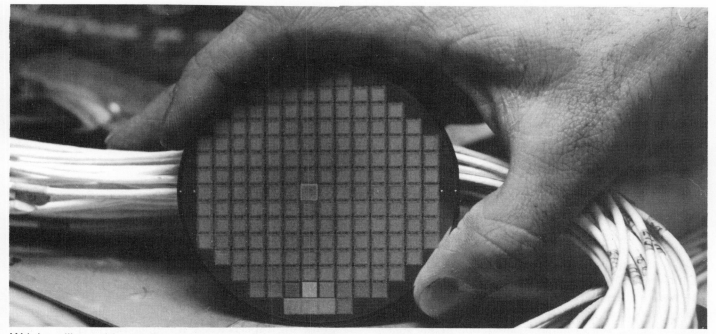

Wright will provide totally new opportunities for human relationships (or isolation) in the future. The potential implications of inhabitating and sharing fantasy worlds of our own creation are both promising and scary. But, as Wright explains, whether you see the prospects with hope or misgiving "depends essentially on your view of human nature."

So far, the discussion has focused on social interaction in small groups, but people also have opportunities to participate in society on a much broader scale. In modern democracies, for instance, few of us are directly involved in formulating legislation, but nearly everyone has the opportunity to campaign for a favorite cause and to vote in elections. Some observers are concerned, however, about the ability of ordinary citizens to make informed choices in a scientific and technological age. This important topic is addressed in the next two articles in this section and opposing perspectives are presented. In "America's Ignorance of Science and Technology Poses a Threat to the Democratic Process Itself," Paul E. Gray argues that scientific and technical illiteracy threatens the survival of democracy. An opposing view is presented by Morris Shamos in "The Lesson Every Child Need Not Learn." He argues that mass scientific literacy is unachievable and unnecessary.

Ronni Rosenberg, in "Debunking Computer Literacy," looks at the issue of whether "computer literacy" as taught in public schools will turn students into "productive workers, informed citizens and wise decisionmakers in the information society." She concludes that present computer literacy programs cannot achieve these goals and that "fundamental educational problems cannot be solved by technological means."

Looking Ahead: Challenge Questions

Can you identify some marginal groups or people who might achieve greater social acceptance and participation through computer networking? Which groups might be hurt even further?

If virtual reality becomes a mass medium, could or should it be regulated as television is today? Why or why not?

CHALLENGING THE MYTH OF DISABILITY

WHEN DISABLED CHILDREN AND ADULTS ARE GIVEN ACCESS TO COMPUTERS, IT BECOMES CLEAR HOW THESE MACHINES CAN, INDEED, CHANGE LIVES

Alan Brightman

Manager of Special Education and Rehabilitation at Apple Computer, Inc., Alan J. Brightman received his PhD in education from Harvard University. His newest book is, Independence Day: Designing Computer Solutions for Individuals with Disability, *1991.*

A computer can change your life. When I first came to Apple more than five years ago, that was one of the phrases I heard most often. The advertising and, particularly, the marketing staff repeated this slogan frequently. I can remember, however, that no matter how much I heard it and no matter how often I saw it on bumper stickers and buttons, it rang a little false to me. It seemed that if it were true a plastic box could change your life, then that was *more of a comment on your life than on the plastic box.* What kind of a life must you have if it could be changed so easily?

Five years later, I still hear the same words. Frankly, they still sound somewhat overstated, but, in one area at least, I've become a total and passionate believer. Every day across the country, when disabled children and adults are given access to computers, it becomes clear how these machines can, indeed, change certain lives. Often the changes can be at the most fundamental level imaginable.

THE RHETORIC OF DISABILITY

Anyone who has been involved with disabled people for any length of time *must* be extremely observant of (if not actually petty about) the apparently casual use of some common words and slogans. The difference that rhetoric has made in the field of special education and rehabilitation—and in the lives of disabled individuals—has been so insistent, so dramatic, and so consequential, that as professionals in this field we would be blatantly irresponsible if we were not vigilant about the words we use.

Almost 20 years ago, I spent some months in Denmark and Sweden trying to discover, firsthand, why the Scandinavian special education and rehabilitation system was regarded as the most humane and progressive in the world. I returned from that visit (and from subsequent visits) with a refreshing new respect for common sense and, in particular, for the ability to

---

It is not too ambitious to set as our goal fundamentally changing the experience of being disabled.

---

match reality with rhetoric. I was walking in the halls of a school building in Sweden at about 10 or 11 o'clock in the morning. In the corridor there were five or six doorways leading to various classrooms. I remember entering a speech class. It seemed fairly typical. Then I went into a reading class. It looked like a reading class. And then I opened a door to a resource room for retarded students. It was lit only by red bulbs. A juke box was playing. Several pairs of students were on a dance floor. They were dancing. Other students stood or sat at a bar drinking and chatting. A silver ball rotated in the ceiling.

This was a disco. It was literally a classroom in "disconess" held at 10 o'clock in the morning in a resource room of a public school. It all seemed a little strange to me at first. But in the context of both the Scandinavian value system and pervasive Scandinavian rhetoric, I was soon discover that this classroom wasn't strange at all. It made perfect common sense.

The Swedish people believe that school is a place that should help people—all people—fit into society and, as much as possible, to become full participants in it. A discotheque is one of the places in our society where a retarded person might, through some inap-

EDUCOM Review, Winter 1989, pp. 17-23. Copyright © 1989 by EDUCOM. Reprinted by permission of Rickard Associates, FL.

propriate behavior, signal that he or she does not fit in. Therefore, why shouldn't school be the place to learn how to behave in a disco? One needs to know how to ask someone to dance and then to be able to dance, how to order a drink and then to pay (and tip) for it, and how to initiate a casual conversation and then to continue it.

I recall this scene in order to consider the critical implications of rhetoric in the fields of special education and rehabilitation. In Sweden, very clearly, the rhetoric is essentially about *mainstreaming*. When you listen to the Scandinavians speak about mainstreaming (and about normalization), you hear very pretty, very proud words. But their sparkling rhetoric would have remained just that if classrooms such as the one I've described had not sprung forth from those words. From a special education and rehabilitation perspective, it is, therefore, not trivial to ask: What is our rhetoric? Furthermore, what might *our* discos be?

If we examine the development of special education and rehabilitation in this country, we will find that what has largely driven its twists and turns is the engine of rhetoric. Two kinds of rhetoric have historically influenced, if not dominated, the design of our discos in special education and rehabilitation. Yet there is a third kind of rhetoric, a new way of thinking and talking about disability, that I am confident will be more forceful, more dramatic, and simply and finally more correct in bringing us to the future. It should become clear in the midst of this discussion why we, at Apple, believe that it is not too ambitious to set as our goal nothing less than *fundamentally changing the experience of being disabled*, in terms of both the quality of life of the disabled person and how the disability is perceived by the rest of society.

The first, and by far the most prevalent rhetoric, is the rhetoric of platitudes. Disability makes most nondisabled adults somewhat awkward. We feel as if we're not quite ourselves in the presence of others who seem so different, others with whom we have so little practice at interpersonal relations. If we could hear the things we say when we're feeling awkward, we'd probably choose to be silent, but we don't. So we issue forth with the kind of safe platitudes that we might seriously question, if we had more insight. Only children, especially those under the age of 12, tend to be free of our platitudes; they make clear and true attempts at understanding. Here, for example, are the kinds of questions children ask when confronted with disability.

- If that girl's blind, why does she keep her eyes open?
- If I yell into that deaf child's ear, will he hear me better?
- Why does that retarded boy do those stupid things?
- How does a person in a wheelchair go to the bathroom?

These are terrific questions. They are real, visceral, curious, and challenging. More often than not, though, if a child directs any one of them to a teacher in a public school, for example, the teacher's answer is something like: "Don't you think it's time we finished our spelling now?"

It seems that we're simply more comfortable pretending not to notice, or else we're driven by a tremendous need to disavow the *fact of difference* in our society. These kinds of disavowals are by no means limited to verbal platitudes. In the name of providing care to disabled individuals, for example, we have built enormous institutional settings as far away from populated areas as possible. We have also put disabled children either in separate schools altogether or in segregated classrooms, typically in the basement, next to the boiler room. These might be called physical platitudes: way out of sight, comfortably out of mind. These physical platitudes turn out to be a breeding ground for one very curious phenomenon, which can only be described as the active and consistent disregard for common sense. In fact, nowhere, in my experience, has common sense proven to be less common than in institutional settings or organizations designed for disabled people.

Many years ago I worked at a large eastern state school for retarded persons. Some of the severely retarded young adults in one of the wards were apparently chewing on the rugs and causing a significant amount of damage. The institution did not bother to notice either that these day rooms, occupied for endless hours by their students, were devoid of books, games, and other diversions or that there was absolutely nothing else to do there. Instead, each individual was brought to the institutional dentist to have all of his or her teeth removed. Thus, the problem was solved.

In a similar institution, the problem was an increase in the number of pregnancies among mildly retarded women who, as a reward for appropriate behavior, were allowed off the grounds on day passes. It seems that some of the local men were taking easy advantage of these vulnerable women. Unbelievably, the institutional response was to implement a new policy whereby the women could no longer go into town on their own. Instead, they had to be paired with a buddy, another woman who had also earned the right to leave the grounds for a day. Within four months, of course, the pregnancy rate was found to have doubled.

It is significant that this common *nonsense* phenomenon isn't limited to places designed to serve only disabled individuals. Sometimes it can occur spontaneously when a disabled person simply enters a place designed for the mainstream population. In the late 1960s, a good friend of mine lost a leg in a freak boating accident. About a year and a half later, he was called to report to the draft board, and, good citizen that he was, he responded. He presented himself to the orientation interviewer—with his right pant leg pinned up—and sat while she noted his name, address, and other pertinent information. One interview question, though, made him get up and leave: Looking first at his pant leg and then straight into his eyes, the draft board interviewer asked, "Will this disability be of lasting duration?" Common sense seems to take flight in the presence of disability. Our comfortable reliance on the rhetoric of platitudes cannot hide our preference for not noticing.

On the other hand, the second category of rhetoric, ✳ which I call high drama, is the rhetoric of noticing too much. We have always cast disabled individuals as special, as exceptional, and we believe that nothing less than the grace of God has prevented us from becoming like them. Their lives are the stuff of grand themes: Frankenstein, Quasimodo, Captain Hook, Dr. Strangelove, Mr. Magoo, and all of the seven dwarfs (not just the one named Dopey). Their lives are the stuff of pity and heroism, which is to say, the stuff of telethons. Theirs are the lives of intense drama, in which countless obstacles are forever having to be overcome.

Yet none of this high drama is real, at least in the experience of the disabled person. In fact, the hardest thing about being disabled really is not the pain, or the dependence, or the expense, or even the inaccessible bathroom. The hardest thing about being disabled is that you're never perceived as just plain ordinary. The world always sees you as someone peculiar, as someone uncommon, as someone who doesn't quite fit in. When you're disabled, we, the nondisabled, regard you as nonordinary, as extraordinary.

THE REALITY OF DISABILITY

The truth is, however, that being disabled has nothing to do with exaggerated melodramatic themes. It has everything to do, instead, with basic, gritty, mundane details: getting through a day and getting through a life, a real life, and being somebody. Several years ago, I edited a book called *Ordinary Moments*, which was an effort to capture the experience of disability from the disabled person's point of view, from the locker room, as it were, rather than from the poet's desk. A chapter written by a friend of mine in Boston begins by offering some definitions for the word "handicapped."

- Being handicapped is when you're the guest of honor at the "Handicapped Person of the Year" award luncheon and the rest room doors are too narrow for the wheelchair so you have to urinate in a broom closet.
- Or when someone actually says to you: "Oh, you have muscular dystrophy? If that happened to me, I'd kill myself."
- Not being able to turn the radio on. Or the television off.

- Accomplishing microscopic tasks well.
- Going to the museum and getting in free.
- Seeing everything from always only four feet off the ground.
- Hating having to ask. All the time ask.
- Having the ability to sit in one place for nine hours without going mad from restlessness. And after nine hours of not moving, coming home to sit in a different chair for seven hours more.
- Being handicapped is worrying about being handicapped too much.
- But damn it, this room is a mess, and I can't clean it.
- I'm hungry and I can't cook. The window is open and it's freezing outside; I can't shut it. The record player's skipping but the bike's in the way of the player. I hate that scratching noise.
- I can't find a pipe that's not clogged, so I can't even get high. And I don't feel like masturbating.
- The incredible pettiness gets wearying at times. I'm always worrying about getting to bed, getting up, getting into a chair, getting out of a chair.
- Being handicapped creates a pettiness syndrome. All you think about is simple stuff.[1]

So much, then, for the rhetoric of high drama, the rhetoric that has historically justified our treating disabled individuals as little more than objects of charity.

There is a new kind of rhetoric that needs to saturate our thinking and our actions in special education and rehabilitation. While doing so, it must also reflect the true reality of disabled children and adults. Simply stated, it is the rhetoric of expectation. A wonderful poster was put out several years ago by the Spastics Society of Great Britain. In it, a fourth- or fifth-grade child is sitting at a computer that he's operating with a head wand. He looks proud and serious. The monitor screen is covered with lines of text. Across the top of the poster, a bold caption reads: "Just because I couldn't speak, they thought I had nothing to say."

I know a lot of nonvocal people who also have much to say and who, with access to a computer, are, for the first time, finally being heard: across a room, over a phone, even on public assembly stages. I know people who will never be capable of actually seeing a printed page but who are now, with combination braille-text printers, able to share written assignments with sighted classmates. I know some profoundly retarded individuals, as well as mildly learning disabled ones, who are finally discovering that education doesn't need to be a perpetual experience in failure.

Disabled people form a significant part of our world. Close to 40 million children and adults with disability live, work, and play in the United States alone. Close to a million and a half of them are attending colleges and universities today. An additional 750 million disabled people live in other parts of the world. And their number, both in this country and abroad, keeps growing every day. In this country, the growing number of disabled people is largely due to advances in medical technology. In other countries, the increase is caused by such factors as war, malnutrition, and insidious disease. Furthermore, out of every seven disabled people alive today, six were not born that way. Eighty-five percent of people who have a disability today acquired it *after birth*, which is why disabled activists frequently refer to you and me as TABs—Temporarily Able Bodied individuals.

THE CHALLENGE OF DESIGNING FOR DISABLED INDIVIDUALS

For the vast majority of disabled individuals, the microcomputer doesn't simply represent the ability to accomplish tasks a little faster or a little better. It represents the ability to do things previously considered unthinkable. In other words, the computer *can* indeed change lives. It can give new, varied, and multifaceted expression to personal identity and, not incidentally, increase and improve self-confidence and self-esteem.

Consider a 15-year-old child in a wheelchair, who is paralyzed from the neck down and without speech. How is that child typically regarded by his peers? Perhaps even by his teachers? What's truly expected of him? And given how he's probably seen by others, how is he conditioned to see himself? Now we say to that child, "You can raise your eyebrows up and down. You have a movement you can control that enables you to pass instructions along to a computer, so you can do word processing, use a modem, and draw pictures. You can even acquire a voice. For the first time in your life, you can say 'here' when attendance is taken. You can demonstrate what a whiz you are at baseball statistics. You can display your artistic talents. You can become known, in other words, for *who you know you are* rather than for what others have interpreted you to be."

Once we say all this to the child, two things will happen. We will make him aware of astounding new, but very real, possibilities. And we will probably cause this young individual to ask a few questions, such as "How can I make those possibilities real for me?" As a matter of fact, these two things have been the primary concerns of our Office of Special Education and Rehabilitation since we created it four years ago.

- First, we try to generate awareness of how the personal computer can provide new options and opportunities for disabled children and adults.
- Second, we try to fashion a comprehensive response capacity to deal with the inevitable questions about actualizing these options and opportunities.

This twofold agenda of ours is written in the rhetoric of expectations, that is to say, where other people may look at a disabled individual and see only diagnosis, we see promise, usually a great deal of promise. We

have chosen to regard the disabled person as someone who can rather than as someone who *probably* can't. Together with his or her family members, friends, teachers, and coworkers, we approach the disabled person eagerly and hopefully, and we always offer answers.

Over the past four years, Apple has developed a response capacity that we believe is second to none in the industry. Our response capacity is rooted both in a comprehensive and carefully maintained database of adaptive technology and in a growing network of close to 40 community-based resource centers that we have established around the country.

PRODUCT DEVELOPMENT

While the history of Apple's response capacity is instructive, it is more useful here to consider the technology involved in product development.

To understand how we approached the area of product development, you have to understand only one basic premise: *This is not a world that was designed or built with disabled people in mind.* The natural world is difficult enough and there are so many man-made obstacles: curbs, steps, doors that are too narrow, and public phones that are too high. To make matters worse, a premium is put on physical beauty, making it an ideal that everyone should strive for. And if you don't have it, you belong to someone else's world, perhaps with people who can't see enough or know enough to tell that you, too, are imperfect. All of which leads, of course, to those favorite worldwide pastimes: the stigmatization and segregation of others and the creation of deviance yardsticks by which some people can assure themselves they are normal. Nevertheless, particularly over the last 15 years or so, largely because disabled activists have grown tired of being told to "just be patient" and have demonstrated that they can conduct sit-ins and chain themselves to fences just as effectively as nondisabled protesters, the physical world has changed significantly. It's a much easier terrain to navigate today than it was not so very long ago.

When the personal computer entered that terrain, it promised disabled people access to all kinds of new

---

Close to 40 million children and adults with disability live, work, and play in the United States.

---

power and capabilities, provided that they could get access to the machine in the first place. And that's the rub. Even the Macintosh, the computer "for the rest of us," was effectively sealed off, shutting out the disabled. To them, *ease of use* was pretty much a hypocritical concept. It is true that by the time the Macintosh arrived, the Apple II product line had become enormously accessible, mostly because of the hundreds of small third-party manufacturers who developed switches, keyboards, keyguards, printers, and specialized software that enabled people with all kinds of disabilities to use the computer, even though they had to operate it in very different ways. But that wasn't the case with the Macintosh, which in the beginning had many barriers for disabled users.

At first glance, none of these obstacles might seem to be too imposing. Yet a 2-inch curb is enough to prevent a motorized wheelchair from getting up on the sidewalk. For that reason, we set ourselves the task of trying to identify where we needed to build, in effect, *electronic curbcuts* into the computer. Suppose, for ex-

---

For the vast majority of disabled individuals, the microcomputer represents the ability to do things previously considered unthinkable.

---

ample, that you're working with your Macintosh and you make a mistake. Your machine will beep at you, which is a terrific warning signal; however, if you're deaf, the signal is irrelevant. Or consider the repeat key. Most good typists report that it's a wonderful feature. Most good typists, however, don't have poor gross or fine motor skills. If they did, they'd discover the frustration that's caused by not being able to remove their fingers from the keys quickly enough and, as a result, ending up with rows of repeating characters filling up the screen. There are also other obstacles, generally born of an attempt to improve hardware or software technology. For example, most software programs now and again require you to press down two or three keys simultaneously. This is impossible if you happen to be able to type only by using a head wand or a mouth stick, or if you are able to use only one finger. Finally, the mouse is obviously another major problem for the disabled user.

Our challenge, then, was to educate our own designers and engineers about the needs of those users typically ignored in the generic design process. Incidentally, the reason our designers and engineers don't ordinarily think about these users is not because they're instinctively insensitive, but, like most people, they need to be reminded now and then that disabled people make up a significant fraction of the population. Several years ago, we brought together about 20 people from different parts of Jean-Louis Gassee's organization and sat them down in front of an Apple IIe. "You know this thing inside and out," we reminded them. "You made it." Then we put an Apple-works disk in front of them and said, "You all know how to use this." Finally, we asked them to put their hands in their pockets, put a pencil in their mouth, and type a memo. As soon as they decided to take the challenge seriously, the protests began. "How about if

I just turn the machine on first?" one of the participants asked. "It's going to be a little hard to do with this pencil." "Let me just put the disk in the drive first, okay?" asked another.

In a short while, virtually on their own, the group identified a list of more than 60 design features that might prove to be an obstacle for one type of disability or another. Most of these barriers have, by now, been addressed. We've either fixed them or we've found simple ways around them. For instance, on those machines where the power switch is not on the front, a power strip affords the user the same function quite handily. It is probably well-known that the beep and the repeat key are both adaptable from the control panel. By sliding the volume control bar down to zero, a video analog of the beep appears in the form of a menu–bar flash. The repeat key feature, of course, can simply be shut off entirely. Simultaneous pressing of more than one key and full use of the mouse are both possible through the two utilities that are included in *Easy Access*: sticky keys and mouse keys. There is also *Close View*, a system utility that enables you to enlarge screen contents up to 16 times, which is helpful not only for the visually impaired person but also for someone who is necessarily sitting farther than usual from the screen, in a bed or a wheelchair, for example. It is also possible to invert the contents of the screen with this program. Of course, the documentation for *Close View* is presented in large print in the system manual.

There are also a number of much less obvious curbcuts built into the Macintosh. We have no latches on our disk drives, for example, and the drives themselves require that very little pressure be exerted on the disk before they accept it. Also, they push the disk out when it's ejected, giving fingers or mouth tongs something to grasp. In fact, the 3.5-inch disk medium itself proves to be an interesting example of a disability-appropriate device. Its increased storage capacity, for one, means that a user will have to do much less disk swapping. It is encased in hard plastic and can, therefore, withstand the often tortuous slamming to which some users (particularly those with poor gross motor skills) subject it before they insert it into the drive.

In this area, our ultimate goal is to *establish, within the product development group, a permanent filter* that enables our designers and engineers both to recognize that there are many users in the world who are quite different from them and, therefore, to make our *generic* machine as accessible as possible. Apple is concerned with these product design issues for many reasons. In the first place, our engineers consider them important. They understand that the products they build are intended for individuals. That is, after all, Apple's design focus. Disabled users merely happened to strengthen the focus on individuals. So when our product designers realized that they had been ignoring this particular group of individuals, they were almost embarrassed. It was obvious, as well, that they were intrigued by the challenge of inclusion. More pragmatically, perhaps, they began to realize that conveniences that are initially invented and implemented for disabled people very soon become conveniences for nondisabled people as well. For example, many users who work in desktop publishing or graphic design have commented to us on how much easier it is for them to use mouse keys, rather than the mouse itself, to move objects on the screen with precision. The fact that conveniences for one turn out to be conveniences for all shouldn't be that surprising. Consider the simple curbcut on the sidewalk. It was put there specifically for disabled people and now nine out of ten people who use it are, of course, nondisabled.

We'll never be completely finished with this design task. In fact, there can never be a generic disability machine, one that meets the needs of all disabled users. Sometimes features that are useful for one set of

---

The challenge grows ever more urgent as the world of computers moves closer to standardization.

---

needs conflict with another set of needs. Consider the curbcut again. Everyone praised it when it began to become popular and legally required, that is, everyone except certain blind people whose guide dogs had been carefully trained to stop at curbs and were now leading them out into busy streets. Nor is the problem for blind people limited just to real-world curbcuts. From an access point of view, this population represents our biggest product design challenge by far. That challenge grows ever more urgent as the world of computers moves ever closer to standardization on graphical interfaces and multiple windows, things that must be seen in order to be used. At this point, we are actively engaged in pursuing several possible avenues of response.

CONCLUSION

Although I have been thinking about it for 20 years, I still find it difficult to say what our special education and rehabilitation programs might look like if they were to truly fulfill the promise of the rhetoric of expectation.

Perhaps the answer can best be found by understanding and appreciating for *yourself* how your knowledge of computer technology could have a tremendous influence on the lives of disabled individuals. *Spend a few hours at the center for disabled student services on your campus.* Find out why that center exists and what needs are being fulfilled there. Forget for a moment about things like *computer literacy* and come to know at least a few people who are involved in the business of *life literacy*. Find out how the technology you know so well, the technology of diversity, might be creatively applied to very real and very pressing human needs.

You needn't be an expert in special education or rehabilitation to learn quickly how you might forge a mutually satisfying association. All that is necessary is an interest in "hanging around until you've caught on," as Robert Frost defined education. Or, to paraphrase Yogi Berra, "You'll be able to observe a lot just by watching." Then you can build a bridge to a new community, which will prove to be a fertile turf for new ideas. Let it be a two-way bridge and encourage a lot of active traffic on it. It might lead, perhaps, to a brand-new disco.

REFERENCE

1. *Ordinary Moments: The Disabled Experience*, ed. Alan Brightman (Syracuse, N.Y.: Human Policy Press, 1985), p. 81.

Hey You! Make Way for My Technology!

DAVID LYON

DAVID LYON is a free-lance writer who owns an answering machine, a personal computer, and a loud diesel car.

AT 4:30 one morning a large truck sped through my upwardly mobile neighborhood, setting off three automobile anti-theft alarms in its wake. The alarms on a two-tone Datsun and a Volvo station wagon stopped screaming within a few minutes. The piercing device on a beige Mercedes 350 SE whooped until well after 5 A.M. The local police explained that the law doesn't limit such intrusions on good citizens' hours in the arms of Morpheus. It's a fair bet that cars equipped with overly sensitive theft alarms suffer an unusually high incidence of slashed tires. One officer of the law suggested the best remedy might be a .357. "Just blow that sucker away," he advised.

Poetic justice would be served by using a forceful product of the first Industrial Revolution to silence a less brutal but no less obnoxious device from the second. Rudeness is on the rise in the United States, and consumer technology is partly to blame for this erosion of civility.

That may seem a harsh indictment for such seemingly innocuous creations as the telephone answering machine, boom box radio-cassette player, and talking computer chip in automobiles. They are hardly cutting-edge devices, but they are relatively cheap to manufacture and insinuate themselves into every corner of daily life. The result is a decline of civilization as we have known it.

Manners and Machines

Civilization, after all, is governed by a network of rules and regulations that people subscribe to as part of the unwritten social contract. You can think of this system as

> *Rudeness is on the rise, and consumer technology is partly to blame.*

a cement mixer filled with ball bearings. Without a viscous medium in which to churn, the bearings eventually grind each other down to metallic dust. The medium that keeps social friction at a minimum is the code of manners.

But manners require some attention, and the whole point of having machines do a job is to free their users from having to pay attention. As machines multiply our capacity to perform useful tasks, they boost our aptitude for thoughtless and self-centered action. Civilized behavior is predicated on the principle of one human being interacting with another, not a human being interacting with a mechanical or electronic extension of another person.

The simple telephone answering machine—an undeniable aid to the thoughtful person who doesn't want to miss a message—can turn into a devilish instrument if misused. Call screening can become the electronic equivalent of avoiding your neighbor's salutation on the street: the machine's owner can use it to avoid talking to anyone except the chosen few. It has been known to prompt retaliatory rudeness in the form of irate messages from callers who suspect they are not

among the elect. I know of one dinner party host who leaves call screening on throughout the meal, making guests embarrassingly privy to what should remain private communiques.

Yet it is hard to tell which enables people to be more rude: the answering machine that screens out obnoxious calls, or the telephone that permits intrusions at all times of day and night. A.G. Bell probably never envisioned aluminum-siding salespeople, college alumni associations, or lovelorn friends when he devised the telephone. Is anything as satisfying as handing over the phone to a talkative three-year-old to chat with a "telemarketer"?

In the drive to make the telephone ever more useful, the Baby Bells are marketing a service that can make the answering machine seem like an instrument of civility. "Call waiting" is handy for the small business that can afford just one telephone, but in certain hands it permits the ultimate breach of telephone etiquette. I have a (former) friend who used to chat happily with me on the phone until a second call came in to her from a potential suitor. After a few long waits, I would hang up and call back—only to reach her answering machine. Obviously, she cared less about years of friendship than reaching out and touching Mr. Goodcall.

One good thing about telecommunicated rudeness is the opportunity to avoid it. You can always hang up. Too bad there isn't such a simple escape from the most pervasive instrument of uncivil behavior, the automobile. Our forebears probably endured a breed of surly, road-hogging oxen that cut off other drivers' carts, but what whip-wielding teamster could match the arrogance and gall of a BMW driver in city traffic? The various high-tech enhancements of luxury sedans and muscle cars seem to have rendered turn signals inoperative. Does each new vehicle retailing for more than $15,000 contain a brainwave generator that turns a tweedy, bearded professor into a satanic finger-waver the moment he climbs into the lumbar-support driver's seat?

The "best" of these new cars employ outstanding design and state-of-the-art materials to insulate the driver more hermetically than ever from the environment and the other hapless humans who inhabit it. Interaction with the road now seems to follow the rules of the jungle: perversely chaotic righthand turns from left lanes, horn blasts that imitate enraged bull elephants, and rapacious disregard for any flesh that dares interrupt the mating charge of the turbo-powered road warrior behind blinding yellow fog lights.

Technology's Seductive Ways

The automobile and a host of other devices such as the telephoto lens, Walkman radio and cassette deck, and personal computer might be classified as "attractive nuisances." They are fun to use but they can stomp all over politesse. Witness the teenager on a subway car armed with 100 decibels of IC-chip rhythm in the package known colloquially as a boom box.

Most amateur photographers will attest to the value of the current generation of powerful zoom lenses—products of computer-aided design in most cases. An 80-to-200-millimeter zoom lens is usually the first accessory a budding Cartier-Bresson buys. But what cost in dignity does the zoom telephoto lens exact? Where is the civility in photographing the picturesque poor from a comfortable distance of 100 yards or more? Do privacy and respect survive the beach photographer shooting down-home cheesecake with a 1,000-millimeter lens?

Long-lens photography may arise from a generous impulse to avoid intrusion. But the impulse is misguided. It merely keeps the photographer from having to obtain permission from the subject. Similarly, the Walkman listener may be trying to avoid inflicting his or her musical taste on the rest of us, but try getting the attention of someone blissed-out on Vivaldi when he is standing on your foot in a crowd.

The explosion of personal-computer technology has spawned a vigorous rudeness that would be impossible without list and word processing. Once upon a time people wrote real letters to each other; form letters arrived only from companies that promised you could win a Cadillac and have it parked at P.O. Box 800. Now every family with a home computer can generate its own "personalized" holiday form letter. The truly technophilic may include the image of a computer-drawn sleigh on the outside of the folded missive, made possible by drastic improvements in dot-matrix printers and aggressive marketing of desktop publishing.

Practitioners of these "arts" will defend them, no doubt, on the grounds that some communication is better than none. But is a pretense of personal rapport good enough? Some product designers seem to think so, but remember that they are enculturated with the prison-camp lexicon of computer-programming languages.

Faking good manners debases the concept of polite behavior, yet thanks to cheap microcomputers and voice-synthesizing circuitry, fake manners abound. Automobile makers install polite and resonant voices that nag us to close the car door and buckle up. "Fasten your seatbelt *please*," says the voice chip. At supermarket check-out lines, kids dulled by hours of running bar-coded packages over magnetic devices sullenly hand out computer-printed receipts that say "thank you." "Thank you" and "please" have never meant so little.

Nor do the machines that mindlessly supply these markers of civility fool anyone. The automated bank teller that flashes "have a nice day" is an annoyance. Worse yet is the babbling vending machine. When a talking cola machine and a traditional, silent machine stood next to each other at Hampton Beach, N.H., last summer, the silent machine sold out first. Most beachgoers preferred to avoid the mechanized chatter and phony politeness. Score one for civility.

THE DOCTOR IS ON

Seek help from a psychotherapist these days and you could well end up baring your soul to a computer.

LISA DAVIS

Lisa Davis is a staff writer.

"MEN ARE ALL ALIKE."

"In what way?"

"They're always bugging us about something or other."

If this were a normal conversation, say between two women talking over coffee, the next sentence would likely be a simple one—maybe just "Yeah." But this is a conversation between a woman and her therapist.

"Can you think of a specific example?"

"Well, my boyfriend made me come here."

"Your boyfriend made you come here—that's interesting."

"That's interesting"—a more elaborate way of saying "uh huh." Later:

"My father is afraid of everybody."

"Really, everybody?"

"My father is very fearful."

"What else comes to mind when you think of your father?"

"Bullies."

"Does this have anything to do with the fact that your boyfriend made you come here?"

Zap. You can smell the ozone from the electricity of a sudden psychic connection. This is what therapy is all about.

Except that the electricity here is more than mental. The therapist is plugged in. The therapist is a computer.

IT WAS CALLED ELIZA, back in 1966, and it couldn't really understand a word. All its insight, all its intuition were a sleight-of-hand illusion, the result of a set of rules devised by computer scientist Joseph Weizenbaum. As it happened, Weizenbaum hadn't even wanted to create a doc-in-the-box with Eliza—he was just interested in whether a machine could analyze and respond to conversational English. He'd chosen to make his new program mimic a therapist only because he thought that would give Eliza a good chance of bluffing its way through a dialogue.

"I wondered, are there some sorts of conversation where you don't need to know anything?" Weizenbaum says. "An example is cocktail party conversation, where I may be talking about energy conversion and you have no idea what I'm talking about, but you say, 'That's very interesting. Why haven't they thought of that before?'

"And then I came upon the psychiatrist. In some types of psychotherapy, the therapist doesn't respond directly to what the patient says. And if the therapist says, 'Tell me about elephants,' you don't interpret that as an admission of ignorance. You attribute knowledge to a psychiatrist whether he has it or not."

Eliza was able to take advantage of the leeway granted to therapists because Weizenbaum had programmed in a dictionary of key words, each with a set of matching canned responses. If a person used the word "always," for instance, Eliza might request a specific example. If there were no key words, Eliza might say something neutral, like "That's interesting," or it might ask an arbitrary question about some key word used earlier in the conversation. The seemingly intuitive leap Eliza made from bullies to boyfriends was just such a random jump.

The program worked well—so well that even when Weizenbaum tried to explain Eliza's gimmick, people who had used the program would often insist that it really did understand what they were saying. Weizenbaum found that bewildering. What he found appalling was that some therapists looked at his program and called it the future of psychotherapy.

Welcome to 1990. Eliza has spawned at least a dozen computer counseling programs in the past 20 years, and while most are in the research stage, a couple of them are already in use. The Therapeutic Learning Program, for instance, has made its way into about 50 counseling services. In universities, businesses, health maintenance organizations, and psychiatric hospitals, such programs can stand in for a flesh-and-blood therapist for more than half of a patient's sessions, if the patient is willing and the therapist thinks it would be useful. There are even a handful of programs, sold in computer magazines and self-help catalogs, that are meant to be used by the purchaser at home.

A session at the keyboard can sometimes help people whom therapists have been unable to reach, according to psychologist James Reagan, many of whose patients at a Michigan psychiatric hospital use the Therapeutic Learning Program. "One forty-two-year-old woman had been in and out of eight different psychiatric hospitals from the time she was twenty-three," Reagan says. "When the computer asked her what childhood events might be contributing to her problems, she checked off sexual abuse. That was the first time she'd said that. Before, she hadn't been asked the question because people had gotten caught up in her hallucinations, or she'd been asked and had avoided the question. Somehow, the computer made it easier for her to talk about it."

In fact, people are often more willing to make intimate disclosures to a machine than to a counselor, at least in the early stages of therapy—even if the machine later prints out their answers for the therapist's review. In one study, for instance, when patients at an alcohol treatment clinic were interviewed by computer, they admitted to drinking an average of 30 percent more than they acknowledged to a human. Women in another study were much more likely to disclose sexual problems to a computer than to even a female psychiatrist. "The computer doesn't blush," says Reagan. "It doesn't get judgmental, it doesn't approve or disapprove. It's just very patient."

Of course these programs don't blush—

"Was this pregnancy planned? Are you both happy about it? Congratulations!" it says. And it goes on to ask Mary how far along she is and whether she has morning sickness, before steering the couple back to more pertinent questions.

"A surprising number of people would pat the computer," says psychiatrist David Servan-Shreiber, who helped develop Sexpert and in one study videotaped four couples using the program. "I don't know if they even realized they were doing that. If it said something cute, they would pat it on the head."

According to researchers, it's not uncommon to see an emotional relationship, albeit a one-sided one, between user and computer—which is a little odd, considering that in some ways a computer program is just a self-help book scrolling across a screen. Therapy programs can't analyze the unconscious, after all. They can't interpret, can't make connections;

—even those who think of therapy strictly in terms of problem solving—do a lot more than transfer information. They spend time with their patients, they pay attention, and they care. "The basis of psychotherapy is a human interaction, the genuine caring of a therapist for a patient," says Karasu. "Until the computer is able to deliver that, it is not a psychotherapeutic process."

The complaint is one of long standing. In the seventies, programmer Weizenbaum pointed out that a basic tenet of the therapy that Eliza mimicked—or perhaps parodied—is that many people go into counseling to learn that they deserve to be cared about. "Of what help could it possibly be to anyone," Weizenbaum wrote then, "to know that he is worthy of being liked *by a computer?*"

Still, that philosophical question didn't stop Weizenbaum's own secretary from

EXPERT even knows when to schmooze. "Congratulations!"
it says. "Was this pregnancy planned?"

they don't understand a word, any more than Eliza did. In fact, because most of the current programs rely on multiple choice menus, they're *less* likely than was Eliza to give an illusion of comprehending. ("The stress that I feel in my family life has to do with . . ." the Therapeutic Learning Program prompts, offering 18 choices. "Having an affair? Physical abuse? Childcare problems?") Even so, a computer program can start to take on personality: stuffy and pedantic; or perky; or calm, caring, and soothing.

Take Sexpert, for example, being developed for use on home computers by couples experiencing sexual difficulties. Its tone is slightly formal yet somehow reassuring as it discusses emotionally fraught issues. Say Sexpert is talking with John and Mary about their sexual concerns. "It may seem strange to you," the program says, "but there is no generally accepted definition of premature ejaculation. . . . Whether premature ejaculation is the 'diagnosis' or not is a purely academic question in my opinion."

Sexpert even knows when to drop everything and schmooze a little. As the program goes through a thorough checklist of questions, it comes out that Mary is pregnant. Sexpert acts, well, human.

you don't get Freud with the flick of a switch. Instead, the programs play to the strengths of the computer, its logic and ability to teach. That means the programs are well suited to schools of psychology that try to get at emotions by way of a person's thoughts and ideas.

"Maybe you're depressed because you keep telling yourself you're worthless," a program might suggest, explaining that thoughts create moods, a concept central to some types of therapy. Then the computer might invite the user to do a little drill on the emotional repercussions of different thoughts, from "The boss is mad at me. I can't do anything right," to "The boss has a lot of nerve! I won't stand for it!" This is therapy as problem solving, as a learning process: The point isn't for a patient to play out lifelong emotional patterns with the therapist in a process of slow change. Instead, the idea is to focus on a specific problem, learn new tools for dealing with it, and resolve the crisis as quickly as possible.

Ironically, it's the computer's proficiency with this approach that has some therapists up in arms. According to psychiatrist T. Byram Karasu, chair of a treatment committee for the American Psychiatric Association, human therapists

asking him to leave the room so that she could talk to Eliza in private, and it's unlikely to dampen enthusiasm now, especially given the lack of options for people in need of psychological care. According to Kenneth Colby, a psychiatrist who's been at the forefront of the computer therapy field since the days of Eliza, most people with mental health problems in this country get no help, either because they can't afford therapy, can't find it, or can't accept the idea that they need it.

"Computers may be able to do better than therapists with some people," says Colby, "because those people won't see a therapist at all." For people who find the thought of psychological help distasteful, it may be less disturbing to imagine sitting at a computer than lying on a couch. And it costs less, which pleases insurance companies and other health care managers whose eyes stay on the bottom line. (It doesn't hurt the popularity of the programs, either, that they can augment therapists' incomes by increasing the number of patients they can see in a day.)

Right now, the disagreement between computer advocates and critics is a quiet one, muted by the fact that the programs are mostly being used as part of human therapy, not as replacements for it. The real argument may come later, when and if programs start popping up at supermarket checkstands and convenience stores. That prospect worries some *advocates* of computer-aided psychology, let alone its critics. After all, the experience with Eliza showed otherwise sophisticated people ascribing almost magical wisdom to the mind in the machine. Without a human to provide a reality check, even the most well-balanced user could be sent down the wrong path. How much worse if the programs are used by people who are truly psychotic or suicidally depressed?

Already, people suffering from depression can pick up an ambitious self-help program through computer software catalogs and in computer stores. Called Overcoming Depression, it responds to conversational English, picking up where Eliza left off. It was designed by psychiatrist Colby to be used at home, and it makes insightful, useful points about the nature and causes of depression. It's a good teaching tool, but a user drawn into revealing deep pain and need may find that the program's easy grasp of vocabulary promises more understanding than it can deliver.

"MY LIFE IS MISERABLE. *There's no one who cares if I live or die. No one likes me or cares about me at all. I think I just want to kill myself."*

If this were a conversation with a caring friend, the next sentence would probably be full of worry and emotion. But this man is using the program Overcoming Depression.

"In depression, suicide is a permanent solution to a temporary problem. Perhaps you are unable to view your depression as temporary."

"I've felt this way for as long as I can remember."

"We were discussing the pros and cons of suicide. Give me another reason why you are still alive."

Another reason? That's a good conversational ploy for a machine that can't, after all, really get involved. Later:

"What is your main reason for wanting to live?"

"I could be happy if only things were different."

"How come you are so cheerful?"

"I'm not cheerful at all . . . But what can I expect from a stupid computer?"

"Do you really believe you are unintelligent?"

Zap. There's a charge in the air, all right —but it isn't from the excitement of making mental connections. The plugged-in therapist has had a mental short-circuit. But it's the patient who may get burned.

Virtual Reality

Robert Wright

ROBERT WRIGHT *is a senior editor of* THE SCIENCES. *His book,* THREE SCIENTISTS AND THEIR GODS, *is published by Times Books.*

One of my few enduring complaints about reality is that you can't be sure it's really out there. You can contemplate the tree outside your window and feel certain that it occupies three whole dimensions, but you can't say with *complete* confidence that it does. All you can say is that particles of light landing on the surfaces of your eyes form two two-dimensional patterns that, together, give rise to an image of a tree. And thus is it always, with touch, taste, hearing, smell: the only information about three-dimensional reality you have direct access to is a series of two-dimensional maps along the surfaces of various organs. Maps on your skin, maps on your taste buds, maps in your ears, maps up your nose.

Among the evidence that these maps do indeed represent a reality actually out there is extensive agreement among them. If you walk heedlessly toward what the maps on your eyeballs insist is a brick wall, the map on the end of your nose will soon reinforce those reports. If you eat what looks like a raw egg, maps inside your nose, on your taste buds, down your throat—and perhaps back up your throat—will confirm that appraisal. So, if physical reality isn't really there, someone must be working hard to convey the impression that it is, showering our senses with intricately coordinated information on a nonstop basis.

Still, strictly speaking, we can't rule out the possibility that this is the case—that everything out there (including our own bodies as we look down at them) is an elaborately planned and executed illusion, that we are all just brains (or some other thinking medium) sitting, say, in a testing facility for extremely sophisticated video game technology.

I would love to take credit for this observation, but René Descartes said something remarkably like it three and a half centuries ago. Descartes, a doubter by nature, was trying to decide whether we can know *anything* with absolute certainty. After all, for all he knew, his life was actually a dream, brought to him by some grand deceiver. While mulling over this prospect, Descartes was struck by an insight: if reality seems questionable *to him*, then there must be a him for reality to seem questionable to. In short: I think, therefore I am; *Cogito, ergo sum*.

Descartes seems to have found the culmination of his inquiry—this airtight affirmation of his existence—quite gratifying. Personally, I find the entire line of thought enjoyable, but for different reasons. It's not that I now realize I exist (I suspected strongly that was the case long before encountering Descartes's work). Rather, it is the prospect of easy and sustained euphoria. If there *is* a grand deceiver, then there probably is a grand control panel. And if you could get control of the control panel, you could have a very, very good time.

Within the Human Factors Research Division of the NASA Ames Research Center, in California, is something that looks like a motorcycle helmet, except that the visor is opaque and protrudes abruptly at eye level. And within this protrusion are wide-angle binocular lenses connected to two tiny liquid crystal display screens. On these screens, a remote computer displays images of an imaginary environment—a room, say, or outer space, with a space station off in the distance. The images on the two screens differ slightly, by about two and a half inches of perspective, as do the two scenes beamed simultaneously onto real eyes in real life. So a person wearing the helmet sees his imaginary reality— "virtual reality," in the vernacular—three dimensionally.

The computer not only sends data but receives; as many as sixty times a second, it gets updated information about the exact location and orientation of the helmet, then adjusts the visual scene accordingly. If, while wearing the helmet, you walk a few feet and stoop to look at a hat that appears to be lying on what appears to be the floor, you see roughly the same smooth succession of images that you'd see while walking across a real room and stooping to look at a real hat: stretches of wall and floor and ceiling pass by, and the hat grows until it occupies much of your visual field. To the extent that you can suspend disbelief, it will look, even feel, as if you *are* approaching and inspecting a hat.

If you're wearing something called a DataGlove, you can reach down and pick up the apparent hat and flip it over, and see not only the hat turning over but also your hand—or, at least, a rendition of it— doing the turning. The DataGlove has sensors stretched along each finger and across the palm, so that it can report the ever changing location and configuration of your hand to the computer, which then reconciles virtual reality with the data. That includes virtual *auditory* reality: if you tap on what appears to be a table three times, you hear a *tap, tap, tap* that seems to come from its general direction. And NASA's virtual environment doesn't just talk; it listens. Your wish ("Fly me to the space station." "Fly me to the moon") is its command. What's more, if you don't like the looks of the space station, you can create a new one using a virtual paint brush and the computer's program for "object editing." After all, it's *your* virtual reality.

Scott S. Fisher, principal investigator for NASA's Virtual Environment Workstation Project (VIEW), stresses that the virtual environments at Ames are still a bit crude. Walls and floors look less like walls and floors than like trellises, because everything is now rendered with "wireframe" graphics. Still, the illusion is fairly compelling. When you fly, as if by jetpack, from a simulated space shuttle to a simulated space station, you "feel" the motion. When you walk over to a virtual escalator and are whisked to the second floor, you may—as some subjects have reported—experience enough dizziness to wish devoutly for handrails.

And Fisher's expectation is that these illusions will soon become more engrossing. NASA is replacing its trellises with continuous, colored surfaces, and a number of developments in computer graphics point toward even greater verisimilitude. Fractal geometry, which permits concise description of such regularly irregular shapes as trees, mountains, and clouds, is making it easier for computers to simulate changes of perspective "in real time"—as fast, that is, as in real life. And at the Massachusetts Institute of Technology's Media Lab, researchers are making creatures that, in a sense, animate themselves; their movement is governed not by a cartoonist's oversight but by "internal" programs that embody the logic of animal movement. Thus, virtual environments may, before long, be peopled by seemingly autonomous representatives of real or imagined species. And progress in artificial intelligence may well, by the early part of the next century, permit virtual humans to respond to your virtual presence—including your conversation—like plain folks.

Meanwhile, visual maps are being supplemented with tactile maps. The Data-Glove was recently equipped with tiny vibrators in each fingertip, so that if you pick up a virtual hat, you feel it. And VPL Research, of Redwood City, California, the company that built the DataGlove, is developing a whole suit of clothing, for deeper immersion into virtual reality. Where will it all end?

Funny you should ask. The founder and head of VPL, Jaron Lanier, has made a hobby of entertaining such questions. Lanier is not inclined to shy away from extrapolation. Though only twenty-seven, he has been around long enough to recognize that computer science demonstrates a clear trend: things get smaller, more powerful, and cheaper, so the difficult becomes easier and the crude be-

comes refined. If this continues, and progress in computer graphics proceeds apace, then virtual reality should become less and less virtual as time goes by. As Lanier puts it, he "believes" in virtual reality. But for all his enthusiasm, he is not a visionary in the pejorative sense. Because his company works daily to make virtual reality more realistic, he must, and does, maintain a certain sobriety; he is quite aware of the practical problems that stand in the way of a virtual future.

Take tactile feedback. It is one thing to feel the surface of a baseball when you touch it; surface contact can be simulated (grossly, at least) with the DataGlove's fingertip vibrators. But it is quite another thing to feel the *substance* of the baseball —to encounter, upon grasping, the stubborn resistance that keeps it from crumbling. Lanier thinks this resistance might be simulated by building a malleable skeleton into the DataGlove—a grid that, although generally unobtrusive, could, upon electronic command, rigidify enough to force a grasping hand into the shape of a baseball. But, obviously, it is easier to simulate the resistance of some objects than of others; sitting down in a virtual chair will remain a risky business for some time to come.

The reason for this risk—gravity—stirs up other troubles, as well. A real-life baseball, in addition to fighting your hand's squeeze, constantly, if subtly, weighs on you, and your brain senses the slight effects on the alignment of muscles in your fingers, hand, arm, even torso. This proprioception, as the sense of our inner shape is called, is likely to defy simulation for decades; there is no obvious way to simulate the effect of an object's weight on the DataGlove, and intervening more directly in proprioception would entail penetrating the skin and reaching deeply buried nerves. Other internal sensings—the inner ear's detection of imbalance and acceleration, for instance—are similarly problematic.

Finally, there is the nagging question of smell. Electronic synthesizers can generate a wide spectrum of sounds, but there is no comparably powerful means of scent synthesis. With current technology, says Lanier, the best we can hope for is an electronic Scratch-n-Sniff catalogue: prepackaged odors emitted on cue.

All these difficulties suggest that virtual reality and physical reality will remain distinguishable long after all of us have gone to that great video game arcade in the sky. Still, anticipated progress in visual simulation alone may be enough to blur the distinction considerably in the near future. After all, as Lanier notes, the brain is accustomed to reading between the lines; every day it builds an entire, three-dimensional reality out of two-dimensional maps. "We really have to

create a world of illusion in order to deal with the physical world, because we don't have omnipresent sensory capability," he says. "And it's our remarkable capacity to do this that makes virtual reality easier than it should be to achieve." In short, "People really want to believe in reality."

Among the envisioned advantages of harnessing this will to believe is the avoidance of costly real-life blunders. NASA will use virtual reality for training, including the simulation of flight (by jetpack as well as by aircraft). And NASA and the Stanford Medical School are embarking jointly on a project that will place aspiring surgeons in virtual reality; they will cut up virtual patients with virtual scalpels, and the worst that their inexperience will produce is virtual death. Architects, similarly, may want to stroll along a virtual city block, sizing up a building before inflicting it on a neighborhood.

The realm of entertainment, of course, will not go untouched by virtual reality. The technology is bound to make its way into video game arcades, and probably into living rooms, as well. (An Apple Macintosh II can generate rudimentary virtual environments, and personal computers are expected to gain power and sophistication by orders of magnitude in coming years.) It is quite possible that before the turn of the century, people will be able to don body stockings and opaque contact lenses—or, at least, bulky sunglasses— and enter elaborate fantasy worlds: fly a Spitfire high over the English Channel in 1943; fend off Martians in the War of the Worlds in 2010; perform before a packed house on Broadway; or single-handedly create an art museum, conjuring up abstract sculptures at will.

Then there is "air guitar." The inspiration behind the DataGlove was the desire of its inventor, Tom Zimmerman, to create real electronic sounds by playing a nonexistent guitar. Ever since, one of the more commonly envisioned virtual environments has been the virtual rock concert: you walk on stage to the seemingly real thunderous applause of seemingly real fans and begin to generate music with your seemingly real guitar. And there, in the front row, gyrating to your musical genius, are seemingly real groupies. And after the concert....

"Everybody thinks of that," says Lanier. "It's amazing how, when people first hear of this idea, they quickly stray into erotic imaginings about it." And those imaginings stray in short order to some very fundamental questions about what a world with readily available virtual reality would be like. How much work would get done? How much contact with real human beings would the average adolescent experience? How many victims of Dungeons & Dragons syndrome would there be? (The syndrome is characterized by a teenager's spending weeks on end immersed in a phantasmagoria, emerging to shoot his math teacher with his father's hunting rifle, then calmly explaining to police that he was acting on orders from Zataar, the god of final exams.)

Lanier has given such scenarios quite a bit of thought, and he admits that some concern is warranted. "It could become a horribly stultifying metatelevision," he says. "My view is that that would be so dangerous, it would sort of end human culture. It would basically grind creative thought to a halt. I would hate to see kids grow up with something like that."

Nonetheless, he is generally optimistic. Lanier compares the virtual reality of the future to a huge sponge, soaking up human activity; energy that otherwise would have real effects on real people will affect only patterns of light on tiny liquid crystal display screens. To the extent that the energy absorbed is positive—that people use virtual reality creatively—the by-products, such as art, will be good and will be widely accessible even if created in isolation. And to the extent that the energy is negative—well-armed people strolling into Virtual McDonald's and gunning down virtually half the customers—the results will be *relatively* good; no one will actually be killed, and it will be fortunate that there is a virtual world in which to vent such hostilities. "I think the more human energy that is spread into virtual reality, as opposed to physical reality, the better," Lanier says.

Another reason Lanier is optimistic about virtual reality is that he hopes people will not, generally speaking, enter it alone, but, rather, will use it as a medium of communication. Thus, a molecular biologist could conjure up a giant DNA molecule and invite his students to get a feel for its properties. And this is nothing compared with the less formal, more recreational kinds of shared virtual reality— the "collaborative dreams," as Lanier calls them, that result from the joint "editing" of an environment.

Suppose, to pull an example out of thin air, that you wake up one Saturday morning and decide to take a vacation. You slip on your body stocking, put in your opaque contact lenses, set your computer's dial to "lush tropical paradise," and prepare to enter Shangri-la, complete with waterfall, swaying palm trees, and mango juice. But before departing, you place a long-distance call and invite a friend to come along. Your friend slips on his reality togs, and his coordinates are transmitted by satellite to your computer, which plunks his image into your virtual environment and then, by transmitting data back to him, wraps that environment around him. The result is that he can see the virtual you in this virtual paradise and you can see the virtual him. You can walk up to him, shake hands, and talk in vivid terms. When he asks how you've been feeling, you summon a fleeting thunderstorm in metaphorical response. Ask him how his marriage is moving along, and a smoldering volcano appears on the horizon. (At VPL, Lanier has been working on a Visual Programming Language— hence the name VPL—designed to facilitate the conjuring up of such creations.) Having dispensed with the small talk, you decide to indulge in a little recreation —golf, but with a twist: the loser on any hole gets to design the next one (and why settle for sand traps when you can have syrup traps or antigravity traps?). The stakes are high; the loser has to play the nineteenth hole: the volcano.

After the match, the two of you head into the forest and assume the form of lions, tigers, or bears. "I'm interested in it as sort of an emotive tool," Lanier says of virtual reality. "When you're in a virtual reality, you have to decide how you appear. You don't look like your regular self. You can become an animal or a robot or something else. And this is psychologically extremely interesting." (At NASA, Fisher is setting up a virtual environment that can be shared by as many as six people, each with a split identity; person A may choose to appear as a dog in the eyes of person B, a dog biscuit in the eyes of person C, and so on.) The main thing, in Lanier's view, is that virtual reality become "a tool for general communication," not a hi-tech route to solipsism. He seeks a new kind of telephone, not television.

How much hope you hold out for Lanier's vision depends essentially on your view of human nature. Are people, at rock bottom, just animals? If left to their own devices, and freed from the constraining observation of friends, colleagues, and relatives, will they simply regress evolutionarily and indulge their most ancient drives, dividing their time among sex, violence, and ingestion? And will this thrill seeking then become suddenly consequential, spilling over into the real world?

One way to approach such questions is to consider current technologies that qualify, loosely speaking, as virtual realities. Television, for example, is a pseudo-reality, and the viewer's control of it has grown finer with cable networks, satellite dishes, and videocassette recorders. Drugs, too, offer a controlled escape from physical reality; stimulants, such as cocaine, and depressants, such as alcohol, permit euphoria even when there are no real grounds for it, and some hallucinogens, such as LSD, facilitate the wholesale construction of virtual realities.

It goes without saying that many people have failed to exercise these electronic and chemical controls over their fields of awareness with restraint. Indeed, one moral of American life in recent decades is that the easy alteration of perceived reality can be a dangerous thing. Pleasure, after all, was built into us by natural selection for the express purpose of our having to earn it, having to arduously and incrementally alter actual, physical reality—go gather berries, or hunt tigers, or convince someone we're worthy mates. Getting pleasure for free is not something we're designed to do.

As virtual reality is realized in the coming years, many people, no doubt, will use their newfound control responsibly; they will create new forms of art, build bridges of mutual understanding. Others will sink so completely, and so shallowly, into imaginary worlds as to find the real one difficult to inhabit. And others will, after much experimentation with virtual reality and quite a bit of excess, swear off the stuff, concluding that if there *is* a grand deceiver out there, he is better qualified for the job than they.

America's Ignorance of Science and Technology Poses a Threat to the Democratic Process Itself

Paul E. Gray

Paul E. Gray is president of the Massachusetts Institute of Technology

Scientific illiteracy is an increasingly serious problem, threatening the conduct of research in this country, our economic vitality,and the democratic process itself.

We live in a time when science and technology are growing in significance and influence. Physicists probe the extremes of cosmic creation. Biologists lay bare the fundamental processes of life. And engineers challenge previous limits in the design of everything from computer technology to hypersonic aircraft.

For good or ill, our society, our culture, and our lives are becoming more and more dependent on technical knowledge. At the same time, ignorance of science and technology is widespread in the general population, even among the supposedly educated.

The American public-school system may not be entirely responsible for the public's scientific illiteracy, but it will do for a start. On the average, high school students take only one year of science. Fewer than half of them take three years of mathematics. In a recent survey by the International Association for the Evaluation of Educational Achievement, which compared students of various ages with their peers in 17 countries, American 14-year-olds ranked 14th in science and mathematics. Among 17-year-olds, the Americans placed in the bottom quartile in biology, chemistry, and physics, behind students in such countries as Australia, England, Hungary, Japan, Norway, and Poland.

As for the colleges, a surprisingly large number of graduates of traditional liberal-arts programs receive their degrees without any significant study in science or mathematics. In blunt terms, our educational system has produced generation after generation of young people who are ignorant in science and incompetent in mathematics. Many American adults are unable to distinguish between astronomy and astrology, for example, and a distressing number believe that their well-being can be influenced by crystals.

A study of scientific illiteracy conducted in 1986 by the Public Opinion Laboratory at Northern Illinois University found that two-thirds of the adults in a nationwide sample of 2,000 did not understand the terms "molecule," "radiation," or "scientific study," and that three-fourths did not understand the term DNA. Beyond that, more than half of the adults in the study said they believed that scientists had a power that made them dangerous, yet at the same time expressed the belief that leaders and experts should be trusted.

Scientific literacy does not mean expertise. It means the capacity to reason in quantitative terms. It means familiarity with a basic scientific vocabulary and with fundamental concepts about physical and biological processes. In short, it means a reasonable intuition informed by the principles of science.

There should be no need for me to elaborate on the consequences for this country of a general public unable to distinguish sense from nonsense in the domains of science and its applications; of an electorate unable to comprehend the arguments arising at the intersection of science and technology and public policy; or of a work force that cannot meet, let alone understand, the technological standards of their competition abroad. We tolerate this situation at our national peril.

Without a basic understanding of science, how can we, as a people, make well-informed decisions on the technical issues that affect our society? How can we, for example, weigh the risks and benefits of future energy sources or of gene-splicing in animals and plants? I seriously doubt that a democratically based society such as ours can prosper when a significant proportion of its citizens don't have even a vague understanding of the scientific and technological principles that have such influence in shaping and directing that society.

Such ignorance threatens the scientific enterprise, as can be seen in the popular and governmental sanctions against DNA research, against experiments using animals, and against the use of radioisotopes and radiation in medicine and medical research. At the same time, however, the popular expectation is that scientists can, if they would only try, overcome almost any problems literally on demand. For example, many Americans believe that the Strategic Defense Initiative or "Star Wars" could be put in place soon, despite widespread advice from scientists that S.D.I. requirements are quite beyond the limits of both contemporary and foreseeable technology.

Another example is the public response to AIDS, perhaps the most baffling disease life scientists have ever encountered. There is a popular belief that if we throw enough money and manpower at the problem, a "magic bullet" will be found. Scientists should quit wasting time, critics say, on seemingly unrelated basic research on the immune system and its genetic precursors: Just find the AIDS agent and kill it. Easier said than done.

The M.I.T. physicist Philip Morrison has described the likely consequence of continued public ignorance of science. "If we cannot promote the growth of a wider understanding of the world view of science and technology, we endanger not only our own abstract enterprises, but even the essence of democracy . . .For the necessities of economics will eventually enforce a social division into islands of the trained, who understand enough to devise and operate an increasingly complex technology, within a sea of onlookers, bemused, indifferent, and even hostile."

The federal government cannot be expected to turn this situation around alone. The ultimate solutions must be provided not only by political leaders but also by parents, teachers, school boards, educational institutions, and the public at large. We must reform our collective thinking about what we expect young people to achieve in school and college. We must bring science and mathematics back into the mainstream of the American educational system.

In sum, American must come to understand that engineering and science are not esoteric quests by an elite few, but are, instead, humanistic adventures inspired by native human curiosity about the world and desire to make it better. The nation must embrace this broadened concept of science if it is to maintain its vigor as a democracy and as an international leader. To achieve that understanding, schools and colleges need new programs and gifted teachers to provide students with a broad and comprehensive knowledge of both the liberal arts and science and technology.

The next century will make exceptional demands on educators and educational institutions, and we have a responsibility to meet those demands. To insure that we will be able to do so, we must begin now to make the case for a stronger and more sustained national commitment to achieving a level of popular scientific literacy in this country sufficient for the needs of a free and democratic society.

THE LESSON EVERY CHILD NEED NOT LEARN

Scientific Literacy for All Is an Empty Goal

MORRIS SHAMOS

MORRIS SHAMOS is a professor emeritus of physics at New York University, and a past president of both the National Science Teachers Association and The New York Academy of Sciences. In the late 1960s, he directed one of the national elementary-science-curriculum development programs then in vogue. He now leads a consulting firm in the high-technology field and is writing a book entitled THE MYTH OF SCIENTIFIC LITERACY.

LAST YEAR, Edward D. Hirsch, Jr., a professor of English at the University of Virginia, published a list of several thousand terms that, in his view, should be familiar to every thinking citizen in the United States. The list was appended to Hirsch's book, *Cultural Literacy: What Every American Needs to Know*, in which he sought to show that a grasp of such background information is the key to effective communication and, hence, to full participation in our society. It included names, ideas, and objects, literary terms, historical events, and geographical references, ranging in scope from such standard grade school fare as Galileo, 1492, Moscow, and the Second World War to such often forgotten, but not entirely unfamiliar, items as James Clerk Maxwell, 1066, Harper's Ferry, and French Impressionism. Hirsch's approach was useful, not only because it confronted the question of what constitutes a core of factual knowledge, which should be of value to educators generally, but, more important, because it forced the issue of the level of understanding one must have of these terms to share in our culture.

One quality that sets apart Hirsch's list from a list that might have been drawn up, say, three centuries ago is the inclusion of a large number of science-related terms; they make up somewhat more than fifteen percent of the total, and include, for example, *entropy, natural selection,* and *the periodic table of the elements*. This, of course, reflects the growing impact of science on Western culture during the past three hundred years. Indeed, so important has science become that we now speak of scientific literacy as an indispensable element in, if not an actual partner to, cultural literacy as a whole.

The current movement toward scientific literacy actually dates back to the period immediately after the Second World War, when the drive for bigger and better science curricula in the nation's schools began to gain momentum. In 1954, the National Science Foundation, an independent federal agency whose principal function is to support basic and applied research, began funding education programs designed to increase the pool from which science and engineering professionals are drawn. Then, in October of 1957, the Soviets launched Sputnik, the first man-made satellite to orbit Earth. Determined not to allow the Soviet Union to surpass the United States in scientific and technological achievement, Congress increased NSF's education budget, from three and a half million dollars to nineteen million dollars, and eventually to sixty-one million, and enlarged the agency's statutory authority, permitting it to support science, mathematics, and engineering education at all levels, including the elementary grades. At the same time, the National Defense Education Act of 1958 authorized the Office of Education, then part of the Department of Health, Education and Welfare, to make funds available to schools for remodeling laboratory facilities and for acquiring equipment and teaching aids. Several billion dollars was poured into these programs over the next two decades. What had begun as an attempt to train more scientists and engineers soon expanded, at least in the minds of many educators, into an effort to provide all students, and the public generally, with a broad understanding of science and technology.

Science, as a result, became a major feature of the general precollege curriculum in the United States and other highly industrialized nations. Where some state education departments failed to make science courses mandatory for high school graduation, colleges usually accomplished the same end by requiring a minimum scientific background for admission. And the colleges, in turn, perpetuated the notion that science should be part of the lore of educated adults by insisting that most graduates at least be exposed to it.

Notwithstanding the sincerity and efforts of teachers and administrators, these education reforms have proved ineffective. Granted, the public may be more sensitive today than it was forty years ago to some science-based issues—nuclear weapons, the war on cancer, computers—but its current understanding of the facts and principles that underlie such issues is no better than it was just after the war. As measured by any reasonable benchmark, even by Hirsch's vocabulary test, we are still a nation of scientific illiterates, which has led some educators to suggest that shortages of professional scientists and engineers are in store. An even greater threat, say the critics, is the prospect that, unless all citizens become scientifically literate, they will be unable to participate intelligently in a technological society and to perform competently in the workplace, with the result that the United States might soon become a second-rate nation.

During the past several decades, the American education system has been the target of a great deal of criticism, some of it deserved, but in this instance the critics are wrong. For, heretical though it may seem, requiring science courses, no matter how thoughtfully designed, of everyone in grade school, secondary school, and college

 From *The Sciences*, July/August 1988, pp. 14-20.

will not produce a scientifically literate society. What's worse, the rationale for seeking such literacy is ill-conceived: widespread scientific literacy is *not* essential to develop an intelligent electorate, to maintain a science and engineering work force, or to prepare people for life in an increasingly technological society. Science, of course, should be taught in schools, and taught with the best methods and facilities at our disposal, but for reasons other than these.

WHAT, IN FACT, do we mean by scientific literacy? While there exists no clear, widely accepted definition, it is fair to say that the scientifically literate individual falls somewhere between two extremes. At one extreme is the man or woman who understands the foundations, current status, and most of the important problems of at least several of the life and the physical sciences. This understanding need not be operational; that is, to be scientifically literate, one does not have to be able to conduct research or to solve problems in the field. But one should be able to read knowingly (including some of the technical literature), and engage intelligently in discussions, on topics relating to such disciplines. Judged according to this standard, few of us, even among scientists and engineers, could be considered literates, which means only that the criterion is too demanding, not that such literacy is undesirable. At the other extreme is the sort of person envisioned by Hirsch—the individual who has acquired a large glossary of technical terms, perhaps by rote, and a brief definition of each. Here the notion of literacy tends to become somewhat fuzzy. It is one thing to nod in recognition of technical terms when reading or listening to accounts of scientific matters and perhaps in this way feel less estranged from science. But it is quite another to appreciate the significance of such terms and be able to employ them in meaningful discourse. Recognition alone cannot be equated with understanding.

Consider, as an example of how difficult it is to define scientific literacy, the one so often cited as a criterion of such literacy—namely, the second law of thermodynamics. Three decades ago, the physicist C. P. Snow suggested that familiarity with the second law should be equivalent to having read a work of Shakespeare. Using Snow's standard, a scientifically literate person might be expected to know not only that the second law is one of the most important concepts in science but also that it asserts that heat cannot pass unaided from a cool body to a warm body and that one can conclude from this that, because the universe is not reversible, its entropy must be increasing. It is safe to say that such understanding more than satisfies Hirsch's definition of scientific literacy, but it raises more questions than it answers.

What, after all, are thermodynamics, heat, entropy, and reversible processes? Why is the second law considered more important than the first law, which asserts that the total energy of the universe always remains constant? And what of the consequences of the second law: Shouldn't a literate individual understand that entropy is a measure of the orderliness of a system and that an ever increasing entropy means the universe is tending toward greater disorder, or running down, that the concept of entropy provides an arrow of time, so to speak, which permits us to record the past but not the future (probably a silly observation to most people, but one that has profound philosophical implications)?

Where shall we stop? Should we expect a scientific literate to know that living organisms appear to defy the principle of increasing entropy because they seemingly tend toward greater order? But that on more careful analysis the entropy of the overall system that supports the organism, including its food supply and environment, actually increases? Even at this point, there is much more that the truly literate individual might be expected to know—why the scientific community has confidence in the laws of thermodynamics; how the laws apply to practical problems in virtually all the natural and engineering sciences (cell metabolism, heat loss in engines, the corrosion of metals); and why they leave us with a pragmatic warning: Beware of anyone trying to sell you what appears to be a perpetual motion machine. The point is that in science there is much more to most ideas than can be conveyed by a simple definition. Concepts such as the second law cannot be treated in isolation; knowing how they interrelate with other facts and principles is essential if one is to achieve true literacy.

But in a sense, all this is beside the point, since, even by Hirsch's standard, few people can be considered scientifically literate. An upper bound can be placed on the number of people who fit this category by assuming that the group includes scientists and engineers; physicians and dentists; science teachers, writers, and editors; and dedicated readers of popular-science literature. According to the most recent census, these groups total only about four or four and a half million people, roughly 2.4 to 2.7 percent of the country's population. Thus, even by the most generous criterion, fewer than three percent of American citizens *might* qualify as scientific literates. It matters little that a much larger number were exposed to science in school; even if such learning was effective at the time, for most it was soon forgotten.

Remember, too, that this estimate assumes that *all* scientists, engineers, and science teachers fit the definition. Yet we know that most scientists and engineers confine their technical interests to narrow fields, and some science teachers do not even understand what constitutes scientific knowledge. Incredible as it may seem, a recent survey of high school biology teachers in Ohio showed that a quarter of the respondents believe that creationism should be taught along with evolution as a *scientific* theory of the origin of life. Hence, if anything, this estimate probably errs on the high side. A discouraging conclusion, to be sure, but, given the nature of twentieth-century science, we can hardly expect it to be otherwise.

ONE OF THE INTRINSIC PROPERTIES that make science difficult to master is its cumulative nature. Indeed, in the view of many scientists and educators, it is this property that most distinguishes science from other forms of intellectual activity. Progress is not a characteristic of the humanities; one would never claim that Michelangelo was less advanced than Picasso. Contrast this with Isaac Newton's declaration that he saw farther by "standing on the shoulders of giants," or consider the increase in scientific publications since Newton's time. Whereas three hundred years ago only a handful of scientific works were published each year, now at least forty thousand journals, representing about a million scientific papers, are published annually.

Merely deciding what portion of this information is worth knowing is no small task. As an illustration of the disagreements that arise, compare Hirsch's list of science-related terms with a list compiled by Charles L. Koelsche and Ashley G. Morgan, Jr., and included in their 1964 book, *Scientific Literacy in the Sixties*. Koelsche and Morgan gathered information needed by readers to understand popular-science articles, yielding a vocabulary list only slightly longer than Hirsch's. Yet fewer than a third of the terms on the two lists are identical. Since the central precepts of science did not change significantly during the intervening two decades, the sizable difference between the lists suggests a discrepancy between what some members of the scientific community perceive as important and what appears in the public press. And there is no reason to believe that this discrepancy has diminished.

Even if agreement could be reached about vocabulary, other, less tractable obstacles stand in the way of achieving scientific literacy. For one thing, the borders that once sharply separated the sciences are crumbling. No longer can the life sciences be completely understood apart from physics and chemistry: biophysics, biochemistry, and biotechnology were virtually unheard of a century ago; today, they are but a few reminders that the sciences have become more and more interdependent.

What's more, an ever widening chasm has opened between scientific and commonsense world views. Aristotle had no difficulty communicating the kind of teleological explanations of phenomena that were in vogue during the fourth century B.C. To explain the acceleration of a falling body, for example, he needed only to observe that "the traveler hastens as he approaches his destination." Or he might account for a variety of pneumatic phenomena by invoking the idea summed up in the aphorism "Nature abhors a vacuum." This mode of explanation not only appealed to early Greek and Roman scholars but also set a pattern of hopeless confusion in science that persisted until the Renaissance.

Only a hundred years ago, when American colleges and universities came to accept science subjects as appropriate prerequisites for admission, it was possible to speak of the universe as a well-behaved, deterministic mechanism made up of billiard-ball-like atoms. But science has since elaborated this commonsense view, as the English astronomer Arthur S. Eddington pointed out in the introduction to his series of Gifford lectures at the University of Edinburgh in 1927.

Eddington spoke of the "two tables" that stood before him. One was the familiar, commonplace object of the real world: it had dimension, color, substance, and some degree of permanence. The second table—the scientific one—was a total stranger to the real world. According to modern physics, it consisted mostly of empty space (the regions between the nuclei of the atoms of which it was composed) and a staggering number of electric charges (electrons) that moved about with great speed and whose combined bulk amounted to much less than one billionth of the real table's bulk. Yet, despite this strange construction, the table supported such things as books and elbows —because the electric charges within its atoms continual-

ly collided with similar electric charges in the objects placed on it, preventing them from "falling through" the empty spaces.

And physics is not alone in becoming obscure; chemistry, molecular biology, and other fields have moved in that direction, as well. Though scientific inquiry usually begins with observations of the everyday world and concludes by returning to that world in the form of technology, the steps between these two extremes, where the real scientific work is done, are largely unfathomable to all but specialists. We have no commonsense counterparts for photons, genes, novas, or black holes; when scientists talk about these things, they reason by means of models —abstractions that agree with what is known about certain phenomena (or, more often, about their effects) but that are not necessarily meant to be pictures of those phenomena. The most extreme form of such reasoning, and thus the most radical departure from everyday discourse, is mathematics.

As far as most students are concerned, mathematics was invented to complicate, rather than facilitate, the study of science. Granted, some come to appreciate equations as tools for applying scientific laws to particular situations— Newton's laws of motion to the trajectory of a rocket, for instance. But in fact, the primary function of mathematics is not computation; it is discovery. Mathematics is the only language by which statements about nature can be made in symbolic form and then combined according to logical rules to lead to new knowledge of the universe. Classic examples are Galileo's definitions of velocity and acceleration, which, when stated in mathematical form and combined algebraically, enabled him to derive the entire science of uniformly accelerated motion, including the laws of falling bodies and the motion of a projectile. Avoiding mathematics, which seems to be the principal attraction offered by some science courses these days, may be a way of drawing students; but by ignoring the theoretical structure of science, this strategy conveys a false impression of the overall scientific enterprise.

Taken together, the cumulative nature of science and its reliance on descriptions that run counter to common sense, especially on mathematics, make it necessary to devote extraordinary effort to the task of becoming scientifically literate. Most of us, certainly the ninety percent of high school students who do not become scientists, appear to be unwilling to make this effort.

EVEN IF WIDESPREAD scientific literacy were possible to achieve, it is not nearly as essential to success in the twentieth century as is commonly believed. Consider the argument cited most frequently: We live in a scientific age, a time in which we all are touched by the discoveries of science, if not directly, then at least by the technologies that result from them. Many issues and problems facing society—dwindling world food supplies, pollution, nuclear testing, genetic engineering, the Strategic Defense Initiative (Star Wars)—have technological bases. An informed electorate, one that is scientifically literate, would be best able to deal with such issues —to reach independent judgments and elect officials who properly reflect those judgments.

One cannot easily quarrel with such a rationale; it is an

ideal devoutly to be wished. In fact, though, no reasonable amount of scientific training could possibly prepare one to form credible judgments on the wide variety of issues the country faces. What's more, being scientifically informed is no guarantee of certainty. Even professional scientists frequently disagree on science-based public policy issues, and for reasons that can be equally convincing. Take the Strategic Defense Initiative: physicists and engineers have lined up on both sides of the fence regarding the feasibility of almost every aspect of the system, including the target-locating systems, the laser beams that would be used to destroy enemy warheads, and the software that would direct the entire operation.

Another popular argument in favor of scientific literacy is that it better prepares a nonscientist to function in business or professional life. If there is any truth to this, students fail to perceive it, and small wonder: they need only look at their own professional family members and friends, at wealthy businessmen and powerful public officials, at people in the arts and professors of humanities—all successful and respected members of society and most, if not all, illiterate in science. After all, what bearing does a lawyer's understanding of the double helix have on the success of his practice? How many times does a banker call on the uncertainty principle to make an investment decision? Is it necessary that the mayor of New York be versed in plate tectonics to run city hall? Would a knowledge of chaos theory have boosted the careers of Luciano Pavarotti or Laurence Olivier? The same questions could be asked of all educated adults in the work force.

The need to increase the nation's scientific manpower pool to avoid future shortages is a third argument often made in behalf of scientific literacy. Many educators and employers feel that students must decide to go into science before graduating from high school, since few choose to do so afterward. Hence the rationale for developing scientific literacy among all students: the expectation that more will then choose careers in science and engineering. This argument fails on two counts.

First, roughly ten percent of the country's high school freshmen profess a desire to become scientists or engineers, and about half of these actually go on to fulfill that desire. The other ninety percent are not science-bound, nor are they likely to have any direct involvement with science after their formal schooling. Requiring science of all students in the hope that one in twenty or thirty will choose it as a career is hardly an efficient means to this end. Moreover, it has never been demonstrated that a compulsory science curriculum produces more professional scientists than a voluntary course of study. Surely there are more effective and less costly ways of attracting students into the sciences, should this be necessary.

Second, there is no hard evidence of impending manpower shortages. The number of students graduating with science or engineering degrees increased after 1955 at an average annual rate of about five percent, then leveled off during the 1980s owing to a decrease both in demand and in the high school population. Besides being irresponsible, turning out more scientists than the marketplace demands, purely on speculation, is a poor argument for scientific literacy for all. If shortages were certain —say, in technical areas in which the United States might be falling behind such countries as Japan—improving the precollege education of *only* science-bound students would be a far easier and more appropriate goal.

The fourth argument for scientific literacy, the only one with a ring of truth to it, relates to America's technology-oriented economy. Will office workers who can handle computers be in greater demand than those who cannot? Will manufacturers be looking for factory workers who can operate the robots that will displace much of the human labor force? The answer to each question, of course, is yes. But does this mean that general literacy in science will be required? Probably not, as the history of technology clearly shows. We learned to use electronic typewriters, office copiers, video equipment, electronic machine tools, and many other devices through specific on-the-job training or simple written instructions, without knowledge of the machines' inner workings, largely because such devices are specifically designed for use by nonexperts. So it is specious to contend that achieving scientific (or even technological) literacy will better prepare students for tomorrow's job market. Granted, the workplace may come to demand a higher degree of technical sophistication from nonscientists than is now required; the way to meet that demand, however, is not to attempt to make all students technically proficient but to enhance technical-education programs for students who choose them.

If widespread scientific literacy is not necessary for responsible citizenship, economic success, maintaining a pool of scientists, or using machines, is there *anything* that can be said in its favor? There is, and it can be traced to ideas espoused by such nineteenth-century scientists as the biologist Thomas Huxley and the mathematician Jules-Henri Poincaré. Students have the most to gain, said Huxley and Poincaré, if they study science chiefly for the aesthetic and intellectual values it bestows. "The scientist does not study nature because it is useful," wrote Poincaré, in *The Value of Science*, published in 1907. "He studies it because he delights in it, and he delights in it because it is beautiful." Not widely accepted when first proposed, Poincaré's idea may be one whose time has finally come.

During early encounters with science—observing fire, light, magnetism, chemical changes, small animals—students nearly always are fascinated and curious. Then, as time goes by, and as science courses increasingly stress memorization, facts, and the study of subjects for which the student has no personal interest, the magic wears off and is replaced by boredom or, worse, outright rejection. Evidence of this inevitable alienation can be found in every high school science classroom in the United States.

Perhaps there is a lesson here. If the dream of scientific literacy for all now lies shattered, it is because it was an impossible dream to begin with. Acknowledging this might allow us to pursue a goal that appears less ambitious but, in the long run, is more promising. Is it not more desirable to nurture an *appreciation* of science and thereby keep open the possibility of full literacy for some individuals than to force-feed facts and formulas and thereby instill a distaste for science that probably guarantees lifelong ignorance?

Debunking Computer Literacy

COMPUTER-LITERACY EDUCATION COMBINES BAD

SOFTWARE, INADEQUATE HARDWARE, AND VAGUE OBJECTIVES. A BROADER CONCEPT

OF "COMPUTER LITERACY" IS NEEDED.

RONNI ROSENBERG

RONNI ROSENBERG is principal writer at Kendall Square Research Corp. Previously, she was a National Science Foundation postdoctoral fellow at Harvard's Kennedy School of Government, where she assessed the role of computer scientists in public policy. Rosenberg is on the board of directors of Computer Professionals for Social Responsibility. This article is abstracted from her MIT doctoral dissertation, for which she observed computer-literacy courses, interviewed computer-literacy teachers and computer coordinators, and examined dozens of textbooks, course descriptions, and curriculum materials.

COMPUTER literacy will transform students into productive workers, informed citizens, and wise decision makers in the "information society." So say its enthusiasts, and they do not use the term "literacy" accidentally. They believe there is something so special about computer literacy that it should be added to the "short list" of basic skills. The much-publicized report *A Nation at Risk* lists computer science as one of "Five New Basics" for high school students—ranking it with English, math, science, and social studies.

In response, virtually every U.S. school has bought at least one computer, and many of these computers are used to teach computer literacy. A 1985 to 1986 survey by the congressionally mandated National Assessment of Educational Progress concluded that from kindergarten on up, school "computers are used almost exclusively to teach about computers." According to a national study directed by Henry Jay Becker at Johns Hopkins' Center for Social Organization of School and completed in 1989, traditional computer-literacy topics—word processing, spreadsheets, and databases—already comprise half of all school computer use.

Expenditures on computer literacy reflect difficult trade-offs. More time for computer classes, curriculum development, and teacher training means less for other subjects. More money for computers means less for teachers, books, maps, lab supplies, and facility maintenance. In the *New York Times,* David Wilson reported that one California class bought $110,000 worth of electronic equipment with state lottery proceeds "normally earmarked for teacher salary raises." Are the trade-offs justified? Is computer-literacy education achieving results?

The burden of proof is on the advocates, and their bold claims for computer-literacy instruction should be judged by classroom achievements. When this is done, we see that the rhetoric—from educators, the media, parents, manufacturers, and many computer professionals—is unjustified. As a fundamental skill, computer literacy is oversold, misapplied, and basically trivial in most schools.

Nevertheless, the momentum behind it remains strong, but the enthusiasm often indicates more about problems with the system into which the technology is introduced than about the value of the instruction itself. Today's optimism about computer literacy reflects a long-standing fascination with "better living through technology." Computer-literacy education is an instance of the eagerness to see technology as a panacea for all problems and a case of the strong forces that press for adopting a technology in the absence of evidence of its value.

Computer-literacy instruction does not amount to meaningful job training, does not enhance general thinking, and does not produce students who are informed about the role of computers in society. Instead, it teaches shallow recognition of jargon, components, and a few applications on very simple computers. It produces students who may believe themselves to be computer literate but who know nothing about real-world computing.

A different kind of general education about computers could make issues related to computer use clear to a broad audience. Such courses would spend much less time on mechanics and programming-language syntax and much more time examining the benefits and risks of significant computer uses. This level of discourse is appropriate to high school or early college, where it might contribute to meaningful computer-literacy instruction.

Why Computer Literacy Is Taught: The Jobs Argument

Advocates of computer-literacy education make three arguments explicitly and often: jobs, mental discipline, and informed citizens. None holds up under examination.

The first argument is that through such education people will gain the job skills they need to participate in the technological workplace, while the United States will gain the skilled workers it needs to compete economically. But as training for genuine high-tech jobs, computer-literacy instruction fails miserably. Students learn virtually nothing valuable about actual computing.

Course goals that sound substantial on paper often translate in the classroom into mechanical skills. "Knowing how to use a computer" means handling floppy disks. "Knowledge of computer technology" means pointing out the keyboard in a drawing. "Understanding what a computer can do" means brief exposure to word-processing and spreadsheet programs. It is astonishing how little this superficial level of computer-literacy instruction changes from kindergarten through graduate school.

Programming is a major job skill, but programming instruction in computer-literacy classes is especially bad. "This year perhaps a million people will write their first program—probably a BASIC program for a small computer from Apple, IBM, Radio Shack, or Commodore—without anyone explaining to them that there's more to program correctness than intuitive fid-

dling," writes John Shore in *The Sachertorte Algorithm and Other Antidotes to Computer Anxiety*. "They will think of themselves as joining the mainstream of the computer age, when in fact they are being introduced to programming as it was understood twenty-five years ago."

Some of the most scathing indictments of computer-literacy classes come from college computer-science teachers, many of whose students took these courses in high school or earlier. A Harvard professor of introductory computer science told me, "Secondary-school education is doing nothing for these people. They don't know anything about computing. It's a waste of time." He added that computer-literacy students have no advantage over those who never handled a computer.

What's more, experience with the tiny programs that are typical of computer-literacy instruction does not scale up to large, real-life applications, whose complexity demands different strategies and poses different problems. One textbook talks about "controlling the computer with quality programming," but teachers rarely have an opportunity to become proficient programmers. Nor are students made aware that their exposure to programming is superficial.

Further, the jobs argument overrates the high-tech job market. Employment demanding significant computer skill is not increasing rapidly. In the computer-industry region of Massachusetts, layoffs are now common. Contrary to the belief of some computer-literacy advocates, few jobs require significant computer skills. Most jobs that *involve* computers, such as grocery-store checkers operating bar-code readers, strain the definition of computer-related technology and require no knowledge *about* computers.

When we hear about the need for workers to operate modern equipment, especially computers, the implication is that workers must be technically savvy and highly intelligent, but the skills actually needed rarely relate to computers. For instance, a *New York Times* article about company training states, "The sleek computerized equipment . . . requires . . . a lot more thinking." The article goes on to define the skills needed—for example, reading graphs and changing percentages to decimals—in other words, elementary math. In fact, managers who talk about their need for "highly skilled workers" often mean workers who can read, write, do basic math, interact socially, and maintain good work habits, such as showing up on time. These skills are crucial, and many high school graduates lack them.

That lack may account for want ads calling for applicants with experience with a specific word-processing or spreadsheet program. Because employers feel that applicants are so weak in basic education that on-the-job training would be difficult, they specify each skill a job requires.

At best, computer-literacy education prepares people for low-level jobs, and without well-trained teachers, adequate hardware, or tolerable software, schools are ill-equipped to provide even this vocational education. If classes focused on general concepts, schools would have less need for current technology. But the focus of most courses is on a school's particular hardware, and most affordable hardware is extremely limited in what it can do. Technical limitations in turn can limit educational objectives. For example, some word-processing programs for small machines restrict students to short papers.

The Mental-Discipline Argument

Separate from the vocational argument is the hype embodied in the assertion that computers are the "Wheaties of the mind." In this view, interactions with computers demand and nurture logical, rational, and organized thinking.

The "mental-discipline" argument rests on the assumption that intellectual skills gained through computer interactions will transfer to other areas of learning. This argument is most often linked to programming instruction. For example, in a 1985 survey, computer-literacy coordinators in Wisconsin and Illinois said that all students have something to gain by learning to write simple programs. "Computer programming provides a logical, systematic framework for problem solving."

However, psychologists point out that it is exceptionally difficult to transfer cognitive skills. Attempts to prove that such benefits arise from learning programming are inconclusive. Careful studies conducted by researchers at the Bank Street College of Education in New York City uncovered no support for the mental-discipline argument.

One Bank Street study compared elementary school students who had no programming experience with those who spent 30 hours learning programming over the course of a school year. Researchers found no difference in the two groups' planning skills. In another Bank Street study, researchers examined the development of thinking skills among high school students with no programming experience, one year of experience, and two years of experience. They found no significant differences in several measures of skill transfer from programming to dissimilar activities.

On the other hand, that study and others reached troubling conclusions about programming mastery, which presumably is a prerequisite to cognitive transfer from programming. Few computer-literacy students who studied programming could formulate correct algorithms, which are the intellectual basis of all programs, and some students failed to understand even programs they completed. Studies of precollege programming students have revealed significant misconceptions about what a program is. And most studies

claiming evidence that programming instruction improves problem-solving ability suffer from serious methodological flaws. For example, one group of researchers failed to account for special attention the teacher gave only to programming students.

As
TRAINING FOR
HIGH-TECH JOBS,
COMPUTER-LITERACY INSTRUCTION
FAILS MISERABLY.
STUDENTS
LEARN VIRTUALLY NOTHING
ABOUT ACTUAL
COMPUTING.

What's more, programming does not, strictly speaking, require good organizing or planning skills, although it does benefit greatly from them—as do many activities. Disorganized people can write disorganized programs that nonetheless can work. Like any task, programming can be done carefully or sloppily, and sloppy programming does not turn a person into a well-organized thinker.

The Informed-Citizens Argument

Third, it is argued, only computer-literate citizens can participate fully in a society where computers are ubiquitous. Students who are not exposed to computers will be left behind.

Although computers are omnipresent, it does not follow that we all must know how they work. Few of us need to be "electric-motor literate," yet we run electric motors every day. We use cars, televisions, and telephones, but we learn to operate them incidentally. Similarly, people can easily learn to operate word-processing or spreadsheet programs if and when they need to.

Moreover, the limited exposure that characterizes computer-literacy classes gives people only the most superficial control over the technology. Students exposed to word processing may be able to format and print text—a convenient and practical skill—but they learn nothing to help them understand or intelligently assess computer uses. The descriptions of some courses highlight software as a way to remove the mystery surrounding computers, but classes often do the opposite. A teacher-training class was fascinated with the ability of computers to alphabetize lists, and a student asked how the computer could do this. Shrugging her shoulders, the instructor responded: "I don't know. How does it know to be a word processor? It's magic!"

Further, many courses and texts explicitly teach positive attitudes about computers, belying their stated goal of nurturing informed, critical attitudes. Discussions of the impacts of computers ignore or skirt the limitations, weaknesses, and risks of major uses. For instance, students may learn that FBI computers store information about criminals, but they do not hear that much of the data is inaccurate, incomplete, or outdated.

"Social impacts" is a catchall sometimes fit into computer-literacy classes. In *Basic Computing F,* a sixth-grade workbook published by Scholastic, Inc., the section on "People and Computers" consists of four cartoons. From a list of captions below each picture, the student selects the most appropriate one. The correct answers are: "Many people believe that computers can do everything, but computers cannot work without people"; "Computers are not only for playing games"; "The word bug has a special meaning in computer language"; and "Some people think that computers want the same things as humans." This one exercise is the entire coverage for the "skill" of "recognizing social and other nontechnical implications of computers."

Schools may do harm by turning out people whose model of computation is simplistic but who nonetheless believe themselves to be computer literate. For instance, much computer-literacy education teaches that computers just follow instructions and never make mistakes. *Basic Computing E,* another elementary-school text, says, "Computers can only do what people tell them to do in a program. If a computer does not get clear instructions, it won't do anything. If something is wrong in a program, the computer will tell you by saying ERROR."

This is comforting but dangerously misleading. The massive systems that run real applications differ qualitatively from the tiny programs and machines that computer-literacy students encounter. Many complex computer systems are so large and have been worked on by so many people for so long that no individual or small group of people understands their workings. Thus, while the Social Security Administration was planning a major system upgrade in the early 1980s, programmers were afraid to touch the existing software. They could not confidently make one change without risking further unpredictable changes. Such systems can manipulate information in ways that are entirely unexpected by their programmers.

Teachers, Priorities, and Computer Literacy

If computer-literacy education is so problematic, why has it flourished? The theme that has dominated teachers' comments to me is that they feel pressured to use computers. They feel pressure from the market-place, where texts and ads send powerful messages about the necessity to use computers in schools. They feel pressure from parents, who are bombarded with newspaper and magazine stories linking good parenting to buying a computer. And they feel pressure from administrators who, according to the director of a computer-literacy lab, "get the computers first, then apply pressure on teachers to use them, instead of identifying an educational need and asking if a computer could help with that."

Teachers complain that many parents judge education solely by the number of computers in the classroom. One computer coordinator told me, "You open a new computer lab, the PTA comes in, they'll have an open house, and the parents marvel at the fact that there's all sorts of equipment. People feel good about that because it's something concrete." But, the teacher concluded, "it's much more difficult to say how valuable that computer lab is going to be in that child's education."

As a result of pressures, computer-literacy classes focus inappropriately on the technology, not on how computers may contribute to education. For instance, despite widespread agreement that most educational software is abysmal, the market is booming. Teachers complain that software is confusing, incomplete, writ-

ASKED TO EXPLAIN HOW COMPUTERS CAN ALPHABETIZE LISTS, AN INSTRUCTOR RESPONDED, "I DON'T KNOW. HOW DOES IT KNOW TO BE A WORD PROCESSOR? IT'S MAGIC!"

ten at the wrong grade level, based on poor pedagogy, accompanied by inadequate documentation, and not field tested. A common complaint is that educational software appears to be written by people who have never entered a classroom. In fact, some software publishers are book publishers who know little about software. One software publisher told me that his company loves the school market "because it is so easy," but the only educational software that is easy to produce is bad software.

A reflection of the technology focus is the tendency to buy computers before thinking about software and to buy hardware and software before thinking about preparing teachers. Curriculum development comes later still, if at all. Pursuing the steps in this reverse order almost guarantees that the technology, introduced as an add-on, will not serve educational needs.

Schools lack the time to consider if computer-literacy education fits into overall priorities. Normally, a topic can be added to a curriculum only if it replaces something. What is computer literacy more important *than,* when so many high school graduates have appalling gaps in basic education? A secondary-school teacher questioned the proper place for computer education among educational priorities: "I have nothing against teaching the kids computers in school. . . . But the thing I want to know is, can those kids add and subtract without computers?" She continued, "If you don't even ever show a kid a computer, but he can read well, if he can think and has good math skills, he can pick up a computer manual any time he wants and figure out how to use it."

Some advocates say that computer literacy need not come at the expense of other instruction if it is integrated into an existing curriculum, but that is harder than creating separate courses. And because curriculum-development resources are insufficient, even the integrated approach usually amounts to squeezing the usual computer-literacy topics into other courses—for example, adding word processing to English class.

School districts and states often require computer-literacy instruction without adequately funding curriculum development, software purchases, teacher training, and maintenance. Teachers are caught in the middle. *Power On!,* the 1988 Office of Technology Assessment (OTA) report on education and information technology, notes that few education students feel ready to teach with computers. Henry Jay Becker says teachers cite their own lack of knowledge as the most serious problem in educational computing, and most rate their computer training as mediocre.

No wonder: some teachers who are required to teach computer literacy receive no training at all. The OTA found that two-thirds of K–12 teachers receive fewer than 10 hours of computer training. What training is available typically consists of a few hours of workshops that impart a minimum of mechanical knowledge. And the workshops are often taught by people who know little about educators' needs—for example, the employees of stores that sell computers to schools.

Sometimes, the information is misleading or simply wrong. In one class that I observed, the instructor defined a computer operating system as a program that "directs the flow of electricity." Actually, it's a collection of software that facilitates the creation of programs and enables people to interact with the computer system. Logo, described as "like an operating system, another set of instructions to the computer," is actually a programming language that lets people unambiguously describe computational processes and data. This was a graduate class for teachers who subsequently would lead computer-literacy classes.

Similarly, educational texts trivialize computer knowledge. *Precollege Computer Literacy,* by David Moursund, tells teachers they "already know a great deal about computers . . . just by living in this society," while David Klassen notes in *AEDS Journal* that playing video games constitutes "considerable computer experience." But people whose interaction with computers is limited to receiving computerized bills or reading computer-typeset publications learn nothing substantive about computers through these interactions.

Still, some teachers remain enthusiastic about computers. A primary reason is that computers and computer classes look attractive compared with the usual precollege academic environment. Consider the working conditions described in an Institute for Educational Leadership study. Many primary and secondary schools are decaying physically—the backdrop is often leaking roofs, burned-out lights, and broken toilets. Schools have serious shortages of textbooks, reading kits, desks, dictionaries, science equipment, lab workbooks, typewriters, basic office equipment, and even pencils and paper.

No wonder, then, that several of the teachers I met were thrilled that their school would get a computer because it could print lesson plans: money was available for computers but not copiers. Many primary and secondary school teachers consider their work environments unsupportive and demoralizing. In contrast, when computers are introduced, teachers receive equipment, attention, and perks, such as the opportunity to attend conferences. In a Boston primary school, I saw two students using a computer while 10 researchers observed, videotaped, audiotaped, transcribed, and photographed them.

Because teachers lack control over important aspects of their jobs, some naturally want to jump on the bandwagon early enough to control a new technology. Because they feel beleaguered by a society that criticizes their work, some respond to the public's enthusiasm about computers. Because they work in deteriorating environments, some take advantage of a resource that administrators, parents, and legislators buy willingly. Teachers' reactions reflect what is bad about education more than what is good about computers.

However, there are signs that the unfulfilled promises of computer-literacy education are causing a backlash. Many teachers resent the pressures, and they find that students are getting bored with mediocre software. One computer coordinator said, "It's like pulling teeth to get people to use computers." Kim Natale, the 1984 Colorado Teacher of the Year, made a similar observation: "Two or three years ago, the kids were all excited about using the computers. Now they say, 'Oh, do I have to?'"

Real Computer Literacy

Underlying the fervor for computer-literacy education is the laudable belief that it will foster a population that encourages computer applications to satisfy social needs and resists applications with unwanted implications. Achieving this goal requires instruction that imparts an understanding not of how computers work but of how society applies them. That means discussing the context into which the technology fits and focusing on case studies of large, complex, real-world systems.

Consider the 1988 episode in which the USS *Vincennes* shot down an Iranian passenger plane in the Persian Gulf. A narrow perspective focuses on the ship's computerized sensors. A wider perspective includes the *Vincennes* personnel who operated intelligence-processing equipment and made decisions based on its output. The widest perspective considers the context in which the incident took place—in a politically unstable location, in an ongoing military crisis (the ship had been under attack), and in a setting very different from the open seas for which the computerized intelligence system was designed. This wide perspective teaches an important general principle: unexpected problems arise when a computer-driven system is used in unusual ways.

A broad view of social, economic, and political factors is the cornerstone of a meaningful computer-literacy program. From such a vantage point, some common themes emerge naturally. For instance, part of a course could be devoted to debunking the myth of computer infallibility. Computers can do only what people understand well enough to describe in algorithms. This is one basis of concern about Star Wars, whose computers would have to respond to unpredictable events. Students would learn how hard, at times impossible, it is to model even simple tasks.

Students should consider not only the astonishing power of computers but also their limits. For instance, simulations, a very important application, depend on their designers' judgment about what aspects of reality to include and leave out. Since a simulation is only as good as its underlying assumptions, even systems tested extensively in simulations can fail in a real test. As Karen Duncan, an information-systems consultant, noted in *Communications of the ACM* (the Association for Computing Machinery), "It's dangerous to put blind faith in systems that try to model complicated realities. It could be disastrous to mistake skill in piloting a simulated oil tanker or running a simulated nuclear plant with mastery of the real thing."

ABC News has reported that courts have used computer-graphics simulations. In one case based on unspecified data—perhaps eyewitness accounts—a simulation "demonstrated" that the defendant was not liable for an automobile accident. Afterward, a juror said that the simulation was critical because she could "see what happened." But what the juror saw was an abstract representation of what happened. We can have no confidence in simulations without knowing the source of the data and who is responsible for the simulation.

Real computer literacy would include discussing the ethics of creating and using computer systems. For instance, what are the ethical implications of widespread computer monitoring of office workers? What are the implications of the automated decision-making systems that already operate in many domains, from the battlefield to law enforcement to medical diagnosis? Who—or what—is responsible for the decisions?

Technological Band-Aids

Dramatic claims about the benefits of computer-literacy education echo claims for the revolutionary academic value of earlier technologies. Computers are but the latest in a long line of "educational technologies," following radios, phonographs, stereoscopes, movies, adding machines, reading machines, teaching machines, and television. Many of these devices now gather dust in schools, and some teachers suggest that computers soon will follow them into the storage closets.

Although no one advocates that schools install a computer as an end in itself, technology often monopolizes educators' attention. And when instruction focuses on technology, nontechnological questions are hard to ask—questions about teacher preparation, parental involvement, the value of the teaching profession, how to meet the early-education requirements of poor and disadvantaged students, and the lack of real literacy among school graduates.

The unchallenged assumption that computer education is worthwhile, even essential, precludes people questioning *whether* computers can truly contribute to education. Instead, the concern is with relatively superficial questions, such as which hardware and software to buy.

A primary-school teacher told me that computer-literacy education, as it exists today, is like "trying to put a Band-Aid on what's wrong with the school system." Euphoria about computers must not become a smokescreen diverting attention from fundamental educational problems that cannot be solved by technological means.

Ethical and Legal Issues

Given the diversity and complexity of a modern society, it is inevitable that groups and individuals will clash over social, political, and economic interests. Most social conflict is of the kind found in the debate of the political forum, the competition of the marketplace, and the labor/ management negotiation table. These types of conflict are socially approved and desirable because they provide appropriate opportunities for the expression of dissent and the exercise of choice—vital elements of the democratic process.

Unfortunately, as we all know, conflict can also be expressed in ways that threaten life, property, privacy, and basic human rights. Computers have emerged as an increasingly important factor behind such dangers. In this section and the following section, we look more closely at two facets of social conflict—the ethical/legal dimension and concerns over individual privacy in the information age.

The first article highlights the important ethical issue of truthful representation. "Seeing is believing" is a maxim few of us question. In "Photographs That Lie: The Ethical Dilemma of Digital Retouching," J. D. Lasica discusses the ethical dilemmas of digitally retouching photographs. This technique makes it possible to distort visual information, and raises the possibility that we may be unable to judge the believability of what we see in photographs in the future.

Our information society has spawned some unanticipated problems over intellectual property rights. Traditionally, information has been treated as a public good rather than a private resource—except under circumstances where individuals may copyright written works or patent inventions. Today, most commercial software is copyrighted which means it is illegal to make copies without the permission of the copyright holder. However, unauthorized copying of software is common. And as Janet Mason explains in "Warning: Here Come the Software Police," firms that allow their employees to pirate software can face stiff penalties.

Some software producers feel copyright does not offer them strong enough protection and are applying for software patents, a practice that has generated opposition from within the computing community itself. In "Software Patents," members of the League of Programming Free-

dom outline their objections to this practice. They argue, among other things, that the Patent Office lacks the expertise to properly evaluate software applications, patent searches are prohibitively expensive and unreliable, and software patents are legally questionable. They claim, moreover, that granting patents will impair the creativity and development of the software industry.

A movement against intellectual property rights is being led by Richard Stallman who insists that all software should be free. Some of his initiatives towards this end include the Free Software Foundations, the GNU project, and the Copyleft software licensing agreement. Details about Stallman's efforts and successes are provided by Simson Garfinkel in "Programs to the People."

An example of unethical and increasingly illegal behavior is the oft glamorized practice of "hacking" or gaining unauthorized access to computers. This can cause severe injury to organizations and individuals even if the perpetrator takes pains to avoid damaging the computer or data. Other dangers arise from deliberate attacks on the integrity of data or computer systems. During a four-year period in the late 1970s and early 1980s, more than two dozen computer installations in Europe were attacked by terrorists. CLODO, a French underground organization, targets the computers of multinational corporations. In Italy, the Red Brigade bombed the Motor Vehicle Industry and destroyed records of who owned cars or trucks and who had driver's licenses.

But one need not resort to terrorism or physical damage to cripple a computer system. As hundreds of articles in the mass media have made clear, computers can be programmed to sabotage themselves with "viruses." A rash of publicity surrounding computer viruses was spurred by the "Internet" virus planted by a Cornell graduate student in November 1988. Though the damage was unintentional, the virus disrupted the operations of an estimated 6,000-plus computers on the Internet Network. In response, several prominent computing organizations issued statements on computer ethics, and condemned the placing of an unauthorized code in computers. In "Legally Speaking," the topic is explored in depth by two legal scholars who discuss issues related to civil and criminal redress for damages caused by viruses. The civil issues are presented by Pamela Samuelson in "Can

Hackers Be Sued for Damages Caused by Computer Viruses?" Criminal issues are covered by Michael Gemignani in "Viruses and Criminal Law." A case study of a successful civil suit and criminal prosecution for a computer virus is offered by Edward Joyce in "Time Bomb: Inside the Texas Virus Trial." Joyce articulately outlines the problems encountered in prosecuting computer crime in general.

As the articles in this section show, there is a high level of ambiguity over which types of computer activities constitute criminal behavior. There is little doubt that a bank employee who uses a computer to embezzle millions of dollars from customer accounts is engaged in a criminal act. However, many other types of cases are less clear. Some examples are provided by Greg Costikyan in "Closing the Net." He focuses on issues related to the content of messages published on computer networks and electronic bulletin boards, and argues that investigations of such activities have been "overzealous." They may even isolate the freedom of the press.

Looking Ahead: Challenge Questions

Should all software be free? Why or why not?

As several articles point out, it is difficult to detect, investigate, and prosecute computer-related crime without some technical knowledge of computing. According to Bryan Kocher, past president of the Association for Computing Machinery, some computer expertise is necessary to make good computer laws in the first place. He observes that legislatures tend to have "many lawyers, morticians, and tavern keepers, but few computer professionals." This lack of computer experts could lead to some very bad laws, argues Kocher. Do you agree? Why or why not?

Photographs That Lie

The Ethical Dilemma Of Digital Retouching

By J. D. Lasica

J. D. Lasica is a features editor and columnist at the Sacramento Bee.

A few years ago I wandered into a seminar touting the wonders that technology would bring to the photographs of tomorrow. Up on the screen, a surreal slide show was in progress. One slide showed Joan Collins sitting provocatively on President Reagan's lap. *Click.* Joan was now perching, elfishly, on the president's shoulder. *Click.* Reagan had grown a third eye. *Click.* Now he was bald. *Click.* And so on.

A representative from the Scitex Corporation, a Bedford, Massachusetts, company that manufactures digital retouching equipment, said that computers could now alter the content of photographs in virtually any manner. The slides had all been produced electronically—with no trace of tampering.

The audience, clearly dazzled, tossed off a dozen or so questions about whether the machines could do this or that. Finally a hand shot up. "Nobody's said a word about the potential for abuse here. What about the ethics of all this?"

"That's up to you," said the representative.

Welcome to journalism's latest ethical nightmare: photographs that lie.

In the past few years, this razzle-dazzle digital artistry has begun to turn up at the nation's largest newspapers, magazines and book publishing houses. The trend has a lot of people worried.

Consider what has taken place already:

• Through electronic retouching *National Geographic* slightly moved one of the Great Pyramids at Gîza to fit the vertical shape of its cover in 1982.

• An editor at the *Asbury Park Press*, the third-largest newspaper in New Jersey, removed a man from the middle of a news photo and filled in the space by "cloning" part of an adjoining wall. The incident prompted the paper to issue a policy prohibiting electronic tampering with news photos.

• The *Orange County Register*, which won a Pulitzer Prize for its photo coverage of the 1984 Summer Olympics, changed the color of the sky in every one of its outdoor Olympics photos to a smog-free shade of blue.

• The editors of the book *A Day in the Life of America* could not choose a cover photo from the thousands of pictures taken by the world's leading photojournalists. They solved the problem electronically by taking a photo of a cowboy on horseback, moving him up a hillside and, for good measure, enlarging the crescent moon. "I don't know if it's right or wrong," says co-director David Cohen. "All I know is it sells the book better."

• For one of its covers, *Popular Science* used a computer to place an airplane from one photo onto the background of another aerial photo. And a number of magazines have combined images of people photographed at different times, creating composites that give the false appearance of a single cover shot.

• The *St. Louis Post-Dispatch* used a Scitex computer to remove a can of Diet Coke from a photo taken of Ron Olshwanger, winner of the 1989 Pulitzer Prize for photography.

Faster than you can say "visual credibility gap," the 1980s may be the last decade in which photos could be considered evidence of anything.

"The photograph as we know it, as a record of fact, may no longer in fact be that in three or five years," warns George Wedding, director of photography for the *Sacramento Bee.*

Jack Corn, director of photography for the *Chicago Tribune*, one of the first papers to buy a Scitex system, says the stakes are enormous. "People used to be able to look at photographs as depictions of reality," he says. "Now, that's being lost. I think what's happening is just morally, ethically wrong."

Digital technology's impact will be no less dramatic in other areas.

Within a decade, consumers will be able to buy a hand-held digital camera that uses a microchip instead of film, allowing the owner to "edit" photos. Soon you'll be able to remove your mother-in-law from that otherwise perfect vacation snapshot.

In the cinema, some experts are predicting the day when long-dead movie stars will be re-animated and cast in new films. "In 10 years we will be able to bring Clark Gable back and put him in a new show," John D. Goodell, a computer graphics consultant, told the *New York Times*.

Beyond such fanciful applications of digital technology, Goodell raises a dark scenario: Consider what might happen if the KGB or a terrorist group used such technology to broadcast a fabricated news bulletin about a natural disaster or an impending nuclear attack—delivered by a synthetic Dan Rather.

More likely than an assault by the Islamic Jihad on our airwaves will be an assault on our trust in visual images. Will photos be admissible evidence in a courtroom if tampering cannot be detected? Can newspapers rely on the truthfulness of any photo whose authenticity cannot be verified? As the price of these machines comes down, what will happen when the grocery-store tabloids start using—or abusing—them?

In television, too, the potential for abuse is great. Don E. Tomlinson, assistant professor of journalism at Texas A&M University, foresees the day when news producers try to re-create news events that they failed to capture on camera using exotic technology whose use was once confined to cinematic special effects. Airing such a simulation on a nightly newscast could confuse viewers about whether they're watching the real thing.

Tomlinson goes so far as to suggest that an unscrupulous TV reporter might use digital technology to fabricate an entire story because of ratings pressure, for career advancement or simply to jazz up the news on a slow day. A shark lurking near a populated beach, for example, could be manufactured using file footage and a digital computer.

While digital machinations on television may pose the greatest threat to the credibility of visual images in the long run, today the war is being waged in print.

Ironically, publishers are snapping up these systems not for their photo-altering capabilities but for economic reasons.

Newspapers and magazines are using digital computers to achieve huge savings in labor and materials, enhance the quality of color photo reproduction, push back editorial deadlines (because of the time saved) and transmit color separations to remote printing plants via satellite.

Among the publications already employing the technology are *Time*, *Newsweek*, *U.S. News & World Report*, *USA Today*, *Newsday*, the *Atlanta Journal* and *Constitution*, the *Providence Journal-Bulletin* and, most recently, the *New York Times*. (Incidentally, while Scitex is the industry leader in producing these machines, it is not alone in the field. Crosfield Electronics of East Rutherford, New Jersey, and Hell Graphics Systems of Port Washington, New York, also manufacture digital retouching systems.)

"People have no idea how much alteration is going on," says Michael Morse of the National Press Photographers Association. "When you're looking at that *Redbook* or *Mademoiselle* or *Sports Illustrated* tomorrow, there's a good chance somebody has done something to that picture."

Of course, some of this photo modification is familiar terrain. Pictures have been faked since the earliest days of photography in the 1850s. Retouching photos by hand was once common practice in many newsrooms, and photographers can change the composition of a black-and-white print in the darkroom. But over the years, ethical standards have tightened. Today retouching a news photo is forbidden at most publications, and faking a photo can be grounds for dismissal.

As the tools of the trade change, however, the rules of the game evolve as well. Altering a photo has never been so fast and seamless. Digital systems allow an editor or art director to capture, display, alter, transmit and publish a picture without it ever seeing photographic paper.

A photographer in the field is now able to capture an image on a light-sensitive semiconductor chip and send it to the newsroom via telephone line, microwave or even satellite. The image—a collection of hundreds of thousands of pixels, similar to the makeup of a TV screen—is then reassembled on the video monitor of a picture editing station, or "electronic darkroom," where an editor can size it, crop it, enhance the contrast and tone and correct minor flaws. From there the image is sent to a color laser plotter, which converts the pixels into signals of zeros and ones (representing the densities of magenta, cyan, yellow and black printing inks) and produces a color separation. While conventional processing reads a transparency or photo by exposing it to light, electronic scanning creates an instant digital representation of an image. *Voilà!* A process that would normally take hours is accomplished in minutes. With a plaything this seductive, it's

easy to understand the temptation to "improve" a news photo at the stroke of a few keys.

Rolling Stone magazine used a digital computer to erase a pistol and holster slung over the arm of "Miami Vice" star Don Johnson after he posed for a 1985 cover shot. Editor Jann Wenner, an ardent foe of handguns, ordered the change; using a computer saved the time and expense of having the cover re-shot.

Unquestionably, this high-tech process is here to stay. The question thus becomes: Where do you draw the line?

"If someone wants to remove a tree from a photo or move two people closer together, that's crossing the line," says Dennis Copeland, director of photography for the *Miami Herald*. "The media's image has been hurt because of those few people who've abused the technology."

While a spot survey of editors, art directors and picture editors at major newspapers nationwide found no one who supported the notion of using digital technology to tamper with the integrity of a documentary news photograph, there was far greater acceptance of using it to create conceptual or illustrative photos.

The distinction is far from academic. Documentary photographs aim to portray real events in true-to-life settings. Conceptual photos are meant to symbolize an idea or evoke a mood. Because a studio shot of, say, a truffle is more akin to a still life than to the hard-edge realism of photojournalism—indeed, because the shot is staged in the first place—art directors and page designers are given wide latitude in altering its content.

What is happening, many photographers and picture editors fear, is that the distinction between the two styles is blurring, partly due to the new technology. Scott Henry, chief photographer for the *Marin County* (California) *Independent-Journal*, detects in photojournalism "a quiet shift toward pictures as ornamentation or entertainment rather than reportage."

And George Wedding of the *Bee* says of tampered photographs, "Fabricated images that look authentic on first glance sometimes taint the believability of the pictures around them."

Wedding sees a trend toward increased reliance on conceptual photos, caused in part by the recent influx into newsrooms of art directors and designers who take their visual cues from art schools and the advertising field, where manipulation is the name of the game. "These people have not been taught the traditional, classic values and goals of documentary photojournalism," he says.

Joseph Scopin, assistant managing editor for graphics at the *Washington Times* (which uses the Scitex system), thinks those fears are overblown. "If you run a photo of someone holding a 4-foot-tall, 300-pound strawberry, it's pretty obvious to the reader we're playing with the images," he says.

Sometimes, however, the distinction can be lost on the reader.

The *Asbury Park Press* ran into that difficulty in 1987 when it ran a cover story in its "Health and Fitness" section on a new kind of beef with lower cholesterol. Says Nancy Tobin, the paper's design director, "We had a head-on shot of a cow munching hay and a studio shot of a beautiful salad, and [we] combined the two images on Scitex. People came up to us afterward and said, 'How'd you get that cow to eat that salad?' We labeled it *composite photo illustration,* but some people were left scratching their heads."

Readers may grow more accustomed to digital photography's use as it spreads from the feature sections to the rest of the paper. Last summer the *Hartford Courant* ran a Page One color photo that showed how the city's skyline will look after several new skyscrapers go up; the feat was accomplished with *Newsday*'s Scitex equipment. Experts say it won't be long before newspapers' real estate pages display computer-created photos, rather than rough "artist's conceptions," of planned developments.

But some observers worry that increased use of digital retouching will make readers skeptical about the integrity of even undoctored images.

"People believe in news photographs. They have more inherent trust in what they see than what they read," says Kenneth Kobre, head of photojournalism studies at San Francisco State University. "Digital manipulation throws all pictures into a questionable light. It's a gradual process of creating doubts in the viewer's mind."

It was precisely that concern that led *National Geographic*, the magazine that moved a pyramid, to rethink its position. Jan Adkins, former associate art director, explains: "At the beginning of our access to Scitex, I think we were seduced by the dictum, 'If it can be done, it must be done.' If there was a soda can next to a bench in a contemplative park scene, we'd have the can removed digitally.

"But there's a danger there. When a photograph becomes synthesis, fantasy rather than reportage, then the whole purpose of the photograph dies. A photogra-

pher is a reporter—a photon thief, if you will. He goes and takes, with a delicate instrument, an extremely thin slice of life. When we changed that slice of life, no matter in what small way, we diluted our credibility. If images are altered to suit the editorial purposes of anyone, if soda cans or clutter or blacks or people of ethnic backgrounds are taken out, suddenly you've got a world that's not only unreal but surreal."

Adkins promises that, at *National Geographic* anyway, "the Scitex will never be used again to shift any one of the Seven Wonders of the World, or to delete anything that's unpleasant or add anything that's left out."

But even if other publications begin to show similar self-restraint, critics warn, digital technology is making additional inroads that threaten the credibility of visual images.

Already, there are a half dozen software programs on the market, such as "PhotoMac" or "Digital Darkroom" for the Macintosh, that allow the user to edit photographs digitally. The programs retail for about $700.

And then there is the digital camera, a sort of hand-held freeze-frame video camera that should be in stores within a decade, at a price within reach of the average buyer. What disturbs many people about this device is that the original image exists in an electronic limbo that can be almost endlessly manipulated. The camera differs from Scitex digital retouching equipment, which works with an original photo or negative.

"The term *photographic proof* may already be an archaic term," says the *Bee*'s Wedding. "You used to be able to hold up a negative and see that the image is real. With the advent of digital technology, you're going to hold up a floppy disk and you're not going to see anything."

Adds Tobin of the *Asbury Park Press*: "This is scaring everyone, because there's no original print, no hard copy. From the moment the shutter is snapped, it exists only as a digitized electronic impulse. Talk about the ability to rewrite history! It literally will be possible to purge information, to alter a historic event that occurred five years ago because no original exists.

There's enormous potential for great wrong and great misuse."

Scitex spokesperson Ned Boudreau says the digital industry addressed such concerns long ago. "To hear the critics tell it," he says, "it's like we've unleashed Joe McCarthy all over again. We haven't."

He says safeguards, such as an archiving system that stores originals where no one can get at them, can be built into the digital equipment. At present, however, manufacturers do not provide such options unless requested.

John Derry, director of graphic services for Chromaset, a San Francisco creative-effects studio that has used digital retouching for dozens of corporations' advertising campaigns, thinks Americans will learn to accept the technology as it becomes pervasive. "Maybe it's generational," he says. "My mother could never tell the difference between videotape and movies, between the hard, sharp edge of Johnny Carson and the soft look of motion picture film.

"As we move into this new technology, perhaps there will be people who won't be able to discern electronically manipulated images from undoctored images. But I think most of us are already pretty savvy about this stuff. If you show someone a picture of Reagan punching Gorbachev, most people won't think it's real. They'll think, Oh, look at this doctored photo. How'd they do that?"

None of this assuages the critics of digital technology, but even its detractors concede this much: It's not the technology itself that's the culprit. Machines aren't ethical or unethical; people are.

"You've got to rely on people's ethics," says Brian Steffans, a top graphics photography editor at the *Los Angeles Times*. "That's not much different from relying on the reporter's words. You don't cheat just because the technology is available."

Wedding of the *Bee* is less sanguine about the future of news photography: "I hope that 10 years from now readers will be able to pick up a newspaper and magazine and believe what they read and see. Whether we are embarking on a course which will make that impossible, I don't know. I'm afraid we have."

WARNING: HERE COME THE SOFTWARE POLICE

Are you sure your firm's
employees haven't made illegal copies
of computer software?
Really sure?

Janet Mason

Janet Mason is a freelance writer in Philadelphia who writes frequently on business and computer topics.

Todd Weiss (not his real name), a chief executive officer of a *Fortune-500* financial institution, recently received a $35,000 lesson in the perils of computer software piracy. Like many CEOs, he had believed that the anti-piracy statement his employees signed annually would thwart illegal copying at his company. He also had thought that the signed statements would protect him from software-vendor lawsuits. On both accounts he was wrong.

In the corporate world, commercial software is no longer locked securely away in the information systems department. Thanks to the rise of the personal computer, commercial software is found throughout the far reaches of corporate offices. Today any employee with access to a PC—from managers and executives to clerks and warehouse employees—can make an illegal duplicate of commercial software in less than two minutes. Ron Palenski, general counsel of the software industry group, Adapso, estimates that one out of every two copies of software used by corporations is illegal. In the United States alone, says the U.S. Trade Representative's Office, the software industry is suffering $40 million annual losses because of software piracy.

Recently, the software industry has decided that it will no longer turn the other cheek to this drain on its profits. The result:

Companies across the nation must now beware of the software police. Since September 1989, the Software Publishers Association (SPA), a Washington, D.C.-based organization representing 565 software vendors, has filed 36 lawsuits and conducted 40 audits against corporations, computer dealers, electronic bulletin boards, and individuals who allegedly have illegal copies of software. Several software companies are also taking independent legal action against companies misusing their products.

The software vendors' ammunition is the United States Code Section 17 Copyright Law—commonly known as the shrink-wrap license—which says that once the purchaser breaks the seal of the software package he can make copies of the software only for backup or archival purposes. It is illegal for the software copies to be used by various people simultaneously, without a separate license. Companies and individuals who break this agreement can be liable for as much as $50,000 for each illegal copy of the software.

The SPA enforces the copyright protection law by way of the corporate audit, such as the one conducted against Weiss's company, and through fines averaging between $20,000 and $50,000. The SPA targets a company based on tips from callers to its piracy hotline and the extent of the alleged violations. The hotline is advertised in trade publications, at trade shows, and in SPA literature. Although no reward is offered for tips, the hotline receives approximately 20 calls a day.

From *Across the Board*, October 1990, pp. 40-45. Reprinted by permission of the author and The Conference Board, 845 Third Avenue, New York, NY 10022.

Once a firm is targeted, the SPA contacts it to warn it of the upcoming audit. Audits are voluntary, but less than 4 percent of companies refuse to cooperate: If they do, the SPA will take them to court.

The audit itself is frequently inconvenient and protracted. A company must escort SPA inspectors throughout the premises to check floppy disks and the hard disk drives in employees' PCs for unauthorized software. Then investigators begin reconciling the companies' purchase records with those of the vendor—a procedure that can take from six days to six months. It's a process that can be eye-opening for the executives involved.

When Todd Weiss's company underwent an SPA audit, he greeted Mary Jane Saunders, SPA's general counsel, at the door by saying: "We can afford to buy our software and we do." Sitting down at the first computer with the audit team, the CEO found that the hard disk, which stores information, including software, contained eight illegal commercial packages. By the time the third computer was audited, revealing electronic games as well as illegal software, says Saunders, "Weiss realized that he didn't know what his employees were doing with their PCs."

With the increase in lawsuits and audits, the responsibility of preventing software piracy falls to the senior managers of a company. Many of these executives believe—as Weiss did—that their companies are protected from lawsuits by the written policies against software piracy that are included in company code of ethics statements or information systems department documents. Although these documents are usually signed by all employees when first hired or on a

---

Facts on File's anti-piracy policy did nothing to protect the company in court from a multimillion-dollar lawsuit.

---

yearly basis, they are useless as protection unless accompanied by stringent enforcement policies. Facts On File Inc., a New York-based publishing firm, found this out firsthand last year when they were slapped with a multimillion-dollar lawsuit; the company's anti-piracy policy, which was unenforced, did nothing to protect it in court.

Management neglect of software piracy implicitly condones the practice, says Saunders. Oftentimes, unbeknownst to senior executives, employees bring in a favorite software package that is not provided by the company and copy it for co-workers. This "backdoor" type of piracy is more prevalent than management-condoned piracy, Saunders says, but that doesn't let management off the hook. "The only employees more suspect than others," she says, "are employees who aren't educated in copyright law—and it's up to management to educate them."

Top management sometimes unwittingly encourages software piracy by cutting corners on their budgets. "An executive might say that there is no reason for the accounting department to have word processing software," Saunders says. "But the fact is that sooner or later every employee has to write a letter." Illegal copies may also circulate if employees prefer to use software other than the company standard for a specific task.

In some instances, the SPA has found that top management does sanction software piracy. "In one case," recalls Saunders, "an employee called and told us that the information systems director at his company was making illegal copies." When the concerned employee complained to top management, he was told: "Don't worry, the software police won't get us." Managers may also condone the practice in a less blatant way—by ignoring the fact that it's occurring. "Software piracy is like personal telephone calls," says a high-level information systems executive with a leading retail institution, "people aren't supposed to do it but some do." This executive, who wishes to remain anonymous, says he views spot checks of employees' hard disks as "draconian."

Invasive as the checks may be, the alternative of multimillion-dollar lawsuits and the attendant publicity is even less appealing. As the senior management of Facts on File learned, lawsuits are expensive and embarrassing. From the software companies' point of view, they are also necessary. Saunders says that although each illegal copy does not constitute a lost sale for the software industry, the piracy rate is high enough to damage the industry by limiting research and development funds and driving up retail prices. To mitigate the damage, companies are beginning to litigate aggressively.

"Often a company will buy one copy of our software and make illegal copies from it," says Curt Blake, general counsel of Aldus Corporation. "They are our customers so we don't want to alienate them, but we also don't want our property stolen." Aldus, a Seattle-based software developer of Page-

Maker, a popular desktop publishing package, is a member of the SPA and also conducts litigation on its own.

One of the SPA's largest piracy suits was filed this May against the National Business Academy. Working in conjunction with Federal impoundment marshals, the SPA raided three California locations—Glendale, Vanuys, and Englewood—of the nationwide computer training company and seized 600 pirated disks. The illegal software represented a quarter of a million dollars in unauthorized programs from Lotus Development Corporation, Microsoft Corporation, and WordPerfect Corporation.

At the time of the raid, the SPA had affidavits of piracy activity from a former administrator, student, and teacher. "Since 1986 the company has trained 4,000 students," says Saunders. "We think they gave copies of illegal software to every one of those students. Even though software vendors all give reduced rates to training companies, the company chose to teach students on unauthorized software. In doing so, it also communicated to students that it's okay to pirate software."

In addition to the 600 disks that it found, the SPA alleges that the school gave away 3,400 pirated programs to former students. The SPA estimates damages at $250 for each pirated copy of Lotus and WordPerfect and $100 for each copy of Microsoft's disk operating system, all of which adds up to a $2.5 million lawsuit.

To educate corporate consumers on the hazards of pirating, Adapso, the software industry group, sends interested companies its "Thou Shall Not Dupe" brochure, which explains copyright law. The SPA distributes a similar brochure, which several software companies send out with new releases of their product. The SPA also provides self-auditing kits for companies that want to take matters into their own hands.

A number of companies have already developed effective anti-piracy programs out of a sense of ethics and good management. They realize that unlike those who have legally purchased software, users of pirated software do not receive technical support, instruction manuals, or software updates from the vendors. Many of these companies keep an inventory of their software and, for the purpose of comparison, conduct periodic audits of their employees' hard disks. Audits are often overseen by individual department managers.

At EDS, the Dallas-based provider of information technology services, each local manager maintains the inventory of soft-

ware for his division. The actual auditing of the employees' hard disks is done quarterly by a corporate-level auditing team. At Chemical Banking Corporation, each business unit has one or more data security managers responsible for preventing software piracy. An official auditing department conducts random spot-checks of employees' hard disks in each department. Like EDS,

Some companies conduct random spot-checks of employees' hard disks in an effort to stop piracy.

Chemical Banking Corporation includes an anti-piracy stipulation in its company code of ethics.

"Our company treats software just like any other company property," says Jim Mayer, senior vice president and processing services director of Chemical Bank. "When we sign a license with a commercial software vendor, that package becomes a company asset that needs to be protected," he says. "An employee pirating software is equivalent to an employee walking out of the building with a typewriter."

In general, companies are vigilant about insuring that employees sign the anti-piracy statements, but are lax when it comes to enforcing stipulations. Saunders of SPA says that although 90 percent of *Fortune*-500 corporations have anti-piracy contracts, fewer than 40 percent enforce the regulations through inventory controls and spot-checks of hard disks.

The software vendors' crackdown on corporate offenders has caused an old question to resurface: If companies don't want their software pirated, why don't they put in some type of technical barrier? Up until the mid-1980s, vendors did routinely include copy-protection devices in their software. These devices were simply a computer code written in the software that prevented users from making more than one or two backup copies.

The problem with the technology was that much of the copy-protected software required users to insert the original disk into the computer each time they used the program—even if they had a hard disk drive. This cumbersome procedure made copy-protected software unpopular with consumers. A further problem was that not all of the software packages were compatible with the various computer models. As a result, some copy-protected software would not run on certain IBM-compatible personal computers.

The EC's Crackdown On Software Piracy

As corporate audits and court action prove increasingly effective in protecting software copyrights at a national level, the U.S. software industry is now turning its concern toward proposed changes in copy-protection law in the European Economic Community. The EEC's proposed copyright-protection law claims to be compliant with U.S. law but is not, says Michael Brown, president of Central Point Software Inc. According to Brown, under the proposed directive, European consumers will not have the right to break technical copy protection on commercial software, even to make backups of software.

In the United States it is legal to make an unlimited number of archival or backup copies as long as they are used only by the licensed user. Consumers have plenty of legitimate reasons to make extra copies, says Brown. Software programs can be easily erased by reformatting, placing the disk near a magnetic field, or spilling coffee on it. Brown himself has somewhat more at stake than the consumer: The proposed EEC legislation would make one of Central Point Software's products, Copy II PC, which unlocks copy protection on commercial software, illegal.

Mary Jane Saunders, general counsel of the Software Publishers Association (SPA), says, however, that a clause has been added to the directive that would protect software packages such as Copy II PC. The proposal's language, she says, was changed in recognition of the need for consumers to make legitimate backup copies.

Although the backup debate looks like it may be resolved, another sticky area remains—reverse engineering. Reverse engineering, which involves breaking down a software program to its machine code to discover how it has been made, is often done by computer programmers who hope to improve on the program to create new software products. The EEC copyright proposal would make reverse engineering illegal in Europe.

Michael Brown argues that reverse engineering, which is done routinely in the United States, is inevitable. "This is how good software is built," Brown says. "People build on other products. It's like taking a toaster apart and building a better one."

Saunders of SPA disagrees. "When people read the machine code, they know everything about the product they need to know to create cheap imitations of it," she says. "This isn't fair to software vendors who put in the time, creativity, and money to develop the program."

Although the copyright section of the EEC document will not be decided until March of next year, Saunders is confident that the prohibition on reverse engineering will pass. "It's backed by key figures in the U.S. House and Senate as well as by business leaders," she says.

—J.M.

The software industry responded to customer complaints by abandoning copy-protection devices for all their products except those sold overseas or occupying certain niche markets. Computerease Soft Inc., for instance, protects its niche-market applications for the typesetting industry with a software copy-protection device but leaves its word-processing software package unprotected.

To some extent, software companies have resigned themselves to software piracy; the alternative often is going out of business. "There are companies starting up all the time," says Donn B. Parker, a senior management consultant at SRI International, "and they are ready to jump in when established companies do something unfriendly, such as putting copy restrictions on software."

Vendors are also skeptical about safeguarding their software with copy-protection technology because computer hackers often find it easy to break. Michael Brown, in fact, launched a successful software business in 1982 with Copy II PC, a copy-protection-breaking software package. In its first year his company, Central Point Software Inc., sold several hundred thousand copies of Copy II PC, which was promoted as a legitimate backup device rather than as a pirating tool. "In the early days of copy protection, you had to go back and get the original disk whenever you wanted to use the software program," says Brown, "and users wanted to make backup copies on their hard disks." Because few software vendors use copy-protection technology today, Copy II PC has become an almost nonexistent part of Brown's business, purchased primarily by consumers with games and home-computer programs, which are still commonly copy protected.

Paradoxically, copy-protection technology has markedly improved since software vendors discontinued using it. "Although there's always a modicum of inconvenience with copy protection," says David Mosby, president of Softguard Systems Inc., "current technology allows copy-protection software to run smoothly on a variety of IBM-compatibles. Also, newer devices do not require that the user insert the original disk each

---

Piracy lawsuits and audits are causing companies to be more concerned about copy protection than vendors are.

---

time." Software packages that use Softguard's copy-protection product take the average consumer about two extra minutes to install. Softguard is also working on making its security product more effective. Within the next year it plans to introduce a program that can be customized by each software vendor, making it more difficult for hackers to break. Currently, each vendor uses the same program, which is periodically updated by the company.

Although few are predicting a widespread return to copy protection, vendors may be

forced to provide such security for their corporate clients. Piracy lawsuits and audits, says Charles Adler, a spokesman for Software Security Inc., "are causing corporations to be more concerned about copy protection than vendors are." To address their anti-piracy needs, Software Security is planning to introduce a combination software and hardware device that will attach to each personal computer in a company and will sell for about $30.

Software vendors are also attacking piracy on the PC networking front. Both Softguard Systems and Lotus Development Corporation sell products that include a security device that prohibits a company from adding new people to its personal computer network unless it purchases a networking license upgrade. David Schnepper, a software architect with Ashton Tate Corporation, which uses Softguard Systems' product, LANmark, says LANmark "does not prevent the user from copying the software, but it does prevent users from adding unlicensed users onto the existing PC network."

Given the corporate trend toward PC networking, anti-networking products are likely to have more of a future in the battle against software piracy than copy-protection devices. For corporations, however, the best protection against the software police rests not in any security device, but in rigorous enforcement of their anti-piracy statements.

Software Patents

Is this the future of programming?

The League for Programming Freedom

This article is a position paper of the League for Programming Freedom, an organization opposed to software patents and interface copyrights and whose members include, among others, Marvin Minsky, John McCarthy, and Robert S. Boyer. Richard Stallman and Simson Garfinkel helped prepare this article for publication. You can contact the League through Internet mail (league@prep.ai.mit.edu) or at 1 Kendal Square #143, P.O. Box 9171, Cambridge, MA 02139.

Software patents threaten to devastate America's computer industry. Newly granted software patents are being used to attack companies such as Lotus and Microsoft for selling programs that they have independently developed. Soon new companies will be barred from the software arena — most major programs will require licenses for dozens of patents, and this will make them infeasible. This problem has only one solution: Software patents must be eliminated.

The Patent System and Computer Programs

The Framers of the United States Constitution established the patent system so that inventors would have an incentive to share their inventions with the general public. In exchange for divulging an invention, the patent grants the inventor a 17-year monopoly on the use of the invention. The patent holder can license others to use the invention, but may also refuse to do so. Independent reinvention of the same technique by others does not give them the right to use it.

Patents do not cover specific computer programs; instead, they cover particular techniques that can be used to build programs, or particular features that programs can offer. Once a technique or feature is patented, it may not be used in a program without the permission of the patent holder — even if it is implemented in a different way. Since a program typically uses many techniques and provides many features, it can infringe many patents at once.

Until recently, patents were not used in the software field. Software developers copyrighted individual programs or made them trade secrets. Copyright was traditionally understood to cover the implementation details of a particular program; it did not cover the features of the program, or the general methods used. And trade secrecy, by definition, could not prohibit any development work by someone who did not know the secret.

On this basis, software development was extremely profitable and received considerable investment, without any prohibition on independent software development. But this scheme of things is no more. A few U.S. software patents were granted in the early 1980s, stimulating a flood of applications. Now many patents have been approved and the rate is accelerating. Many programmers are unaware of the change and do not appreciate the magnitude of its effects. Today the lawsuits are just beginning.

Absurd Patents

The Patent Office and the courts have had a difficult time with computer software. The Patent Office refused until recently to hire computer science graduates as examiners, and in any case does not offer competitive salaries for the field. Patent examiners are often ill-prepared to evaluate software patent applications to determine if they represent techniques that are widely known or obvious — both of which are grounds for rejection. Their task is made more difficult because many commonly used software techniques do not appear in the scientific literature of computer science: Some seemed too obvious to publish while others seemed insufficiently general.

Computer scientists know many techniques that can be generalized to widely varying circumstances. But the Patent Office seems to believe that each separate use of a technique is a candidate for a new patent. For example, Apple has been sued because the HyperCard program allegedly violates patent number 4,736,308, a patent that covers displaying portions of two or more strings together on the screen — effectively scrolling with multiple subwindows. Scrolling and subwindows are well-known techniques, but combining them is apparently illegal.

The granting of a patent by the Patent Office carries a presumption in law that the patent is valid. Patents for well-known techniques that were in use many years before the patent application have been upheld by federal courts.

For example, the technique of using *exclusive-or* to write a cursor onto a screen is both well-known and obvious. (Its advantage is that another identical *exclusive-or* operation can be used to erase the cursor without damaging the other data on the screen.) This technique can be implemented in a few lines of a program, and a clever high-school student might well reinvent it.

Reprinted from *Dr. Dobb's Journal*, November 1990, pp. 56, 58, 62, 65-67, 70-73.

But it is covered by patent number 4,197,590, which has been upheld twice in court even though the technique was used at least five years before the patent application. Cadtrak, the company that owns this patent, collects millions of dollars from large computer manufacturers.

English patents covering customary graphics techniques, including airbrushing, stenciling, and combination of two images under control of a third, were recently upheld in court, despite the testimony of the pioneers of the field that they had developed these techniques years before. (The corresponding United States patents, including 4,633,416 and 4,602,286, have not yet been tested in court, but they probably will be soon.)

All the major developers of spreadsheet programs have been threatened on the basis of patent 4,398,249, covering "natural order recalc," the recalculation of all the spreadsheet entries that are affected by the changes the user makes, rather than recalculation in a fixed order. Currently Lotus alone is being sued, but a victory for the plaintiff in the case would leave the other developers little hope. (The League for Programming Freedom has found *prior art* that may defeat this patent, but this is not assured.)

Nothing protects programmers from accidentally using a technique that is patented — and then being sued for it. Taking an existing program and making it run faster may also make it violate half a dozen patents that have been granted, or are about to be granted.

Even if the Patent Office learns to understand software better, the mistakes it is making now will follow us into the next century, unless Congress or the Supreme Court intervenes to declare these patents void.

However, this is not the whole of the problem. Computer programming is fundamentally different from the other fields that the patent system previously covered. Even if the patent system were to operate "as intended" for software, it would still obstruct the industry it is supposed to promote.

What is "Obvious"?
The patent system will not grant or uphold patents that are judged to be obvious. However, the system interprets the word "obvious" in a way that might surprise computer programmers. The standard of obviousness developed in other fields is inappropriate for software.

Patent examiners and judges are accustomed to considering even small, incremental changes as deserving new patents. For example, the famous Polaroid vs. Kodak case hinged on differ-

ences in the number and order of layers of chemicals in a film — differences between the technique Kodak was using and those described by previous, expired patents. The court ruled that these differences were unobvious.

Computer scientists solve problems quickly because the medium of programming is tractable. They are trained to generalize solution principles from one problem to another. One such generalization is that a procedure can be repeated or subdivided. Programmers consider this obvious — but the Patent Office did not think that it was obvious when it granted the patent on scrolling multiple strings as described above.

Cases such as this cannot be considered errors. The patent system is functioning as it was designed to do — but with software, it produces outrageous results.

Patenting What is too Obvious to Publish
Sometimes it is possible to patent a technique that is not new precisely because it is obvious — so obvious that no one would have published a paper about it.

For example, computer companies distributing the free X Window System (developed by MIT) are now being threatened with lawsuits by AT&T over patent number 4,555,775, covering the use of "backing store." This technique is used when there are overlapping windows; the contents of a window that is partly hidden are saved in off-screen memory, so they can be put back quickly on the screen if the obscuring window disappears (as often happens).

The technique of backing store was used in an earlier MIT project, the Lisp Machine System, before AT&T applied for the patent. The Lisp Machine developers published nothing about this detail at the time, considering it too obvious. It was mentioned years later when the programmers' reference manual explained how to turn it on and off.

The Lisp Machine was the first computer to use this technique only because it had a larger memory than earlier machines that had window systems. Prior window system developers must have dismissed the idea because their machines had insufficient memory space to spare any for this purpose. Improvements in memory chips made development of backing store inevitable.

Without a publication, the use of backing store in the Lisp Machine System may not count as *prior art* to defeat the patent. So the AT&T patent may stand, and MIT may be forbidden to continue using a method that MIT used before AT&T.

The result is that the dozens of companies and hundreds of thousands of users who accepted the software from MIT with the understanding that it was free are now faced with possible lawsuits. (They are also being threatened with Cadtrak's *exclusive-or* patent.) The X Window project was intended to develop a window system that all developers could use freely. This public service goal seems to have been thwarted by patents.

Why Software is Different
Software systems are much easier to design than hardware systems of the same number of components. For example, a program of 100,000 compo-

Computer scientists are trained to generalize solution principles from one problem to another

nents might be 50,000 lines long and could be written by two good programmers in a year. The equipment needed for this costs less than $10,000; the only other cost would be the programmers' living expenses while doing the job. The total investment would be less than $100,000. If done commercially in a large company, it might cost twice that. By contrast, an automobile typically contains under 100,000 components; it requires a large team and costs tens of millions of dollars to design.

And software is also much cheaper to manufacture: Copies can be made easily on an ordinary workstation costing under $10,000. To produce a hardware system often requires a factory costing tens of millions of dollars.

Why is this? A hardware system has to be designed using real components. They have varying costs; they have limits of operation; they may be sensitive to temperature, vibration, or humidity; they may generate noise; they drain power; they may fail either momentarily or permanently. They must be physically assembled in their proper places, and they must be accessible for replacement in case they fail.

Moreover, each of the components in a hardware design is likely to affect the behavior of many others. This greatly complicates the task of determining what a hardware design will do: Mathematical modeling may prove wrong when the design is built.

By contrast, a computer program is built out of ideal mathematical objects whose behavior is defined, not modeled approximately, by abstract rules. When an *if* statement follows a *while* statement, there is no need to study whether the *if* statement will draw power from the *while* statement and thereby distort its output, nor whether it could overstress the *while* statement and make it fail.

Despite being built from simple parts, computer programs are incredibly complex. The program with 100,000 parts is as complex as an automobile, though far easier to design.

While programs cost substantially less to write, market, and sell than automobiles, the cost of dealing with the patent system will not be less. The same number of components will, on the average, involve the same number techniques that might be patented.

The Danger of a Lawsuit

Under the current patent system, a software developer who wishes to follow the law must determine which patents a program violates and negotiate with each patent holder a license to use that patent. Licensing may be prohibitively expensive, as in the case when the patent is held by a competitor. Even "reasonable" license fees for several patents can add up to make a project infeasible. Alternatively, the developer may wish to avoid using the patent altogether; but there may be no way around it.

The worst danger of the patent system is that a developer might find, after releasing a product, that it infringes one or many patents. The resulting lawsuit and legal fees could force even a medium-size company out of business.

Worst of all, there is no practical way for a software developer to avoid this danger — there is no effective way to find out what patents a system will infringe. There is a way to try to find out — a patent search — but searches are unreliable and in any case too expensive to use for software projects.

Patent Searches are Prohibitively Expensive

A system with 100,000 components can use hundreds of techniques that might already be patented. Since each patent search costs thousands of dollars, searching for all the possible points of danger could easily cost over a million. This is far more than the cost of writing the program.

The costs don't stop there. Patent applications are written by lawyers for lawyers. A programmer reading a patent may not believe that his program violates the patent, but a federal court

may rule otherwise. It is thus now necessary to involve patent attorneys at every phase of program development.

Yet this only reduces the risk of being sued later — it does not eliminate the risk. So it is necessary to have a reserve of cash for the eventuality of a lawsuit.

When a company spends millions to design a hardware system, and plans to invest tens of millions to manufacture it, an extra million or two to pay for dealing with the patent system might be bearable. However, for the inexpensive programming project, the same extra cost is prohibitive. Individuals and small companies especially cannot afford these costs. Software patents will put an end to software entrepreneurs.

Patent Searches are Unreliable

Even if developers could afford patent searches, these are not a reliable method of avoiding the use of patented techniques. This is because patent searches do not reveal pending patent applications (which are kept confidential by the Patent Office). Since it takes several years on the average for a software patent to be granted, this is a serious problem: A developer could begin designing a large program after a patent has been applied for, and release the program before the patent is approved. Only later will the developer learn that distribution of the program is prohibited.

For example, the implementors of the widely used public domain data compression program *compress* followed an algorithm obtained from *IEEE Computer* magazine. They and the user community were surprised to learn later that patent number 4,558,302 had been issued to one of the authors of the article. Now Unisys is demanding royalties for using this algorithm. Although the program is still in the public domain — using it means risking a lawsuit.

The Patent Office does not have a workable scheme for classifying software patents. Patents are most frequently classified by end results, such as "converting iron to steel," but many patents cover algorithms whose use in a program is entirely independent of the purpose of the program. For example, a program to analyze human speech might infringe the patent on a speedup in the Fast Fourier Transform; so might a program to perform symbolic algebra (in multiplying large numbers); but the category to search for such a patent would be hard to predict.

You might think it would be easy to keep a list of the patented software techniques, or even simply remember them. However, managing such a list is nearly impossible. A list compiled in

1989 by lawyers specializing in the field omitted some of the patents mentioned in this article.

Obscure Patents

When you imagine an invention, you probably think of something that could be described in a few words, such as "a flying machine with fixed, curved wings" or "an electrical communicator with a microphone and a speaker." But most patents cover complex detailed processes that have no simple descriptions — often they are speedups or variants of well-known processes that are themselves complex.

Most of these patents are neither obvious nor brilliant; they are obscure. A capable software designer will "invent" several such improvements in the course of a project. However, there are many avenues for improving a technique, so no single project is likely to find any given one.

For example, IBM has several patents (including patent 4,656,583) on workmanlike, albeit complex, speedups for well-known computations performed by optimizing compilers, such as register coloring and computing the available expressions.

Patents are also granted on combinations of techniques that are already widely used. One example is IBM patent 4,742,450, which covers "shared copy-on-write segments." This technique allows several programs to share the same piece of memory that represents information in a file; if any program writes a page in the file, that page is replaced by a copy in all of the programs, which continue to share that page with each other but no longer share with the file.

Shared segments and copy-on-write have been used since the 1960s. This particular combination may be new as a specific feature, but is hardly an invention. Nevertheless, the Patent Office thought that it merited a patent, which must now be taken into account by the developer of any new operating system.

Obscure patents are like land mines: Other developers are more likely to reinvent these techniques than to find out about the patents, and then they will be sued. The chance of running into any one of these patents is small, but they are so numerous that you cannot go far without hitting one. Every basic technique has many variations, and a small set of basic techniques can be combined in many ways. The patent office has now granted more than 2000 software patents — 700 in 1989 alone. We can expect the pace to accelerate. In ten years, programmers will have no choice but to march on blindly and hope they are lucky.

Patent Licensing has Problems, too

Most large software companies are trying to solve the problem of patents by getting patents of their own. Then they hope to cross-license with the other large companies that own most of the patents, so they will be free to go on as before.

While this approach will allow companies such as Microsoft, Apple, and IBM to continue in business, it will shut new companies out of the field. A future start-up, with no patents of its own, will be forced to pay whatever price the giants choose to impose. That price might be high: Established companies have an interest in excluding future competitors. The recent Lotus lawsuits against Borland International and the Santa Cruz Operation (although involving an extended idea of copyright rather than patents) show how this can work.

Even the giants cannot protect themselves with cross-licensing from companies whose only business is to buy patents and then threaten to sue. For example, the New York-based Refac Technology Development Corporation,

a company that represents Forward Reference Systems (owners of the patent for *natural order recalc*), recently sued Lotus Corporation. *Natural order recalc* is Refac's first foray into the software patent arena; for the past 40 years, the company has negotiated licenses in the fastener and electronic component industries. The company employs no programmers or engineers.

Refac is demanding — in the neighborhood of — five percent of sales of all major spreadsheet programs. If a future program infringes on 20 such patents — and this is not unlikely, given the complexity of computer programs and the broad applicability of many patents — the combined royalties could exceed 100 percent of the sales price.

The Fundamental Question

According to the Constitution of the United States, the purpose of patents is to "promote the progress of science and the useful arts." Thus, the basic question at issue is whether software patents, supposedly a method of encouraging software progress, will truly do so, or will retard progress instead.

So far we have explained the ways in which patents will make ordinary

software development difficult. But what of the intended benefits of patents: More invention, and more public disclosure of inventions? To what extent will these actually occur in the field of software?

There will be little benefit to society from software patents because invention in software was already flourishing before software patents, and inventions were normally published in journals for everyone to use. Invention flourished so strongly, in fact, that the same inventions were often found again and again.

In Software, Independent Reinvention is Commonplace

A patent is an absolute monopoly; everyone is forbidden to use the patented process, even those who reinvent it independently. This policy implicitly assumes that inventions are rare and precious, because only in those circumstances is it beneficial.

The field of software is one of constant reinvention; as some people say, programmers throw away more "inventions" each week than other people develop in a year. And the comparative ease of designing large software systems makes it easy for many people to do work in the field. A pro-

Once a program is developed, it can be patented. Software developers are now faced with a number of problems that will blunt their creative activity: the cost of patent searches, the struggle to find a way to avoid known patents, and the danger of lawsuits.

grammer solves many problems in developing each program. These solutions are likely to be reinvented frequently as other programmers tackle similar problems.

The prevalence of independent reinvention negates the usual purpose of patents. Patents are intended to encourage inventions and, above all, the disclosure of inventions. If a technique will be reinvented frequently, there is no need to encourage more people to invent it; because some of the developers will choose to publish it (if publication is merited), there is no point in encouraging a particular inventor to publish it — not at the cost of inhibiting use of the technique.

Overemphasis of Inventions

Many analysts of the American and Japanese industry have attributed Japanese success at producing quality products to the fact that they emphasize incremental improvements, convenient features, and quality rather than noteworthy inventions.

It is especially true in software that success depends primarily on getting the details right. And that is most of the work in developing any useful software system. Inventions are a comparatively unimportant part of the job.

The idea of software patents is thus an example of the mistaken American preoccupation with inventions rather than products. And patents will further reinforce this mistake, rewarding not the developers who write the best software, but those who were first to file for a patent.

Impeding Innovation

By reducing the number of people engage in software development, software patents will actually impede innovation. Much software innovation comes from programmer's solving problems while developing software, not from projects whose specific purpose is to make invention and obtain patents. In other words, these innovations are byproducts of software development.

When patents make development more difficult, and cut down on development projects, they will also cut down on the byproducts of development — new techniques.

Could Patents Ever be Beneficial?

Although software patents are in general harmful to society as a whole, we do not claim that every single software patent is necessarily harmful. Careful study might show that under certain specific and narrow conditions (necessarily excluding the vast major-

ity of cases) it is beneficial to grant software patents.

Nonetheless, the right thing to do now is to eliminate all software patents as soon as possible, before more damage is done. The careful study can come afterward.

Clearly, software patents are not urgently needed by anyone, except patent lawyers. The prepatent software industry had no problem that was solved by patents; there was no shortage of invention and no shortage of investment. Complete elimination of software patents may not be the ideal solution, but it is close, and is a great improvement. Its very simplicity helps avoid a long delay while people argue about details. If it is ever shown that software patents are beneficial in certain exceptional cases, the law can be changed again at that time — if it is important enough. There is no reason to continue the present catastrophic situation until that day.

Software Patents are Legally Questionable

It may come as a surprise that the extension of patent law to software is still legally questionable. It rests on an extreme interpretation of a particular 1981 Supreme Court decision, Diamond vs. Deihr. (See "Legally Speaking" in *Communications of the ACM*, August 1990.)

Traditionally, the only kinds of processes that could be patented were those for transforming matter (such as for transforming iron into steel). Many other activities which we would consider processes were entirely excluded from patents, including business methods, data analysis, and "mental steps." This was called the "subject matter" doctrine.

Diamond vs. Deihr has been interpreted by the Patent Office as a reversal of this doctrine, but the court did not explicitly reject it. The case concerned a process for curing rubber — a transformation of matter. The issue at hand was whether the use of a computer program in the process was enough to render it unpatentable, and the court ruled that it was not. The Patent Office took this narrow decision as a green light for unlimited patenting of software techniques, and even for the use of software to perform specific well-known and customary activities.

Most patent lawyers have embraced the change, saying that the new boundaries of patents should be defined over decades by a series of expensive court cases. Such a course of action will certainly be good for patent lawyers, but it is unlikely to be good for software developers and users.

One Way to Eliminate Software Patents

We recommend the passage of a law

to exclude software from the domain of patents. That is to say that, no matter what patents might exist, they would not cover implementations in software; only implementations in the form of hard-to-design hardware would be covered. An advantage of this method is that it would not be necessary to classify patent applications into hardware and software when examining them.

Many have asked how to define software for this purpose — where the line should be drawn. For the purpose of this legislation, software should be defined by the characteristics that make software patents especially harmful:

- Software is built from ideal infallible mathematical components, whose outputs are not affected by the components they feed into.
- Ideal mathematical components are defined by abstract rules, so that failure of a component is by definition impossible. The behavior of any system built of these components is likewise defined by the consequences of applying the rules step by step to the components.
- Software can be easily and cheaply copied.

Following this criterion, a program to compute prime numbers is a piece of software. A mechanical device designed specifically to perform the same computation is not software, because mechanical components have friction, can interfere with each other's motion, can fail, and must be assembled physically to form a working machine.

Any piece of software needs a hardware platform in order to run. The software operates the features of the hardware in some combination, under a plan. Our proposal is that combining the features in this way can never create infringement. If the hardware alone does not infringe a patent, then using it in a particular fashion under control of a program should not infringe either. In effect, a program is an extension of the programmer's mind, acting as a proxy for the programmer to control the hardware.

Usually the hardware is a general-purpose computer, which implies no particular application. Such hardware cannot infringe any patents except those covering the construction of computers. Our proposal means that, when a user runs such a program into a general-purpose computer no patents other than those should apply.

The traditional distinction between hardware and software involves a complex of characteristics that used to go hand in hand. Some newer technologies, such as gate arrays and silicon compilers, blur the distinction because they combine characteristics associated with hardware with others associated with software. However, most of these technologies can be classified unambiguously for patent purposes, either as software or as hardware, using the criteria above. A few gray areas may remain, but these are comparatively small, and need not be an obstacle to solving the problems patents pose for ordinary software development. They will end up being treated as hardware, as software, or as something in between.

Fighting Patents One by One

Until we succeed in eliminating all patenting of software, we must try to overturn individual software patents. This is very expensive and can solve only a small part of the problem, but that is better than nothing.

Overturning patents in court requires *prior art*, which may not be easy to find. The League for Programming Freedom will try to serve as a clearing house for this information, to assist the defendants in software patent suits. This depends on your help. If you know about *prior art* for any software patent, please send the information to the League (see the accompanying text box.)

If you work on software, you can personally help prevent software patents by refusing to cooperate in applying for them. The details of this may depend on the situation.

Conclusion

Exempting software from the scope of patents will protect software developers from the insupportable cost of patent searches, the wasteful struggle to find a way clear of known patents, and the unavoidable danger of lawsuits.

If nothing is changed, what is now an efficient creative activity will become prohibitively expensive. The sparks of creativity and individualism that have driven the computer revolution will be snuffed out.

To picture the effects, imagine that each square of pavement on the sidewalk has an owner and that pedestrians must obtain individual licenses to step on particular squares. Think of the negotiations necessary to walk an entire block under this system. That is what writing a program will be like in the future if software patents continue.

*Computer whiz Richard Stallman
is determined to make software free—even
if he has to transform the industry
single-handedly.*

Programs to the People

Simson L. Garfinkel

Simson L. Garfinkel is a free-lance science writer and a doctoral candidate in the MIT Media Laboratory. He is writing a book about Richard Stallman and Project GNU.

ACCORDING to the Software Publisher's Association (SPA), more than half of all programs currently in use are illegal copies. SPA estimates that unauthorized copying costs the software industry nearly $2 billion a year in lost revenue. The crooks aren't just pimply-faced pirates or vendors in Southeast Asia copying programs and shipping them back to the United States. Rather, all of us are to blame—small offices buying one copy of a word processor and using it on two computers, or people copying a program from work for use at home. After all, a copy of a program works as well as the original, so why pay?

Richard M. Stallman, president of the Cambridge-based Free Software Foundation (FSF), believes companies that sell programs give their customers the choice of being criminals or bad neighbors. People can break the law by copying programs for friends, or they can force friends to go and buy their own. "Imagine if somebody was going around your neighborhood saying 'I will give you all of these wonderful things if you promise not to let your neighbors have them,' " says Stallman. "To many people, that person would be the Devil." Six years ago, when he started the work his foundation supports, his motivation was to be part of a software-sharing community in which people can freely give copies of programs to their friends: "I decided that I was going to do it even if I had to write all the software myself."

What might have been an impossible task for anyone else was just a matter of punching in coding for Stallman, who many consider to be one of the world's greatest and most prolific programmers. Already he has helped create dozens of programming tools, many of them vastly superior to their commercially available counterparts, and broad acceptance by users has convinced several companies, such as Hewlett-Packard and Digital, to include his programs with their computer systems. At the forefront of his achievements is EMACS, a powerful program used by hundreds of thousands of people throughout the world. EMACS lets programmers perform an extensive range of tasks—from editing files to playing games—and they can alter it to their own liking and add their own features.

Moreover, the free-software movement Stallman has spearheaded is taking off. He has convinced hundreds of programmers to contribute their time and efforts. Most of the programs these people have produced are small improvements to other free programs that are already available, but others have been substantial projects, conceived, developed, and distributed as free software. Also, FSF has attracted more than $600,000 worth of gifts in cash and computer equipment. And last summer, Stallman was awarded a "genius grant" from the MacArthur Foundation in recognition of his work.

Stallman wants to create a family of free software so good that companies who do not use it could be driven out of business. In the process, he hopes to free computer users and return youthful hacker idealism to the computer world.

He may just do it.

Back to the Source

Programs, which allow computers to be word processors today and electronic spreadsheets or payroll-printers tomorrow, are something like a cross between a cookbook recipe and a mathematical proof. Each line of a program contains a set of instructions for the computer to execute at a certain time; around the instructions are comments that explain how the program works. Programmers call the collection of instructions and comments the "source code," and in the early days of computing, companies almost always provided it with the programs they sold. Programmers read the code to learn how programs worked and modified it to fix problems and add features. They even built new programs by taking parts from old ones and reassembling them.

But as the business of computing exploded in the 1970s and 1980s, companies began restricting access to source code so that competitors couldn't see how a program worked and write their own versions. Richard Stallman thinks that was a big mistake. Making source code available again is key to his free-software movement. He likes to explain why it's so important by telling the story of the first two laser printers at the MIT Artificial Intelligence Laboratory, where he was a researcher from 1971 until 1983.

The laser printers of the mid-1970s were the size of today's compact cars. When Xerox gave the AI lab a Xerox Graphics Printer, the only place for it was in the lab's ninth-floor machine room. Researchers connected the printer to the local area network that the lab was developing, and soon anybody in the building could print a 100-page document by typing in a few commands.

That worked fine, except that sometimes the printer would run out of paper or jam, and dozens of other jobs would pile up. Other times there would simply be a lot of people wanting to print long documents, and the person who needed to print a single page would have to run up and down the stairs or babysit the printer until that page appeared. But since the programmers at the lab had the source code to the program that ran the printer, they could add features that solved these problems. Soon the printer was helping the lab run smoothly. "It would send you a message when your document had actually been printed," recalls Stallman. "It would send you a message if you had anything queued and there was a paper jam."

All this changed in 1978, when Xerox replaced the machine with a new laser printer called a Dover but wouldn't share the printer's source code with the lab. "We wanted to put those features into the Dover program, but we couldn't," Stallman says. Xerox wouldn't put the features into the program either. "So we had to suffer with paper jams that nobody knew about."

Keeping source code proprietary hurts users in a wide variety of other ways as well. Say a real estate company with an accounting-system program that allows for 10 checking accounts suddenly finds itself in charge of 13 properties. The program may not be able to handle the additional accounts, and if the company doesn't have the source code, it will either have to change accounting practices or find a new program. If the real estate firm lacks the source code, it may not even be able to hire an outside programming firm to make the necessary changes. "It is a monopoly because only one company can provide you with fixes or updates or changes to that program," says Robert J. Chassell, FSF's treasurer. "It's like you bought a car but there was only one mechanic who was permitted to work on it, and he lived in another city. Americans and American law have been against monopolies for years and for good reason—it is bad for both industry and the public."

Although consumers theoretically have the choice of being able to buy a different program, that choice is often illusory. "People have spent money on a specific program, but more significantly, they have become habituated to it," explains Chassell, who was trained as an economist at Cambridge University in England. "The expense of changing to a new program is not buying it: the expense is unlearning one program and relearning a second one."

To add to the cost, most programs store their data files in a format that is not compatible with competing programs. Most people, says Chassell, will put up with two or three major problems with a program rather than make a change.

The Rise of UNIX

Until recently, people had the same problems switching between computers made by different companies that they have today switching between different application programs. The problem had to do with the operating system, the master control program that orchestrates the functions a computer performs: every computer had a different one, and all of them were incompatible. Computers made by IBM used an operating system called VM, while those made by Prime used PRIMOS. Digital Equipment Corp. had a variety of different operating systems—sometimes more than one for each computer that it sold.

For the hardware manufacturers, this was good business, because even if a company lost its competitive edge, it would still have a captive base of users who would have to keep buying its computers to run their old programs. And these users could be counted on to pay just about anything the company asked. From the users' point of view, this state of affairs was simply a fact of life. It added to costs, and there was nothing they could do about it. But for computer researchers, such "closed systems" were a nightmare.

If someone developed a program on one computer, those who had other kinds of machines had no access to any of the research that person had done.

Today, "open systems," which let users mix hardware and software components built by different vendors, are changing the computer industry. Compatibility makes more services and products available, while competition cuts prices. Open systems are, in fact, central to Stallman's mission to liberate software, though he can hardly be credited with originating the idea. At its core is a special operating system called UNIX and a programming language called C, both developed at Bell Labs in the 1970s.

UNIX, a pet project of AT&T researchers Ken Thompson and Dennis Ritchie, evolved into a programmer's dream. The system was composed of compact programs called tools, each of which performed a single function. By putting tools together, programmers could do complicated things. The operating system mimicked the way that programmers think. C, the programming language UNIX programs were written in, was created by Ritchie expressly to make them "portable"—that is, able to run on different computers. And unlike other portability schemes under development at the time, C was designed to be sleek, simple, and fast.

Nevertheless, problems remained. UNIX, which the AT&T researchers had developed on DEC computers, handled data a little differently than the operating system on IBM computers—which meant that UNIX programs, even if they were scrupulously written in C, didn't always work on an IBM. The Honeywell operating system was a little different still, creating a whole new set of obstacles. Programs that worked on one machine would mysteriously fail on others.

Then somewhere around 1976 Thompson and Ritchie made a breakthrough. They decided that although writing their programs in C was certainly a good idea, it wasn't enough. What they really needed to do, they reflected, was to move UNIX itself—after all, an operating system is just another program, and users could simply run UNIX instead of the system the computer manufacturer had supplied. It was a radical idea in an age when every computer and its particular operating system seemed to be inextricably linked.

By this time, UNIX had become more than just a research curiosity. As early as 1973, some 25 Bell Labs computers were running it, and the operating system soon spread outside of the telephone company. By 1977, more than 500 sites were using it, 125 of them at universities, among them the University of California at Berkeley.

UNIX took a new turn at Berkeley that shows just how much can be done when a source code remains available to users. Like other schools, Berkeley had paid $400 for a tape that included the complete source code to the operating system. But instead of merely running

UNIX, two bright graduate students, Bill Joy and Chuck Haley, started making changes. In 1977, Joy sent out 30 free copies of the Berkeley Software Distribution (BSD) UNIX, a collection of programs and modifications to the UNIX system.

Over the next six years, the BSD UNIX grew into an operating system of its own that had significant advantages over AT&T's. For example, a programmer using the BSD UNIX could switch between multiple programs running at the same time. AT&T's UNIX allowed the names on files to be no more than 14 letters long, but on Berkeley's they could stretch out to 255 letters. Berkeley also developed software to connect many UNIX computers together using high-speed networks. If there had been a popularity contest between the two systems, the BSD UNIX would have won hands down. And Berkeley never charged more than a modest duplication fee for its software.

Yet Berkeley didn't make a dent in AT&T's sales: since the university's system was based on UNIX, anybody who wanted to run it first had to purchase a source-code license for UNIX from AT&T. What's more, the company was beginning to realize the true value of the operating system it had spawned. In 1977, a commercial source-code license for UNIX cost $17,000, but by 1981, that price had jumped to $43,000.

Educational source-code licenses for UNIX were still under $1,000, so many universities bought the AT&T license, put the system that went along with it on the shelf, and ordered the BSD UNIX from Berkeley. But the businesses that were turning to UNIX couldn't justify spending tens of thousands of dollars just for a source code. Instead, they spent the few hundred dollars AT&T charged for versions of UNIX that didn't include the code. These firms couldn't make changes or see how programs were written, but they could still write their own applications.

Software War

Back at MIT, Richard Stallman and the AI lab had had their own brush with commercializing software—with very different results. In the late 1970s, the lab was peopled with students, professors, and staff that had drifted in during their high school or college days and never left. This tightly knit community of hackers seemed to live for programming alone. In many ways, what united them was that the lab had built its own computer, the Lisp Machine, and a whole new operating system designed for AI applications.

Progress in developing software for the Lisp Machine was swift: whenever somebody discovered a bug, it was fixed. If people wanted to add a feature to a program—make it do something useful that it hadn't done before—they went right ahead.

Encouraged by the academic success of their

machine, a group of hackers left the lab in 1980 to set up a company to commercialize the computer. They called it Lisp Machine Inc. (LMI). Soon a second group left and set up a company called Symbolics. Both companies licensed the Lisp Machine operating system from MIT, and a clause in their contracts specified that any improvements they made had to be returned to the Institute. So although competition between the two companies was fierce, they shared everything they learned. Any time anyone made an advance, everyone in the embryonic industry benefited. The hackers at the AI lab saw the cooperation between Symbolics, LMI, and MIT as a model for software development.

Then in 1982, Symbolics' lawyers reread their licensing agreement with MIT and discovered that while they had to give any new software they created back to the Institute, they didn't have to grant MIT the right to redistribute those ideas. Programmers at Symbolics developed a new feature for the operating system and refused to let MIT share it with LMI. Although the feature wasn't in itself a major advance, Symbolics' new policy was the death knell to software sharing.

"Stallman and I went into a crash mode," recalls Richard Greenblatt, the Lisp Machine's inventor. They refused to accept Symbolics' terms, and decided to reinvent the company's new feature for themselves. "We hacked around the clock for two solid weeks and finally put a comparable feature into the MIT sources."

For the following two years, Stallman took every improvement that Symbolics' programmers made and rewrote it for the operating system used by MIT and LMI. Programs that took Symbolics months to write he would rewrite in a matter of days. The only reason he did it, he says, was to punish Symbolics for breaking its promise to share software. He called it "the war."

But while he fought the war, Stallman's beloved AI lab fell apart. All the old hackers slowly left, siphoned off by LMI and Symbolics. "Machines would break and there was no one to fix them anymore—they had to be turned off and abandoned," he remembers. "It was a society that could no longer keep itself going. I was the last one who could keep it going, but I couldn't, because one person wasn't enough."

He also came to realize that his fight had little significance. The evolution of computer systems had bypassed the Lisp Machine, which was too specialized and expensive to produce. Stallman saw that the real enemy was not Symbolics but the entire software industry that was restricting access to source code.

In 1984, he decided that it was time to start a counterattack: "Instead of continuing to punish those who had destroyed the old software-sharing community, I wanted to start a new one." He quit his job at MIT. More than anything else, he didn't want a repeat of the Lisp Machine debacle—spending years on a project just to have it pulled out from under him and licensed to a company on MIT's terms. Then he sat down and started the task of building a new operating system.

What's GNU?

He called his brainchild GNU, a recursive acronym meaning GNU's Not UNIX.

As early as 1984, UNIX appeared to be on its way to becoming the operating system of the future. It was taking over the computer research world and making strong inroads in commercial computer systems. Versions of it were already available for most computers—from microcomputers to supercomputers—and engineers were rapidly adapting it to others. UNIX could even run on the lowly IBM PC. Stallman reasoned that a free version of the operating system, written completely from scratch, would have a large user base eager to accept it.

★★★★★★

Richard Stallman's mission to liberate all software began at MIT's Artificial Intelligence Laboratory back in 1982, when fellow hackers reneged on their tacit promise to share their ideas. Today, the movement he has spearheaded has taken off.

★★★★★★

But GNU would *not* be UNIX, even though all GNU software would also run on UNIX. Most significantly, the source code for any GNU program would be available to anyone who wanted it, and people would be able to freely redistribute their own copies of the software—both identical copies for friends and enhanced copies, like Berkeley's version of the original UNIX.

Stallman's main worry was that some company would take the operating system he wrote, make some changes, and then say that their "improved" programs were separate inventions and proprietary. To prevent that, he invented a new kind of licensing agreement, the "Copyleft," which lets people do anything they want with the software except restrict others' right to copy it. As Stallman says, "Forbidding is forbidden." The Copyleft furthermore requires that anybody who distributes a GNU program make its source code available for a nominal fee. And if any piece of a Copylefted program is included into another program, the entire resulting program is Copylefted.

Although Stallman expected that other programmers would eventually help him out with his project, at first he was on his own. When he discovered that nobody else had been assigned to his old office at the AI lab, he started sneaking back at night: he needed a computer to write GNU, and the machines at the lab were available. Soon he was working there days as well. Patrick H. Winston, the AI lab's director, knew about it, but he didn't say anything, since he saw Stallman's resignation as largely symbolic. If Stallman was going to continue writing good programs that other people in the lab could use, Winston wasn't about to tell the 13-year veteran to leave.

Within a year, Stallman's first program was out: GNU EMACS, which edits programs and does a much better job of it than the standard editor that comes with UNIX. EMACS is so powerful that people can use it to write programs, try them out, read electronic mail, browse through online documentation, find programming mistakes with the help of a debugger (also written by Stallman), and even play games. Programmers immediately saw the caliber of the promised GNU software and shared the program with their friends.

And then, just as Stallman had hoped, they started fixing his bugs and adding new features. The hard thing about writing a major program like EMACS, he explains, is starting it. Once the first version is available, people play with it and easily make substantial contributions. By producing just one crop of free software, Stallman bootstrapped a movement that has grown in momentum as the software has improved. Today hundreds of significant subsystems for EMACS have been contributed from around the world, and programmers have adapted it to more than 50 different kinds of computers. It runs on everything from desktop microcomputers to Cray supercomputers.

The success of EMACS led Stallman to found the Free Software Foundation, which gives a tax deduction to companies and individuals who want to contribute to Project GNU. Stallman describes it as "a charity for writing computer programs," and from that perspective, it has been highly successful, receiving $267,782 in donations in 1989 alone. The foundation also earned $330,377 from the sale of manuals and computer tapes containing GNU programs. Moreover, Stallman and the other FSF programmers no longer sneak around to use the AI lab's computers, since they have a fleet of high-performance workstations donated by Hewlett Packard, Thinking Machines, Sony, and even Bell Laboratories. Companies have donated cash as well, and paid for technical staff to spend a year in Cambridge working with Stallman.

The foundation uses the money it garners to pay its staff of fourteen, which includes nine programmers and three technical writers. Even though Stallman works for free, he doesn't expect everybody else to do the same. Nevertheless, FSF programmers earn only $25,000 a year, which is one-half to one-third the salary they would command on the open market. Paying low wages lets FSF take on more staff members, and it guarantees that they're all committed to the cause.

A Programming Coup

In the workstation and minicomputer market, GNU has already caught on strong. Many computer companies that sell UNIX-based systems—including Convex Computer Corp., which makes mini-supercomputers, and DEC—already include GNU software as part of their standard operating-system distribution. Data General and NeXT, Inc., the billion-dollar startup of Apple Computer's founder Steve Jobs, use GNU as the basis of their workstation line. About the only territory that remains untouched by GNU—and by UNIX as well—is the personal-computer market: the UNIX that runs on the IBM PC often costs more than $1,000 for a usable configuration. But the situation is due to change. As soon as the core of GNU is operational, something that Stallman expects before the end of 1991, GNU software will run on any personal computer based on the Intel 386 microprocessor—what is quickly becoming the standard machine—for free.

If EMACS made the computer world suspect that Project GNU was a force to be reckoned with, what clinched the matter was Stallman's second GNU program, something called the GNU C Compiler (GCC). Compilers are those critical programs that translate source code into "machine code," or language that a machine can use. But not all compilers are equal. Given the same source code, different compilers will produce different machine code. A certain compiler may generate machine code that is more efficient than another's, or it may make mistakes, so that its machine code doesn't work properly.

Stallman knew that he had to write a good C compiler; otherwise people wouldn't want to use it. But he didn't intend to write one of the best. Because it is free software, GCC simply *became* one of the best. Stallman implemented ideas that had been in textbooks for years, and then, since the compiler was distributed with the source code, programmers all around the world helped make it better.

Today the machine code GCC generates is more reliable than that from other commercially available compilers. The reason, say its users, is that people who discover bugs can figure out the fixes themselves by looking through the source code. All the bug reports—and the fixes—end up back on Stallman's workstation. New releases of the compiler come out nearly every month instead of every year, as is the case with most commercial software.

GCC can also generate code for more than 11 different kinds of microprocessors, while most commercial compilers are tailored to a specific microprocessor. Before Stallman wrote GCC, nobody believed a compiler that generated code for more than one kind of machine could be efficient, but Stallman's compiler is efficient indeed: it consistently produces machine code that runs 20 to 30 percent faster than the code from other commercially available compilers.

"The only way for other commercial compilers to continue to exist in the face of GCC is to offer features that GCC does not," says Don Seeley, a senior systems programmer at the University of Utah. "The many vendors whose compilers are not even current with old technology will lose. New compilers must be at least as good as GCC, or the market won't accept them."

It was rave reviews like Seeley's that convinced Ralph W. Hyver, who now manages Hewlett-Packard's Information Architecture Group, to give FSF a $100,000 cash grant and another $350,000 in equipment. Helping Stallman made sense, says Hyver, because many of the research groups that Hewlett-Packard was supporting were using GNU software. The company was also using GNU programs internally.

Another convert is NeXT. All of the software that it delivers with its computers is compiled with GCC. "The issue for us had nothing to do with proprietary versus non-proprietary," says Bud Tribble, NeXT's vice-president of software engineering. "We benchmarked many compilers, and found the GCC code produced to be excellent. The internal structure of GCC was also very clean and allowed us to extend it in several ways. If there had been another 'non-free' compiler that was better, we probably would have used it instead."

Conflicting Definitions of Freedom

Nevertheless, other companies have been reluctant to use GNU software. Some have spent millions of dollars developing their own C compilers and may feel threatened by a compiler Stallman developed essentially by himself. Engineers at Sun Microsystems, for example, refuse to even talk about GCC anymore. "They have all spoken with people about GCC in the past and believe that comparing our compilers with GCC quickly becomes a fairly unproductive philosophical discussion," says Erica Vener, a spokesperson for the company. "Bottom line, Sun is in the business of selling the products it develops."

But ironically, it is probably the Copyleft, more than anything else, that is preventing more widespread adoption of GCC and other GNU programs. Most companies aren't comfortable with the idea of selling a program only to have the customer turn around and make a copy for a friend. And they don't like the requirement that the source code be made available to anybody who asks for it.

At Berkeley, UNIX developer Mike Karels says that the software he writes is actually more free than Stallman's. Since the mid-1980s, Karels and the other researchers at Berkeley's Computer Systems Research Group (CSRG) have been working to isolate their programs from AT&T's. And it has paid off. By now, a "significant fraction" of their code has been "written from scratch," Karels notes. Berkeley gives those programs away to companies that do not have AT&T source-code licenses and imposes essentially no restrictions. The companies, in other words, may modify and resell the software without providing the source code to their customers.

Throughout the 1980s, CSRG developed a set of programs for networking computers. Firms bought the software, sometimes altered the source code and added features as they saw fit, and marketed the finished product. Today nearly every UNIX manufacturer sells a version of the Berkeley networking software, and some companies have even placed the programs into integrated circuits that are used inside IBM personal computers. Karels says none of that would have happened if Berkeley had required that the networking source code be made available to customers: companies would have been frightened away by the idea that they would somehow lose their competitive edge. And he adds that many users aren't interested in seeing the source code anyway.

Unfortunately, Berkeley's terms also mean that customers who buy Karels's programs from vendors have to rely on the vendors for bug fixes. This matters the most with security problems. In 1988, for instance, the infamous computer worm written by Robert T. Morris got through a hole in Berkeley's network mail program and shut down thousands of computers across the country. The fix, like many security-related fixes, required changing a single line of the mail program, and it was distributed over the network within a few hours after the worm had been stopped. But it was useful only to those schools and businesses that had the source code. Others had to get new versions of the mail program from their vendors, some of whom took more than a month to distribute them.

"We have been pushing for vendors to ship source code for security-critical functions," Karels says. But vendors haven't complied.

The Question of Support

Advocates of FSF believe it is precisely because of the Copyleft that GNU software will eventually dominate the computer industry. And, they say, by voting with their checkbooks, people are already forcing manufacturers to abandon their proprietary operating systems. Given the opportunity to use free software, many computer users might soon refuse to purchase anything else.

The pressure will become even more intense once FSF follows through on its plan to produce a spreadsheet program for workstations and advanced PCs that competes with Lotus's best-selling 1-2-3. Although at first the GNU spreadsheet will lack many of the features of

1-2-3, they will surely be added over time. Soon the only competitive advantage of 1-2-3 will be its name.

But who would pay for programmers to eat if all software were free? The same people that are now, says Stallman. Most programs are written for internal use, not for resale, and that will continue, he argues. A company that pays a programmer to write a word processor for drawing up reports and other such applications shouldn't care if that program is shared with another company—especially if the second company gives bug fixes and improvements back. GNU software will make programmers more productive, since they won't have to write each new application from scratch, Stallman points out. He's looking toward a future in which companies that sell computer programs earn their money not by using the copyright law to prevent people from making copies, but by offering services like support and training. If you had a personal computer, for example, you would pay company programmers to add extra features or help you use the ones already provided.

Naturally, not everyone is enthusiastic about the idea. "It is nice to say that we should just sell support and give away the software, but why?" asks Tom Lemberg, vice-president of Cambridge-based Lotus Development Corp. "The way our economic system works is that people who create value are able to get value by selling it."

Other critics note that in fact product support for GNU software has been lacking so far—and that this could prevent businesses from wholeheartedly adopting the programs. "Digital supports people in mass quantities," says Jon Hall, one of Digital's product managers for ULTRIX Workstation Software. "Thousands of customers at one time. Some of the customers are not even computer literate, much less UNIX literate." He contends that Digital can provide that level of support only by charging for its software and using the copyright system to prevent people from making their own copies.

But companies that exclusively supported free software would have lower costs. Michael Tiemann, who wrote a compiler for the G++ programming language, is banking on that idea: last January he founded Cygnus Support, a firm that writes, sells, and supports Copylefted software. Tiemann believes that wholesale adoption of GNU programs will be inevitable once there's a company willing to sign its name on the dotted line, charge an annual fee, and guarantee to fix any bugs and answer any questions a customer might have. Cygnus is that company.

In its first year of operation, Cygnus signed over a million dollars in support contracts. One of the clients is Intel, which needed a C compiler for a new microprocessor that it has developed. "They want to ship GCC as their standard compiler, but companies that they sell to are concerned that it is not a supported product. So they contracted with us to do the support for it," says David Wallace, another Cygnus founder. "We are also starting to get calls from people whose potential clients are telling them 'if it doesn't run the GNU software, we are not going to buy your hardware,'" he adds.

Wallace acknowledges that it will take years to wean the computer industry away from proprietary software. Yet he maintains that Stallman isn't just a fluke programmer, and that GCC is not just a lucky success. "The free-software part isn't a gimmick," he points out. "It is the very thing that makes the software so good."

legally speaking

Can Hackers Be Sued for Damages Caused by Computer Viruses?

The law can be a rather blunt instrument with which to attack a hacker whose virus has caused damage in a computer system. Among the kinds of damage that can be caused by computer viruses are the following: destroyed programs or data, lost computing time, the cost of system cleanup, and the cost of installing new security measures to guard against a recurrence of the virus, just to name a few. The more extensive and expensive the damage is, the more appealing (at least initially) will be the prospect of a lawsuit to seek compensation for the losses incurred. But even when the damage done is considerable, sometimes it may not be worthwhile to bring a lawsuit against the hacker whose virus has damaged the system. Careful thought should be given to making a realistic appraisal of the chances for a meaningful, beneficial outcome to the case before a lawsuit is filed.

This appraisal must take into account the significant legal-theory and practical difficulties with bring-

ing a lawsuit as a way of dealing with the harm caused by a hacker's virus. This column will discuss both kinds of difficulties. A brief synopsis of each type of problem may be helpful before going into detail about each. The legal theory problem is essentially this: There may not yet be a law on the books or clearly applicable legal precedents that can readily be used to establish a right to legal relief in computer virus situations. The law has lots of experience with lawsuits claiming a right to compensation for damage to persons or to tangible property. But questions may arise if someone seeks to adapt or extend legal rules to the more intangible nature of electronically stored information. The practical difficulties with using the law to get some remedy for harm caused by a hacker's virus can be even more daunting than the legal theory problems. Chief among the practical difficulties is the fact that the lawsuit alone can cost more than can ever be recovered from the hacker-defendant.

To understand the nature of the legal theory problems with suing a hacker for damage caused by his or her virus, it may help to understand a few basic things about how the law works. One is that the law has often evolved to deal with new situations, and evolution of this sort is more likely when fairness seems to require it. Another is that the law generally recognizes only already established categories of legal claims, and each of the categories of legal claims has its own particular pattern to it, which must be matched in order to win a lawsuit based on it. While judges are sometimes willing to stretch the legal category a little to reach a fair result, they are rarely willing to create entirely new categories of law or stretch an existing category to the breaking point. Because of this, much of what lawyers do is pattern-matching and arguing by analogy: taking a given set of facts relevant to a client's circumstances, sorting through various possible categories of legal claims to determine which of them might apply to the facts at hand, and then developing arguments to show that this case matches the pattern of this legal category or is analogous to it.

Whenever there is no specific law passed by the legislature to deal with a specific issue, such as damages caused by computer viruses, lawyers look to more general categories of legal claims to try to find one that matches a particular client's situation. "Tort" is the name used by lawyers to refer to a category of lawsuits that aim to get money damages to compensate an injured party for harm caused by another person's wrongful conduct. Some torts are intentional (libel, for example, or fraud). Some are unintentional. (Negligence is a good example of this type of lawsuit.) The harm caused by the wrongful conduct may be to the victim's person (as where someone's negligence causes the victim to break a leg) or property (as where a negligent driver smashes into another car, causing it to be "totaled"), or may be more purely economic losses (as where the victim has to incur the expense of renting another car after his or her car has been destroyed by a negligent driver). In general, tort law permits a victim to recover money damages for all three types of injuries so long as they are reasonably foreseeable by the person who causes them. (Some economic losses, however, are too remote to be recoverable.)

Among the categories of traditional torts that might be worth considering as the basis of a lawsuit seeking compensation for losses caused by a computer virus is the law of trespass. Though we ordinarily think of trespass in connection with unlawful entry onto another's land, the tort of trespass applies to more situations than this. Intentional interference with someone's use of his or her property can be a trespass as well. A potential problem with the use of trespass for computer virus situations, however, might be in persuading a judge to conceive of a virus as a physical invasion of a computer system. A defendant might argue that he or she was in another state and never came anywhere near the plaintiff's computer system to show that the trespass pattern had not been established. The plaintiff would have to counter by arguing that the virus physically invaded the system, and was an extension of the defendant who was responsible for planting it.

Another tort to consider would be the law of conversion. Someone who unlawfully "converts" someone else's property to his or her own use in a manner that interferes with the ability of the rightful owner to make use of it can be sued for damages by the rightful owner. (Conversion is the tort pattern that can be used to recover damages for theft; *theft* itself is more of a criminal law term.) As with trespass, the law of conversion is more used to dealing with interferences with use of tangible items of property, such as a car. But there would seem to be a good argument that when a virus ties up the computing resources of a firm or university, it is even more a conversion of the computing facility than if some component of the system (such as a terminal) was physically removed from the premises.

Even if a claim, such as conversion, could be established to get damages for lost computer time, that wouldn't necessarily cover all of the kinds of losses that might have been caused by the virus. Suppose, for example, that a virus invaded individual accounts in a computer system and sent out libelous messages masquerading as messages from the account's owner or exposed on a computer bulletin board all of the account owner's computer mail messages. Libel would be a separate tort for a separate kind of injury. Similarly, a claim might be made for invasion of privacy and intentional misrepresentation to get damages for injuries resulting from these aspects of the virus as well.

So far we have been talking mostly about intentional torts. A hacker might think that he or she could not be found liable for an intentional tort because he or she did not intend to cause the specific harm that resulted from the virus, but that is not how tort law works. All that is generally necessary to establish an intentional tort is that the person intended to do the conduct that caused the harm, and that the harm was of a sort that the person knew or should have known would be reasonably certain to happen as a consequence of his or her actions. Still, some hackers might think that if the harm from their viruses was accidental, as when an "experiment" goes awry, they might not be legally responsible for the harm. That is not so. The law of negligence allows victims of accidental injury to sue to obtain compensation for losses caused by another's negligence.

Negligence might be a more difficult legal claim to win in a computer virus case because it may be

---

The law of negligence allows victims of accidental injury to sue to obtain compensation for losses caused by another's negligence.

---

unclear exactly who had what responsibilities toward whom under the circumstances. In general, someone can be sued for damages resulting from negligence when he or she has a duty to act in accordance with a standard of care appropriate to the circumstances, and fails to act in accordance with that standard of care in a particular situation. Standards of care are often not codified anywhere, but depend on an assessment of what a reasonable person would do in the same set of circumstances. A programmer, for example, would seem to have a duty to act with reasonable care in writing programs to run on a computing system and a duty not to impose unreasonable risks of harm on others by his or her programming. But the owner of the computing system would also have a duty of care to create reasonable safeguards against unauthorized access to the computing system or to some parts of the computer system because the penchant of hackers to seek unauthorized entry is well-known in the computing community. The focus in a negligence lawsuit, then, might not be just on what the hacker did, but on what the injured party did to guard against injury of this sort.

Sometimes legislatures pass special laws to deal with new situations such as computer viruses. If a legislature was to consider passing a law to provide remedies for damages caused by computer viruses, there would be a number of different kinds of approaches it could take to formulate such a law. It is a tricker task than one might initially suppose to draft a law with a fine enough mesh to catch the fish one is seeking to catch without creating a mesh so fine that one catches too many other fish, including many that one doesn't want to catch.

Different legislative approaches have different pros and cons. Probably the best of these approaches, from a plaintiff's standpoint, would be that which focuses on unauthorized entry or abuse of access privileges because it limits the issue of wrongful conduct by the defendant to access privileges, something that may be relatively easy to prove. Intentional disruption of normal functioning would be a somewhat more demanding standard, but would still reach a wide array of virus-related conduct. A law requiring proof of damage to data or programs would, again from a plaintiff's standpoint, be less desirable because it would have stiffer proof requirements and would not reach viruses that merely disrupted functioning without destroying data or programs. The problem of crafting the right law to cover the right problem (and only the right problem) is yet another aspect of the legal theory problems posed by computer viruses.

Apart from the difficulties with fitting computer virus situations in existing legal categories or devising new legal categories to reach computer viruses, there are a set of practical difficulties that should be considered before undertaking legal pursuit of hackers whose viruses cause damage to computer systems.

Perhaps the most important set of practical difficulties with suing a hacker for virus damages is that which concerns the legal remedy one can realistically get if one wins. That is, even if a lawyer is able to identify an appropriate legal claim that can be effectively maintained against a hacker, and even assuming the lawyer can surmount the considerable evidentiary problems that might be associated with winning such a lawsuit, the critically important question which must be answered before any lawsuit is begun is what will one realistically be able to recover if one wins.

There are three sets of issues of concern here. One set relates to the costs of bringing and prosecuting the lawsuit. Lawsuits don't come cheap (and not all of the expenses are due to high attorney fees). Another relates to the amount of damages or other cost recoveries that can be obtained if one wins the lawsuit. It's fairly rare to be able to get an award of attorney's fees or punitive damages, for example, but a lawsuit becomes more attractive as an option if these remedies are available. Also, where the virus has spread to a number of different computer systems on a network, for example, the collective damage done by the hacker may be substantial, but the damage to any one entity within the network system may be sufficiently small that, again, it may not be economically feasible to maintain individual lawsuits and the collectivity may not have sufficiently uniform interests to support a single lawsuit on behalf of all network members.

But the third and most significant concern will most often be the ability of the defendant to write a good check to pay the damages that might be awarded in a judgment. Having a judgment for one million dollars won't do you any good if it cost you $10,000 to get it and the defendant's only asset is a used computer with a market value of $500. In such an instance, you might as well have cut your losses and not brought the lawsuit in the first place. Lawyers refer to defendants of this sort as "judgment-proof."

While these comments might suggest that no lawsuit should ever be brought against a young hacker unless he or she has recently come into a major inheritance, it is worth pointing out the law does allow someone who has obtained a judgment against another person to renew the judgment periodically to await "executing" on it until the hacker has gotten a well-paying job or some other major asset which can be seized to satisfy the judgment. If one has enough patience and enough confidence in the hacker's future (or a strong enough desire for revenge against the hacker), there may be a way to get some compensation eventually from the defendant.

Proof problems may also plague any effort to bring a successful lawsuit for damages against a computer hacker. Few lawsuits are easy to prove, but those that involve live witnesses and paper records are likely to be easier than those involving a shadowy trail of electronic signals through a computer system, especially when an effort is made to disguise the identity of the person responsible for the virus and the guilty person has not confessed his or her responsibility. Log files, for example, are constantly truncated or overwritten, so that whatever evidence might once have existed with which to track down who was logged onto a system when the virus was planted may have ceased to exist.

Causation issues too can become very murky when part of the damage is due to an unexpected way in which the virus program interacted with some other parts of the system. And even proving the extent of damages can be difficult. If the system crashes as a result of the virus, it may be possible to estimate the value of the lost computing time. If specific programs with an established market value are destroyed, the value of the program may be easy to prove. But much of the damage caused by a virus may be more elusive to establish. Can one, for example, recover damages for economic losses attributable to delayed processing, for lost accounts receivable when computerized data files are erased and no backup paper record was kept of the transactions? Or can one recover for the cost of designing new security procedures so that the system is better protected against viruses of this sort? All in all, proof issues can be especially vexing in a computer virus case.

In thinking about the role of the law in dealing with computer virus situations, it is worth considering whether hackers are the sorts of people likely to be deterred from computer virus activities by fear of lawsuits for money damages. Criminal prosecution is likely to be a more powerful legal deterrent to a hacker than a civil suit is. But even criminal liability may be sufficiently remote a prospect that a hacker would be unlikely to forego an experiment involving a virus because of it. In some cases, the prospect of criminal liability may even add zest to the risk-taking that is involved in putting a virus in a system.

Probably more important than new laws or criminal prosecutions in deterring hackers from virus-related conduct would be a stronger and more effective ethical code among computer professional and better internal policies at private firms, universities, and governmental institutions to regulate usage of computing resources. If hackers cannot win the admiration of their colleagues when they succeed at their clever stunts, they may be less likely to do them in the first place. And if owners of computer facilities make clear (and vigorously enforce) rules about what is acceptable and unacceptable conduct when using the system, this too may cut down on the incidence of virus experiments.

Still, if these measures do not succeed in stopping all computer viruses, there is probably a way to use the law to seek some remedy for damages caused by a hacker's virus. The law may not be the most precisely sharpened instrument with which to strike back at a hacker for damages caused by computer viruses, but sometimes blunt instruments do an adequate job, and sometimes lawsuits for damages from viruses will be worth the effort of bringing them.

Pamela Samuelson
Visiting Professor
Emory Law School
Atlanta, Ga.

Viruses and Criminal Law

Harry the Hacker broke into the telephone company computer and planted a virus that he expected would paralyze all telephone communications in the United States. Harry's efforts, however, came to naught. Not only did he make a programming error that made the virus dormant until 2089 instead of 1989, but he was also unaware that the telephone company's computer was driven by a set of preprogrammed instructions that were isolated from the effects of the virus. An alert computer security officer, aided by automated audits and alarm systems, detected and defused Harry's logic bomb.

A hypothetical situation, yes, but not one outside the realm of possibility. Let us suppose that Harry bragged about his feat to some friends in a bar, and a phone company employee who overheard the conversation reported the incident to the police and gave them Harry's name and address. Would Harry be guilty of a crime? Even if Harry had committed a crime, what is the likelihood that he could be convicted.

Before attempting to answer these questions, we must first know what a crime is. A crime is an act that society, through its laws, has declared to be so serious a threat to the public order and welfare that it will punish anyone who commits the act. An act is made criminal by being declared to be a crime in a duly enacted statute. The statute must be clear enough to give reasonable notice as to what is prohibited and must also prescribe a punishment for taking the action.

The elements of the crime must be spelled out in the statute. In successful prosecution, the accused must have performed acts that demonstrate the simultaneous presence of all of the elements of the crime. Thus, if the statute specifies that one must destroy data to have committed an alleged crime, but the act destroyed no data, then one cannot be convicted of that crime. If the act destroyed only student records of a university, but the statute defines the crime only for a financial institution, then one cannot be convicted under the statute.

All states now have criminal statutes that specifically address certain forms of computer abuse. Many misdeeds in which the computer is either the instrument or object of the illicit act can be prosecuted as more traditional forms of crime, such as stealing or malicious mischief. Because we cannot consider all possible state and federal statutes under which Harry might be prosecuted, we will examine Harry's action only in terms of the federal computer crime statute.

The United States Criminal Code, title 18, section 1030(a)(3), defines as criminal the intentional, unauthorized access to a computer used exclusively by the federal government, or any other computer used by the government when such conduct affects the government's use. The same statute, in section 1030(a)(5)(A), also defines as criminal the intentional and unauthorized access to two or more computers in different states, and conduct that alters or destroys information and causes loss to one or more parties of a value of at least $1000.

If the phone company computer that Harry illicitly entered was not used by the federal government, Harry cannot be charged with a criminal act under section 1030(a)(3). If Harry accesses two computers in different states, and his action alters information, and it causes loss to someone of a value of at least $1000, then he can be charged under section 1030(a)(5)(A). However, whether these conditions have been satisfied may be open to question.

Suppose, for example, that Harry plants his logic bomb on a single machine, and that after Harry has disconnected, the program that he loaded transfers a virus to other computers in other states. Has Harry accessed those computers? The law is not clear. Suppose Harry's act does not directly alter information, but merely replicates itself to other computers on the network, eventually overwhelming their processing capabilities as in the case of the Internet virus on November 2, 1988. Information may be lost, but can that loss be directly attributed to Harry's action in a way that satisfies the statute? Once again, the answer is not clear-cut.

And what of the $1000 required by the statute as an element of the crime? How is the loss measured? Is it the cost of reconstructing any files that were destroyed? Is it the market value of files that were destroyed? How do we determine these values, and what if there were adequate backups so that the files could be restored at minimal expense and with no loss of data? Should the criminal benefit from good operating procedures on an attacked computer? Should the salaries of computer personnel, who would have been paid anyway, be included for the time they spend to bring the system up again? If one thousand users each suffer a loss of one dollar, can one aggregate these small losses to a loss sufficiently large to be able to invoke the statute? The statute itself gives us noguidance so the courts will have to decide these questions.

No doubt many readers consider questions such as these to be nit-picky. Many citizens already are certain that guilty parties often use subtle legal distinctions and deft procedural maneuvers to avoid the penalities for their offenses. "If someone does something wrong, he or she should be punished and not be permitted to hide behind legal technicalities," so say many. But the law must be the shield of the innocent as well as a weapon against the malefactor. If police were free to invent crimes at will, or a judge could interpret the criminal statutes to punish anyone who displeased him or her, then we would face a greater danger to our rights and freedoms than computer viruses. We cannot defend our social order by undermining the very foundations on which it is built.

The difficulties in convicting Harry of a crime, however, go beyond the questions of whether he

has simultaneously satisfied each condition of some crime with which he can be charged. There remain the issues of prosecutorial discretion and the rules of evidence.

Prosecutors have almost absolute discretion concerning what criminal actions they will prosecute. That a prosecutor can refuse to charge someone with a crime, even someone against whom an airtight case exists, comes as a shock to many citizens who assume that once the evidence exists that someone has committed a crime, that person will be arrested and tried.

There are many reasons why a prosecutor may pass up the chance to nail a felon. One is that the caseload of the prosecutor's office is tremendous, and the prosecutor must choose the criminals who pose the greatest danger to society. Because

able about computers, few judges and even fewer jurors are. The presentation of the case, therefore, will be more difficult and time consuming, and the outcome less predictable. I am familiar with a case that took hundreds of hours to prepare and resulted in a conviction, but the judge sentenced the convicted criminal to pay only a small fine and serve two years probation. With such a result, one cannot be surprised that prosecutors ignore computer criminals when there are so many felons that courts obviously consider more worthwhile.

Suppose, for the sake of argument, that we have a prosecutor who is willing to seek an indictment against Harry and bring him to trial. Even then, computer-related crimes can pose special evidentiary problems. Remember that to convict Harry,

---

Even if the prosecutor is quite knowledgeable about computers, few judges and even fewer jurors are. The presentation of the case, therefore, will be more difficult and time consuming, and the outcome less predictable.

---

computer crimes are often directed against businesses rather than persons and usually carry no threat of bodily injury, they are often seen as low priority cases by prosecutors. Even computer professionals themselves do not seem to think that computer crime is very serious. In a 1984 survey by the American Bar Association, respondents rated computer crime as the third least significant category of illicit activity, with only shoplifting and illegal immigration being lower. With such attitudes among those responsible for computer security, who can blame prosecutors for turning their attention to crimes the public considers to be more worthy of law enforcement's limited resources?

Underlying the assessment of priority is a general lack of understanding about computers among prosecutors. Thus, a prosecutor would have to spend an unusual amount of time to prepare a computer crime case as opposed to a case that dealt with a more traditional, and hence better understood, mode of crime. Moreover, even if the prosecutor is quite knowledge-

the prosecutor must convince a jury beyond a reasonable doubt that Harry committed an act in which all of the elements of the crime were found simultaneously. The elements of the crime cannot be found to exist in the abstract; they must be found to apply specifically to Harry.

Apart from having to prove that the act caused the requisite amount of damage and that the computers used were those specified by the statute, the prosecutor would have to show that Harry committed the act and that he did so intentionally and without authorization. Because Harry was using someone else's account number and password, tying Harry to the crime might be difficult unless unusual surveillance was in place. A gunman and his weapon must be physically present at the teller's window to rob the bank, but a computer criminal may be thousands of miles away from the computer that is attacked. A burglar must physically enter a house to carry off the loot and may, therefore, be observed by a witness; moreover, it is generally assumed that someone carrying a television set out of a darkened house in the middle of the night is up to no good. By contrast, a computer criminal can work in isolation and secrecy, and few, if any, of those who happen to observe are likely to know what he is doing.

The evidence that ties the computer criminal to the crime, therefore, is often largely circumstantial; what is placed before the jury is not eyewitness testimony, but evidence from which the facts can only be reasonably inferred. Although convictions on the basis of circumstantial evidence alone are possible, they are often harder to obtain.

Adding to the prosecutor's difficulties in getting convincing evidence about Harry's acts are the unsettled constitutional issues associated with gathering that evidence. Does Harry have a reasonable expectation that his computer files are private? If so, then a search warrant must be obtained before they can be searched and seized. If Harry's files are enciphered, then must Harry furnish the key to decryption, or would he be protected from having to do so by his Fifth Amendment right against self-incrimination? The evidence that would convict Harry won't do the prosecutor much good if it is thrown out as having been obtained by impermissible means.

In the face of these difficulties, some have introduced bills into Congress and into some state legislatures that prohibit planting a virus in a computer system. But drafting a responsible computer crime bill is no easy task for legislators. The first effort at federal computer crime has proscribed, and even imposed heavy penalties for, standard computing practices. It did not clearly define what acts were forbidden. It was so broad that one could have been convicted of a computer crime for stealing a digital watch, and it did not cover nonelectronic computers. The bill was never enacted.

If we want a statute that targets persons who disrupt computer systems by planting viruses, then what do we look for in judging the value of proposed legislation?

Is the proposed statute broad enough to cover activity that should be prohibited but narrow enough not to unduly interfere with legitimate computer activity? Would an expert be able to circumvent the statute by designing a harmful program that would not be covered by the statute? Does the proposed statute clearly define the act that will be punished so as to give clear notice to a reasonable person? Does the act distinguish between intentional acts and innocent programming errors? Does the statute unreasonably interfere with the free flow of information? Does it raise a First Amendment free speech problem? These and other questions must be considered in developing any new computer crime legislation.

Where do I personally stand with regard to legislation against viruses, logic bombs, and other forms of computer abuse? It is not enough to say I am against conduct that destroys valuable property and interferes with the legitimate flow of information. The resolution of legal issues invariably involves the weighing of competing interests, e.g., permitting the free flow of information v. safe-guarding a system against attack. Even now, existing criminal statues and civil remedies are powerful weapons to deter and punish persons who tamper with computer systems. I believe that new legislation should be drawn with great care and adopted only after an open discussion of its merits by informed computer professionals and users.

The odds are that Harry the Hacker will never be charged with a crime, or, if charged, will get off with a light sentence. And that is the way it will remain unless and until society judges computer crimes, be they planting viruses or stealing money, to be a sufficiently serious threat to the public welfare to warrant more stringent and careful treatment. If such a time comes, one can only hope that computing professionals and societies such as the ACM will actively assist legislatures and law enforcement officials in dealing with the problem in an intelligent and technologically competent manner.

Michael Gemignani
Senior Vice President and Provost
University of Houston at Clear Lake
Houston, TX 77059

TIME BOMB

INSIDE THE TEXAS VIRUS TRIAL

Edward J. Joyce

Edward J. Joyce is a writer and consultant based in Lexington, KY.

> *Three years ago, Donald Gene Burleson was a highly regarded programmer at a large brokerage and insurance firm. Today, he stands convicted as a felon following what has been called the country's first "computer virus" trial. Here is the inside story of events leading to his prosecution and conviction as a computer saboteur.*

On Saturday morning, September 21, 1985, a computer operator at the Fort Worth, TX, headquarters of USPA & IRA Inc. sat down at his console to access the company's IBM System/38. To his initial puzzlement, he discovered that he could not perform routine maintenance functions. His annoyance turned to shock when he found that his security level had been changed. A short time later, accounting personnel who were working on preliminary financial reports at some of the 75 terminals connected throughout the system encountered an even more serious problem: About half of the firm's sales commission detail records—168,000 of them—had vanished.

Something awful had happened. The brokerage and insurance firm (its full name is United Service Planning Association, Inc. and The Independent Research Agency for Life Insurance Inc.) hadn't experienced a data loss of anything near that magnitude since acquiring the System/38 four years earlier. The commission records are critical to the generation of paychecks for the company's sales representatives, then numbering 400 in offices worldwide.

Several members of the USPA's Information Services staff, headed by William C. Hugenbert Jr., vice president

and director of MIS, were immediately summoned to the computer center. The first clue that they were up against something more than a routine hardware or software failure came when the operator examined the system log and noticed that the computer had been accessed from an on-site terminal at 3 a.m. that morning—a time when no one should have been in the locked building. Although there was no sign of forced entry, the police were called and notified of an apparent trespass.

Information management staffers, meanwhile, mapped out a detailed recovery plan. "Our first priority was to reconstruct the 168,000 sales commission detail records so field representative could be paid, and troubleshoot the causes of the problems later," recalls one of the staffers. They immediately took an internal "snapshot" of the System/38, copying the entire contents of its disks, both data and programs, to 15 tapes. Then they meticulously restored the sales records from backup tapes. The recovery took the entire weekend.

Early Monday morning, when the first few employees to arrive switched on their desktop terminals, things appeared to be operating normally. Within 10 minutes, however, the System/38 suddenly and inexplicably

Reprinted from *Computer Decisions*, December 1988, p. 43, by permission.

115

crashed. The weary analysts and programmers donned their troubleshooting caps again. This time, they discovered they were up against far more than a data restoration problem.

Someone recalled that during the weekend, while they were troubleshooting the missing sales records, one listing had come off the printer showing a CL (control language) program containing a single instruction: "power-down system." Because they were preoccupied with restoring data, no one paid much attention to the instruction at the time. When the system crashed Monday morning, however, they recovered the listing and examined it more closely. Tracing back through the code, they found that it was invoked by the selection of a menu option for a commonly used data retrieval application. Specifically, if anyone attempted to retrieve data from a certain file, the system would inevitably be taken down.

The power-down program was stamped with a creation date of September 3, 1985—almost three weeks prior to the problem. Staff analysts then went back to the system log and discovered that other programs, all designed to interact with one another and disrupt normal data processing operations, had also been created on the same day.

They would later refer to this latticework of destructive programs—at least one written in RPG—as "trip wires and time bombs." The series included instructions that would be triggered automatically if a certain area of the computer's memory was not reset to a predefined value. This routine was designed to wipe out two sections of memory at random, then duplicate itself, change its own name, and execute automatically one month later unless the memory area was reset. The destructive program—what would today be called a virus—had not been activated, but it was clear, in the words of one of the investigating analysts, that "the system could not be trusted."

At this point, USPA's I/S staff opted for a total restoration of the system from scratch to "decontaminate" it. "We had no idea of the extent of the damage or how many backup tapes were infected," one of the staffers explained later in court, "so we reloaded all software, including utilities, applications, and vendor products, from original copies. We even had IBM deliver a fresh copy of the CPF operating system."

Two days later, the totally rebuilt system was up and running for good. Company officials then turned their attention to the security breach and related problems.

From the time the first shreds of evidence pointing toward sabotage surfaced, suspicions centered on one individual. Donald Gene Burleson, a senior programmer who also functioned as the firms's computer security officer, had been fired on Thursday, September 18. He was, according to one former coworker, "a damned good systems programmer, very intelligent." Said another, "He could do anything with a computer." But associates also described Burleson as "arrogant and evasive" and "a fanatic who regularly rebelled against authority."

The latter terms were applied in the context of Burleson's role as a follower of the now-jailed tax protestor Irwin Schiff, who preaches on the fundamental unconstitutionality of the federal income tax. Burleson is said to

have carried on his own war against the government at USPA by using the company computer to write and store documents related to personal tax matters.

USPA doesn't allow such personal use of its computer system. When Burleson's unauthorized use of the system was discovered, he was called on the carpet by the company officials. Burleson flatly denied using the system for personal business. Thus, according to later court testimony, what began as a routine personnel reprimand escalated into a major confrontation. Noted one USPA observer, "A reasonable person would have admitted the transgression, promised not to do it again, and the matter would probably have been dropped. But his boldfaced lying created an atmosphere of mistrust that was unbecoming of a security officer, so he was fired."

It was a vengeful Burleson, company officials later charged, who entered the computer center at 3 a.m. on the following Saturday, blew away the 168,000 sales commission records, and activated the disruptive code sequences he had placed weeks before.

USPA officers acknowledge that the 40-year-old programmer surrendered a set of building keys at the time of his termination and that they expunged his password on the same day, per standard operating procedure. Some later heard that he had duplicate keys in his possession, and that he gained access to the system on the morning of September 21 through an unauthorized "backdoor" password. As a security officer, they point out, Burleson himself had responsibility for administering system passwords.

What USPA considered to be the smoking gun in its developing case against the fired programmer was the record of daily system logs that showed the development and planting of sabotage routines. There was no doubt that the programs had been edited and compiled repeatedly on September 3, during normal business hours, by someone working from the terminal in Burleson's private office. That person had logged on under Burleson's personal identification code.

Burleson claimed he was out of the office on September 3, even though company records, including the minutes of one meeting, show he was present. "The only way someone else could have worked from that terminal throughout that day, as the logs show, is if he had been sitting on Burleson's lap," quips a USPA source. But Burleson denied it all from the start, insisting that anyone could have walked into his office and planted the code in an attempt to frame him.

As company officers pondered their next move, they received a surprise notice from their former employee: *He* was suing *them* in small claims court for improperly withholding taxes from his last paycheck. USPA swiftly filed a countersuit seeking compensation for costs incurred as a result of the September 21 escapade. Although USPA had apparently suffered no permanent damage or loss of data, it figured that it had spent $12,000 for employee overtime, new locks, and related expenses to recover from the sabotage. In the ensuing civil suit, heard in June 1986, the company won a judgment against Burleson in that amount.

Long before the case went to civil court, it had attracted the attention of Davis McCown, a 30-year-old

VIRUSES, PESTS, AND POLITICS: STATE OF THE ART

Two months after the trial of Donald Gene Burleson, a computer "virus" again broke into the nation's headlines. This time the furor was the result of a violation of an electronic-mail system running under Unix on Arpanet, a nonclassified network set up by the U.S. Department of Defense in which a number of research facilities and universities participate.

The author of the invading program was Robert T. Morris Jr., a 23-year-old Cornell University graduate student. He is the son of the chief scientist at the National Security Agency's National Computer Security Center. The senior Morris, a former researcher at AT&T's Bell Laboratories, worked on the original Unix operating system.

Corporate computer security experts are quick to make a distinction between headline-garnering student exploits and the threat of real sabotage by invasive programming. The Morris program, they point out, was technically not a virus, but a subset that security experts now call a pest.

"A pest may have most of the characteristics of a virus," says Harry DeMaio, information security products manager for Deloitte Haskins & Sells in New York, "but it does not attach itself to other software, and therefore is harder to detect. And where a virus is usually designed to attack memory or storage, a pest simply multiplies to the point where its own ongoing replication chokes system resources."

Another classic pest, DeMaio points out, was the Christmas message program that brought down IBM's headquarters system last year.

That pest, which was eventually traced to a West German university, did exactly what the Morris pest did to 6,000 Unix nodes on Arpanet: It congested IBM's computers to the failure point.

The Arpanet breach by a student—even one called brilliant by his acquaintances—does raise a point: If Donald Burleson was able, according to the findings of a Texas jury, to plant a self-replicating, self-concealing virus program in an IBM System/38 three years ago, what is the real potential for malicious state-of-the-art programming today?

"I wouldn't say there has been any great leap forward in systems programming capability," says DeMaio. "It's the tremendous growth of connectivity that constitutes a greater threat." Given the current rate of networking activity, much of it carried out ad hoc outside the purview of the corporate I/S staff, there is a high probability that many organizations have already lost track of parts of their connective scheme. DeMaio, who put in 30 years with IBM and was the company's top security consultant, adds that organizations are "heading further into an environment where the entire business is run on the computer—there's much greater dependency so there's more destructive potential."

What worries the experts most about viruses is that when they are discovered, it's almost always by accident, so the total extent of the problem remains unfathomed. Also, a high percentage of known infestations have been either initiated or protracted by

unwitting users' provision of seemingly benign software as "carriers" of bugs.

"Viruses can reinfect programs that have been cleaned up," states Fred Cohen, a professor at the University of Cincinnati and publisher of pioneer studies on computer viral phenomena. "They can survive many generations of program changes and upgrades. Even the most thoroughly verified program might become infected in its executable form. Typical change control mechanisms do not stop or detect this."

The network security problem is massive and will, despite an already developing ground swell of attempts by end-user organizations and other vested interests to spike it, inevitably lead to demands for new levels of centralized I/S intervention and control. Eric Allman, original developer of the electronic-mail program on Arpanet, left a "backdoor" access in place that Morris apparently discovered and exploited, just as Donald Gene Burleson had used his own back door into the security scheme he designed. "By making something harder to break into it also makes it harder to use, [so] there's a constant trade-off," Allman told *The New York Times.*

Corporate I/S can thus expect a new outbreak of political friction over connectivity-based security issues. Since the courts have been leaning toward holding top management responsible in recent cases involving information security breaches, however, it might not be hard to get some attention.

—Robin Nelson

assistant district attorney in the Tarrant County section of economic crime. McCown believed criminal charges could be filed against Burleson under an untried Texas statute voted into effect on September 1, 1985. The statute, known as the "harmful access to a computer" law, makes it a felony offense to "intentionally and knowingly cause a computer to malfunction or interrupt the operation of a computer; or alter, damage, or destroy a computer program stored, maintained, or produced

by a computer without the effective consent of the owner." The statute had not yet been tested in court, and McCown felt that he had the acid test.

In the past, prosecutors have had only limited success in prosecuting computer crimes. Such cases are usually presented before a court under various criminal mischief laws, but there is frequently no physical evidence of any crime. Prosecutors often try to negotiate out-of-court settlements when the details of computer cases

4. ETHICAL AND LEGAL ISSUES

'We had no idea of the extent of the damage or how many backup tapes were infected, so we reloaded all software.'

appear too technical for a typical jury to grasp. However, laws similar to the Texas statute, defining computer mischief itself as a crime, have now been passed by 48 states and the federal government.

McCown first presented the USPA case before a grand jury that handed down an indictment of Burleson in January 1986. The indictment was invalidated, however, because of a misspelled name; then, a initial re-indictment was quashed by a defense motion challenging the wording in a section dealing with the deleted commission records. A second re-indictment finally stuck. The trial finally got underway on September 6, 1988.

Generally, such protracted delays work in favor of defendants—witnesses tend to forget, evidence is lost or misplaced, and so forth. In this instance, the delay worked in the prosecutor's favor. "The district attorney did a remarkable job of becoming familiar with the intricacies of USPA's computer system during that time," noted one observer familiar with the case. "He did a lot more homework than the defense."

"I had taken some computer and programming courses in college, and my wife is a systems analyst at General Dynamics," McCown explains. "Over the years, I've had a lot of exposure to computers." McCown adds that he received valuable assistance in preparing his case from USPA's I/S staffers, who helped him sort through endless listings and supplied him with a set of System/38 operating system manuals for reference during the proceedings.

As the trial unfolded, the media played the case as a watershed event. *USA Today* headlined it as the "first computer virus trial." Coverage also appeared in *Time, US News & World Report, Business Week,* and Associated Press accounts in newspapers throughout the country. It was, in fact, hardly the first time anyone had gone to court because of computer code tampering. But the specificity of the new law coupled with the current computer virus hysteria undoubtedly hyped the level of interest.

Burleson's defensive strategy was based on deflecting two of the prosecution's primary arguments. He called David Kinney, a Los Angeles-based consultant, as an expert witness to testify that there were no signs of embedded software anomalies—no virus codes—in the USPA computer at the time of the incident. Burleson also produced a signed credit card receipt indicating he had been more than 200 miles from the Fort Worth area the day the software time bombs and trip wires were allegedly planted from the terminal in his office.

Kinney, a former IBM employee who was involved in the original development of the System/38, was paid by Burleson to examine parts of the tape "snapshot" USPA made of its flawed system on September 21. The trial judge had ruled previously in Burleson's favor on the question of access to the tapes for preparation of his defense. During subsequent cross-examination, however, McCown was able to demonstrate that Burleson gave Kinney only those tape segments covering uncontaminated parts of the system, and avoided showing him sections containing the introduced code.

It was during Kinney's testimony, according to McCown, that the term "virus" got introduced into the proceedings. "We were staying away from it," McCown recalls, "trying to keep our definitions very precise. I wouldn't have applied it as loosely as he did." From that point on, however, the Texas Virus Trial was in full swing.

McCown then showed the jury that the credit card receipt establishing Burleson's whereabouts on September 3, 1985, was printed on a form that American Express did not introduce until 1987, thereby pegging it as a forgery. Burleson's defense was crumbling.

"The defense lawyer hoped to cloud the jury's understanding of the computer evidence—what he called 'technical mumbo jumbo'—and plant a reasonable doubt in their minds as to the guilt of the defendant," McCown recalls. "But the majority of the jury panel understood the technical issues. And once we proved that Burleson had fabricated the evidence to support his alibi for September 3, he didn't have a leg to stand on."

On September 19, 1988, the jury of six men and six women deliberated for six hours before finding Burleson guilty of a third-degree felony. A month later, he received a sentence of seven years' probation and was ordered to pay USPA $11,800 for the civil judgment awarded in 1986.

Karen Burns, a senior programmer/analyst at Texas-New Mexico Power Co. in Fort Worth and one of three computer professionals on the jury, says she had no trouble following the "technical mumbo jumbo" during the proceedings. "The district attorney did an excellent job," Burns says. "At one point he even showed the jury a hexadecimal dump of object code and made it understandable. Regardless of the spoken testimony, however, the computer logs contained sufficient evidence to show the defendant's guilt. In effect, the computer proved he did it."

Kinney, however, maintains that the incriminating computer logs could easily have been doctored by another USPA employee to frame Burleson. "The evidence was grossly inadequate to prove or disprove the guilt of the defendant," argues Kinney, who thinks the case could be dismissed for insufficient evidence by a higher court.

Burleson's attorney, Jack Beech, insisted that his client is innocent and says he will appeal the decision. But Beech also confided that he hadn't expected anybody to be able to successfully prosecute the case because of the technical nature of the evidence. "I had to learn a completely new language," says Beech of his own experience during the trial. "When I cross-examined witnesses and would ask them something like 'What was deleted?,' they'd hem and haw around, then throw three or four [technical] words at me, and ask if I meant physically deleted or something else. I'll probably go take a computer course next time around."

Besides the possible appeal, Burleson could find himself back in court for another reason. McCown says his office is considering filing perjury charges against Burleson based on the fabricated credit card receipt.

Following Burleson's conviction, USPA's president, Lamar C. Smith, was asked to comment. "We are gratified by the decision of the jury members, and wish to compliment them for their sagacity," he said. "Additionally, the Tarrant County District Attorney's office should be commended for its vigorous and expert prosecution of the case. Our MIS director, who was the prosecution's best witness, and his staff fully supported the DA's efforts." Smith then added that the incident had never compromised any sensitive data, such as client records.

MIS Director William Hugenberg cites company policy in declining to comment on the Burleson conviction or any changes in computer security at USPA since 1985. However, one step USPA is known to have taken involves physical security: Six months after the episode, the company substantially upgraded its physical security system when it moved into a new building, now patrolled during off hours by a guard. In addition, current users of its corporate system are pointedly reminded of the consequences of unauthorized access every time they log on. The following message appears along with the password prompt on the screen of each terminal: "The unauthorized use of this Computer System or its contents and/or the attempt to gain unauthorized access thereto constitutes a violation of the Texas Penal Code."

Juror Burns believes there are several lessons for information managers in the USPA experience. "Generally, computer security consciousness has increased dramatically in recent times—at my company, for example," she says, "When USPA had its problem in 1985, its security was probably average for an installation of that size. Considering the events presented in the trial, though, I'd caution MIS directors to review and possibly upgrade physical security. Also, system security responsibilities should be delegated to several individuals."

No company relishes involvement in the kind of unpleasant, highly publicized legal battle that a computer tampering case can bring. With public attention being drawn to the sensational aspects of sophisticated computer

'Once we proved Burleson fabricated the evidence to support his alibi, he didn't have a leg to stand on.'

viruses that can migrate between, as well as within, systems, the temptation to keep the lid on such incidents can be strong. McCown, however, stresses that I/S managers must cooperate fully with authorities to bring the perpetrators of computer crime to justice. "I'm concerned that many companies never prosecute these crimes," he says. "They may be put off by what customers will think, afraid they won't get a conviction, and would just as soon prefer to sweep the dirt under a carpet and forget about it. If everyone takes this attitude, computer crooks won't ever have to worry about suffering the legal consequences of their crimes."

McCown says USPA didn't hold back. "On the contrary," he notes, "the company fully supported our efforts in the case and is to be commended for shouldering its civic responsibility." Over a period of several weeks after the Burleson verdict was delivered, McCown got calls from nine different enforcement officials from across the country, plus one in Canada. All of the officials wanted advice on the prosecution of computer crimes that are under active investigation.

Perhaps the most important security issue brought to light by this case is that of hiring practices and employee background checks. Although Burleson committed his alleged crime in 1985 and lost the civil suit in 1986, he apparently had no problem staying employed at other data processing shops. Even at the time of his criminal trial, Burleson was working as a programmer at a Dallas telemarketing company and was reportedly dismissed by the firm only after his picture appeared in a newspaper story about the trial.

On the day he was sentenced, as he walked from the courtroom, Burleson was asked if he intended to remain employed in the computer industry. His answer came without hesitation: "I sure do," he said.

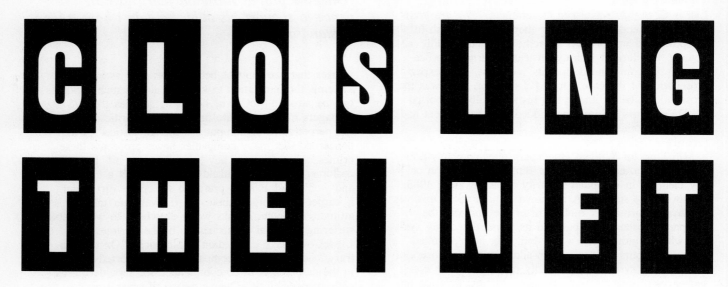

CLOSING THE NET

Will overzealous investigations of computer crime render freedom of the press technologically obsolete?

GREG COSTIKYAN

Greg Costikyan is a writer of fiction and nonfiction who has designed 23 commercially published games.

Back in early February, newspapers across the country reported that computer hackers were interfering with emergency calls over the 911 communications network. The reports said the hackers had penetrated the system using information from a secret computer document.

The scare grew out of an indictment by a grand jury in Lockport, Illinois. On February 7, Craig Neidorf and Robert Riggs were indicted on seven counts of wire fraud, violation of the Computer Fraud and Abuse Act of 1986, and interstate transportation of stolen goods.

Prosecutors alleged that Neidorf and Riggs had conspired to steal, using fraudulent methods, a confidential and proprietary document from the Bell South telephone company. This document, it was claimed, could allow computer hackers to disrupt the 911 emergency network.

The arrest of Neidorf and Riggs was only the beginning. The Secret Service, which has authority over crimes involving government computers, had embarked on a vast, nationwide investigation of hacker activity: Operation Sun Devil.

Imagine the night face of North America, shining not with cities but with lines of light showing the transmission of data. Brightest are New York City, the financial capital, and California, the technological capital, with Wash-ington, D.C., a close third. The lines that crisscross the country are telephone wires and cables, microwave transmissions, and packet-switching networks designed for computer communication. Here and there, beams dart into space to reflect off satellites and back to earth.

The computer networks in this country are huge. The largest are entities like UseNet and InterNet, which link every academic computing center of any size and are accessible to every scientist, university student, and faculty member in the nation. The networks also include government-operated systems, such as MilNet, which links military computers that do not carry confidential information. And there are the commercial services, such as Dow Jones News/Retrieval, SportsNet, CompuServe, GEnie, and Prodigy. CompuServe is the largest of these, with half a million subscribers.

In addition to these massive entities are thousands of tiny bulletin board services, or BBSes. Anyone with a computer and a modem can start a BBS; others can then call it up and use it. BBSes offer, in miniature, essentially the same services that the commercial nets offer: the ability to chat with others by posting messages to an electronic bulletin board and the ability to upload and download software and text files. There are more than 5,000 BBSes in the United States, most of them operated for fun. Few charge their users. In my local calling area alone, I know of BBSes for writers, gamers, Macintosh enthusiasts, gays, and the disabled—and I'm sure there are others.

The vast majority of BBSes deal with unexceptionable topics. But some boards deal with questions of computer security. These attract hackers.

Naturally, hackers discuss their hobby: breaking into computers. Usually, however, bulletin board discussions are general in nature. Hackers are not stupid, and they know that posting credit card numbers or the like is evidence of criminal activity. By and large, BBS discussions rarely, if ever, contain information that would be illegal if published in print form. It's not illegal, after all, to tell your readers how to commit illegal acts. If it were, books like *The Anarchist's Cookbook* and *Scarne on Cards* (and half the murder mysteries in print) would be banned.

The laws dealing with electronic transmissions, however, are far from clear. And the methods used to enforce these vague laws set a dangerous precedent for abridging freedom of speech.

In the future, the Net—the combination of all the computer networks—will be the primary means of information transmission, with print publication merely its adjunct. The Net will replace the press, and users of the Net must enjoy precisely the freedoms enjoyed by the press. If users of the Net have to worry about police surveillance, if censorship is rife, if the state forbids mere discussion of certain topics—then the liberty for which the Founders fought will have been destroyed, not by war or tyranny, but by mere technological change.

From the government's point of view,

the arrest of Neidorf and Riggs did not end the threat to the 911 network. The document they had stolen was not a single piece of paper that could be returned to its rightful owner. It was an electronic document that Riggs had downloaded from a Bell South computer.

Riggs belonged to a hacker group called the Legion of Doom, whose members shared information. It was likely that others in the group had copies of the 911 document. Worse, Riggs had uploaded the 911 document to a bulletin board service in Lockport, Illinois. Neidorf had downloaded the file from the Lockport BBS. Anyone else who used the same BBS could have downloaded it, too, meaning that dozens of people might have this dangerous information. Worse yet, Neidorf had published an edited version of the Bell South document in an issue of his underground computer magazine, *Phrack*.

Unlike conventional magazines, *Phrack* never saw a printing press; it was distributed electronically. After preparing an issue, Neidorf would dispatch it, via various computer networks, to his address list of 1,300 names. Any recipient could then upload the magazine to a bulletin board or to one of the academic or commercial nets. That meant thousands, perhaps millions, of people had access to the information in the Bell South document.

We may imagine that the Secret Service was gravely concerned about the potential threat to emergency services. If not, their subsequent actions are hard to fathom.

On March 1, 1990, employees of Steve

Jackson Games, a small game company in Austin, Texas, arrived at their place of business to find that they were barred from the premises. The Secret Service had a warrant, and the agents conducting the search wouldn't let anyone in until they were done.

The agents ransacked the company's offices, broke a few locks, and damaged some filing cabinets. They searched the warehouse so thoroughly, says company founder Steve Jackson, that afterward it "looked like a snowstorm," with papers strewn randomly. The agents confiscated three computers, a laser printer, several pieces of electronic equipment (including some broken equipment from a storeroom), several hard drives, and many floppy disks. They told Jackson they were seizing the equipment "as evidence" in connection with a national investigation.

Among the equipment seized was the computer through which S.J. Games ran a BBS to communicate with customers and freelancers. It had never been a congregating point for hackers and was about as much a threat to the public order as a Nintendo game.

The loss of the equipment was bad enough. Worse, the Secret Service seized all existing copies—on hard drives, floppy disks, *and* paper—of S.J. Games' next product, a game supplement called GURPS Cyberpunk. The loss of that data shot Jackson's publication schedule to hell. Like many small publishers, S.J. Games runs on tight cash flow. No new products, no income. No income, no way to pay the bills.

Over the next several weeks, Jackson was forced to lay off about half of his 17 employees. By dint of hard work, he and his staff managed to reproduce the data they'd lost, mostly from memory. S.J. Games finally published GURPS Cyberpunk as "The Book Seized by the Secret Service." It has sold well by the (low) standards of the field.

Jackson estimates the raid has cost him more than $125,000, a sum a small company like his can ill afford. (The company's annual revenue is less than $2 million.) He was nearly put out of business by the Secret Service.

What justified the raid and the seizures? Apparently, this: The managing editor of Steve Jackson Games is Loyd Blankenship. Blankenship ran The Phoenix Project, a BBS of his own in the Austin area. Blankenship consorted with hackers. He was fascinated by the computer underground and planned to write a book about it. He may or may not have once been a hacker himself. He certainly knew and corresponded electronically with admitted members of the Legion of Doom.

But perhaps Blankenship's worst luck was this: An issue of Neidorf's *Phrack* magazine included an article titled "The Phoenix Project." As it happens, that article had nothing to do with Blankenship's BBS of the same name. But the Secret Service was well aware of the contents of *Phrack*. Indeed, the revised indictment of Neidorf and Riggs, issued in July, cited the article by title. The same morning that the Secret Service raided Steve Jackson Games, agents awakened Blankenship and held him at gunpoint as they searched his house. They seized his computer and laser printer as "evidence."

Consider the chain of logic here. Robert Riggs is accused of a crime. Riggs belongs to a group. Loyd Blankenship is friends with other members of the group, though not with Riggs himself. Steve Jackson Games employs Blankenship. Therefore, the Secret Service does grievous financial injury to Steve Jackson Games. This is guilt by association taken to an extreme.

Neither Blankenship, nor Steve Jackson Games, nor any company employee, has ever been charged with so much as spitting in a public place. The Secret Service refuses to comment, saying only that S.J. Games was not a target of the investigation.

The company is now receiving legal help from the Electronic Frontier Foundation, an organization devoted to promoting civil liberties in electronic media. The Secret Service has returned most—but not all—of the company's seized equipment. Some of it is broken and irreparable. The government has made no offer of restitution or replacement.

On May 8, 1990, the Secret Service ex-

ecuted 28 or more search warrants in at least 14 cities across the country. The raids involved more than 150 agents, plus state and local law enforcement personnel.

According to a press release from the U.S. Attorney's office in Phoenix, the operation targeted "computer hackers who were alleged to have trafficked in and abused stolen credit card numbers [and] unauthorized long-distance dialing codes, and who conduct unauthorized access and damage to computers." The agency claimed the losses might amount to millions of dollars. In later releases and news reports, that figure was inflated to tens of millions of dollars.

Nationwide, the government seized at least 40 computers and 23,000 disks of computer information. In most cases, the subjects of these searches have remained anonymous. Presumably, they have either been advised by counsel to remain silent or have been so intimidated that they wish to attract no further attention.

John Perry Barlow reports in *Whole Earth Review* that the Secret Service held families at gunpoint while agents charged into the bedrooms of teenage hacker suspects. He adds that some equipment seizures deprived self-employed mothers of their means of support. These reports remain unconfirmed. It's clear, however, that the Secret Service closed down a number of BBSes by the simple expedient of seizing "as evidence" the computers on which those BBSes operated.

Bulletin board services are venues for speech. They are used mainly to exchange information and ideas. Nothing in the nature of the technology prevents the exchange of illegal ideas. But in a free society, the presumption must be that, in absence of proof to the contrary, the use of a medium is legitimate. The Secret Service has not indicted, let alone convicted, the operators of any of the BBSes closed down on May 8.

If law enforcement officials suspect that a magazine, newspaper, or book publisher may be transmitting illegal information, they get a warrant to search its files and perhaps a restraining order to prevent publication. They don't, however, seize its printing presses to prevent it from operating. A clearer violation of freedom of the press could hardly be imagined. Yet that is precisely what the Secret Service has done to these BBSes.

One of the BBSes closed down was the JolNet BBS in Lockport, Illinois, which Neidorf and Riggs had used to exchange the 911 document. Ironically, JolNet's owner, Richard Andrews, had triggered the investigation by noticing the document, deciding it was suspicious, and notifying the authorities. He had cooperated fully with the investigators, and they rewarded him by seizing his equipment.

The Ripco BBS in Chicago was among

those raided by the Secret Service. Operated by Bruce Esquibel under the handle of "Dr. Ripco," it was a freewheeling, wide-ranging board, one of the best known BBSes in the Chicago area. Speech was extraordinarily free on the Ripco board.

"I felt that any specific information that could lead to direct fraud was not welcome and would be removed, and persons who repeated violating this themselves would be removed from the system also," Esquibel writes. But just about anything else was open for discussion. Hackers did indeed discuss ways of breaking into computers. And the Ripco board contained extensive text files, available for downloading, on a variety of subjects to which some might take exception. For instance, there was a series of articles on bomb construction—material publicly available from books such as *The Anarchist's Cookbook*.

Along with the computer on which Ripco operated, the Secret Service seized two other computers, a laser printer, and a 940-megabyte WORM drive, an expensive piece of equipment. The additional seizures mystify Esquibel. "My guess is that after examining the rat's nest of wires around the three computers, they figured anything plugged into the power strip must have been tied in with [the rest] in some way," he says.

The Secret Service has yet to return any of Esquibel's equipment. He has yet to be charged with any crime, other than failure to register a firearm. (He had three unlicensed guns at his office; he informed the Secret Service agents of this before they began their search.) Says Esquibel, "The government came in, took my personal property to determine if there was any wrongdoing somewhere. It seems like a case of being guilty until proven innocent....It's just not right....I am not a hacker; [I don't] have anything to do with credit cards or manufactured explosives. Until the weapons charge I never had been arrested, and even my driving record has been clean since 1978."

It appears that the Secret Service has already achieved its goal. The Ripco board was a place where "dangerous" speech took place, and the agency closed it down. Why bother charging Esquibel with a crime? Especially since he might be acquitted.

Secret Service agents searched the home

of Len Rose, a computer consultant from Baltimore, on May 8. The agents not only seized his computers but confiscated every piece of electronic equipment in the house, including his fax machine, along with some family pictures, several boxes of technical books, and a box containing his U.S. Army medals.

On May 15, Rose was indicted on four counts of wire fraud, aiding and abetting wire fraud, and interstate transportation of stolen goods. Among other things, the indictment alleged that Rose is a member of the Legion of Doom, a claim both he and admitted Doomsters vociferously deny.

The interstate-transportation charge is based on the fact that Rose was in possession of source code for Unix, an operating system used by a wide variety of minicomputers and computer workstations. (Source code is the original text of a program.) In theory, Unix is the property of AT&T, which developed the system. AT&T maintains that Unix is protected as a confidential, unpublished work. In fact, AT&T has sold thousands of copies across the country, and every systems programmer who works with Unix is likely to have some of the source code lying around.

The wire-fraud counts are based on the fact that Rose sent a copy of a "Trojan horse" program by electronic mail. Trojan horse programs are sometimes used by hackers to break into computers; they are also sometimes used by system managers to monitor hackers who try to break in. In other words, a Trojan horse program is like a crowbar: You can use it to break into someone's house, or you can use it to help renovate your own house. It has both legitimate and illegitimate uses.

Rose is a computer consultant and has dealt with security issues from time to time. He maintains that his Trojan horse program was used solely for legitimate purposes—and, in any case, would no longer work, because of changes AT&T has made to Unix since Rose wrote the program. Rose is not charged with actually attempting to break into computers, merely with possessing a tool that someone could use to break in. In essence, the Secret Service found Len Rose in possession of a crowbar and is accusing him of burglary.

By seizing Rose's equipment, the Secret Service has effectively denied him his livelihood. Without his equipment, he cannot work. Rose says he has lost his home, his credit rating and credit cards, his business, and some of his friends. He can no longer afford to retain his original attorney and is now represented by a public defender.

Rose's difficulties are compounded by a theft conviction arising from a dispute with a former client regarding the ownership of computer equipment. Nevertheless, it seems brutal for the Secret Service to deny him the means to support his family and to pay for an effective defense. Investigators must long ago have gleaned whatever evidence his equipment may have contained.

Ultimately, the case against Neidorf and

Riggs fell apart. In June, the grand jury issued a revised indictment. It dropped the charges of violating the Computer Fraud and Abuse Act and added seven new counts of wire fraud, some involving electronic mail between Neidorf and Riggs. Neidorf was charged with two counts of wire fraud for uploading issues of *Phrack* to JolNet. In other words, mere distribution of his publication was deemed to be "fraud" because *Phrack* contained material the Secret Service claimed had been obtained by fraudulent means. The new indictment also reduced the "value" of the document Riggs allegedly stole from more than $70,000 to $20,000.

On July 9, Riggs pleaded guilty in a separate indictment to one count of conspiracy in breaking into Bell South's computer. Sentencing was set for September 14—after Neidorf's trial was to begin. Riggs agreed to be a witness for the prosecution of Neidorf.

On July 28, Neidorf's trial began in Chicago. Within four days, it was over. The prosecution's case had collapsed.

Under cross-examination, a Bell South employee admitted that the stolen document was far from confidential. Indeed, any member of the public could purchase a copy by calling an 800 number, requesting the document, and paying $13—far less than the $20,000 claimed value or the $5,000 minimum required to support a charge of transporting stolen goods across state lines.

Testimony also revealed that the contents of the document could not possibly allow someone to enter and disrupt the 911 network. The document merely defined a set of terms used in telecommunications and described the procedures used by Bell personnel in setting up a 911 system.

Riggs, testifying for the prosecution, admitted that he had no direct knowledge that Neidorf ever gained illegal access to anything; that Neidorf was not himself a member of the Legion of Doom; and that Neidorf had not been involved in the initial downloading of the document in any way.

In short, Neidorf and Riggs had not conspired; therefore, Neidorf should not have been charged with the fraud counts. The only value of which Bell South was "deprived" by Riggs's downloading was $13; therefore, he was, at worst, guilty of petty theft. The interstate-transportation counts were moot, since the "stolen goods" in question were worth less than the $5,000 minimum.

Not only was there no case against Neidorf—there also was no case against Riggs. The government dropped the case against Neidorf. Riggs, however, had already pleaded guilty.

The computer nets do need policing.

Computer crooks can steal and have stolen millions of dollars. But a balance must be struck between civil liberties and the legitimate needs of law enforcement. The laws as currently constituted are inadequate from both perspectives, and the Secret Service seems determined to interpret them with a callous disregard for civil liberties.

To attack computer crime, prosecutors primarily use the statutes dealing with wire fraud and interstate transportation of stolen goods, the Computer Fraud and Abuse Act of 1986, and the Electronic Communication Privacy Act of 1986. The wire fraud statute prohibits the use of the telephone, wire services, radio, and television in the commission of fraud. The courts have, logically, interpreted it to apply to electronic communications as well.

The interstate transportation statute prohibits transportation of stolen goods valued at $5,000 or more across state lines. Neidorf's lawyer moved to dismiss those counts, claiming that nothing tangible is transported when a document is uploaded or downloaded. The judge ruled that tangibility was not a requirement and that electronic transmission could constitute transportation. The Computer Fraud and Abuse Act prohibits knowingly, and with intent to defraud, trafficking in information that can be used to gain unauthorized access to a computer.

The Electronic Communications Privacy Act makes it a crime to examine private communications transmitted electronically. Among other things, it requires law enforcement agencies to obtain search warrants before opening electronic mail. It is unclear whether electronic mail files on a BBS's hard drive are covered by a warrant that permits seizure of the hard drive, or whether separate warrants are needed for each recipient's mail.

The reliance on fraud statutes to fight computer crime presents problems. Fraud is the use of chicanery, tricks, or other forms of deception in a scheme to deprive the victim of property. Most attempts by hackers to gain illegal access to a computer do involve chicanery or tricks, in some sense—the use of other people's passwords, the use of known bugs in systems software, and so on. Much of the time, however, a hacker does not deprive anyone of property.

If the hacker merely signs on and looks around, he deprives the computer operators of a few dollars of computer time at worst. If he downloads a file, the owner still has access to the original file. If the file's confidentiality has value in itself—as with a trade secret—downloading it does deprive the owner of something of value, but this is rarely the case.

We need a "computer trespass" statute, with a sliding scale of punishments corresponding to the severity of the violation. Just as burglary is punished more severely than trespass, so a hacker who steals and uses credit card numbers ought to be punished more severely than one who does nothing more than break into a computer and examine a few public files. In the absence of such a scheme, law enforcement personnel naturally try to cram all computer violations into the category of fraud, since the fraud statutes are the only laws that currently permit prosecution of computer crimes. As a result, petty crimes are charged as felonies—as with Neidorf and Riggs.

Legitimate users and operators of computer networks need to be protected from arbitrary seizures and guilt by electronic association. The criminal code permits law enforcement personnel to seize equipment used in a crime or that might provide criminal evidence, even when the owner has no knowledge of the crime. But the purpose of such seizures is to allow the authorities access to evidence of criminal activity, not to shut down businesses. Searchers need not remove computer equipment to inspect the files it contains. They can sit down and make copies of whatever files they want on the spot. Even if they expect some piece of incriminating material to be hidden particularly well—for example, in a specially protected file or in a ROM chip—it is unreasonable to hold onto the seized equipment indefinitely.

And it's clearly wrong to seize equipment that cannot, by any stretch of the imagination, contain incriminating data. In both the Steve Jackson and Ripco cases, the Secret Service seized laser printers along with other equipment. Laser printers have no permanent memory (other than the factory-supplied ROM chips that tell them how to operate). They print words on paper, that's all. They cannot contain incriminating information.

Even computers themselves cannot possibly constitute evidence. When you turn off a computer, its memory dies. Permanent data exist only on storage media—hard drives, floppy disks, tape drives, and the like. Even if law enforcement personnel have some compelling reason to take storage media away to complete a search, they have no reason to take the computers that use those media.

Just as a computer is not evidence because it once carried incriminating information, a network is not a criminal enterprise because it once carried data used in or derived from fraudulent activity. Yet under current law, it seems that the operator of a bulletin board is liable if someone posts an illegal message on it. Say I run a BBS called Mojo. You dial Mojo up and leave Mario Cuomo's MasterCard number on the board, inviting anyone to use it. Six people sign on, read the message, and fly to Rio courtesy of the governor before I notice the message and purge it. Apparently, I'm liable—even though I had nothing to do with obtaining Cuomo's credit card number, never used it, and strenuously object to this misuse of my board.

Such an interpretation threatens the very existence of the academic and commercial nets. A user of UseNet, for instance, can send a message to any other user of UseNet. The network routes messages in a complex fashion—from Computer A to Computer B to Computer C, and so on, depending on what computers are currently live, the volume of data transmitted among them, and the topography of the net itself. The message could pass through dozens of computers before reaching its destination. If someone uses the message to commit fraud, the system operators of every computer along its path may be criminally liable, even though they would have no way of knowing the contents of the message.

Computer networks and BBSes need the same kind of "common carrier" protection that applies to the mails, telephone companies, and wire services. Posting an illegal message ought to be illegal for the person who posts it—but not for the operator of the board on which the message appears.

The main function of the Net is to promote communication. People use it to buy goods, research topics, download software, and a myriad of other things as well, but most of their computing time is spent communicating: by posting messages to bulletin boards, by "chatting" in real time, by sending electronic mail, by uploading and downloading files. It makes no sense to say that discussion of a topic in print is OK, but discussion of the same topic via an electronic network is a crime.

Yet as currently interpreted, the law says that mere transmission of information that someone *could* use to gain access to computers for fraudulent purposes is itself fraud—even if no fraudulent access takes place. The Secret Service, for instance, was willing to indict Neidorf for publishing information it thought could be used to disrupt the 911 network—even though neither Neidorf nor anyone else actually disrupted it. We must clearly establish that electronic communications are speech, and enjoy the same protections as other forms of speech.

The prospects for such legal reform are not bright. Three times in this century, technological developments have created new venues for speech: with radio, with television, and with cable. On the grounds of scarcity, government restricts freedom of speech on radio and television; on the grounds of natural monopoly, government regulates speech on cable. Recent events, such as the conviction of former Cornell graduate student Robert T. Morris for introducing a virus into the nationwide ARPANet, have aroused worry about hacker crimes. But concern for the rights of legitimate users of computer nets has not received the same level of publicity. If anything, recent trends lean toward the adoption of more draconian laws—like the Computer Fraud and Abuse Act, which may make it illegal even for computer security professionals to transmit information about breaches of security.

The Net is vast—and growing fast. It has

already changed the lives of thousands, from scientists who learn of new breakthroughs far more quickly than if they had to wait for journal publication, to stay-at-home writers who find in computer networks the personal contact they miss without office jobs. But the technology is still in its infancy. The Net has the capacity to improve all our lives.

A user of the Net can already find a wide variety of information, from encyclopedia entries to restaurant reviews. Someday the Net will be the first place citizens turn to when they need information. The morning paper will be a printout, tailored to our interests and specifications, of articles posted worldwide; job hunters will look first to the Net; millions will use it to telecommute to work; and serious discussion will be given to the abolition of representative government and the adoption of direct democracy via network voting.

Today, we are farmers standing by our country lanes and marveling as the first primitive automobiles backfire down the road. The shape of the future is murky. We cannot know what the Net will bring, just as a farmer seeing a car for the first time couldn't possibly have predicted six-lane highways, urban sprawl, the sexual revolution, and photochemical smog. Nonetheless, we can see that something remarkable is happening, something that will change the world, something that has the potential to transform our lives. To ensure that our lives are enriched and not diminished, we must ensure that the Net is free.

Individual Privacy in the Information Age

While computer crime and sabotage pose a clear danger to the property and safety of individuals or organizations, another serious—though largely unperceived—threat arises from the application of computers to problems of societal management. One possibility is that a malign power might use computers to impose an Orwellian "Big Brother" type of totalitarian rule over an unwilling populace. In the spring of 1989, the People's Republic of China used all the information technology at its disposal to identify and search out dissidents who participated in prodemocracy demonstrations. News reports of foreign journalists as well as telephone and facsimile messages to and from China were intercepted and studied by the government in its search for "counterrevolutionaries." The government also used its control of information technology to make sure that its citizens got only the "official" version of events. In light of these developments, it is tempting to ask whether the full integration of computing technology into Chinese society was a tool for or against the people. This question is explored in *The New Republic* editorial, "Our Chip Has Come In."

Information technology in the hands of the governed can be a powerful tool against government oppression, however. For example, more than one observer has noted that a good "democracy barometer" is the number of telephones relative to the size of the population; the higher the telephone to people ratio, the more democratic the society. The argument is that where there are many telephones, it is simply too hard for a government to keep track of who's calling whom or what they're talking about. (There are still very few telephones in China.) The technological empowerment argument has, of course, been extended to computing. When ordinary people have access to computing, information can be generated and spread very quickly. As encouraging as this is, the proliferation of computers, electronic data bases, and networking does pose threats to individual privacy.

Some of these dangers are quite unintended and may accompany legitimate and socially desirable uses of information technology. One such threat comes from the problems associated with managing the huge, powerful organizations that pervade modern society. A German sociologist, Max Weber (1864–1920), argues that the magnitude and complexity of modern social enterprises would be impossible without big organizations. It is not uncommon for organizations to have capital resources and budgets in the millions of dollars or to employ thousands of people or serve millions of clients spread across continents. Just keeping track of and effectively managing resources in such organizations can be a nightmare. Also,

once established, organizations can take on a life and momentum of their own. Unfortunately, organizations sometimes pursue their legitimate interests in ways that conflict with the rights and freedoms of individuals or other organizations.

All of the articles in this section highlight conflicts of interest between organizations and individuals. In "Is Nothing Private?" the kinds of personal information in the electronic data banks of government agencies, commercial business, and credit bureaus are described. Also discussed is how electronic records are being sold and matched against other sources of data, and a brief overview of U.S. legislation intended to protect the privacy of electronic data on individuals is provided. An excellent illustration of unintended computer-organizational threats is presented in "Absolutely Not Confidential." Clark Norton describes the threat to individual privacy posed by computerized medical databases in this article.

In "Read This!!!!" Jill Smolowe discusses how information in one type of electronic data base is used by mass marketers to send out "junk mail." As Smolowe explains, junk mail has its virtues—for both businesses and consumers. But it also generates a great deal of garbage, annoys a number of people, and because it relies on computerized personal information, it raises concerns about privacy. David Churbuck elevates the "junk information explosion" issue to another plane and discusses junk phone calls, junk fax messages, and junk electronic mail in "Prepare for E-Mail Attack." He also describes some new and forthcoming technologies that will enable people to deflect unwelcome electronic intrusions. One of these new tools is "Caller ID," a telephone accessory that displays the number of incoming phone calls. In the final article, Jeff Johnson reviews advantages and disadvantages of Caller ID. He concludes that, for business, the advantages are great. For individuals, its benefits are doubtful and the service may erode rather than protect their privacy.

Looking Ahead: Challenge Questions

Freedom of information is necessary to ensure a democratic society but it can also threaten individual privacy. In order to resolve this contradiction, Yoneji Masuda has proposed that the right to privacy is an outmoded social value. He proposed that the "human right to protect secrets . . . change into a human duty or ethic to share information." What are the pros and cons of Masuda's proposal?

Must we give up our right to personal privacy for the sake of the "Information Society"? Why or why not?

IS NOTHING PRIVATE?

COMPUTERS HOLD LOTS OF DATA ON YOU—AND THERE ARE FEW LIMITS ON ITS USE

Last spring, the long arm of American Express Co. reached out and grabbed Ray Parrish. After getting his credit card in January, the 22-year-old New Yorker promptly paid bills of $331 and $204.39 in February and March. Then he got a surprising call. His credit privileges were being suspended, an American Express clerk informed him, because his checking account showed too small a balance to pay his April charge of $596. A contrite American Express now says it should have asked before peeking, and it reinstated Parrish after he paid his bill from his savings and cash on hand. But that was beside the point. "I felt violated," says Parrish, who has kept his card because he needs it. "When I gave them my bank account number, I never thought they would use it to routinely look over my shoulder."

Well, Ray Parrish, welcome to the Information Age. Over the past couple of decades, computers have collected a vast store of data on average people. Like Parrish, who gave American Express the right to snoop when he signed its credit card application, everyone has parted with the most private details in applying for mortgages, drivers' licenses, even telephone service. Few people realize that this information is largely unprotected by rules, laws, or codes of ethics. Instead, it is free to be pored over, analyzed, and sold and perhaps paired with other data to draw an intimate profile based on a person's daily habits. Says Robert Ellis Smith, editor of the Washington (D.C.) newsletter *Privacy Journal:* "For very little cost, anybody can learn anything about anybody."

Much of this information begins its journey at one of the three leading credit bureaus, the companies that verify for lenders the creditworthiness of prospective borrowers. Between them, TRW in Orange (Calif.), Equifax in Atlanta, and Trans Union Credit Information in Chicago have 400 million records on 160 million individuals. All guard their information. It's hard to steal. But it's easy to buy. The credit bureaus themselves sell at least 300 variations of it, broken down by such categories as sex, age, and income. They sell lists of people they think may go bankrupt and then sell consumers who worry about being on such lists their own credit reports. Beyond that, they supply so-called superbureaus, a second tier of perhaps 200 credit agencies that generally serve small customers ignored by the Big Three. And by reputation, at least, the superbureaus tend to sell to almost anyone.

To test that, one of BUSINESS WEEK's editors signed up with two superbureaus, identifying himself as an editor at McGraw-Hill Inc. He told one fib: that he might be hiring an employee or two and would need their credit reports. After a perfunctory check, both bureaus gave him carte blanche—and revealed the surprising breadth of their files (page 132). Provided with just the names and addresses of two of his colleagues, one superbureau produced their credit reports—including their Social Security numbers that the editor didn't have—for $20 apiece. The superbureau manager warned that one colleague's mortgage was ominously large, then offered to fax the reports.

The second arrangement was more open-ended. For a $500 initial fee, the editor got access via his home computer to the superbureau's data base. Free to explore, he again checked on his colleagues, at about $15 per report. Then, he ran two names whose prominence might have set off alarms if the credit agency audited the use of its files. One was Representative Richard J. Durbin (D-Ill.), the other Dan Quayle.

'WE HELP.' There were no alarms. A request for plain Dan Quayle at an Indiana address listed in an old *Who's Who in the Midwest* turned up an "a.k.a. J. Danforth Quayle" with a Washington-area address. There was nothing juicy. The Vice-President charges more at Sears, Roebuck & Co. than at Brooks Brothers. He has a big mortgage. His credit card number at D. C. area Merchants Bank is.... Sixteen digits long. But Quayle is not amused. "We find the invasion-of-privacy aspect of the credit situation disturbing," says a spokesman. "Further controls should be considered."

As the credit bureaus point out, there are plenty of legitimate uses for financial histories—especially now. With individual bankruptcies rising 25% annually, to about 80,000 this year, and with about 4% of all consumers not paying credit card and mortgage bills, lenders are becoming more wary. "The better we get, the more we help them reduce losses," says Richard D. C. Whilden, executive vice-president and general manager of TRW Information Systems Group. James O. Perkins, president of the credit bureau division at Equifax, adds that when Equifax projects an individual's bankruptcy, based on up to 40 factors such as his payment history and how fast he's running through lines of credit, "lenders are usually surprised." But about 90% of the time, he adds, Equifax is right.

For marketers, moreover, the credit bureaus are "a remarkable asset," says William L. Edwards, an analyst for Volpe, Covington & Welty, an investment company in San Francisco. "They have files on nearly every consumer in the largest consumer market in the free world." As much as $2 billion will be spent this year finding the right people to pitch products to. And in a wasteland of inaccurate lists, says Denison Hatch, editor of the newsletter *Who's Mailing What,* "the credit bureaus are offering up-to-date, technologically driven information." Now, it's possible to buy the names of Hispanics who earn $500,000 a year and have $10,000 available on their credit cards. Or the names of every person within a 50-mile radius of Dallas with $1 million in the bank. With few

exceptions, selling such information is perfectly legal. And profitable. The credit bureaus' margins before taxes from this end of the business run about 25%.

But should credit information be as easy to buy as knickknacks at a weekend bazaar? If all that results is more

junk mail, it's hard to find fault. But what if the consequences are greater? It's just a short step to "behavorial manipulation," says George B. Trubow, a privacy expert and professor at John Marshall Law School in Chicago. And there are other nagging issues.

THE RIGHT TO PRIVACY: THERE'S MORE LOOPHOLE THAN LAW

His bank cost Theodore Cizik his job. In 1983, the former controller at a New Jersey company sided with his employer in a dispute with Midlantic National Bank/North—just after he applied for his own loan there. When Cizik wouldn't budge, he claims, the bank got even. It told Cizik's boss that he had a Rolls-Royce and Mercedes—assets he had wanted kept secret but had listed on his loan application—and the bank suggested that he had been moonlighting. Fired from his $45,000 job on that pretext, he says, Cizik sued the bank, and ultimately settled out of court.

Cizik's case highlights a startling fact: Almost no information is private. Only rarely, moreover, can individuals find out that information on them is being used. With about 10 privacy laws on the books, how can that be? The laws are narrow, and full of holes.

'BORK BILL.' The Fair Credit Reporting Act of 1970 is a case in point. It sounds good. It gives individuals the right to see and correct their credit reports and limits the rights of others to look at them. But it has five exceptions, including a big one: Anyone with a "legitimate business need" can peek. Legitimate isn't defined.

Then there's the Right to Financial Privacy Act of 1978. It forbids the government to rummage through bank-account records without following set procedures. But it excludes state agencies, including law enforcement officials, as well as private employers. And more exceptions are tacked on every year. Says John Byrne, the federal legislative counsel for the American Bankers Assn.:

"There's not a lot to this act anymore."

The best protection, in fact, is for customers of video stores. In 1987, a Washington (D. C.) weekly, *The City Paper*, published a list of videotape titles borrowed by Robert H. Bork, then a U. S. Supreme Court nominee. Outraged, lawmakers passed the Video Privacy Protection Act of 1988. Called the Bork Bill, it bars retailers from selling or disclosing video rental records without a customer's permission or a court order. While this is a breakthrough of sorts, privacy advocates say it's silly to pass such laws when medical and insurance records remain unprotected. Others find it ironic that the government itself continues to reveal more than anyone else.

For instance, the Privacy Act of 1974 was supposed to bar federal agencies from sharing information on U. S. citizens, a practice called matching. But it's O. K. to share information if the

disclosure is consistent with the purpose for which the stuff was collected. That's called the routine use exception. In 1977, Health, Education & Welfare Secretary Joseph A. Califano Jr. crafted the exception to help root out welfare cheats by letting HEW review federal payroll records (page 76). His reasoning: Efficiency is a goal of all federal agencies. So they can share data to ensure it.

WATCHING WATCHERS. Today, matching remains alive and well. When Congress passed last year's Computer Matching & Privacy Protection Act, which regulates the way federal agencies verify eligibility for benefits or recoup delinquent debts, it gave the government explicit permission to perform frequent matches. It tossed a bone to the subjects of matches. Before their benefits can be cut off, an agency needs two pieces of proof for its findings. And it has to notify individuals who are under suspicion.

Every bit helps, of course, but reformers want more. George B. Trubow, the former general counsel to the White House Right to Privacy Committee, wants a federal data protection agency to "watch the watchers." David F. Linowes goes further. The former chairman of the U. S. Privacy Protection Commission, which was set up by the Privacy Act, is in favor of rules without exceptions. And he would give individuals $10,000 in punitive damages every time an abuse occurs. An interesting idea. But not one that Congress is likely to buy soon— at least not outside of video stores.

By Michele Galen, with Jeffrey Rothfeder, in New York

THE MAJOR LAWS ON PRIVACY

FAIR CREDIT REPORTING ACT (1970) Bars credit agencies from sharing credit information with anyone but authorized customers. Gives consumers the right to review their credit records and be notified of credit investigations for insurance and employment.
▶ But the law lets credit agencies share information with anyone it reasonably believes has a "legitimate business need"

PRIVACY ACT (1974) Bars federal agencies from letting information they collect for one purpose be used for a different purpose.
▶ The law's exceptions let agencies share data anyway

RIGHT TO FINANCIAL PRIVACY ACT (1978) Sets strict procedures when federal agencies want to rummage through customer records in banks.
▶ But the law doesn't cover state and local governments. And a growing list of exceptions let the FBI and U.S. attorneys grab files

VIDEO PRIVACY PROTECTION ACT (1988) Prevents retailers from disclosing video-rental records without the customers' consent or a court order. It also forbids the sale of the records.
▶ Privacy supporters want the same rules for medical and insurance files

COMPUTER MATCHING & PRIVACY PROTECTION ACT (1988) Regulates computer matching of federal data for verifying eligibility for federal benefits programs or for recouping delinquent debts. Requires the government to give individuals a chance to respond before taking adverse action.
▶ Limited in scope, the law leaves many potential matches unaffected, including those done for law enforcement and tax purposes

DATA: BW

The information the credit bureaus end up with usually has been provided for a specific use—in American Express' case, to help customers establish a credit record. "It's disturbing to see companies" repackage and sell it without approval, says Jonathan Linen, president of the Direct Marketing Group at American Express, since that tells competitors who his best customers are. And when individuals "find out what's going on," adds Ken McEldowney, director of San Francisco-based Consumer Action, "they are appalled."

Karen Hockman certainly was. Last fall, she told a caller trying to sell long-distance service from ITT that she doesn't make many out-of-town calls. "I'm surprised to hear you say that," she recalls him saying. "I see from your phone records that you frequently call Newark, Delaware, and Stamford, Conn." A spokesman says ITT "has very little control" over the 13 telemarketing companies working for it. But that's no comfort to Hochman, a direct-mail consultant in New York. "I was shocked, scared, and paranoid," she recalls. "If people are able to find out who I call, what else could they find out about me?"

Like viruses and hackers, it's a modern dilemma. "Computers have outstripped our ability and that of our laws to safeguard privacy," says David F. Linowes, a University of Illinois professor. He chaired the 1977 U.S. Privacy Protection Commission, which warned that use of computers for collecting and sharing personal information was getting out of hand. Indeed, with the cost of computing dropping rapidly and data flowing more freely, it won't be long, say privacy advocates, before practically anyone can do it. That will worsen a problem already noted by Priscilla Regan, chief researcher at Congress' Office of Technology Assessment (OTA): Most citizens have little idea what files on them exist, and it's "nearly impossible for individuals to learn how these records are being used."

'MELTDOWN.' At least 10 federal laws ostensibly protect individual privacy. But most of them are weakened by fist-size loopholes (see page 129). During the Reagan Presidency, moreover, the Federal Trade Commission, which oversees the credit bureaus, suffered what some staffers call a "regulatory meltdown" that left the Fair Credit Reporting Act (FCRA) of 1970 unattended. With a flat budget for eight years—a decline if adjusted for inflation—"the agency can hardly survive," says Albert A. Foer, an FTC staffer in the Ford and Carter Administrations and now chief executive at Melart Jewelers Inc. In Washington. The FTC's Credit Practices Group, the FCRA watch-dog, has lost nine of its 42 staffers.

This isn't especially surprising, given the government's own record as a snoop. That started on a large scale in 1977, the year that Joseph A. Califano Jr. decided to make the Health, Education & Welfare Dept. more efficient. Califano's idea was to compare thousands of files of welfare recipients with government payroll records—and root out double-dippers. This meant bending the 1974 Privacy Act, which prohibits federal agencies from sharing information without an individual's consent. But Califano insists it was worth it. He claimed millions in savings, which "kept Great Society programs from being cut."

The assertion of great savings has been widely disputed. Doubters cite the case involving a nurse who, at 32, was forced to quit her job in Washington, D. C., and go on welfare after she contracted cervical cancer in 1977. Months later, with the cancer under control, she returned to work and tried, unsuccessfully, to have her welfare payments stopped. Then, in September, 1978, she was caught in one of Califano's Project Match stings. She was indicted with 15 others who allegedly stole an average of $6,000 each by accepting welfare while holding a job.

In the end, the nurse and three others were cleared, four people pleaded guilty to misdemeanors, and six to felonies. The most repaid by any of them was $2,000. "When you consider the court-appointed attorney's fees, the salaries of those doing follow-up investigations, and the cost of court time," says Evan Hendrix, editor of the newsletter *Privacy Times*, "this was not a very cost-effective match." As recently as 1986, a General Accounting Office study of a few dozen data-matching projects reached a similar conclusion. In particular, it lambasted savings estimates, saying that agencies weren't able to detail the costs they incurred to generate the benefits.

By then, however, computer matching had "become an industry in Washington," says an aide at the House Government Operations Committee. In 1984, the last time OTA did an audit, government agencies were computer-matching more than 2 billion records in 110 programs. Some matches seem frivolous: The Selective Service Administration has compared its files with birthday party lists kept by some chains of ice cream parlors, looking for 18-year-olds who haven't registered.

But most matches are serious. The Credit Alert System at the Housing & Urban Development Dept., for instance, lets banks check HUD records to see if mortgage applicants are in default on Federal Housing Administration loans. Washington also shares with the credit bureaus files on people who owe the government money. And until the Social Security Administration dropped the practice this year, it had for 10 years let companies such as Citibank, TRW, and Chilton Corp. compare their files against the SSA's to ensure the accuracy of Social Security numbers on credit records. TRW was about to run 140 million such matches when Senator David H. Pryor (D-Ark.) complained during hearings last April, calling it "the largest breach of privacy in [SSA] history."

The Federal Bureau of Investigation generated similar reactions in 1987, when it proposed a modernization of its information system, the National Crime Information Center (NCIC). Among other things, the project, known as NCIC 2000, would have linked FBI criminal data banks with computerized records at airline reservation systems, car rental companies, creditors, credit bureaus, insurance companies, and phone companies. Moreover, NCIC 2000 would have cross-matched government data banks at the Internal Revenue Service, the Social Security Administration, and the Immigration & Naturalization Service.

POLICE STATE? NCIC 2000 raised many civil-liberties questions—including the specter of a police state. So, Representative Don Edwards (D-Calif.), whose House Judiciary subcommittee on civil and constitutional rights oversees the FBI's data-base efforts, asked the American Civil Liberties Union, among others, to comment. Based on the ensuing criticism, the FBI's plans were toned down, though a source who watches the agency says "there are other efforts under way that deserve attention." For example, he claims that the FBI is collecting financial records of individuals, including brokerage-house orders and electronic-funds transfers between banks, through electronic surveillance of data transmissions over phone lines. Now, the Edwards panel has asked the FBI to tell it if this is happening.

Two decades ago, the credit bureaus themselves saw the potential for abuse in the data they gathered. They were so stingy with it, in fact, that not until the FCRA was passed were individuals given the right to see their own files. TRW's code of ethics at the time declared that "credit information shall be treated by both TRW Credit Data and its subscribers as confidential. Lists of names shall not be compiled . . . for sale." Today, TRW's absolute rules have been replaced by a more flexible Privacy Review Board. And the company sells lots of lists.

What happened? "The marketplace changed," says Edward A. Barbieri, a TRW vice-president and general manager of TRW's credit-data services division. Not just banks, but direct marketers, retailers, and even charities were ravenous for information. Rising costs for postage, paper, and in-person sales calls were one reason. So was the potential for better-focused sales calls.

'GREAT OPPORTUNITY.' Credit bureaus get most of their information automatically. At least once each month, the nation's banks and retailers, among others, give the bureaus computer tapes or electronic files detailing the purchasing and payment activities of nearly every consumer in the U.S. Dotting these files are mortgage and credit-card payments and balances, income, family makeup, employment histories, driving records, bank balances, descriptions of legal tangles, and Social Security numbers—good raw material for fashioning new products. "It's a great opportunity for us," says John A. Baker, senior vice-president for marketing services at Equifax. "We don't have to do a lot to grow fast."

Last year, Equifax' operating income from sales of credit and marketing data rose 17%, to $61.5 million, on an equal increase in revenues, to $259 million. Those operations contributed 35% of Equifax' overall revenues but 75% of its profits. Credit and marketing revenues of $335 million at TRW and $300 million at Trans Union were each up about 10% last year.

The credit bureaus have two strategies for keeping the growth going. One is acquisitions. In less than five years, TRW has bought 33 other credit agencies, including last year's $330 million purchase of Chilton, which added 140 million files to TRW's computers. Equifax has put nearly 104 smaller credit bureaus on its network. Trans Union has brought aboard 23 and opened offices in 25 new markets. Together, the number of credit bureaus controlled by the Big Three has doubled during the 1980s to more than 200, giving them data on more than 90% of the U.S. adult population. This helps with the other growth strategy: Selling new products developed by repackaging credit-bureau data. Technology analyst Louis Giglio at Bear, Stearns & Co. says this can produce net margins of more than 30% on the incremental revenues.

It's in stretching for new products that the credit bureaus may stimulate controversy. In the past, they were uncomfortable selling to just anyone anything approaching the all-inclusive credit reports that banks get. Instead, they would sell lists of names that fell within the parameters that a retailer, for instance, provided: men between 40 and 45 with incomes of $100,000.

CROSSING THE LINE? Then, last year, TRW developed the Financial Lifestyle Database. For as little as 10¢ per name, any customer—mail-order house, phone solicitor, or fringe political group—can buy names, addresses, and phone numbers of people categorized by their income, whether they have credit cards, and how much credit they have available. This product raised eyebrows even in the industry. "It gets too close to the credit report," says Baker at Equifax. Equifax sells lists based on credit records but categorizes people more generally, by above-average, average, or below-average credit activity. TRW says that Equifax is just splitting hairs.

There is also criticism of a product called Hawk, a Trans Union offering that weeds out frauds. It runs names submitted for credit approval against a data base of phony addresses, Social Security numbers, and telephone numbers gathered from check-cashing offices, mail drops, telephone-answering services, government agencies, and credit reports. *Privacy Journal* editor Smith claims that if Hawk gives an incorrect assessment, an undeserved cloud of suspicion could hover over an innocent person. But Trans Union President and CEO Allen J. Flitcraft dismisses these concerns. "A huge percentage [of Hawk] is accurate," he says.

Even when there's no controversy, credit-bureau products are getting more precise. Last year, Equifax paid $21 million for National Decision Systems, which sells computerized breakdowns of neighborhoods and towns with profiles of the residents' spending habits. It derives this from census data and surveys, among other sources. National plans to incorporate Equifax' credit data into its data base. And that "will take us down

NEVER MIND YOUR NUMBER—THEY'VE GOT YOUR NAME

Trapped—that's what most Americans are when it comes to ending up in credit reports and a variety of other data bases. There are avoidance schemes, such as guarding your Social Security number. But only one strategy really works: Pay cash. Avoid credit. Don't sign up for government programs. Walk, don't drive. Live under a rock. In short, for most ordinary people. There is no way out.

Early on, the Social Security number was the culprit—the tag for information on individuals. Originally, citizens had to disclose their number only when dealing with the Social Security Administration. But by the early 1960s, the Internal Revenue Service and other government agencies could demand the number for use in their identification systems. By the mid-1970s, states could ask for it on driver's license applications. Soon, universities, banks, and employers used it for identification, too. About then, the credit bureaus were converting to computers. And the Social Security number was a handy way to index their files.

The bureaus still use it a lot. Consumers usually can't borrow wads of money without providing the number and having their spending habits checked. But increasingly, the Social Security number is just a convenient aid. Americans apply for credit so often, and use their credit so much, that credit reports are updated monthly. The news that you paid on time pops up with your name and address attached. And the frequency of this makes the reports as good a tool as any number for keeping track of you.

Consumers will feel the effect as the credit bureaus develop new products. As they try to grow, one of their goals is to sell more data on lifestyles in addition to credit reports. They buy subscription lists, census records, real estate and insurance information, and marketing surveys. Mail-order pharmacies provide lists of their regular customers and the vitamins and drugs they use. Even charities sometimes give out lists of their best contributors. None of these records has a Social Security number attached. But every one has a name and address. Now things have come full circle: Provide someone's name, and the credit bureau will come up with the Social Security number that goes with it.

The ease of tracking people by name may help the concept of targeted marketing, new in the past few years, to blossom in the future. Already, it's possible to produce crude profiles predicting what goods individuals may buy and where—at the mall or at local shops. The next step, as the technique is refined, is to anticipate what products a family will be ready for next— from shoes to vacations or minivans—and try to influence even earlier the way decisions are made. In *1984*, the George Orwell classic, Big Brother was a political dictator. In 21st century America, he may be a marketing whiz.

Stephen Phillips in Cleveland

to the level of offering information on the habits of individual households," says Richard Abraham, National's financial services marketing director. Marketers no longer will think of two neighbors as similar because their houses are and each has two kids. National will know that one heavily uses his five Visa cards and the other has none.

Where all this will end is hard to tell. With few laws restraining the credit bureaus, critics pick at a few controversial practices. For instance, the FTC is now mustering an attack against prescreening, in which a company selling a product or offering a credit card gets a credit bureau to identify the best candidates on a list of potential customers. "Consumers don't understand that for each ad stuffing their mailbox, a company without their knowledge or permission has asked a credit bureau to review their file," says Anita Boomstein, a New York lawyer who specializes in banking and consumer financial services.

LOBBYING MACHINES. Over the years, an

FTC rule that a marketer must make an offer of credit to everyone who survives a prescreen has been watered down by staff decisions. Now, the agency wants to turn back the clock. The Big Three have objected that prescreening is working just fine—and they've cranked up their lobbying machines. "The credit bu-

THE BIG THREE CREDIT BUREAUS

Companies	1988 revenues	Number of individual files
		Millions
TRW	$335	155
TRANS UNION	300	155
EQUIFAX	259	100

DATA: COMPANY AND ANALYST REPORTS

reaus tend to know their local congressmen very well," says Kenneth McLean, who as an aide to former Senator Wil-

liam Proxmire crossed swords with them and lost over efforts to limit their activities. Thus, consumer activists fear that when the five-member FTC rules this fall, prescreening will survive unchanged.

There's little chance of restraining the superbureaus either. The Big Three whisper that they would like them shut down. But their hands are tied, they say. "We're especially vulnerable to antitrust complaints," says Equifax' Baker, "when we refuse to allow smaller companies to subscribe to our services." The FTC will be of little help. "We're very concerned about the superbureaus," says Jean L. Noonan, the agency's associate director for credit practices. "I've heard allegations that they're far too lax." But she concedes that the FTC lacks the investigative muscle to prove it.

That might change with George Bush in the White House—or it might not. Last month, Henrietta F. Guiton, director of the President's Council on Consumer Affairs, convened credit-industry leaders, consumer and civil-liberties ac-

THE SCOOP ON SNOOPING: IT'S A CINCH

The stories are everywhere: A real estate agent gives a good client a couple of credit reports. A banker checks on a potential tenant for a friend. How hard is it, I wondered, to get into the credit files of someone else, even someone I've never met? The answer: not hard at all.

I decided not to test the Big Three credit bureaus—TRW, Equifax, and Trans Union. They're the most secure, and they probably knew me as a reporter. A better bet seemed to be small credit agencies, called superbureaus, that buy and resell information from the Big Three and other sources and are often accused of being leaky. They're in the yellow pages under Credit Agencies. And they advertise in magazines written for private eyes and spooks.

Identifying myself as a McGraw-Hill Inc. editor who might be hiring someone, I spoke to nearly a dozen superbureaus before settling on two. One, on the East Coast, ran searches for me. I gave a name, I got a report. I had to speak with someone by phone to do it, which dissuaded me from checking on, say, Elizabeth Taylor. But any ordinary names—I used two colleagues'—would have worked. I signed a form required by the Fair Credit Re-

porting Act, declaring myself a customer authorized to buy credit reports. My signature was accepted by fax, which isn't legally binding.

Another superbureau was more enticing. Its promotional literature listed a dozen services, from "instant nationwide tracing of Social Security numbers" to "over 250 million credit- and driver-history files on individuals." And I could get it all, using my own personal computer, for one low sign-up fee of $500. I paid with my personal credit card.

This company made me send in a written application—a heartening sign. Except that no one read it, apparently. Asked for a McGraw-Hill federal identification number—the corporate equivalent of a Social Security number—I made up two different ones on the same form. Asked for McGraw-Hill's bank-account locations, credit references, and the company's correspondence with the federal government, I said we couldn't disclose those. I was told to submit the application anyway, leaving spaces blank as necessary.

Maybe the blanks aroused suspicion—an investigator would be by to see me, I was told. The jig was up, I thought. My office is too small and plain for a big shot. And at work, I don't even have the personal computer

needed to use the superbureau's service—just a terminal on a network.

GUESSING WORKS. But there was no need to worry. We met in the foyer, and the questions were easy. When was the building built? Did McGraw-Hill own or lease it? I didn't know, but I guessed. The last requirement was a photograph of the place. Just like the one to the left, without me.

At home, from my own PC, I found the superbureau's menu a snoop's delight. Besides credit files—including credit-card numbers—there were Social Security numbers and addresses. And driving records. And credit reports on thousands of businesses.

I learned about loopholes, too. If I wanted reports for employment purposes, the subjects would have to be notified in accordance with federal law. "Can I get around this?" I asked. "When you go on-line," said my superbureau contact, "just ask for 'credit reports' as opposed to 'employment-purpose credit reports.' Then no one will have to know anything."

I'm out of the snooping business now, especially since this article blows my cover. It was fun while it lasted, but here is the sobering thought: If I can do all this, anyone can. And maybe the next time, the target will be me.

Jeffrey Rothfeder in New York

tivists, and congressional staffers to discuss if privacy is being abused by the sale of information. Afterward, Guiton said: "There's a problem here, because consumers don't want information about them used for any other purpose than the one it was collected for." But she's unsure how she'll advise the President.

New laws could stop the snoops—but not unless the public is aroused. And for now, it is apathetic. Robert H. Courtney Jr., a computer-security expert, discovered this some years ago. Then a manager at IBM, Courtney sent researchers out to a New York street to ask passersby if they thought modern technology was invading privacy. "Nearly 90% said yes," says Courtney. The next day, on the same street, his group offered a credit card with a favorable interest rate. The application asked for a Social Security number, information about other credit cards, and bank-account numbers and balances. "About 90% of the people filled it out without hesitating," says Courtney, "leaving no spaces blank." The message is hard to ignore: If people feel that nothing is private, then probably nothing is.

By Jeffrey Rothfeder in New York, with Stephen Phillips in Orange, Calif., Dean Foust in Atlanta, Wanda Cantrell in Chicago, Paula Dwyer in Washingon, and Michele Galen in New York

READ THIS!!!!!!!

Some call it direct mail, others know it as junk, but Americans love the paper flood washing over them as much as they say they hate it

JILL SMOLOWE

Does your hand clutch reflexively for the wastebasket when you encounter an invitation for a "21-day free trial period"? Do you feel a numbing sensation when confronted by a hysterical series of !!!!! or uppercased exhortations: THIS IS YOUR CHANCE!!!!! ONLY YOU CAN HELP!!!!! ORDER NOW!!!!! ? Have you begun to regard with suspicion bordering on paranoia every piece of mail marked OFFICIAL or V*A*L*U*A*B*L*E D*O*C*U*M*E*N*T*S I*N*S*I*D*E? Do the words "You May Already Have Won . . ." provoke in you an overwhelming desire to nuke the mailman?

THEN DON'T TURN THE PAGE!!! THIS ARTICLE IS *specially designed for* YOU!!! You will receive valuable information that you can use in your home or business!!! For absolutely no extra charge, you can . . .

The flood has already begun, and in this holiday season it will be greater than ever. During the past year, 63.7 billion pieces of third-class mail found their way into mailboxes across the nation. For tens of millions of Americans, the seasonal tide, as faithful as the first snow or the appearance of tinsel and colored lights, has started to rise. Letter boxes are filled to bursting with envelopes of every size and color, living rooms and kitchens are suddenly cluttered with mail on all available surfaces, and wastebaskets are overflowing with the sale not made.

The producers of this mountain of missives call it direct mail or mail order. The U.S. Postal Service refers to the onslaught as "bulk business mail." But to most people the deluge of material that descends on them each year is just plain junk mail, a typically American sobriquet that recognizes its vast and disorderly variety, its cheeky aggressiveness and its easy ability to raise hackles. Whatever its name, it is an extraordinary by-product of democratic civilization. Catalogs, catalogs, catalogs. Political flyers. Charitable solicitations. Environmental entreaties (on recycled paper, naturally). Sweepstakes packets. Magazine subscription offers. Investment brochures. Anything-of-the-month promotions. Coupons. Shopping guides. Freebie newspapers. Gewgaw samples.

And yet this vast variety is regarded by its recipients with ambivalence, not to say schizophrenia. The plain fact is that Americans love the stuff as much as they hate it. Last year 92 million Americans responded to direct-market pitches, a 60% jump in just six years. According to Marketing Logistics of Lincolnshire, Ill., a direct-marketing publisher, a grand total of $183 billion was shelled out for mail-order purchases and donations. Curse it though Americans may, the great outpouring of third-class communication can provide an antidote to loneliness, access to hard-to-find goods and a convenient answer to a housebound or time-pressed shopper's prayers. Careful study of this stack offers a handy citizen's guide to the most urgent political, environmental and social issues of the day. Cast in the best light, direct mail is *the* great American transcontinental linkup. It binds one nation, under Ed McMahon, indivisible, with bonus coupons and toll-free shopping for all.

For better or worse, America is married to the mails as a cost-efficient way of disseminating that most prized of 20th century commodities: information. Today more money is invested in direct-mail pitches, promotions and appeals than is spent on advertising in magazines or on radio or network television. The ensuing competition drives direct-mail marketers ever higher (and lower) to distinguish their message from the rest. To target potential customers more accurately, they compile and swap lists that provide increasingly detailed information about individual consumers, a practice that raises citizen concerns about privacy.

The biggest complaint of consumers, though, is that there is so much paper invading their homes. Over the course of a lifetime, the average American professional will devote eight entire months to sifting through mail solicitations. Third-class mail is now a nearly 4 million-ton colossus that accounts for 39% of all U.S. postal volume. This year about 41 lbs. of junk mail have been generated for each adult American. Of the pile that reached mailboxes, an estimated 44% landed in trash cans, unopened and unread. Many of the rejects were "prospecting letters," mailings that fish for new clients and often hook only a 2% response—plenty, by industry standards, to justify the flow.

The prodigality leaves environmentalists seething about the direct-mail bombardment, which consumes millions of trees each year. Conservationists also fume that the discards amount to 3% of the total clutter in the nation's landfills. And just how do they try to enlist public support? By mail, of course. The environmental watchdog organization Greenpeace USA sends more than 25 million pieces annually. Earlier this year the Environmental Defense Fund put out a direct-mail fund raiser (on recycled paper) that offered, in exchange for membership, a copy of the best-selling *50 Simple Things You Can Do to Save the Earth.* The book's No. 1 suggestion for planetary rescue is "Stop junk mail!"

The rallying cry is being taken up by federal and state legislators who feel that the problems caused by direct mail are multiplying out of control. A key concern is the alleged threat to individual privacy, which many fear is infringed upon by the direct marketers' aggressive collecting of trade information about the finances and spending habits of potential customers. Democratic Congressman Charles Schumer of New York plans to resubmit a bill to Congress next year that aims to prohibit the use of credit information for marketing purposes. At present, many credit agencies tap into sensitive data to compile lists that can then be rented by direct-mail marketers.

The Deceptive Mailings Prevention Act of 1990, which was signed this month by President Bush, bans mail solicitations that masquerade as government notices and prey particularly upon the fears of the elderly. Last January a New York State law went into effect that barred retail stores from keeping records of the addresses and phone numbers of customers who use credit cards. The practice is intended to verify identifications, but it is increasingly used to compile mailing lists, which are then rented.

Direct-mail practitioners counter that their product is the solution, not the problem. Mail-order shopping helps the environment, they argue, by keeping consumers out of cars, saving gas and motor oil and reducing air pollution. On the issue of privacy, they contend that direct mail is the least intrusive way to reach consumers. "It's not like a commercial where you have to wait a whole minute for the evening news to continue, or a billboard that blocks the scenery, or the telephone call that gets you out of the bathtub," says copywriting maestro Bill Jayme of Sonoma, Calif. "If you're not interested, you just throw it out." Says Denison Hatch, publisher of the industry newsletter *Who's Mailing What!:* "Junk mail is a good offer sent to the wrong person."

Proponents contend that direct mail is the most efficient way to organize and rally support for public causes. "How else do you communicate with people?" asks Peter

Bahouth, executive director of Greenpeace USA. "For better or worse, it's the lifeblood of the community." Advocates argue that direct mail actually fosters democracy. "It is a very decentralizing force," says Roger Craver of Falls Church, Va., who raises money through the mails for liberal causes. "In many ways, it has revolutionized American politics."

Certainly it has revolutionized the way Americans conduct business. Once upon a time, direct mail evoked only two names: Montgomery Ward and Richard Sears. Ward, a Midwest traveling salesman, had a simple idea: "Sell directly to the consumer and save them the profit of the middleman." In 1872 he published a one-page listing of 163 items, from red flannel cloth to oilcloth table covers, and mail order as we know it today was born. Fourteen years later, Sears, a Minnesota railroad-station agent, decided to mail a few $12 watches to his peers for $14 apiece. When the ploy

---

CONTENTS REQUIRE IMMEDIATE ATTENTION

Copywriters estimate that they have only four seconds to get a consumer's attention with direct mail. Hence great care is devoted to the design of the envelope, the crucial outer garment that direct-mail watchdog Denison Hatch likens to "hot pants on a hooker." It may be deliberately oversize or emblazoned with URGENT warnings in bold red letters. It can be laser printed to make a boxholder's name appear handwritten, or stamped with an eye-fetching cancellation mark. "My job," explains Ted Kikoler, a Toronto graphic designer who works primarily for U.S. firms, "is to make people read the words, by hook or by crook."

The gurus of the direct-mail copywriting trade are the Sonoma, Calif., team of Bill Jayme and Heikki Ratalahti. Over the past 20 years they have used their wiles to help launch more than a score of publications, including *Bon Appétit, Smithsonian* and *Mother Jones.* Jayme and Ratalahti's marketing packages, which cost $30,000 to $50,000 each, share four characteristics: an irresistible envelope, a personalized typewritten letter, a brochure intended to give an as yet nonexistent product an aura of legitimacy, and a response card. Jayme and Ratalahti know that people do not read direct-mail pitches carefully, so they adhere to a simple axiom: state the message, repeat it—then repeat it again.

There are plenty of other tricks to the trade. Most pitches rely on sentences that are short, punchy and startling. ("Hatch chicks in your bra!" says an offering for *Countryside* magazine.) The intimate second person "you" is usually invoked in the first sentence and sprinkled liberally throughout the rest of the pitch. Prices are rarely rounded. (A $29.95 price tag helps people believe

the item is still in the "$20 range.") Pitches often run to several pages. (Says Kikoler: "The more you tell, the more you sell.") The message is often printed on toned paper because warm colors apparently evoke a warm response. And usually there is a postscript. Some writers claim that the P.S. gets more attention than the body of the pitch letter.

Gimmicks are a must. Mailings often include stickers or buttons to "involve" the consumer. "It starts to reduce the amount of logic readers use," explains Kikoler. "They tend to become more childlike." Katie Muldoon, president of HDM Muldoon, a New York City direct-marketing agency, has discovered that an offer to cut prices 50% works better than a 65% discount, which consumers consider too good to be true. Disabled American Veterans has found that when gummed, individualized address labels are included, the response rate (35%) is almost twice that for mailings without stickers.

Is all this highly manipulative? Of course. "They really know how to push our hot buttons," says copywriter David Lusterman of San Anselmo, Calif. "I'm very jaded." Counters pitchman Jayme: "Junk mail gives everyone the chance to say, 'Yes, I exist. They're still writing to me—and dammit, I wish they'd stop!'" —*By Jill Smolowe. Reported by Elizabeth L'Hommedieu/San Francisco and Michael Riley/Washington* worked, Sears hooked up with a Chicago watchmaker named A.C. Roebuck to establish a mail-order business. By 1927 Sears, Roebuck was mailing 75 million letters and catalogs.

Over the next six decades, the explosion of merchandise catalogs was so immense that competition from more specialized retailers finally demolished one of its originators: in 1985 Montgomery Ward left the catalog business. Today's big sellers include J.C. Penney, L.L. Bean, Lands' End and Sears. In 1989 Bean, the famous Maine purveyor of outdoor gear, took in almost 90% of its $600 million net sales from the 116 million catalogs it mailed. Wisconsin's Lands' End sold $545 million worth of clothing and domestic items last year through its 90 million catalogs. "It's always fun to have them arriving at the door," says Lands' End president Richard Anderson. "It's like having Christmas every day."

But even the most tolerant consumer might feel like Scrooge in the face of so much postal excess, no matter how worthy the touted product or cause. Last year the Red Cross responded to Hurricane Hugo and the San Francisco earthquake by mailing 12 million appeals, twice the organization's usual annual outpouring. Disabled American Veterans sent 38.5 million fund-raising pieces. In the case of some nonprofit organizations, as much as 90% of all funds raised through mail campaigns are applied to more mailings to raise more money.

Even so, direct mailers maintain that junk mail is the most cost-efficient way to reach out to customers. They claim that a single mailing on average draws 10 times as many responses as newspaper ads and 100 times as many as TV ads. Plus, they note, they can judge the effectiveness of a mailing with far greater precision than most other advertisers can.

Small wonder so many advocacy groups turn to the mails. Take the American Association for Retired People and the National Rifle Association, two of the nation's most powerful lobbies and, not by coincidence, two of the largest direct mailers. In addition to the literature it sends its 32 million members, the A.A.R.P. each year puts into the mail stream 50 million pieces simply prospecting for new adherents. The N.R.A. generates up to 12 million pieces monthly. Each group has the capacity to flood Capitol Hill with thousands of letters when it feels its interests are threatened. Earlier this year the N.R.A. sent out 10 million "membership alert" mailings, urging gun owners to oppose legislation that sought to ban semiautomatic assault weapons and impose a waiting period on the purchase of handguns. Neither restriction passed Congress.

Cynics might say such pitches know no better target, since the Senate and House are two of the country's biggest users of the mails. Through the franking privilege, which enables members of Congress to use their signatures as postage, elected officials can deluge voters with mail at taxpayers' expense. During the past presidential election year, 805 million pieces of political literature spewed from Capitol Hill, at a cost of about $113 million.

Critics contend that little of that outpouring went for its authorized purpose: to enable elected officials to conduct a dialogue with constituents. Most of it, they argue, went to help incumbents consolidate their hold on power. The outcry has given rise to some reforms. House and Senate members up for re-election are prevented from issuing mass mailings just prior to elections. This year the Senate prohibited members from transferring individual franking allocations to colleagues, and the House agreed to restrict franking funds to about $180,000 for each representative.

Commercial and nonprofit direct mailers have to work much harder than members of Congress to address their pitches to specific audiences. To sing their siren songs effectively, they rely on a bewildering variety of list compilers, list brokers and list managers. In short, the mail-order

Holding Back the Tide

If you feel you are drowning in direct mail, there are ways to stem the flow. For one thing, you can take the initiative in notifying companies when you don't want your name included on rental lists. You can substantially reduce direct-mail deliveries to your home by sending your name and address to the Direct Marketing Association's Mail Preference Service at 11 West 42nd Street, P.O. Box 3861, New York, N.Y. 10163-3861. Equifax Inc. of Atlanta will soon offer a nationwide, $10 pick-and-choose service at 1-800-289-7658 that will enable you to screen out various categories of direct mail.

Even with these precautions, you're still unlikely to achieve a completely uncluttered existence. So why not make your peace with direct mail by joining the battle for a cleaner environment? Many mail pitches are printed on recyclable paper. Rather than reaching for the wastepaper basket, deposit today's discards in the nearest recycling bin. ■

industry is teeming with precisely the sort of people Montgomery Ward set out to eliminate: middlemen.

The listmakers wed advanced computer technology to an ever expanding data base to churn out highly specialized rolls of potential customers. They aim to know not only *where* you are but also *who* and *what* you are. By cross-indexing lists obtained from credit agencies, political parties, mail-order companies and other organizations, a direct-mail specialist can merge and compare the data to identify the groups you belong to, the car you drive, the party you vote for, the amount you paid for your house. All this helps direct marketers identify the goods, services and causes that might be of interest to you—and whether you are a good credit risk.

Much of the information is frighteningly easy to obtain. A guide published by the Quill Corp. of Lincolnshire offers public-domain prospecting tips for listmakers. Among other things, it suggests taking a look at marriage licenses, birth certificates, voter registrations, sporting and business licenses and the membership rolls of schools, churches and civic organizations. Quill advises that these lists can often be obtained through local government offices.

Amassing such information is a major investment of time and money. Hence many marketers turn to *Direct Mail List Rates and Data,* the industry's Domesday Book, to mine existing lists. This 4-in.-thick volume, published bimonthly by Standard Rate & Data Service of Wilmette, Ill., at an annual cost of $317, features descriptions of 10,258 rental mailing lists. The tome does not provide specific names and addresses of customers-in-waiting, but it indicates who owns compiled lists and which rolls include the names of people who responded to mailings. These "response lists" are the jewel in the direct-mail crown. According to marketing lore, if your name is on a response list, chances are good you'll buy again.

The name-trading game is now an estimated $3 billion business in itself. Rental lists, which cost anywhere from $50 to $150 per 1,000 names, are bartered not only by most mail-order houses and many nonprofit organizations but also by a few public utilities and telephone companies. List owners typically pay a 20% commission to a list broker and 10% to a list manager. Even with those overheads, some concerns make more money from the rental of their lists than from the sale of their products.

Once acquired, customer lists can be fine-tuned to an exacting degree. Suppose a financial-services company wants to identify potential clients for home-equity loans. Good list brokers will first define an audience, say, people who own $100,000 homes, have lived in them for 10 years or more and are likely to have built up substantial equity in the dwelling.

Brokers then cast a wide net. They might draw on Census Bureau data, which are available to the public, to identify geographical areas where homes fall into the targeted price range. They can tap into lists from major compilers, like Donnelley Marketing of Stamford, Conn., whose data base details the buying habits of 80 million households, or into various computerized systems that identify neighborhoods by consumer behavior. They might pay credit agencies like TRW of Cleveland and Equifax Inc. of Atlanta to draw up sophisticated demographic models, consumer profiles and potential customer lists. A thorough computer sorting of all these sources—which sometimes includes information from up to 100 lists—will then turn up a list of customers who might respond positively to a pitch for a home-equity loan.

Zap! The direct mailer can then aim a solicitation at a letter box with a precision bordering on the scientific. While some people find the attention flattering, others consider it insidious. "There's something kind of creepy about companies knowing more about you than your own family, and compiling and trading information about you behind your back," says Robert Ellis Smith, editor of the watchdog newsletter *Privacy Journal.* Direct marketers strongly deny that they are intruders. "Nobody wants dossiers compiled about them," says Michael Manzari, president of Kleid Co., a New York City concern that brokers and manages lists. "We're not doing that. We're identifying markets." As a result of their care, goes the argument, less unwanted mail is inflicted on consumers. Says Katie Muldoon, president of a New York City direct-marketing agency: "If the mailbox is going to be crowded, we want to make sure it's stuff people want."

Still, direct mailers are growing more sensitive to consumer concerns about increasingly interwoven data bases. A few direct mailers refuse to rent their lists to other mailers. Among the holdouts: the Red Cross, *Reader's Digest* and AT&T, which posts close to 300 million pieces of promotional mail annually.

Some trade or offer names for rent but otherwise keep information about their customers under tight wraps. Lands' End offers no information about individuals when it passes on their names. "We are fanatical about keeping information about customers in the office," says Michael Atkin, the company's marketing vice president. The Time Inc. Magazine Co., which publishes TIME and sends out close to 35 million pieces of promotional mail each year, rents its customer lists. But they are made available only to buyers who agree to strict conditions, such as refusing to use telephone appeals for any of the acquired

names. The company, like many others, will not rent a list until it sees and approves the proposed mailing.

Such safeguards help make the direct-mail flood more selective, but it is likely to continue to spread. In fact, the glut may grow exponentially as relatively cheap technologies increase the numbers of marketers who can tap into the stock of consumer information. Last month Lotus Development Corp. of Cambridge, Mass., introduced a Macintosh-compatible software data base culled from more than 7 million U.S. companies. The $695 package will enable small concerns to enter the business-to-business direct-market mainstream. Another Lotus data base, due early next year, will allow small businesses to tap into the consumer market as well. Says Henry Hoke Jr., publisher of *Direct Marketing* magazine: "It's brought the mailing-list business to Main Street."

Despite the scorn the pitches often elicit, there are indications that consumers don't mind the junk deluge as much as they sometimes say. A national survey released last June by Equifax found that direct-market mailings stimu-

lated 54% of all Americans to make at least one purchase. One of every six Americans has made six or more purchases through the mail. By contrast, only 15% have bought at least one item through TV home-shopping clubs, and only 14% have responded to telephone solicitations.

A U.S. Postal Service survey of 5,000 families made two years ago found that 60.3% of respondents did not mind getting "advertising mail" that did not interest them, so long as the pile included some pieces that caught their eye. Not surprisingly, households with incomes of $65,000 and up received more of this mail than other income groups—and also wanted less. Although the elderly, particularly the homebound, often rely on mail-order shopping, the over-70 crowd felt that they received too much advertising mail. Younger consumers tended to want more.

Some peeves cut across all demographic lines. One typical complaint is that checks, credit cards and other valuables can get lost in the mounds of paper that consumers toss out daily. Another common gripe: duplicate mailings. While some of the replication is carelessness on the part of direct mailers, the overlap is testimony to the number of times that consum-

---

Too Many Busy Signals

What's less bulky than direct mail but just as likely to surround you with carefully crafted pitches? Answer: computerized machines that can automatically call and relay messages to thousands of telephone owners daily, and facsimile machines that can send reams of information to unsuspecting offices.

Already, 180,000 businesses use automatic-dialing systems to deliver prerecorded sales pitches to as many as 7 million people each day, according to the House Energy and Commerce Committee, and 2 million U.S. offices employ fax machines to transmit more than 30 billion pages of information—much of it unsolicited—per year.

Consumers complain that calls from these "electronic salesmen," who get their names by purchasing mailing lists, constitute an invasion of their privacy. They are concerned that solicitations that continue even after a recipient hangs up can have serious consequences for fire stations and emergency rooms, which the dialers can reach unintentionally. What irks people most is having to pay for solicitations they never asked for. Those with car phones and pagers are charged for every minute they use a telephone line, whether or not they initiated the call, and fax-machine owners pay up to 10¢ a sheet for the special paper the machines use to print out messages, including ones they did not request.

More than a dozen states have passed legislation to stem the electronic barrage. Some versions ban or restrict the hours in which automatic dialers can be used. Others—notably Connecticut, Florida, Maryland and Oregon—prohibit unsolicited fax-machine advertisements outright. Constitutional lawyers argue that fax bans might violate the senders' free-speech rights, but Congress may take action. Democratic Representative Edward Markey of Massachusetts is sponsoring a bill that would make it illegal to send fax solicitations or automatically dialed, prerecorded phone pitches to people who have notified a clearinghouse that they do not want them. The White House says the number of complaints doesn't seem to warrant such legislation. ∎

ers' names are bought and sold in the direct-mail marketplace. Many consumers also resent notices advising them that they have been preapproved for a credit card. "How do they *know* that I'm a sound credit risk?" they wonder.

Consumer resistance to direct mail appears to be rising. Last May the New York Telephone Co. enclosed a form in the monthly bills for its 6.3 million residential customers, asking if they wanted their names removed from a list that it intended to rent to other direct mailers. A surprising 800,000 people wrote to demand that they be removed from the offering. The 3,500-member Direct Marketing Association, a group that has been monitoring, boosting and charting the industry since 1917, reports that more than 1 million people have signed up for a service that aims to eliminate subscribers' names from national direct-mail lists.

Sensing the backlash, direct mailers are beginning to rethink their more profligate tactics. "People simply don't have the time to sift through a lot of unwanted and unnecessary pieces of mail," says Bill Davis, who runs the Database Marketing Corp. in Burlington, Mass. "If you treat your own customers with a sort of throw-it-against-the-wall-and-hope-a-little-of-it-sticks approach, you're actually alienating them." There is also a new economic reason to reassess the scope of the mail flow. Next February postal hikes could raise third-class costs by as much as 33%. (The current rates provide the Postal Service with revenues of $8.1 billion; additional revenues are generated when customers send in their checks and receive their purchases through the mail.)

Direct mailers who want to demonstrate their sensitivity to environmental concerns about the mail volume might emulate Smith & Hawken, a San Francisco Bay Area business that markets specialty garden tools. Since its founding 11 years ago, the company has donated 10% of its pretax profits to environmental causes. Last year 80% of the company's $50 million in sales was generated by orders placed through 20 million nonrecyclable catalogs. Co-founder Paul Hawken decided that a greater effort was needed. He has publicly pledged to print all Smith & Hawken catalogs on recycled paper, use only soy-based inks and plant two trees for every one cut down in S&H's publishing effort. He has further promised to let customers know to whom S&H rents its lists and to offer them a chance to remove their names from the rolls.

Other publications and mail-order houses routinely duplicate that last offer. But by the time a written demurral is processed, consumers may find that their names have cropped up on several new lists. One much needed reform would be for direct mailers to provide adequate time for customer-deletion requests to roll in before rental lists roll out.

The intriguing, enticing, exasperating mountain of direct mail is not about to go away. The fact is Americans like it too much and find it too useful. After all, while a trip to a junk-free mailbox might be less irksome, it would also be less helpful and interesting. The challenge, for senders and consumers alike, is to look hard at the flood of third-class communication and find ways to maintain the dialogue at a reasonable pitch. —*Reported by Thomas McCarroll/ New York, Michael Riley/Washington and Elizabeth Taylor/Chicago*

Prepare for E-mail attack

Wonders of technology brought cheap communications. Great, but one consequence is a bad case of information overload—a nuisance for consumers, a headache for marketers.

David Churbuck

Direct mail operators send so many "urgent" mailgrams that most people don't even open the envelopes now. Solicitors hit you at night with so many phone solicitations that you shelled out the extra bucks for an unlisted number. Then they got through with random dialers. So you bought an answering machine. And now they've invaded your computer and your fax machine with junk mail. Is there no peace?

This is the information age that the futurists talked about, the day when telephone technology, fax machines and electronic mail would make communication cheap and plentiful. Too plentiful.

Says Mitchell Kapor, the former chairman of Lotus Development Corp.: "It's a well-known phenomenon in large corporations that when you come back from a long weekend you'll find 50 pieces of electronic mail in your mailbox, spend hours going through it, and end up with most of it being stuff you don't want to see." Kapor protects himself at home with an unpublished telephone number, and opts for a public electronic mail address for his computer. Yet the unwanted messages still come through.

So many unwanted messages are floating around that the wanted ones sometimes get lost in the shuffle. And so we have what could perhaps be called a war of access, fought on a battleground of chips and software. Everyone, it seems, is screaming for your attention. Among the callers' weapons are electronic white pages, power dialers that can do 20,000 calls a day, and systems that hunt down unpublished fax numbers.

Defensive strategies? These include PBX switchboards with software to route unwanted calls into answering machines and call blockers that reject calls from specific unwanted numbers. Tomorrow's strategies will include software that filters out sales pitches from electronic mail by looking for telltale words like "insurance" and "financial planner."

The ultimate gatekeeper for the busy executive or the very private individual is, of course, another human being. But secretaries and butlers are expensive. For most people, then, the answer to junk communications will be found in call blockers, software filters and screening devices that enable communication targets to dig an electronic moat around themselves.

The roots of this emerging electronic warfare are to be found in the very success of semiconductors, which have made talk cheap. But with information, more can be less— a phenomenon once quantified by MIT Professor Ithiel de Sola Pool. Tracking various media from 1960 to 1977, De Sola Pool found that there has been a rapid growth (9% annually) in data made available in the form of periodicals, television, radio, phone calls, mail, faxes and telexes. At the same time there has been a much slower growth (3% annually) in data consumed. Out there at the margin, in short, only about a third of the extra information is getting through. We are suffering from information overload. The transmission of information, while becoming cheaper, is becoming less efficient. The De Sola Pool study concluded that even while transmission costs are dropping, it is costing more to send a message and have it sink in.

While senders are spending more to reach out, some receivers are spending more not to be touched. Survey Sampling, a Fairfield, Conn. research firm, says 28% of all U.S. households have an unlisted number. Los Angeles is 56% unlisted.

New Jersey Bell, which already charges customers $12.50 a year for the privilege of not having their numbers published, is offering another defense this year, Caller ID, in some parts of its territory. For $78 a year plus a onetime charge of $60 for a readout device, a residential customer sees the number of the caller when his phone rings. If he recognizes the number, he picks up; if he doesn't, he might ignore the call or maybe let an answering machine get it.

For $48 a year New Jersey Bell will accept a list of up to six calling numbers that will be blocked from your phone altogether; the callers get a central-office recording telling them to buzz off. Depending on how many stockbrokers, bill collectors and ex-spouses you are trying to avoid, six may fall far short of your needs. But New Jersey Bell's services are just the opening wedge of call-blocking technology. If a $60 device can capture phone-number data from the phone line for display, another device could sit between a telephone and a personal computer, trapping and storing incoming phone numbers. There it could be compared against an unlimited list of *numeri non grati*. Perhaps, as Caller ID spreads to other Bell companies (Nynex plans to offer the service as well), some entrepreneur will market software that can identify the sleazier phone solicitors—penny stock touts, for example—and cut them off.

Businesses are already figuring ways to turn Caller ID into an offensive weapon, says a telephone consultant who is advising them. In New Jersey, commercial accounts can identify calling phone numbers for $102 a year. Obvious scheme: Advertise, say, a free book on municipal bonds with a phone number to call, then capture the callers' numbers and feed them to ravening cold-call brokers.

Don't forget that the strongest weapon in the arsenal of people making calls is phone numbers. Getting those numbers along with your name, address, zip code and any other personal information (the more personal the better) is big business. List brokers thrive by leasing computer tapes containing magazine circulation lists, product warranty registration lists and other information to direct marketers.

Technology makes this process a bigger problem. Nynex is selling, for $10,000, a compact disc containing 10 million white page listings for its New York and New England service area. The discs are updated monthly and include a little more information than the paper white pages: names, addresses, zip codes and, of course, phone numbers. Chief customers for Nynex' disc: bill collectors, banks and law enforcement agencies.

Once the marketer has a million numbers, what does he do with them? Feeds them into a power dialer, also known as a junk-call machine. About $38 million worth of the power dialing equipment was sold in 1988, according to William Reed at Link Resources, a New York market research firm. This notwithstanding about 30 state laws supposedly restricting them. (Massachusetts has a law requiring phone companies to make available to operators of power dialers a list of phone customers who have asked to be spared such solicitations. But the law does not require the junk call operators to get the list, much less to honor it. In Florida a 1987 law bans phone machines from calling people with pitches for "tangible" goods like aluminum siding. "Tangible," however, does not cover the activities of stockbrokers and insurance salesmen.

Boston-area-based Davox Corp. says one purchaser of its CAS-1000 system, which supports 64 phone lines and 32 customer service representatives, was able to dial 20,000 numbers and make 4,000 contacts in one day. Those dialers aren't cheap. A midlevel Davox system—one that supports 16 lines and 8 to 10 agents—is priced at $125,000.

As telemarketers spend more for offense, their audience will have to step up defensive outlays. One manager of a bed-and-breakfast in San Francisco uses a device called PriveCode to stop his phone from ringing. "I was tired of being offered free dancing lessons," he says. "With a phone in every room, every time they rang the house sounded like it was taking off to the sky."

PriveCode asks callers for their access number, which they punch in with a touch-tone phone. The inn's guests have a code that makes the phone rings come in bursts of four. The booking agent uses a code that rings three times. The manager's friends have yet another code that sets off two rings. The single-ring code is for "special occasions," he says. Dance lesson pitchmen can't make the phone ring at all.

PriveCode was invented by IMM Corp. in Philadelphia, which, alas, doesn't sell it anymore. It was a marketing failure, partly because of its high price (about $300 for a single extension) and partly because it doesn't also have a message-taking option for people who don't know the code. But experts say it would be easy to build a ring-blocking device into the current generation of $100 answering machines, which already use codes to read back messages to the owner calling in from another phone.

Another defensive technology has been around for a long while but is much more feasible with modern software-controlled PBXes, or switchboards. Keep two phone extensions. One rings when a stranger dials your company and asks to be connected to you. That extension is shunted to a secretary. The other extension is known to people you want to hear from. You pick up that extension yourself, saving the inconvenience of a screening by your secretary. Software-driven switchboards facilitate this dodge immensely. For one thing, they can easily change your private extension number if it leaks out to outsiders. For another, they can shunt the cold-callers to a low-cost dump such as a voice mailbox. If corporate executives of the future can win this little electronic battle, they can probably make do with fewer secretaries.

But marketing people, desperate for new leads, are fighting back: Offensive software is moving ahead. A Norcross, Ga. company, Digital Publications, is selling a program and 5,000-name database that allows publicists to mass-distribute faxed press releases automatically at night, at a cost of 10 cents each, much cheaper than the average 80 cents paid per mailed press release. Mr. Fax, a fax supply company in Irvine, Calif., has accumulated a large database of fax numbers by offering cameras and Sony Walkmans for lists of fax numbers. Such lists are one reason fax users are inundated with mail—and paying for the insult, since suppliers are on them.

Defense against junk fax assaults: Don't let out your fax numbers. Soon, however, fax marketers will have a powerful retaliatory weapon, inspired by the "demon dialer" of the movie *War Games.* Zoom Telephonics in Boston plans to release in March a $595 modem that can be programmed to randomly dial thousands of numbers, hunting for responses that betray the characteristic signals of a fax machine beginning to receive. The fax numbers are stored for later retrieval.

Now what do you do? So far only a few fax manufacturers have added a feature that demands an access code before permitting a transmission to begin. But such features may soon become standard on all machines rather than options.

Electronic mail—messages sent from computer to computer—presents a more complicated battlefield. It's more powerful than letter mail and potentially more invasive. Why so? With a fax message, you don't know whether or not the intended recipient got the message or read it, but some electronic mail systems, for instance, permit the sender to attach a "receipt" to a message so he'll know when you've read it and can follow up with a phone call. Defense: Forward the message to yourself and then read it. The receipt won't be triggered.

E-mail still has a way to go before it replaces the post office—or snailmail, as its detractors call it. However, it is already formidable. The number of messages over public systems (such as CompuServe and MCI Mail) reached about 500 million in 1987. Coopers & Lybrand predicts that number will reach 2 billion in 1992. On private, corporate electronic mail systems, there were about 1 billion messages in 1988, and there could be over 10 billion by 1992.

When the first corporate electronic mail systems were installed in the 1970s, users noticed a disquieting phenomenon: unwanted messages. "Someone in a branch office hires a new salesman and sends a message to everyone in the company, including the chairman," says Walter Ulrich, a partner at Coopers & Lybrand in Houston. "That clutters everyone's mailbox. It is so simple to simply address the message to 'everyone' that there is abuse.

Without electronic mail that branch manager would never think of making the same announcement, running off 10,000 Xerox copies and then mailing it out." As chairman of the privacy and security subcommittee of the Electronic Mail Association, Ulrich is monitoring ways to cope with this problem of overuse.

Help is on the way. Professor Thomas Malone at MIT's Sloan School of Management is leading a project called the Information Lens, a system of filters, defined by the user, that scans incoming mail and sorts it into "folders" according to user-defined criteria. Mail from the boss will be flagged as urgent if the user has so programmed the system. The Lens can also identify messages from electronic pests by the way the user handles them, and can route them into an electronic trash can or low-priority folder.

General broadcasts, like junk mail, can be regarded as useless by many recipients, who would prefer not to receive impersonal communications. The Lens, rather than posting a copy of a broadcast message in everyone's in-box, puts it into an electronic pool of other broadcast messages.

Members of the system can tell the Lens to search the pool for items of interest, retrieve them, and save them in a personal file. In this system the receiver has more control over the communication channel than the sender.

"Imagine various kinds of pricing schemes," says Malone. "On a simple level a sender is charged for sending messages and charged more for sending a message to many people. You can imagine some more elaborate schemes: One would be a toll for getting information into your mailbox. You won't be willing to look at messages from random strangers unless they are willing to pay to get that information into your mailbox.

"That way I have a certain kind of filter that says it has to be worthwhile to the sender to get it to me. Such a system increases the incentive for the sender to target his communications more directly."

Professor Nicholas Negroponte, director of MIT's Media Lab, envisions a world of "reverse advertising." "I tell my computer to tell the world that I want to buy a windsurfer for under $800, and the windsurfer world responds with bids." Don't call us, we'll call you. Now we're talking.

ABSOLUTELY NOT CONFIDENTIAL

"**I**nsurance companies used to hire sleazy private eyes to find out what diseases people had and what they were taking for them. Now there's a record for everything—and a way to get almost any record."

Clark Norton

Clark Norton is a freelance writer in San Francisco.

SKIING CROSS-COUNTRY through a campus park one winter's day, University of Michigan graduate student Frank G. Palermo* found himself perched atop a steep slope. Heart racing, he pushed off and sped downhill, only to come to a wrenching halt when his ski tips dug abruptly into the thin crust. The leather strap on his left ski pole snapped; so did his left thumb. Palermo wound up at the University Hospital in Ann Arbor, where his doctors decided to operate. In preparation, they summoned his medical records from his family physician in Detroit.

According to Palermo's file, he was a walking medical minefield. "You appear to have had your gallbladder removed at age two," the doctors told him. "You've had kidney stones, a broken nose, and recently broke your leg." Palermo was perplexed; except for the broken nose, the list of mal-

* *This name has been changed.*

adies was news to him. A phone call solved the mystery: It seems his family doctor had carelessly lumped his medical history in with those of his grandfather and cousin—both also named Frank G. Palermo.

Palermo laughs now about the snafu. But imagine another scenario, one that easily could have occurred had he not been able to set his medical records straight: Palermo applies for individual health insurance and signs a standard waiver authorizing the insurer to obtain copies of his medical files. With a supposed history of internal disorders and broken bones dating back to age two, he's clearly a bad risk and his application is rejected. Meanwhile—again acting on the waiver Palermo signed—the insurance carrier feeds its findings to a computer bank that shares medical data with hundreds of other insurance companies.

By Clark Norton. Reprinted from *Hippocrates,* The Magazine of Health & Medicine, March/April 1989, pp. 52-59. Copyright © 1989, Hippocrates Partners.

Now say that his grandfather or cousin had problems more controversial than gallstones or a broken leg. Some psychiatric care, perhaps. Drug abuse. Or—an increasingly daunting prospect today—a positive test for HIV, the virus associated with AIDS. In addition to being rejected for insurance, Palermo suffers a series of unaccountable setbacks. He applies for a postgraduate program—and is turned down. He sends out job applications—and is never called for an interview. And when Palermo finally lands a second-rate job, he co-workers buzz about his "condition." He loses any chance of career advancement. Palermo never suspects that it is his medical records—leaked to the world, containing mistakes he doesn't even know about—that have left his life in a shambles.

Palermo was lucky; he was able to head off trouble. But if you don't know what's in your own medical records and who has access to them, you might find yourself in just such a horror story.

"More and more people are demanding your medical records," says Stuart A. Wesbury, president of the American College of Healthcare Executives. "Attorneys. Employers. Insurers. Government agencies. Media."

"Insurance companies used to hire sleazy private eyes to find out what diseases people had and what they were taking for them," says Evan Hendricks, publisher of *Privacy Times* newsletter in Washington, D.C. "They don't need to do that any more. There's now a record for everything—and a way to get almost any record." This point was dramatically illustrated in November 1986, when a reporter somehow obtained the medical record of the late right-wing lawyer Roy Cohn from the National Institutes of Health and published it in *Harper's* magazine, complete with information confirming that Cohn had AIDS.

The awful irony is that depending on where you live, you may have far more difficulty getting your medical records than would any of those groups on Wesbury's list. Twenty-one states currently have no law guaranteeing patients access to their hospital and physicians' office records. Only 23 states and the District of Columbia let patients see both kinds of records. And even in those states, obtaining records can be so costly or time-consuming that many people give up in frustration.

LIKE MOST AMERICANS, you've probably assumed your medical records were confidential—protected by ethics and the law. At one time, you would have been right.

"We used to have a medical system that was confidential," says retired Harvard School of Medicine neurosurgeon Vernon Mark, whose father, grandfather, and great-grandfather were also physicians. "The patient went to a doctor, the doctor made a diagnosis, and the diagnosis stayed with the doctor. My father used to treat a lot of people who had sexually transmitted diseases. For him to reveal that kind of information would have been unthinkable."

Though physicians still swear an oath not to reveal patient information, old-fashioned medical confidentiality has become a notion quaint as the house call-gradually eroded by court decisions and a victim of the industrialization of medicine.

The courts have ruled, for instance, that when the welfare of society is at stake, medical information can be released without the patient's consent or knowledge. In the case of sexually transmitted diseases, as an example, doctors are now required to report patients who have venereal disease to state public health departments. In most states, doctors also must report gunshot wounds or cases of suspected child abuse. Psychiatrists often are required to alert the police if they believe a patient is dangerous. The courts have ruled that hospital review boards may use patient records to flush out bad doctors. Researchers rely on medical information for public health purposes such as tracking down Legionnaire's disease. Lawyers frequently depend on medical records to document cases of malpractice. Police and grand juries are sometimes permitted to use records to gather medical evidence to catch or indict criminals.

But privacy has fallen hardest to the demands of the big business of medicine. Insurance companies, employers, and government agencies now foot an estimated 70 percent of all the medical bills in this country. They want to know where their money's going, and to find out they scrutinize the records that doctors and hospitals keep on all of us.

To be sure, much of this record-sharing is legitimate, even beneficial. Who could argue with the need to ferret out child abusers, to uncover fraudulent doctors, to hold down medical costs? University of Chicago surgeon Mark Siegler says these exceptions to total medical confidentiality, which he calls a "decrepit concept," have led to better health care for all.

The trouble is that the demands for information have grown so much that the orderly flow has become a nearly unchecked torrent. In a single month, the Stanford University Hospital medical records department receives 1,500 requests for medical records information—from insurers, physicians, attorneys, federal and local law officers with subpoenas, and other sources.

YOU MAY BE THE ONE who unknowingly starts the flood. For the privilege of having health insurance, you most likely have signed a waiver on a claim form that says something like this: "I authorize any physician, hospital, or other medical provider to release to [name of insurance company] any information regarding my medical history, symptoms, treatment, examination results, or diagnosis." With that in hand, if your insurer wants to know why your doctor charged $600 for a physical, it can delve into your records without telling you.

And that's one place where the leaks may start springing: The doctor's office can turn the insurer's request into a breach of confidence, simply out of expediency. As San Francisco personal injury lawyer Bennett Cohen explains, "If an insurance company wants records to see if someone has an asthma condition, and that patient also saw the same doctor for a VD infection five years ago, the insurer gets that information, too. No one in the doctor's office is going to go through fifteen visits and segregate out the records relevant to asthma, and—legitimately, I suppose—the insurer doesn't want to rely on a nurse or receptionist to figure out what's pertinent to what."

Hospitals, too, may release more than the insurer needs to know, barraged as they are by requests for records. "It's up to the hospitals to ask insurance companies, 'What do you need that for?'" says Wesbury. "But each policy is a little different. It's very difficult to identify precisely what information is needed." Hospitals also contribute their own unique leaks. "Charts travel all over," says Molly Cooke, an internist and head of the ethics committee at San Francisco General Hospital. "Thirty to forty people may look at one during treatment: X-ray technicians, dietitians, occupational and physical therapists, social workers, medical students, pharmacists. If the patient has an unusual illness, the number may be much higher. And the fact is that total strangers could also look at charts, the way most hospitals leave charts lying around. Then there are the 'elevator conversations' among doctors—who because they're in a hospital simply forget they're talking about someone in public."

In practice, your records may not even go directly from the doctor or hospital to the insurance company. Many insurers use a consumer reporting agency, which also gathers information for groups such as mortgage lenders and marketing research firms, to collect authorized records from doctors and hospitals. One such company, Equifax Services, handles 1.5 million transactions per day for its 60,000 customers, which include all the major North American insurance carriers. Equifax says it doesn't keep any of the medical information it collects for insurers. However, such firms depend on computers and sometimes on computer data banks—none of which has ever been heard to utter the Hippocratic Oath, and all of which may invite electronic break-ins.

One data bank that has long given consumer advocates the willies is the Medical Information Bureau, a Boston-based nonprofit association representing about 800 of North America's insurance companies. The bureau stores computerized medical data—and some nonmedical information such as bad driving records or hazardous hobbies—on 13 million North Americans. If you have ever filled out an application for individual health or life insurance, or for additional coverage on your group insurance plan, you may be on file.

Here's how the system works: When you apply for insurance, you sign an authorization (this is different from the claim form waiver) allowing the company to gather material on you from sources such as the Medical Information Bureau, government agencies, consumer reporting groups, even

interviews with neighbors. Your application will say whether that insurer uses the bureau.

If the company finds anything it thinks might interest other insurers—weight, blood pressure, electrocardiograph readings, and X-ray results are among the most common items—it feeds the data to the bureau. Later, upon request, the bureau relays the information to any other member company; except for government agencies with a subpoena, only member companies can use the data. The bureau doesn't check the information for accuracy, and it stays in the computer seven years.

While the Medical Information Bureau runs the "Big Computer in the Sky," as one attorney dubs it, your fellow employee or office supervisor may present an even more immediate threat at the video display terminal down the hall. With computers enabling employers to handle claims in-house, four-fifths of the nation's 1,500 largest firms now run or finance their own insurance programs. That means that when you submit a claim, the personnel office, and maybe your boss or others, will discover that you have had, say, an abortion. Some larger companies now have safeguards such as separating employee medical records from other records.

More than privacy is at stake here. Chicago psychiatrist Jerome Beigler, former chairman of the American Psychiatric Association's Committee on Confidentiality, says that his investigations found several cases across the country in which schoolteachers had been fired or demoted after undergoing psychiatric treatment billed through their employers' insurance. "The irony is that those with the courage to get treatment jeopardize their careers," Beigler says, "while others who could be much worse off take it out on their students instead." An estimated 15 percent of all employees with company-run insurance programs pay for covered psychiatric treatment themselves, because they fear repercussions from their employers.

Similarly, Los Angeles substitute teacher Allan Rodway's decision to take an AIDS test before marriage cost him his job—and more. According to the lawsuit Rodway filed, the University of Southern California Hospital mistakenly told the Los Angeles School District that Rodway had AIDS, causing him to be suspended. California law prohibits releasing such information without written patient consent. Rodway regained his job through out-of-court negotiations, after his doctor wrote a letter stating that the teacher did not have AIDS. Even so, according to Rodway's deposition, the disclosure caused his fiancée to leave him and his church to shun him.

An employer or insurance company may not even be the last stop in the journey of a runaway medical record. It wouldn't be hard, say privacy experts, for those not involved in your health care to get their hands on your records: The ubiquitous use of computers and data banks, and the frequency with which records are passed among insurers and employers, offer plenty of chances for someone to intercept private information. (The Medical In-

CAN YOU GET YOUR MEDICAL RECORDS?

State	Doctor	Hospital	Mental Health	Comments
ALABAMA	No law	No law	No*	*Records releasable by court order
ALASKA	Yes	Yes	Yes	
ARIZONA	No law	No law	Yes*	*Unless harmful to patient
ARKANSAS	No law	No law	No law	
CALIFORNIA	Yes	Yes	Yes	
COLORADO	Yes	Yes	Yes*	*Unless harmful to patient
CONNECTICUT	Yes	Yes	Yes	
DELAWARE	No law	No law	No*	*Records releasable to attorney or by court order
D.C.	Yes*	Yes*	Yes**	*Access guaranteed by case law, not state law **Unless harmful to patient
FLORIDA	Yes	Yes*	Yes	*Except psychiatric progress notes and consultation reports
GEORGIA	Yes	Yes	Yes	
HAWAII	Yes	Yes	Yes	
IDAHO	No law	No law	Yes*	*Applies to patients of state institutions; unless harmful to patient
ILLINOIS	Yes	Yes	Yes	
INDIANA	Yes	Yes	Yes	
IOWA	No law	No law	Yes	
KANSAS	No law	No law	Yes*	*Unless harmful to patient
KENTUCKY	No law	No law	Yes	
LOUISIANA	Yes	Yes	No*	*Records releasable to attorney or relative
MAINE	No law	Yes	Yes*	*Patient may have to be supervised while reviewing records
MARYLAND	No*	Yes	Yes	*Release is at doctor's discretion
MASSACHUSETTS	Yes*	Yes	Yes*	*Unless harmful to patient
MICHIGAN	Yes	Yes	Yes*	*Unless harmful to patient
MINNESOTA	Yes*	Yes	Yes	*Unless harmful to patient
MISSISSIPPI	No law	Yes	No*	*Patient authorizes release, but law doesn't specify release to patient directly
MISSOURI	Yes	No law	Yes*	*Unless harmful to patient
MONTANA	Yes*	Yes*	Yes*	*Uniform Health Care Information Act passed in 1987; unless harmful to patient
NEBRASKA	No law	No law	No*	*Patient authorizes release, but law doesn't specify release to patient directly
NEVADA	Yes	Yes	Yes*	*Patient allowed to see records at least every three months; unless harmful to patient
NEW HAMPSHIRE	No law	No law	No law	
NEW JERSEY	Yes	Yes*	Yes	*Access guaranteed by state department of health regulation, not state law
NEW MEXICO	No law	No law	Yes*	*Unless harmful to patient
NEW YORK	Yes	Yes	Yes	
NORTH CAROLINA	No law	No law	Yes*	*Unless harmful to patient
NORTH DAKOTA	Yes	Yes	No	
OHIO	No law	Yes	Yes*	*Unless harmful to patient
OKLAHOMA	Yes	Yes	No*	*Patient not entitled to records unless court-ordered, but practitioner may consent to release
OREGON	No*	No*	Yes**	*Release is at discretion of private institutions and doctors; public institutions must release records **Unless harmful to patient
PENNSYLVANIA	No law	Yes	Yes*	*Unless harmful to patient; patient may have to be supervised while reviewing records
RHODE ISLAND	No law	No law	No law	
SOUTH CAROLINA	No law	No law	No law	
SOUTH DAKOTA	Yes	Yes	Yes*	*Unless harmful to patient
TENNESSEE	No law	No*	No**	*Patient must show "good cause" to get records **Patient can designate person to receive records
TEXAS	Yes*	Yes	No law	*Unless harmful to patient
UTAH	No*	No*	No**	*Releasable to attorney **Releasable to family or friends
VERMONT	No law	No law	No law	
VIRGINIA	No law*	No law*	Yes**	*In a lawsuit, patient has right to records; attorney general opinion extends this right to non-suit situations **Unless harmful to patient
WASHINGTON	No law	No law	No*	*Patient can designate person to receive records
WEST VIRGINIA	Yes	Yes	Yes	
WISCONSIN	Yes	Yes	Yes	
WYOMING	No law	No law	No law	

A "yes" in any column means state law specifically guarantees patient access. A "no" means state access law doesn't include patients. The comments column gives restrictions. Other hurdles, such as copying fees, usually exist. Don't give up if you live in a state that has no law or doesn't grant access. Your doctor may let you see your records anyway. If not, have them sent to a more cooperative physician. Or get a lawyer to make the request for you. If your records are kept by a federal facility, such as a VA hospital, you're guaranteed access.

Hippocrates research by Mary James.

formation Bureau, however, is well known for its thorough computer security, and Equifax says that none of its medical information is stored in data banks.) Experts suspect interception happens, but have little real evidence. In 1983, though, a group of Wisconsin teenagers proved that it could when they electronically gained access to some 6,000 records at New York's Memorial Sloan-Kettering Cancer Center. The consequences might have been disastrous: Among other duties, the computer helped regulate radiation doses for patients. Some have warned that medical snake-oil salesmen could similarly acquire computerized mailing lists of patients—organized neatly by ailment—to bombard the afflicted with pitches for quack remedies.

If you're thinking there must be laws that will protect you against such abuses, don't count on it. What exists on the federal level covers only federal agencies, such as Medicare, or federally funded programs, such as drug rehabilitation services. The Privacy Act of 1974, for example, does require federal agencies to get written patient consent before releasing records outside the agency. But an agency can get information from a doctor or hospital without telling the patient. And it needs no consent to pass someone's records around within the agency—the Centers for Disease Control could pass a record to the Alcohol, Drug Abuse, and Mental Health Administration, for instance, because both are part of the Public Health Service.

Employers and insurers are covered by state laws, but they are usually scattershot. In most states, doctors and hospitals cannot release a medical record without the patient's consent. An indiscreet doctor can lose his or her license or be sued. (However, that blanket waiver you sign on the claim form gives health care providers all the consent they need.) In Louisiana, hospitals and doctors have to give patients, on request, a copy of anything they have provided to any company, agency, or individual. About a dozen states—including Georgia, Illinois, and California—permit patients to inspect and copy insurers' records. Rhode Island requires that an insurer's authorization waiver must state that no disclosure will be made without patient permission. Alaska, Ohio, and Wisconsin let employees see or copy medical records held by their employers; Connecticut and Michigan let employees correct such information. But few, if any, state laws go beyond the employer or insurer. "The lack of control over what insurance companies and others do with records is the single biggest weakness in medical privacy law today," says Robert Ellis Smith, publisher of the *Privacy Journal* in Washington, D.C.

If the legal jumble seems like a bad dream, the possibility of mistakes can turn it into a nightmare. With each pass from doctor to insurer to employer, with each clerk who types your records into yet another computer file, with each change of doctors or insurance companies, errors can flare up like herpes and are just about as impossible to eradicate. No one knows how often mistakes occur, but

THEY'VE GOT A FILE ON YOU

CHARLES ZIMMERMAN probably could have gotten disability insurance without any trouble if he hadn't bragged about his healthy habits. But when an investigator for the insurance company asked the 32-year-old Boston engineer whether he smoked, "I proudly said, 'I have a very clean lifestyle—I don't smoke or drink,'" says Zimmerman. "I thought he'd be impressed."

Instead, he was . . . interested. Never drank? Did Zimmerman ever attend Alcoholics Anonymous? Zimmerman, being an honest sort, said yes. And was denied insurance. He applied to a second insurance company, and was offered coverage for 25 percent above the normal rate. That's when Zimmerman learned there was a file on him at the Medical Information Bureau, the data bank used by the country's major life and health insurance companies. In that file, there was a little symbol that meant Zimmerman was an alcoholic.

Now as Zimmerman says, he doesn't know if he can rightly be called an alcoholic. Drinking had never threatened his job, had never led to any medical or legal problems. He had simply decided, six years ago, that he was drinking too much, and had done something about it. "I told them, 'There is no medical history here—my only symptom ever was a hangover.'"

Zimmerman eventually got insured at normal rates, and—though it took a year—he also got the bureau to remove the disputed symbol from his file. But his experience highlights concerns about the data bank that holds information on about 13 million of North America's insured.

The Medical Information Bureau was founded in 1902 to guard against the wily applicant who, denied insurance at one company, would lie to a second in order to pass muster. It's a simple setup: If an insurance company finds an applicant has a health-threatening condition, such as high blood pressure or heart disease, it alerts the

data bank. The bureau requires its members to independently verify all information. (A 1977 investigation found that 80 member companies had not been following this rule; now, says president Neal Day, such incidents are rare.)

It's hard for an outsider to know whether these internal rules are followed, though, because the data bank isn't stringently regulated. According to privacy experts, most state laws governing the bureau lack punch, if they exist at all. On the federal level, the Fair Credit Reporting Act would empower a rejected applicant to find out just what is in that file—except that the act specifically excludes medical information. That leaves self-regulation. According to Day, the agency acts as though all its dealings were covered by the Fair Credit Act.

By the grace of the bureau, then, you can find out what's in your file. It will send you a form that asks for your name, birthdate, birthplace, present address, and a promise, under penalty of fines and imprisonment, that you are who you say you are. When you return the form, it'll send you within 30 days any nonmedical information it may have on you—for instance, that your medical records note that you're a skydiver. Any medical information goes to a health care professional of your choice.

If you find any mistakes, there's a simple procedure to follow—although Zimmerman's experience shows that it's not always a speedy one. First, the agency will ask for a re-investigation by the insurer that originally filed the erroneous information; you may want to send the insurer a statement from your doctor. If the bureau decides you're correct, it will make the appropriate changes. If you're dissatisfied with the response, your only recourse is to send the bureau a statement of dispute, which will become an inseparable part of your file.

Write or call: Medical Information Bureau, P.O. Box 105, Essex Station, Boston, MA 02112, 617/426-3660. —*Lisa Davis* they do happen: Out of the 7,000 patients who ask for their files from the Medical Information Bureau each year, 200 request corrections in their records. Sometimes the damage—both physical and economic—from these errors can be devastating.

Midwesterner Scott Dillon* has been haunted by such a mistake for more than two decades. While attending medical school in the mid-1960s, Dillon, who was considering a career in psychiatry, opted to undergo psychoanalysis as a routine part of his training. During this time he visited the student health service for treatment of severe headaches and back pain. The doctor in charge, discovering that Dillon was seeing a psychiatrist, concluded that the pains were psychosomatic. Dillon was sent to a psychiatrist-in-training, who wrongly told him he was manic-depressive.

The diagnosis followed him like an insistent mosquito. Desperate to ease his pain, Dillon allowed doctors to give him powerful antidepressants and shock treatments. The effects were worse than the supposed illness. Dillon dropped out of medical school, and several graduate schools later rejected his applications. Worst of all, Dillon didn't receive the timely treatment he needed for what eventually were diagnosed as genuine physical ailments: severe allergies and a degenerative disease of the spine. As a result, he was left half-crippled. He later learned that the medical school had sent his medical record, complete with psychiatric diagnoses, along with his academic record to all the graduate schools to which he had applied. The misdiagnoses were eventually expunged from his record, but he believes he carries their stigma to this day.

If you want to have any say about what's in your records and who gets them, here's what you have to do: Get a copy of your own medical records from your doctor and make sure they're accurate and complete. Before 1959, no court recognized that patients had the right to have access to their own medical records. Today, it may not always be easy to get your records, but at least you have a fighting chance. "The issues of third-party access and patient access go hand in hand," says Smith of the *Privacy Journal*. "How can you give informed consent to insurance companies examining your records if you don't know what's in them?"

"Everyone should have a copy in their bureau drawer, and take them along whenever they go to the doctor," says Doris Haire of the Washington, D.C.–based National Women's Health Network. If something is inaccurate or missing, she says, you should go to the responsible doctor or hospital and ask for a correction. You may have to agree to undergo certain tests or examinations in order to remedy the mistakes.

You can also practice a little preventive medicine on your insurance policy. On the claim forms, try rewording the waiver this way: "I authorize my

*This name has been changed.

records to be released only from [the pertinent hospital or doctor] for the dates [the date of your hospitalization or appointment] as relates to [the condition covered by that claim]."

On the application, you can limit the authorization by adding a notation that says the company can obtain information only for the period up to and including the current date. That way, the company doesn't have perpetual permission to collect anything it wants, anytime it wants. Keep in mind, however, that insurers may tell you to take your business elsewhere. And, while George Annas of the Boston University School of Public Health says the technique works well for many, he also says, "If it's life insurance, they have you over a barrel. They want everything. And they won't insure you unless they get it."

Under the Federal Fair Credit Reporting Act, however, you are entitled to the sources of any medical information an insurer has used to deny you coverage. Likewise, you can get any information that the Medical Information Bureau may have on you. Also, you might want to contact your local chapter of the American Medical Record Association (call 312/787-2672, extension 256) to learn whether your state has laws to help you get your records from employers, insurance carriers, and others.

One option that all states permit—albeit a rather drastic one—is to sue your doctor if you catch him or her red-handed in a breach of confidentiality. "But if you really want to keep your privacy, that's a self-defeating proposition," Annas says. "As soon as you bring a lawsuit, your record becomes public."

Perhaps the best news for your medical secrets is a model bill drafted by the national Conference of Commissioners on Uniform State Laws, a group that tries to iron out inconsistencies and gaps in state laws. (Each state can enact this law; it doesn't need ratification by a majority of states).

The proposed law would allow patients to get their own records, require that anyone other than doctors or hospitals get patient consent before obtaining records, and limit access by subpoena. If outsiders couldn't present compelling evidence of need, records keepers could not be held liable for refusing their request. The act specifies some key exceptions—such as allowing access to bona fide researchers, financial auditors, or emergency rooms —that may leave open some of the same old loopholes. And it doesn't tackle the crucial problem of the release of medical information by insurance companies and others.

Montana is the only state to adopt the law so far, and while other states may soon follow, it's probably best not to wait on them. When it comes to protecting your own medical privacy, there's really only one good rule to follow: Don't count on anyone else to do it for you.

Our chip has come in

Apparently Orwell got it wrong. Or, at least, half wrong: he understood that new information technologies would profoundly affect the direction of history, but his forecast of the direction was off by around 180 degrees. In *1984*, TV cameras and colossal (low-tech) databases served mainly to tighten state control over speech and thought, to strip the individual of power. But in 1989 (and 1988, and 1987), information technology has had the opposite effect. Witness Russia and, now, China. Whatever has happened in China by the time you read this—whether the forces of liberalization or of reaction have won the day—the Chinese are, in the long run, squarely on the road toward greater freedom. Indeed, it is beginning to look as if, in the information age, there is no other road.

We are not talking only, or even mainly, about satellite dishes. Much has been said about the role of TV in China's remarkable springtime adventure, quite a bit of it true: yes, the knowledge that the world was watching probably made the government reluctant to crack down on student protesters early on; yes, TV had helped blow the winds of *glasnost*, not to mention genuine Western democracy, eastward in the first place; yes, TV helped the demonstrations proliferate, from Beijing to Shanghai to Hong Kong—almost as if masses of Asians were replicating themselves via satellite. So, yes, TV may, in some significant but still unclear way, load the dice in favor of democracy. On the other hand, as the Chinese showed by pulling the plug on Dan Rather, TV is susceptible to centralized control. It is becoming less so, as cameras and satellite dishes become smaller and cheaper; but for now, TV is not intrinsically a technology of the individual.

More fundamentally democratizing, in the decades ahead, will be the personal computer and ancillary technologies. The modern economy, everyone now knows, is fueled by information; as economic development proceeds, the portion of the work force that makes its living by manipulating information, or by making or maintaining machines that manipulate information, grows inexorably. To compete economically, a nation must give its workers—its people—information machines that are by nature decentralizing and empowering: computers, printers, modems, fax machines. Through them, people gain sources of information—and *become* sources of information—that are hard for the government to control. The fundamental myth of totalitarian communism (that the people all agree) collides with the crucial reality of capitalist democracy (that they don't) and yields the dilemma now facing leaders in Moscow and Beijing: let the people think for themselves and speak their minds, and recognize the diversity of their opinions—or smell your economy rot.

Of course, history was on the side of democracy long before the microchip was invented a few decades ago by two entrepreneurial American scientists. (Marx, like Orwell, was one for two: yes, history is headed inexorably toward the vindication of a specific political philosophy; no, it's not your philosophy.) Capitalism has always been the most productive economic system around, and its freedom of enterprise has always seemed to imply a certain freedom of thought and expression, though some repressive capitalist nations have succeeded in keeping the connection between the two quite tenuous. What the microelectronic revolution has done is strengthen this connection. For despots, the cruel logic runs like this: your economy cannot compete unless it is a decentralized and free one; once decentralized, it still cannot be very competitive unless it is riddled with small, cheap, potent information processors, each capable of serving as a printing press, a database, a transmitter, a receiver; once your economy is so riddled, your society is so riddled; once your society is so riddled, hang on to your hat.

The remarkable thing is that this logic is just beginning to kick in, and already the ferment is considerable. Though the newly vibrant and diverse Soviet press is fueled partly by personal computers, these machines remain rare and precious things in Russia. Indeed, if they weren't, all the news about Orwell being published overground would barely matter; once home computers are common, any body of writing, with or without the Party's seal of approval, can reproduce wildly, via laser printer or modem. In China, too, the information revolution is young by Western standards. In fact, the recent upheaval has been a striking testament to the power of low-tech organizing: bicycle messengers and posters, leaflets and word of mouth (albeit amplified by loudspeaker) have coordinated the actions of a million people. This is the frightening thing from the point of view of aspiring Chinese dictators: of the information revolution's one-two punch—TV and widely decentralized computerization—only the first punch has been delivered, and already the place is a shambles.

In spite of the foregoing, there are several reasons not to break out the champagne. First, there is a certain amount of evidence that doesn't fit neatly into sunny, technologically deterministic forecasts. Dictators like Manuel Noriega have resolutely ignored television's damning images, and capitalist tyrannies, as in South Africa, have successfully squelched them—and kept a lid on internal dissent. For the time being, at least, this is doable. Still, the smart money says that as IBM, Apple, and NEC continue to infiltrate the working world, and TV technology undergoes further miniaturization, the separation of political and economic liberalization will become increasingly untenable.

A second reason not to celebrate democracy's world championship prematurely is that democracy is a funny thing. When it works, it is clearly superior to any other form of government. But it seems only to work easily in select environments (principally, so far, northern and western ones). When democracy and capitalism suddenly appear in cultures without a history of both, turbulence can ensue. There is no reason to expect the miracle of modern technology to change that. Around the world, the will of the people will almost certainly find greater and more frequent expression, but there is no reason to bet that this expression will assume the orderly form that makes Americans so partial to it. (There are senses, in fact, in which the information age *complicates* the functioning of a mature democracy, such as ours.)

One can imagine, then, a world in which sporadic, destabilizing thrusts of popular will fight an ever more violent battle with repression. And remember: the communications revolution has brought blessings for the repressor as well as the repressed; computers do have the *potential* for effecting totalitarian control. If the government of a modern economy wanted to centrally collect the various computerized information about each citizen—every long-distance phone call, every book bought on credit, every hotel stayed in, every videotape rented—it could fairly cheaply come to know a disturbing amount about everyone. In America, the people don't *want* the government to have that sort of access, so it doesn't. The hope is that increasingly, other governments, too, will find it hard to do things their people don't want them to do.

Still, there is a chance—a slim one, it seems, but a chance—that Orwell will be vindicated in the end, that the darker side of information technology will win out. This is the second good news/bad news joke brought to us by the seeming disintegration of modern communism. The first is that once the Iron Curtain begins to crumble, everyone realizes that a bipolar world had the virtue, at least, of being simple; the fluidity of geopolitics in a post-cold war, multipolar era may in some ways be frightening. The second joke is that totalitarian communism could well crumble only to be replaced by something not necessarily better: an enduring chaos, in which individual liberty doesn't clearly prevail and yet isn't systematically and quietly stifled, but rather is periodically beaten down only to rise up again—an ongoing, high-tech battle between good and evil.

Maybe it is just as well to go ahead and have some champagne after all. Once the latest party is over, there will be much work to do.

Caller Identification: More Privacy or Less?

Jeff Johnson—CPSR/Palo Alto

Jeff Johnson is a researcher at Hewlett-Packard in Palo Alto, CA. He serves on the executive committee of the CPSR Board of Directors, and he was active in the organization of the CPSR conference on "participatory design." CPSR Washington Office Director Marc Rotenberg also contributed to this article. They both encourage CPSR members to submit their own views on Caller ID to either the National or Washington, D.C., offices of CPSR.

Which privacy right is more important: the right to prevent your telephone number from being disclosed to others, or the right to know who is calling you? As telephone companies across the U.S. prepare to introduce a service called Caller Identification (Caller ID), and as opponents of the service raise concerns about privacy implications, that is how the issue is being framed.

Caller ID works as follows: whenever a telephone whose owner subscribes to the service is called, it is provided with the number of the calling telephone. What the called telephone *does* with that number depends, of course, upon what it is *designed* to do with it. Most of the telephones in use now couldn't do anything with the information. Most Caller-ID compatible telephones would simply show the calling number in a small display while the telephone is ringing and during the ensuing conversation. Fancier telephones would compare the number to a stored list, either to determine the caller's name so they can display that instead of the number or to decide how to handle the call, *e.g.,* to ignore the call, activate a telephone-recorder, play a caller-specific message, or ring the telephone. More advanced telephones, integrated into computer systems, might send the number to a database, either to add it to a list of callers or to retrieve other information about the caller.

An important point about Caller ID is that whether your telephone number is given to people you call depends upon whether *they* subscribe to the service, not whether you do. Subscribing lets you see the numbers of people who call you.

Caller ID has been available in private PBX telephone systems for internal calls for several years. It was made available to many businesses offering "800" numbers two years ago. Within the past year, telephone companies have begun to make Caller ID available to residential customers. By 1992, telephone companies are expected to have it available nationwide.

Proponents of Caller ID maintain that knowing who is calling is useful information that can help prevent telephone calls from being as intrusive as they now are. They argue that if someone interrupts you by calling you, you have a right to know who they are. Furthermore, they claim, you have a right to know *before* you pick up the telephone, so you can decide if you want to let that person interrupt you. Also, Caller ID is touted as a way to reduce the incidence of obscene or harassing calls, since the perpetrators of such calls rely upon anonymity.

Apart from allowing telephone users to control telephone interruptions and deter crank calls, proponents claim that Caller ID has other advantages. For example, it allows people to have telephones that can be "programmed" to handle calls from different people differently. For example, calls from relatives can be sent to the telephone recorder, calls from friends can ring through, calls from fellow bridge club members can be greeted by a message stating the place and time of the next meeting, and calls from others can be ignored entirely. Caller ID also enables "Call last caller back" for cases in which, for example, the telephone rings while you are in the shower, or is ringing when you come home with your arms full of grocery bags.

From *The CPSR Newsletter,* Winter/Spring 1990, pp. 1-6. Reprinted by permission of the author and The Computer Professionals for Social Responsibility, Palo Alto, CA.

Criticism of Caller ID

Critics of Caller ID claim that its benefits are outweighed by its violation of everyone's right to control to whom they give their telephone number. They argue that if someone wants your number, they should ask you for it rather than getting it without your consent. Caller ID opponents point to a number of legitimate types of telephone calls for which anonymity is important; *e.g.*, people calling AIDS or child-abuse hot lines or police tip lines, social workers and medical workers calling patients from home, probation officers calling their charges, people calling businesses who don't want their number added to a telemarketing database.

Caller ID opponents also claim that the benefits of Caller ID are less than claimed anyway, because:

1. Caller ID may result in an overall *increase* in unwanted calls, since many businesses will use it to compile lists of customers for use in telemarketing.

2. Having Caller ID won't really reduce the intrusiveness of telephone calls. Once you've stopped what you were doing to go to the phone to see if you want to answer it, you've already been interrupted. Furthermore, it is difficult to tell from a displayed number who is calling, especially quickly enough to decide what to do before the caller gives up; people with number-display telephones will end up answering most calls anyway.

3. Most of the benefits of Caller ID can already be achieved in other ways, without revealing anyone's number without their consent. Telephone calls needn't be so intrusive. Our compulsion to answer the telephone when it rings is what should be changed: people should feel freer to get unlisted numbers and screen calls through answering machines. If the telephone company can give you the caller's number then they can trace crank and obscene calls. They can also provide "Call last caller back" without telling you the number.

Caller ID advocates rebut that the benefits of the service are real, and that those who oppose it are just "technological reactionaries" out to impede progress. Some Caller ID proponents counter critics' concerns about privacy by claiming that the service doesn't violate anyone's privacy rights, since *the telephone company*, not the telephone user, "owns" telephone numbers.

Caller ID critics respond that pro-Caller-ID arguments are just a smoke-screen; Caller ID's true beneficiaries, and its main promoters, are businesses who see it as a valuable tool for collecting telemarketing data, telephone service companies who will sell the service to businesses, and telephone equipment manufacturers who look forward to a situation in which most of the telephones in the country are suddenly obsolete.

Caller ID Controversy

This is an issue over which there has been, and will continue to be, heated debate. (One indication that Caller ID is a hot topic is that it was the subject of a recent discussion on "Nightline," the ABC News talk show that deals exclusively, it seems, in controversial issues. Similarly, a column on the subject by William Safire in *The New York Times* [December 11, 1989] drew many letters to the editor.) Telephone companies reportedly realized that some people, especially those with "unlisted" numbers, would not appreciate their numbers being disclosed by Caller ID. Nonetheless, telephone companies did not anticipate that the controversy over the service would reach the level it has. As has been said, Caller ID has been available for various types of non-residential telephone service for quite a while. Only after telephone companies began to introduce it for residential customers did significant opposition begin to appear.

Though Caller ID has been approved for imminent availability by Public Utility Commissions (PUCs) in some areas of the U.S. and is already available in others (*e.g.*, New Jersey), approval has rarely been uncontested. Consumer advocacy organizations, state public advocate offices, state legislators, and the American Civil Liberties Union are usually among the vocal critics of Caller ID. In areas where opposition is strong, PUCs have delayed approval or imposed complicated restrictions and conditions. In California for example, the PUC and the state assembly required that a blocking option be provided so that callers can prevent their numbers from being displayed. Pennsylvania's PUC also required a blocking option, but yielding to telephone company arguments that having such an option defeats the purpose of Caller ID, restricted its use to law enforcement officials, crime witnesses, victims of violent crimes, and others who deal with violent people. That decision has been appealed in the Pennsylvania courts by the state Consumer Advocate. Meanwhile, Senator Kohl (D-WI), has introduced a bill in Congress to require a blocking service nationwide. In the face of such complicated regulations, some telephone companies have delayed introducing or even asking for permission to introduce Caller ID until the debate cools down.

Clearly, the idea of revealing callers' telephone numbers without their consent bothers some people, and clearly, the prospect of not having the benefits of Caller ID disturbs others. The arguments for and against Caller ID raise several issues. In what follows, several are explored in detail.

Who Owns Telephone Numbers?

First, who really owns the rights to people's telephone numbers? Certainly, telephone companies can and do distribute people's telephone numbers in the various directories that they provide. This includes reverse-directories, which customers (usually businesses) can purchase to determine peoples' names and addresses from their telephone numbers. Some directories are or soon will be available in on-line form, facilitating their use in the construction of databases.

But what about "unlisted" numbers? Doesn't the extra money a person pays for an unlisted number buy them exclusive distribution rights? Yes and no. Unlisted numbers are not included in directories, but *are* given out via Caller ID to whomever the holder of the unlisted number calls (provided the call recipients subscribe to the service).

If you give the number of a friend to a third party without asking your friend, your friend may not like it, but you certainly would not have violated any law. A telephone company's disclosure of your number to a third party is, it might be argued, exactly analogous. However, it might also be argued that automatic or electronic disclosure of telephone numbers differs from person-to-person disclosure and *is* illegal. For example, in Pennsylvania, the ACLU argued that Caller ID violates that state's wiretap law, which forbids the use of devices that capture a caller's telephone number. One might also base a counter-argument not on the medium of disclosure but rather on who obtains the number. For example, one might claim that, while telephone companies can distribute directories to customers, they cannot sell lists of telephone numbers to private investigators.

So what are we to conclude about who "owns" a telephone number? Just that the issue is yet unresolved.

Does Caller ID Enhance Privacy?

Next, let's examine the claimed benefits of Caller ID and the corresponding counter claims of critics. For individuals (*i.e.*, residential telephone users), the question is: would having Caller ID enhance their privacy?

New Jersey Bell reports that the number of obscene and threatening telephone calls reported has dropped sharply since Caller ID was introduced last year. Though it is in their interest to be able to report this, it is a result that presumably could be checked. Suppose it's true. Suppose the reduction in such calls is 80%. Given that such calls represent a tiny fraction of all annoying calls, how important is it compared to an increase, say of 25%, in telephone sales solicitations, which Caller ID may well bring about?

What about Caller ID's other claimed benefits? One thing that clearly limits Caller ID's usefulness to individuals is the fact that telephone numbers identify telephones, not people. Knowing the number of the calling telephone doesn't necessarily tell you who is calling. Crank callers could

simply use pay telephones to avoid detection or worse, *other* people's telephones, getting *them* into trouble. You would have no way of knowing who at a given number was calling you. If you had Caller ID, you might reject a call from your spouse stranded somewhere with a broken-down car or from someone who has discovered your injured child because you didn't recognize the number.

Another limiting factor on the overall benefit of Caller ID is the cost of the service and of the necessary equipment. Though a small percentage of the population can afford sophisticated telephones that automatically categorize numbers and handle them accordingly, most Caller-ID compatible telephones in people's homes will be of the simplest variety. Telephones or telephone attachments that do anything more than show the calling number will be extremely rare. So, for most people, the usefulness of Caller ID will depend upon how quickly and easily they can decide, based upon a displayed number, what to do when the telephone rings. I find the arguments of critics—that by the time you're looking at the number you've already been interrupted and that there will be a temptation to answer most calls "just in case"—quite convincing. If they are right, Caller ID will, for average citizens, be little more than a toy that lets them answer the telephone, "Hello, Fred."

One thing proponents and critics of Caller ID agree upon are its telemarketing benefits; what they disagree upon is whether those benefits are worthwhile. According to Calvin Sims, a reporter for *The New York Times*, "Phone companies expect the service to be popular among businesses, which could link it to computer files of customer records." This expectation is already being realized: as stated earlier, many businesses offering "800" numbers already have Caller ID, allowing them to capture the numbers of callers. It will soon be available for companies offering "900" services. Sims says that "American Express uses an AT&T system that lets service representatives see a caller's name and account information before they answer the telephone." With reverse-directories available from telephone companies, businesses could use captured telephone numbers to fill-out their marketing databases.

Caller ID Alternatives

Having examined the benefits of Caller ID, let's consider some alternatives that might provide some of the same benefits without the cost to public privacy.

New Jersey Bell says that Caller ID reduces obscene and harassing calls, and calls it "the best technology" for doing so. Is it? Do you really want to know the telephone number of an obscene caller? Your telephone company can certainly get it if you report the disturbance. Shouldn't they and the police be the ones to handle such problems? Obscene and threatening calls would also be "sharply reduced" if telephone companies simply encouraged people to report them and made it clear that tracing numbers is trivial. Even if tracing numbers is not trivial now, any telephone company that can provide Caller ID could *make* it trivial.

Setting aside criminal calls, let's consider alternative ways to reduce "ordinary" unwanted calls. I'll begin with ways that are available now, then discuss some possible technological alternatives to Caller ID.

As stated earlier, we can simply not answer the telephone when we don't want to be disturbed. Bells can be muted; telephones can be unplugged; answering machines work as well when we are at home as when we are out. If those solutions seem dishonest or require too much behavior modification on our part, consider this: for $69.95, you can buy a device that adds a 3-digit access code to your telephone number; those who don't know it hear a perpetually-ringing telephone and you hear nothing. Arguably such a device is *better* than Caller ID: people you give your code to can get through regardless of what telephone they call from, people who don't have your code can't, you avoid repeated interruptions of having to decide when the telephone rings whether to answer or not, and no one's telephone number is disclosed without consent.

Now, let's turn to alternatives that don't yet exist, but could in the near future. I mentioned earlier that one limitation on the value to residential users of Caller ID is that telephone numbers identify telephones and not people. Another problem is that telephone numbers are effective, unique links to households and data records, which is why they are valuable to businesses and other potential violators of privacy. How might we fix these problems?

First, let's consider what *not* to do. The way the problem is stated—"telephones identify telephones and not people"—suggests that a solution might be to create a system in which telephone numbers identify people, not telephones. In other words, each person has a unique ID number, encoded on a card that can be inserted into telephones. In addition to being used for billing and other purposes, a caller's unique telephone-ID number is provided to whoever that person calls. People you call get more accurate information about who is calling them. This is in fact the direction that many phone pundits expect the telephone system to go. It is also precisely the wrong thing to do, because it increases the invasiveness of the technology to individual privacy, and it keeps the burden of decoding numbers on telephone-call recipients.

A much better solution is to change the system so that people are identified to callers only by name, not by a unique ID number. Names are more useful than any sort of number to residential call-recipients because they can

be used directly. They are also *less* effective as links back to the caller because they aren't unique. The names "Fred J. Smith", or even "Caitlin D. Fitzsimmons," by themselves, would not be as useful to businesses as those peoples' telephone numbers. Two ways to supply names to call recipients come to mind: 1) Use the above-mentioned card, but send just the caller's name, not their account number, to the recipient; 2) Allow callers to "type" their names (or abbreviations thereof) using the key pad when they make a call. Method 1 makes giving a false name more difficult, but some people may not like even their name being given to the callee. Method 2 has the advantage that supplying one's name is optional, but lends itself to the use of false names (though that could be handled by agreement between callers and callees, *e.g.*, nick-names).

Of course, neither of these alternatives satisfy the requirements of businesses. They aren't trying to screen calls. They want a link back to the caller. They need the telephone number, *i.e.*, Caller ID itself. The question is: do we want them to have it?

Different Value for Different Users

Though the Caller ID debate has been framed as a matter of whether callers' right to keep their numbers private is more important that callees' right to know who is calling them, that is not the real issue. The issue has to do with the relative costs and benefits of the service for individuals and for businesses. I have argued that the benefits of Caller ID for residential telephone users are minimal. For them, Caller ID is a naive attempt to solve a difficult problem. Trying to decide how to handle calls based upon the number of the calling telephone is like trying to filter out commercials automatically when recording TV shows based upon the volume level (this has been attempted); you still hear a lot of commercials and you miss a lot of program material. I expect that many people will subscribe to the service, naively believing that it will help them screen calls, and then realize that it doesn't and that they are wasting their money.

While the benefits of Caller ID for individuals are doubtful, the costs are not: widespread dissemination of personal information in a society where such information is increasingly traded as a commodity. For businesses, the situation is reversed: the benefits of Caller ID are great while the only costs are money. All citizens pay the privacy cost while only businesses and people who can afford very sophisticated telephones get real benefits.

I would urge telephone companies, in their roles as public utilities, to place less weight upon the needs of businesses and more on those of their residential customers. I would urge them to seek alternatives to Caller ID that are more useful to the public and less invasive to individual privacy.

Computer System Reliability and Safety

The introduction of any new and powerful technology poses unforeseen hazards. In conducting research for a popular magazine article on the history of American technological achievements, engineer/writer Samuel Florman found that nearly every new technological triumph was initially accompanied by disastrous side effects. He learned, for example, that during the early days of steamboat transport, 42 explosions killed 270 persons between 1825 and 1930. These events, and public outrage, led to government-funded research that ultimately resulted in legislation on safety standards. Florman tells a similar story of the early days of railroading, and in particular, railroad bridges:

> In the late 1860s more than 25 American bridges were collapsing each year, with an appalling loss of life. In 1873 the American Society of Civil Engineers set up a special commission to address the problem, and eventually the safety of our bridges came to be taken for granted.

As these examples illustrate, the solution of these terrible problems was not to abandon but to improve technology. Florman summarizes the pattern of technological advance as "progress/setback/renewed-creative-effort."

Computers have been relatively common for a few decades now. Compared with the steamboat and railroad examples above, computers have caused very few serious injuries to humans. Yet, as the articles in this section show, several aspects of computing pose potentially serious risks to health and safety, and to the smooth functioning of society.

The first two articles in this section address the issue of whether computer hardware and other technologies that emit low-level electromagnetic fields (EMFs) are a threat to health. In "The Magnetic Field Menace," Paul Brodeur reviews the findings of studies conducted in several countries. Though there is still insufficient evidence to reach any firm conclusions, computer users are urged to exercise caution until further research is completed. In the next article, Andrew Bassett argues it is premature to become alarmed over electromagnetic fields. He points out that media coverage of EMFs has ignored the "therapeutic uses of such fields [and thus] overlooked the major source of information on bioeffects and safety records." Nevertheless, since both the potential benefits and hazards are still largely unknown, Professor Bassett also urges further study (rather than premature regulation) of EMF technologies.

In addition to hardware concerns, another and potentially greater source of danger stems from the software that controls complex computerized operations. At the individual, organizational, and society levels, we are dependent on computer systems, some of which are so crucial to the preservation of life and/or societal functioning they must be 100 percent reliable. However, as technical systems become more complex, the goal of reliability is increasingly difficult to achieve.

Sociologist Charles Perrow has argued that danger is increased when highly complex technical systems arise from and operate within equally complex social systems. Disaster can occur if either system breaks down. An example of this is the Challenger space shuttle that exploded because rocket seals failed to function properly in cold weather. The engineers who had worked on the rocket system knew of these defects, and when they learned the launch site temperature was significantly below normal, they tried to have the launch delayed. They were unable, however, to get their warnings past "organizational" barriers to those in command. Thus the tragedy that ensued must be seen as a consequence of bureaucratic as well as technical failure.

The next two articles in this section provide examples of malfunction in complex computer systems. Both articles also discuss relevant organizational, political, and labor issues as well as technical problems in producing software that may contain up to several million lines of code. Evelyn Richards' article, "A System on Overload," focuses on the complexity of commercial and military software. In "Programmed for Disaster," Jonathan Jacky focuses on medical computing and discusses how computer safety can be improved through the use of software engineering, formal methods of software analysis, and possible government regulation.

The final article looks at the high-tech weaponry used during the early days of the 1991 Gulf War (Operation

Desert Storm). In "Robowar," Gregg Easterbrook discusses the history of high-tech conventional warfare and suggests that the increased reliability and accuracy of the newest weapons makes them more humane than their predecessors. But, as he also explains, the success of the initial air strikes against Iraq reflected the favorable combination of climatic and social factors as well as technical sophistication.

Looking Ahead: Challenge Questions

As complex computer systems become more widespread, do you think they will become more reliable and thus safer as happened with steamboats and railroads, or will safety risks increase? What political, social, economic, and technical factors should be taken into account when assessing computer risks?

Aside from nuclear or chemical weapons, do advances in weapons systems raise the prospect of more humanitarian warfare in the future? What, besides technical factors, affects the level of humaneness in armed conflict?

THE MAGNETIC-FIELD MENACE

Computer monitors may pose a very real threat to users

PAUL BRODEUR

Paul Brodeur, a staff writer at the New Yorker *since 1958, specializes in medical and science writing. The winner of many national awards for his reporting on the dangers of asbestos, the hazards of enzymes in household detergents, the destruction of the ozone layer, and the effects of electromagnetic emissions, Brodeur's most recent book is* Currents of Death *(Simon and Schuster, 1989).*

As the new decade begins, most Macintosh users and other inhabitants of the vast computer community have become aware that serious questions are being raised about the potentially harmful health effects of electromagnetic emissions from display monitors. However, the issue has been so shrouded by denial on the part of manufacturers and employers, and addressed with such incompetence by state and federal regulatory agencies, that computer users scarcely know what to think about it, who to turn to for reliable information, or how to protect themselves. Meanwhile, industry, government,

and the medical and scientific community are mounting belated attempts to study the problem and reach some consensus about how to deal with it.

Since disease does not develop by consensus but by immutable laws of biology, it seems prudent to review what is known about the harmful biological effects of low-level electromagnetic emissions from display monitors, power lines, and other sources—particularly magnetic-field emissions, which have been linked for more than ten years to the development of cancer—and to understand how this knowledge has been acquired and disseminated. It also seems sensible to determine the strength of magnetic-field emissions from monitors—something that has not been done with accuracy to date—and to relate these emissions, insofar as possible, with what is known about their potential for harm.

For this reason, *Macworld* has undertaken to conduct careful measurements of the strength of the magnetic fields given off by monitors that are commonly used

with the Macintosh. The idea is to provide accurate readings so that Macintosh users can determine for themselves whether they wish to take protective measures in order to reduce their exposure to magnetic fields (see "At Arm's Length").

First Suspicions

Radiation from computer terminals first became an issue in 1977, when officials of the National Institute for Occupational Safety and Health (NIOSH) measured emissions from several display monitors at the *New York Times,* where two young copy editors had developed incipient cataracts after working on the machines for periods of a year or less. The NIOSH officials reported that the electric-field and magnetic-field strengths of the VLF (very-low-frequency) radio-frequency radiation being emitted were too weak to be detected by their instruments at a distance of 4 inches. As it turned out, they were trying to measure the fields in terms of milliwatts per square meter, even though VLF and ELF (extremely-low-frequency) fields can't be accurately measured in this manner.

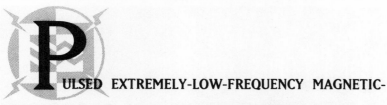

PULSED EXTREMELY-LOW-FREQUENCY MAGNETIC-FIELD LEVELS OF MORE THAN 22 MILLIGAUSS HAVE BEEN MEASURED AT A DISTANCE OF 4 INCHES FROM THE APPLE 13-INCH COLOR MONITOR AND FROM E-MACHINES' COLORPAGE 15

Early in 1980, NIOSH officials measured VLF magnetic-field strengths of almost 9 milligauss (a gauss is a unit of strength of the magnetic field, and a milligauss is $^1/1000$ gauss) near the flyback transformers of several display monitors at newspapers in San Francisco and Oakland, California. The NIOSH officials discounted the health hazard of these fields, claiming that "there is no occupational standard for this frequency and these frequencies have not been shown to cause biological injury."

During the next two years, seven unusual clusters of birth defects and miscarriages involving women who operated video-display terminals (VDTs) were reported in Canada and the United States. Instead of taking their own measurements of the machines in question, however, the health officials who investigated these cases relied on the flawed NIOSH reports and characterized each of the clusters as a chance occurrence. By this time, the regulatory officials and computer manufacturers of both nations seemed to be falling over one another in their haste to absolve computers of any blame.

In March of 1981, the director of Canada's Radiation Protection Bureau declared that VDTs "carry no radiation hazard." Similar claims were made before a congressional subcommittee by the U.S. Food and Drug Administration's Bureau of Radiological Health and by the director of standards for IBM. In October of that year, a senior scientist at the Bell Telephone Laboratories in Murray Hill, New Jersey, declared that computer terminals "do not represent a health hazard from any radiation exposure caused by their use." (At the time, there were well over 100,000 computer terminals in operation in the Bell systems.)

60Hz Hazards Exposed

Unaccountably, no one in industry or government said a word about the pulsed 60Hz electric and magnetic fields that were being emitted by display monitors (see "Cathode-Ray Tubes Explained"), even though there were by then many studies in the medical literature to suggest that the 60Hz alternating-current fields given off by power lines might be hazardous to health. Chief among these studies was one that had been published in March of 1979 in the highly respected *American Journal of Epidemiology* by epidemiologist Nancy Wertheimer and physicist Ed Leeper, who live in Boulder, Colorado. Wertheimer and Leeper had conducted an investigation showing that children in the Denver area who lived in homes near electric distribution wires carrying high current had died of cancer at twice the expected rate. (Since magnetic fields are produced by electric current, distribution wires carrying high current produce relatively strong magnetic fields—invisible lines of force that readily penetrate almost anything that happens to stand in their way, including the human body.)

In their article, Wertheimer and Leeper pointed out that magnetic fields in homes near high-current wires might reach levels of 2 milligauss or more "for hours or days at a time," and that if magnetic-field exposure were responsible for the increased incidence of childhood cancer they had observed, the duration of exposure might be an important factor. They also suggested that the magnetic fields from power lines might be promoting cancer in children by hindering the

ability of the body's immune system to fight the disease.

Instead of taking Wertheimer and Leeper's disturbing findings as a sign that the magnetic-field problem should be thoroughly investigated, the electric-utilities industry tried to discredit their work. But in 1986 the association between magnetic fields from high-current wires and childhood cancer was confirmed by a major study conducted under the auspices of the New York State Department of Health. This investigation reported that "prolonged exposure to low-level magnetic fields may increase the risk of developing cancer in children." Earlier, a similar finding was announced by scientists studying childhood cancer in Sweden. What should have been of profound concern to the manufacturers and users of display monitors was that the incidence of cancer in all three childhood studies was associated with 60Hz magnetic-field strengths of only 2 to 3 milligauss.

Computer Monitors Implicated

The fact that display monitors emit significant radiation in the form of pulsed ELF electric and magnetic fields did not come to light until October of 1982. At that time, Dr. Karel Marha, a biophysicist at the Canadian Centre for Occupational Health and Safety (CCOHS) in Hamilton, Ontario, revealed that Canadian researchers had measured 60Hz magnetic fields greater than 2 milligauss at distances of 12 inches from two display monitors, and fields of approximately 1 milligauss at a distance of 20 inches from several screens. In 1983, CCOHS issued press releases carrying Marha's warning that there was scientific evidence to suggest that pulsed electric and magnetic fields could be more harmful than nonpulsed fields, as well as his recommendation that workplaces be redesigned so that VDT operators do not sit close to their display monitors or to neighboring monitors.

Marha's recommendations were ignored by government health officials in Canada and the United States, who failed to appreciate the possible connection between the potential health hazard of alternating-current 60Hz power-line magnetic fields and that of the pulsed 60Hz magnetic fields given

CATHODE-RAY TUBES EXPLAINED

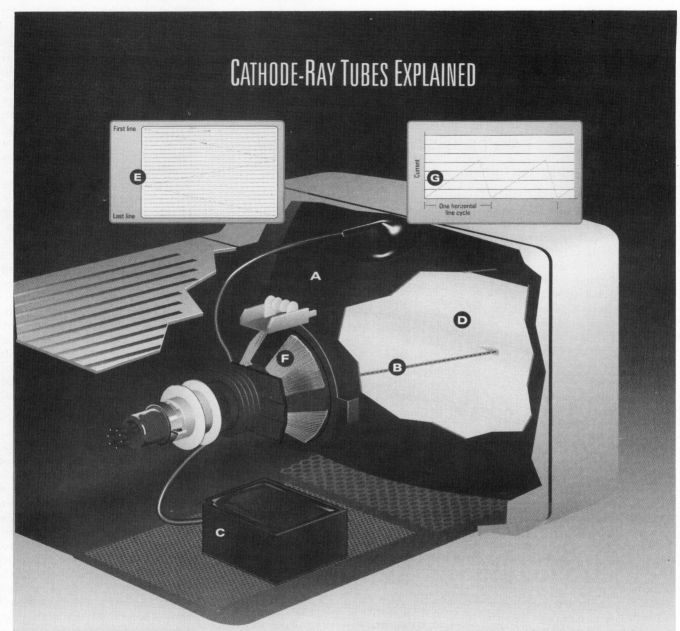

Computer display monitors operate on much the same principle as television sets. An evacuated glass tube containing an electron gun, called the cathode-ray tube (CRT) **(A)**, produces a narrow electron beam **(B)**; a step-up transformer known as the flyback transformer **(C)** then accelerates and directs the beam toward the front of the tube. When the beam strikes the inner surface of the CRT screen, it interacts with a phosphor coating **(D)** on the face of the tube to generate a spot of visible light.

To produce a screen image, the electron beam sweeps from left to right and from top to bottom in a series of raster lines **(E)**. The movement of the electron beam is controlled by deflection coils **(F)** wound like a yoke around the neck of the CRT; electric current flowing through the coils produces magnetic fields that control the electron beam. Increasing current in the horizontal-deflection coil forces the beam from left to right; a drop in current causes the beam to return to the left. Meanwhile, an increase in the vertical-deflection coil's current aims the beam down a line. This pulsing action results in a sawtooth waveform **(G)**.

The horizontal-scan frequency for a typical computer monitor is generally between 10kHz and 30kHz, which falls in the very-low-frequency (VLF) range. Because most monitors operate at 60 to 75 frames per second, their vertical-scan frequency is between 60Hz and 75Hz, within the extremely-low-frequency (ELF) range. Both electric and magnetic fields are generated in the ELF and VLF ranges.

In addition, 60Hz alternating-current (AC) fields originate in the monitor's power transformer. (60Hz AC current flows back and forth 60 times a second.) Since the AC fields decay rapidly over distance, they can usually be measured only in the immediate vicinity of the power transformer.—*P.B.*

SOMEONE SHOULD REMIND THE MONITOR MANU-
FACTURERS THAT SCIENTISTS DON'T KNOW EXACTLY HOW INHALED
ASBESTOS FIBERS ACT TO CAUSE CANCER, AND ONLY FOOLS WOULD
WILLINGLY EXPOSE THEMSELVES TO ASBESTOS

off by display monitors. Moreover, the CCOHS press releases were not picked up by any major newspaper in the United States or Canada. A year later, the medical director of the *New York Times* told a congressional subcommittee that he was aware of "no medical evidence of serious VDT–related health effects." By then, of course, newspapers everywhere had become highly dependent upon computer technology.

Supporting Evidence
In July of 1982, shortly before Marha's announcement that display monitors were emitting potentially hazardous electric and magnetic fields, Dr. Samuel Milham, Jr., a physician and epidemiologist for the Washington State Department of Social and Health Services, published a letter in the *New England Journal of Medicine* that furnished a new insight into the problem. Milham had examined the data for 438,000 deaths occurring between 1950 and 1979 among workers in Washington State and had found that leukemia deaths were elevated in 10 out of 11 occupations involving exposure to electromagnetic fields. His pioneering study provided the starting point for some 20 subsequent investigations here and abroad, which showed that persons whose occupations require them to work in electromagnetic fields—among them electricians, electrical engineers, and telephone- and power-line workers—die of leukemia and brain cancer at a much higher rate than other workers.

For example, a 1984 study demonstrated that a significantly higher than expected number of Maryland men who had died from brain cancer had been employed in electrical occu-

pations, and a 1988 study of men who had died of brain cancer in East Texas revealed that the risk for electric-utility workers was 13 times greater than that for workers who were not exposed to electromagnetic fields.

Additional cause for concern came in November of 1989 with the announcement that a study conducted by epidemiologists at the Johns Hopkins University School of Hygiene and Public Health, in Baltimore, had found an elevated risk of all cancers among cable splicers working for the New York Telephone Company. Indeed, the incidence of leukemia among these men, who often work close to power lines, was 7 times that of other workers in the company. Moreover, measurements of their on-the-job exposure showed that the mean level of the 60Hz alternating-current magnetic-field strengths to which they had been subjected was only 4.3 milligauss. Considering the fact that a pulsed ELF magnetic field level of between 4 and 5 milligauss has been measured at a distance of 12 inches from the Apple 13-inch color monitor and from E-Machines' Color-Page 15, this is a discomfiting finding, to say the least.

Laboratory Studies Concur
While epidemiologists were investigating the incidence of cancer among human beings exposed to low-level electromagnetic fields, other scientists were studying the effect of weak ELF fields on test animals. Chief among them was Dr. W. Ross Adey, a clinical neurologist and neuroscientist, who was formerly the director of the Brain Research Institute at the University of California at Los Angeles and is now associate chief of staff for research at the Jerry L. Pettis Memorial Veterans' Hospital, in Loma Linda, California. During the 1970s, Adey and his col-

leagues discovered that weak ELF electromagnetic fields altered brain chemistry in living cats. During the 1980s they found that low-level electromagnetic fields can interfere with the ability of T-lymphocyte cells—the soldiers of the immune system—to kill cancer cells, which suggests that these fields may be acting as cancer promoters by suppressing the immune system.

In 1988, Adey and his associates demonstrated that weak 60Hz electric fields similar in strength to those that can be found in the tissue of a human being standing beneath a typical overhead high-voltage power line (or, for that matter, in the tissue of someone standing very close to a display monitor) could increase the activity of an enzyme called ornithine decarboxylase, which is associated with cancer promotion.

Back in 1980 and 1981, even as government health officials in the United States and Canada were denying any possible connection between electromagnetic emissions from display monitors and adverse pregnancy outcomes among women who worked with those machines, Spanish researchers were conducting experiments showing that when chicken eggs were exposed to weak pulsed ELF magnetic fields, nearly 80 percent of them developed abnormally, with malformations of the cephalic nervous system being particularly prevalent. The adverse effect of pulsed magnetic fields upon the development of chick embryos was confirmed in 1984 by scientists at the Swedish National Board of Occupational Safety and Health.

Later that year, however, Professor Arthur W. Guy, director of the Bioelectromagnetic Research Laboratory at the University of Washington, in Seattle, who had been hired by IBM to review the literature on the biological effects of VDT emissions, pointed out that the weak magnetic-field pulses used by the Spanish researchers did not match the sawtooth shape of the pulses emitted by computer display monitors, and concluded that there was no valid evidence that monitor emissions posed any health hazard.

Further Indications
Early in 1986, Guy's criticism was addressed in a Swedish study conducted by Dr. Bernhard Tribukait, a professor

of radiobiology in the Department of Radiobiology of the world-renowned Karolinska Institute, in Stockholm. Together with a colleague, Tribukait discovered that the fetuses of mice exposed to weak pulsed fields with the same sawtooth shape as those given off by display monitors experienced more congenital malformations than did the fetuses of unexposed test animals. (This finding was reported by Tom Brokaw on "NBC Nightly News," but went unmentioned by the *New York Times* and virtually every major daily newspaper in the United States.)

In the spring of 1987, Dr. Hakon Frölen, of the Swedish University of Agricultural Sciences, in Uppsala, Sweden, reported that he and a colleague had found a significant increase in fetal deaths and fetal losses by resorption (a phenomenon similar to miscarriage in humans) among pregnant mice exposed to weak pulsed magnetic fields, compared with those occurring in nonexposed test animals. In June, other Swedish scientists reported that radiation similar to that emitted by display monitors could cause genetic effects in exposed tissue samples. An important aspect of all three Swedish studies was that the radiation exposure in each of them had been designed to mimic as closely as possible the sawtooth magnetic-field pulses emitted by VDTs.

Further evidence that weak pulsed magnetic fields might be hazardous to health came in the spring of 1988, when the combined results of a six-laboratory experiment conducted in the United States, Canada, Spain, and Sweden confirmed the earlier finding that such fields could indeed adversely affect the development of chick embryos. Later that year, Frölen found that the fetuses of pregnant mice were most sensitive to pulsed magnetic fields in the early stages of pregnancy, which was consistent with a similar observation by Canadian and Spanish researchers.

At the second international VDT conference, which was held in Montreal in September of 1989, Frölen described a series of experiments in which he delayed exposing pregnant mice to pulsed magnetic fields for up to nine days after conception. The results were striking. All of the mice that were exposed immediately after

conception, or on the first, second, or fifth day after conception, had statistically increased rates of resorption.

Louis Slesin, the editor and publisher of *VDT News*—a newsletter that reports six times a year on the biological effects of display monitors . . . —has emphasized the importance of Frölen's findings, pointing out that the lack of any effect after the ninth day following conception "clearly indicates that the pulsed magnetic fields—not some as-yet-unrecognized factor—are damaging the embryos."

Industry Responses

Meanwhile, the Coalition for Workplace Technology—a powerful lobbying group set up by the Computer and Business Equipment Manufacturers Association (CBEMA) and strongly supported by IBM—had been lobbying since 1984 in various state legislatures against laws designed to protect the health of VDT workers. Computer manufacturers continued to scoff at the idea that their devices might emit hazardous radiation. One industry spokesperson, Charlotte Le Gates, the director of communication for CBEMA, declared that for pregnant operators to ask to be transferred away from VDTs "is like asking to be transferred away from a light bulb."

By using this simile repeatedly, computer manufacturers and their paid consultants in CBEMA and the Center for Office Technology have been unquestionably successful in allaying growing concern among computer users that the emissions from display monitors might be hazardous. The comparison is specious and unscientific, however. A light bulb emits no magnetic field whatsoever—a fact that can easily be ascertained by holding a gauss meter (a device that measures the strength of a magnetic field) to an incandescent light bulb. . . . many display monitors *do* emit magnetic fields that are as strong or even stronger than the magnetic-field levels that have been associated with the development of cancer in children and workers.

Risk Acknowledged

The accumulation of evidence suggesting that the electromagnetic fields

given off by display monitors may be hazardous, together with the fact that there are now some 40 million computer terminals in the workplace, raises the question of why so few epidemiological studies have been conducted in the United States to determine whether monitor emissions are affecting the health of American users. Astonishingly, only one major epidemiological study has so far been conducted in this country. It was performed by researchers at the Northern California Kaiser Permanente Medical Care Program, in Oakland, who conducted a case-control study of 1583 pregnant women who had attended Kaiser Permanente obstetrics and gynecology clinics during 1981 and 1982.

In an article entitled "The Risk of Miscarriage and Birth Defects among Women Who Use Visual Display Terminals During Pregnancy" (*American Journal of Industrial Medicine,* June 1988), Kaiser researchers wrote that they had found that women who worked with VDTs for more than 20 hours a week experienced a risk of both early and late miscarriage that was 80 percent higher than the risk for women who performed similar work without using VDTs. In their conclusion, the researchers stated, "Our case-control study provides the first epidemiological evidence based on substantial numbers of pregnant VDT operators to suggest that high usage of VDTs may increase the risk of miscarriage."

Apple Responds

As might be expected, the results of the Kaiser Permanente study, together with the Swedish experiments demonstrating that the emissions from display monitors can adversely affect the fetuses of test animals, have prompted many computer users to write to computer manufacturers to ask whether their monitors are safe to use. One such letter was sent on November 5, 1989, to John Sculley, chief executive officer of Apple Computer, by Professor Harris Barron, who taught electronic media in art-making at the Massachusetts College of Art in Boston for 25 years. In his letter, Barron told Sculley that he was writing on a Macintosh SE; that his young daughter-in-law, "an avid law school scholar,

ONE DOES NOT NEED TO BE A MEDICAL DOCTOR TO APPRECIATE THAT SUCH ELECTROMAGNETIC PHENOMENA, WHICH HAVE NO COUNTERPART IN MAN'S EVOLUTIONARY HISTORY, MAY WELL PROVE HAZARDOUS TO HEALTH

sits long hours at the terminal of her own SE"; and that "she and her computer-user husband intend to raise a family in the near future." . . . Barron then asked whether his daughter-in-law was at risk from the electromagnetic fields emitted by her monitor and told Sculley that "the results of any studies that Apple has made in this regard would be helpful."

On December 6, 1989, Barron received an unsigned letter from the Apple Customer Relations Department, thanking him for his letter and informing him that some materials were enclosed for his perusal. The enclosed material consisted of an article from the February 1984 issue of *Health Physics*, which said that X-ray emissions from VDTs posed no health problem; some 1984 recommendations by the European Computer Manufacturers Association on how to avoid ergonomic problems from VDT use; a 1983 policy statement issued by the American Academy of Ophthalmology, which said that VDTs presented no hazard to vision; and some 1985 Apple safety data sheets about the testing of toner materials.

On December 11, 1989, Barron wrote Sculley to express disappointment with Apple's response to his initial query. "With your pro forma mailing, I am now armed with *1984* materials, data so antiquated that I would be embarrassed to use it, as would Apple in any of its public relations," Barron said. "Reprints of ergonomic factors, ocular data, toner safety data, and the 'put-to-bed' X-ray issue totally ignored my one basic question on permanent harm from ELF magnetic-field VDT emissions." In conclusion, Barron told Sculley that he intended to prepare a statement about

his correspondence with Apple for circulation to his contacts in higher education, including the National Education Association.

Further Equivocations
On January 9, 1990, Barron received a reply to his second letter from David C. McGraw, Apple's newly appointed manager for corporate environmental health and safety. McGraw apologized for the delay and confusion in getting back to Barron, and assured him that "the pro forma response to your initial letter dated 11/5/89 is not the way Apple wishes to respond to this important issue." He went on to tell Barron that "Apple believes that no increased risk of adverse pregnancy outcome due to VDT work has been demonstrated," and to point out that Apple's position in this regard "is supported by the American Medical Association, the American College of Obstetricians and Gynecologists, the National Institute for Occupational Safety and Health (NIOSH), and the World Health Organization (WHO)."

McGraw said that the Kaiser Permanente study "drew public attention because of what appeared to be an increase in miscarriages among women who use VDTs more than 20 hours per week," but that the researchers who conducted it "were unable to determine the specific cause of the increased rate of miscarriages." He then noted that "similar studies in Canada and Scandinavia have found no relationship between VDT work and adverse pregnancy outcome." McGraw enclosed the results of a recent animal study that had been conducted for IBM and Ontario Hydro by researchers at the University of Toronto, who, unlike Drs. Frölen and Tribukait, had found that pulsed magnetic fields

did not adversely affect the fetuses of test mice. He also recommended that Barron read a compendium entitled *Latest Studies on VDTs,* published in August 1989 by the Center for Office Technology. (This is the new name of the Coalition for Workplace Technology of the Computer and Business Equipment Manufacturers Association, which had previously assured computer users that the emissions from a display terminal were no different than those from a light bulb.)

In January of this year, McGraw sent Barron the names and résumés of three people whom he described as "experts in the field of biological effects of electromagnetic radiation." One was Edwin L. Carstensen, a professor of electrical engineering at the University of Rochester, who has been a paid consultant of the electric-utility industry for nearly 15 years and has testified for power companies in court cases on several occasions. Another was Kenneth R. Foster, a professor in the Department of Bioengineering at the University of Pennsylvania, who has not only discounted the possibility that low-level electromagnetic radiation can have adverse biological effects but has even suggested that restrictions be placed on further investigation of the problem. The third was Eleanor R. Adair, a physiologist at the John Pierce Foundation, in New Haven, Connecticut, who, in spite of dozens of scientific studies published in leading scientific journals around the world demonstrating that weak pulsed electromagnetic fields given off by display monitors and low-level fields emitted by radar and other sources can cause adverse biological effects at field strengths far below those necessary to produce heat, has recently been quoted as saying that she has "never seen one bit of scientific evidence— and let me emphasize the word *scientific*—that ELF or microwave radiation has any nonthermal biological effects."

Answering Critics
Macintosh and other computer users must now decide for themselves whether monitor manufacturers are dealing forthrightly with the issue of display monitor emissions. It is clear that computer users are being asked by manufacturers to extend the presumption of benignity to the pulsed electric and magnetic fields given off

by display monitors, even as scientists continue to investigate the apparent health hazard posed by these emissions. One of the chief rationales behind this strategy is the belief that there is no "conclusive" proof that VDT emissions have any harmful effects on computer users. Another is that no biological mechanism has yet been postulated to show exactly how pulsed magnetic fields might cause miscarriages and cancer. In other words, if scientists can't explain how something is happening, it can't be happening. Someone should remind the monitor manufacturers that scientists don't know exactly how inhaled asbestos fibers act to cause cancer; yet everyone knows that asbestos causes cancer, and only fools would willingly expose themselves to asbestos.

As it happens, a model of how a 60Hz alternating-current magnetic field may cause or promote cancer has been provided by Dr. Harris Busch, an oncologist, who was chairman of the Department of Pharmacology of the Baylor University College of Medicine in Houston for 25 years and was also formerly an editor of the distinguished *American Journal of Cancer Research*. After explaining that a 60Hz alternating-current magnetic field vibrates to and fro 60 times a second, Busch points out that there will be a similar to-and-fro movement on the part of anything magnetic in such a field. According to Busch, this means that "any kind of molecule that is in a person's brain, or in a person's body, is being twisted 60 times a second up and back."

Recently, Dr. W. Ross Adey has made the point that in the case of weak electromagnetic fields given off by display monitors, the tissue responses can take account of the regularity of the repeating pulses and assume the rhythm of those pulses in a phenomenon called *entrainment*, which, in turn, can alter the normal activation of enzymes and cellular immune responses in ways consistent with the promotion of cancer.

One does not need to be a medical doctor to appreciate that such electromagnetic phenomena, which have no counterpart in man's evolutionary history, may well prove hazardous to health.

AT ARM'S LENGTH

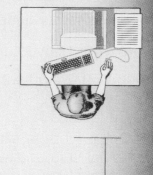

While ELF magnetic-field emissions of roughly 5 to 23 milligauss (mG) were found at 4 inches from the front of monitors commonly used with the Macintosh, *Macworld* found that at 28 inches from the screen, all the monitors tested at less than 1mG. (The ambient ELF magnetic-field emissions measured in the *Macworld* offices ranged from 0.1 to 0.5 mG.) Macintosh users wishing to reduce exposure to pulsed electromagnetic fields should position their display monitors at arm's length (with fingers extended) **(A)**.

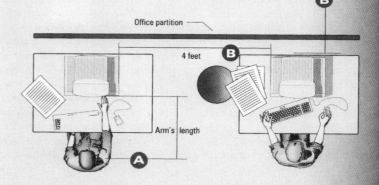

Because magnetic fields emitted from the sides and backs of most monitors are considerably stronger than those given off from the front, users should consider maintaining a distance of at least 4 feet from the sides or back of any other monitor in the workplace **(B)**. Keep in mind that magnetic-field emissions are not stopped by cubicle partitions, walls, lead aprons, or even the human body.

Curiously, there are no standards for ELF magnetic-field emissions, although several countries, Sweden and Canada among them, have developed standards for VLF magnetic-field emissions. A number of vendors—IBM, DEC, and Philips, for instance—market monitors for PCs that meet those standards. For the past two years, Sigma Designs has supplied the European market with monitors for the Mac that meet the VLF standards, and American users can now special order these monochrome and gray-scale 15-, 19-, and 21-inch monitors. Also, any monitor based on a technology other than a cathode-ray tube will have the advantage of not emitting the types of pulsed radiation associated with vertical- and horizontal-deflection coils. . . .

The controversy surrounding low-frequency electromagnetic emissions will continue until further research is completed. In the meantime, prudent avoidance—sitting at arm's length from the front and 4 feet from the sides or back of a monitor—is a sensible solution. *Macworld* is committed to documenting any new developments as they relate to this issue. Stay tuned.

—*Suzanne Stefanac*

Premature Alarm Over Electromagnetic Fields

C. Andrew L. Bassett

C. Andrew L. Bassett is professor emeritus of orthopedic surgery at Columbia University. He has been involved in the development and use of selected time-varying magnetic fields for 30 years.

The past year was marked by a flurry of news articles and commentaries on possible health risks—ranging from reproductive disorders to cancer—associated with the weak, low-frequency electromagnetic fields that emanate from power lines, video display terminals, and most electrically powered household items. Unmentioned in these reports, however, was the extensive use of electromagnetic fields in medical treatments. Ironically, by ignoring the therapeutic uses of such fields, the press overlooked the major source of information on bioeffects and safety records.

The significant body of scientific data amassed during the past 15 years from cellular, animal, and human therapeutic studies indicates that the term "weak, low-frequency electromagnetic fields" is too broad to be useful. Asking whether such fields are good or bad for your health makes no more

Before we start regulating, we need better information on which to base policy.

sense than asking whether chemicals are good or bad for your health. We all recognize that some chemicals (such as vitamins, hormones, and drugs) may be vital to health, and others (such as carbon monoxide and arsenic) can be lethal. What's more, the dosage can be all-important—even an essential vitamin taken in very small amounts may produce no effects at all, and in very large doses be toxic. Similarly, certain portions or combinations of frequencies along the nonionizing electromagnetic spectrum produce beneficial effects, whereas other portions or combinations of frequencies may be deleterious.

Although the underlying phy-

sical principles governing the interactions between living systems and these fields have yet to be elucidated fully, many details of what actually happens at the cellular and subcellular levels have been identified. In certain therapeutic applications, more is known about why pulsed magnetic fields are beneficial than about the action of aspirin.

One particularly significant fact is that with electromagnetic fields, less can be more, and vice versa. Traditionally, biomedical science embraces a "dose-response" model for bioactive agents such as drugs: A small amount of the agent produces no response, and too much yields an adverse or plateaued response, with a range of desired action for doses in between the extremes. Defining a dose-response pattern for weak electromagnetic fields is far more complex. Either too little or too much may produce no response whatsoever, with an all-or-nothing effect in between. In addition, it is not sufficient to specify simply how much (that is, amplitude of induced voltage or current) without identifying factors such as frequency,

From *Issues in Science and Technology*, Spring 1990, pp. 36-39. Copyright © 1990 by the National Academy of Sciences, Washington, D.C.

direction, timing of exposure, and a host of other variables.

Take, for example, the power-line issue. The assumption that the "culprit" is a 60 hertz sine wave magnetic field of a given amplitude is overly simplistic from the beginning. It takes no note of other frequencies and amplitudes introduced by switching transients, power surges, harmonic distortions, and the unique energy patterns induced in transmission lines by solar flare activity.

Furthermore, field distortion, cancellation, augmentation, and altered phasing can result when multiple lines are parallel or angled in clusters. It may even be that the purported ailments linked to living near power lines are chemical in origin; epidemiological studies have yet to examine the role of herbicides used along power line rights-of-way, polychlorinated biphenyls (PCBs), or the byproducts of high-tension arcing.

Without more detailed information on how electromagnetic fields affect humans, it is fruitless to try to set safety standards. In fact, ill-founded standards, which could engender a false sense of security and impede inquiry, might be worse than no standards at all. Until policymakers, scientists, engineers, physicians, and journalists become more conversant with specificity of action, they, and the public, will remain awash in a sea of confusion and concern. Furthermore, the vast potential for expanding therapeutic benefits and limiting possible hazards will continue to be squandered.

The healing fields

Most progress in the therapeutic use of electromagnetic fields has hinged on efforts to mimic nature. Living systems evolved on this planet in a literal sea of natural static and time-varying magnetic fields. When organisms are isolated by magnetic shielding from this weak field environment, their metabolism changes in measurable ways. In fact, the Earth's magnetic field plays a significant role in determining how cells handle calcium ions, a major regulator of cell function. Weak magnetic and electric phenomena are essential in every chemical reaction.

In addition, physical activity produces electromagnetic fields. With every heartbeat or neural response, biomagnetic fields are created. With every step we take, our bones are deformed by mechanical and hydrodynamic forces, which distort the balance of electric charge in the tissues and thereby generate minute voltages.

Research into these human-created fields has made it possible to design pulsed electromagnetic fields (PEMFs) that induce electric currents in bone similar to those caused naturally by deforming forces. During the past 15 years, more than 200,000 patients with bone fractures that have not healed normally have been treated with these PEMFs to induce healing; many of these individuals were saved from amputation after years of disability and numerous surgical failures. These results have been achieved by treating patients at home, with a significant saving in costs over surgical approaches. Recently, selected PEMF patterns have been used successfully to treat young adults with avascular necrosis, a potentially disabling prearthritic hip condition. Moreover, laboratory research data indicate that PEMFs may benefit patients with osteoporosis, severed nerves, chronically unhealed diabetic ulcers, and coronary artery disease. Pilot studies suggest that this form of energy deserves thorough investigation as a means for controlling certain types of cancer. (This is not to suggest that PEMFs are a panacea, only that, like drugs, various patterns can produce a wide range of effects.)

Throughout the sizable, long-term clinical experience with PEMFs, there has been no evidence of hazardous side-effects when they are used properly. Even patients who received daily treatment for 10 years showed no harmful effects. Animal studies found no evidence of adverse effects on conception, reproduction, development, or longevity. Standard Food and Drug Administration toxicologic and teratologic tissue culture investigations have also revealed no risks.

What about hazards?

But if some PEMFs can have beneficial effects, cannot others be harmful? A recent report by Congress' Office of Technology Assessment concluded that little is known about such risk beyond the principle that weak fields can interact with biological processes. Until these phenomena are better understood, the report prudently suggested that exposure be minimized or avoided whenever practical.

But just how can we minimize or avoid exposure to electromagnetic fields without returning to the age of oil lamps? Nonionizing electromagnetic fields are ubiquitous, produced by everything from elevators to vacuum cleaners. Certain types of shielding have been developed, but such protection is impractical and very expensive. Even burying power lines will not shield the fields unless the iron content of the surrounding soil is high. Design changes in electrically powered devices can modify field patterns, but we do not know how much to change them or even in what direction. We cannot establish standards until we know what we want to achieve.

Before we start regulating, we need better information on which to base policy. Current research is scattered and underfunded. The National Institutes of Health devote less than $1 million a year to all aspects of the topic. The Environmental Protection Agency ended most of its research in 1989. The Electric Power Research Institute, an industry group, is exploring the effects of power lines, and IBM is examining video display terminals, but looking at these sources in isolation will not provide the information we need. The Departments of Defense and Energy have investigated the subject, but neither has a broadly based research program.

Many of these efforts have attempted to answer specific questions without having adequate controls for a myriad of interactive physical and biological factors. Research must begin by defining in as much detail as possible the breadth of biological responses that result from various electromagnetic fields, taking into account all the variables that influence these responses. The individuals capable of this task can be found throughout government, academia, and industry, but no single agency has the depth and diversity necessary to direct this research. Therefore, Congress should create a National Bioelectromagnetics Commission with broad interdisciplinary capabilities in physics, biochemistry, biology, engineering, and medicine, to explore the issue thoroughly.

The commission's first duty would be to define what constitutes a valid experiment. Most of what has been done is flawed because it fails to take into account all relevant variables. Over two or three years, the commission could collect the detailed response data at the cellular and subcellular levels necessary to identify new therapeutic applications and potential hazards. With this information, it could begin productive exploration of medical uses and, if necessary, the development of product standards or environmental regulations.

A comprehensive program would cost no more than $100 million a year, an amount already being saved for society by those orthopedic surgeons who use PEMFs instead of surgery to treat certain bone fractures. The potential payoff in clarifying and controlling risks and developing low-cost medical techniques would more than justify the investment. In the process, it will become clear that a revolutionary new method for communicating with cells is at hand. Precise physical control of cellular function and behavior will open unseen horizons for managing human ills and allaying unwarranted concern.

A System on Overload

Our unlimited appetite for software strains our ability to produce it

First of a series

Evelyn Richards
Washington Post Staff Writer

It was exactly 2:25 p.m. last Jan. 15 when, out of the corner of his eye, Jim Nelson spotted an alarming sea of red spreading across the screens of 75 video monitors in the control center of AT&T's vast long-distance network.

The screens normally are filled with bland charts and maps of the United States. For Nelson, the manager of the Bedminster, N.J., center, the red warning signals were an unmistakable sign of crisis.

"We have the big one," an assistant exclaimed.

The nation's largest telephone network had virtually collapsed, frustrating millions of Americans who were blocked from making long-distance calls for nine hours and sending a team of more than 100 phone company technicians on a frantic search for the cause.

They found it in the software that controls the system's computers and electronic switches—a small, undetected error in the web of written instructions that tell the equipment what to do. An unexpectedly heavy flow of calls had overwhelmed a weak point in the system, and American Telephone & Telegraph Co. computers, lacking instructions on how to deal with the unforeseen overload, simply shut down.

The calamity that struck AT&T that Monday afternoon is just the kind that many experts have increasingly come to fear as software reaches deeper into everyday life. In a generation's time, software has emerged as the ubiquitous control system of an automated society, a $125 billion-a-year industry that is an essential underpinning of America's economic and political standing in the world.

Software controls banking and airline reservations networks and is critical to U.S. defense systems. It decides when to buy and sell huge blocks of stock. It is buried inside videocassette recorders and the dashboards and fuel systems of automobiles. It picks lottery winners and flushes toilets in the new Boeing 747-400. It helps physicians select and administer treatments. And, by crunching billions of instructions each second, it can simulate nature to help researchers unravel man's genetic makeup or predict hurricanes.

A miracle of human ingenuity, software instructions translate the tasks requested by humans into electronic commands that computers can follow. Software converted this reporter's keystrokes into letters on a computer screen; other software converted those letters into type for this newspaper page. The computers involved in those operations are lifeless combinations of silicon chips and electronic parts that only software can activate.

Most software routinely performs as expected, but as society demands more and more from software and the computers it controls, errors and failures like AT&T's could easily become more common. According to scores of computer scientists and other specialists, the nation's ability to produce software on time and with high reliability is in jeopardy.

Software problems already affect many sectors of society. One of the most important is the Pentagon, whose increasingly high-tech weapons systems depend—with uneven success—on some of the world's most elaborate computer programs. Another is human health, which can be threatened by faulty software. And at giant corporations, huge investments can be undermined by delayed and over-budget software projects, which are now routine.

The Bank of New York once had to borrow $24 billion overnight from the Federal Reserve, incurring $5 million in instant interest costs, because a software glitch left it without enough funds to balance its account with the Fed. Inadequate software used to process student loans may cost a group of international lenders up to $650 million. Fargo Bank in California vastly overstated the income of 22,000 employees in reports to the Internal Revenue Service because a programming error moved the decimal point two places to the right.

Last year, a mysterious defect paralyzed the American Airlines reservations system for nine hours. Though the carrier located the general problem area, it still isn't certain exactly why the software ran amok.

Perhaps one-quarter of all software projects are so troubled that they are simply canceled in midstream, according to Software Productivity Research, a Cambridge, Mass., consulting firm. The state of Washington, for example, last year pulled the plug on a seven-year, federally backed $20 million automation effort designed to give social service caseworkers more time to spend with their clients. One complaint: The program kept caseworkers waiting 20 minutes for computerized files.

While such problems are multiplying, the supply of new programmers and software designers is declining. After a sharp rise in the late 1970s and early 1980s, interest in computing jobs has plummeted among college freshmen, the fastest collapse ever recorded for a career preference in the 23 years that the University of California at Los Angeles has conducted such surveys. The reason most commonly given: Computer jobs are no longer considered glamorous.

But demand for software is expanding relentlessly, driven by society's insatiable appetite for new uses and the ability of computers to perform calculations at ever greater speeds. Each year, computers have been providing 25 percent more power per dollar, while the productivity of people who produce software has been rising at less than half that rate.

"The amount and quality of software we need is increasing constantly, and our ability to produce it is essentially stagnant. Those two things are on a collision course," warns William Wulf, former head of the National Science Foundation's office of computer and information science. It is "absolutely a problem of much larger dimension than most people realize," says Wulf. The consequence, he fears, will be a slowing of technological progress and in turn a decline in the country's economic competitiveness.

"Software can well become the limiting factor in what we can do in building systems in the future," says Norman Augustine, chairman of Martin Marietta Corp. in Bethesda, Md. The bottleneck could affect "space systems, telephone systems, automobile systems or any other complex technological device," he says.

Other experts warn that, as computers increasingly take over decisions formerly made by human beings, software producers and the public may be placing too much confidence in a technology that defies perfection.

"I'm worried that people are putting too much reliance on computers without enough understanding of the potential risk that they may be adding," says Nancy Leveson, a professor specializing in software reliability at the University of California at Irvine.

Problems with software have claimed a handful of lives, and the potential for software-triggered breakdowns to affect public health and safety "will be much worse in the future than it has been in the past," says John Guttag, an industry consultant and Massachusetts Institute of Technology computer science professor.

Large software systems, in the words of John Shore, a Washington author and software engineer, are "by far the most complex artifact" built by man. It is impossible for designers to predict how complex software will function in every circumstance, and when failures do occur they may never be fully comprehended even by those who crafted the code.

"The programs we construct are effectively too large for humans to understand," says Wulf. "Yet every characteristic of them depends upon the human's ability to understand them, to cope with them."

The challenges confronting the software industry center on the tension between the rigid, precise demands of electronic technology and the spontaneous creativity of programmers and software designers—with their capacity for human error.

Hidden and intangible when in operation, software takes form as the excruciatingly detailed instructions known as computer "code." Generally written by professional programmers, the code is gibberish to the uninitiated. But it actually is a logical structure of step-by-step commands and decisions, bearing some resemblance to English in its use of letters, numbers and symbols. A line of code is akin to a sentence of instruction.

The instructions are either stored electronically in computer chips, like those inside video games, calculators and automobile emission-control systems, or recorded on magnetic disks and tapes linked to computers.

In recent years, software programs have swelled from something easily handled by a lone "hacker"—as computer enthusiasts are known—to systems too large to be grasped by a single mind.

One popular software program for personal computers known as "dBase," designed to manage large amounts of data, was written a decade ago by two programmers and required fewer than 50,000 lines of code. It took a team of more than 100 people three years to write a new, more sophisticated version of the program, and even then the 400,000 lines of code they delivered—six months late—were so laden with defects that publisher Ashton-Tate Corp. of Torrance, Calif., provided buyers a "bug list" of flaws during the 21 months it spent making further corrections.

Still, a program like dBase is a small job compared with the software produced by the aerospace and defense industries. Those projects often run more than 1 million lines—roughly equivalent to the listings in the Manhattan phone book.

As a product of human minds—with their wide variances in skill and judgment—software is not a task easily reduced to tools, mass production or standard parts. Nor is there enough effort to transfer know-how from project to project, causing wasteful duplication.

"The problem is that software has the highest manual labor content of almost any manufactured item in the second half of the 20th century. It's like building pyramids or handcrafting Rolls-Royces," says Capers Jones, chairman of Software Productivity Research.

"We're still building software in many ways the same way we were 30 or 40 years ago," says Max D. Hopper, senior vice president for information systems at American Airlines in Dallas.

Indeed, software development frequently is treated more like an art than a science, with design and testing often dictated more by personal choice than by regimen. Software developers, a fragmented community of independent-minded souls, lack the widely accepted safety standards and engineering discipline applied to the manufacture of mechanical and electrical equipment. Programmers need no license, no particular academic degree and no other official credential to build a software structure, though their creation may be as critical as any bridge or skyscraper.

Software problems begin long before the first line of code is written. In trying to take on tasks or decisions formerly handled by people, or new challenges never before conceived, software must translate all the ambiguity of human thought into rigid commands that a computer can follow.

This means that even before writing code, software developers must try to imagine all the different circumstances to which the computer or electronic equipment ultimately may need to respond, a virtually impossible task. And often the people writing the software have little understanding of the industry that is going to be using it.

"Imagine building a skyscraper and then realizing you forgot to leave space for a water system," says William Scherlis, software technology program manager at the Pentagon's Defense Advanced Research Projects Agency. "That's what happens in software all the time."

There is also the endless temptation to keep tinkering with and adjusting what has largely been completed, a practice that can cause other parts of a program to unravel.

Poor management, as much as anything, is to blame for poor software, experts say. Top corporate managers, many lacking an understanding of software, often don't know how to plan for something they can't see or touch. With little in the way of a standard blueprint to help visualize the outcome of a software effort, many companies and government agencies fail to gauge the challenge or create a structure necessary to see large projects through to completion.

Those in charge of software projects routinely miscalculate the magnitude of their project, a mistake Allstate Insurance Co. officials, for instance, readily acknowledge making.

Allstate, based in Northbrook, Ill., hoped a new computer program would cut as much as 75 percent of the time it takes to devise new life-insurance policies. In 1988, just before the system was supposed to be completed, the company realized the project was badly off track, and it started over. Now it predicts that the work will not be completed until 1992—and at three times the original cost.

"I don't believe we had recognized the level of planning that was needed," says project chief Ben Currier. "I don't think we had the proper management procedures in place."

American Airlines paid a steep price when it tried to add international fares to existing software before managers had the right information at hand. Too late, they discovered the fare-calculation formulas were incorrect and insufficient, causing development time and costs to double and leaving agents unable to function as planned. "We totally screwed up," senior vice president Hopper concedes.

Many companies that develop software for their own payroll, inventory tracking and other essentials of business estimate that they are so backed up in their software development that if they stopped getting new assignments today, programmers would spend the next three years completing their backlog of requests.

A major software failure like the one last January at AT&T can be traced to any combination of human error, design flaws and project mismanagement.

The problem with AT&T's software turned out to be a mistake made in just one line of a 2 million-line program used to route calls. Software is structured much like a road map, with many of the lines directing the software where to go next. The flawed line, or software "bug," in the AT&T program sent the call-processing mechanism to an incorrect place in the code, where the next instruction it encountered made no sense, thus disabling the equipment.

As is often the case, the fatal bug had been injected into the system when AT&T altered the software a month earlier to fix an unrelated flaw. The ability to alter software with relative ease causes many of its problems, since small changes can cause larger disruptions elsewhere.

The glitch surfaced only when telephone traffic was so heavy that two calls happened to arrive at a troubled switch within one-hundredth of a second of each other. Despite months of testing, AT&T had failed to prepare for this exact sequence and pace of events.

The AT&T breakdown underscored the trade-off between achieving greater performance and taking greater risk. Software has evolved as the technological backbone of modern society because, in most cases, it is much quicker and more reliable than humans. Many of today's conveniences are possible only because software has taken over where humans or machines left off, carrying on tasks with amazing speed and without wearing out or tiring. And like humans, software has a seemingly endless capacity to adapt to change.

But ultimately, software's performance depends on humans—on people's ability to turn imprecise human preferences into a master plan that can operate flawlessly, without the benefit of common sense to guide it through unexpected situations. These days, as the people who write software race on an accelerating treadmill to keep up with demand, concerns are rising that they are being pushed too far, too fast.

As the Bell Laboratories vice president who presided over the AT&T software-repair mission, Karl Martersteck knows that dilemma well. "With complexity," he says, "you increase the number of things that can go wrong."

For the Military, Getting With the Program Is Half the Battle

When the contract was first awarded in 1984, the U.S. Army hoped to develop a largely automated battlefield.

Computers would determine what gun to fire at what target, and precisely when. They would select routes for artillery and trucks to travel. They would track troops as they moved across the terrain. Commanders would manage the battle from computer consoles.

After six painful years, the Advanced Field Artillery Tactical Data System (AFATDS) is a monument to the perils of reliance on sophisticated computer software to fulfill complex military assignments. The skeleton of a system that can automate bits and pieces of the battlefield has been created. But synchronizing the whole operation, the Army now acknowledges, is still years—and many millions of dollars—away. Nearly $80 million has produced nothing that is yet usable on a battlefield.

AFATDS (pronounced a-FA-tids), far from the Pentagon's largest software project, captures in miniature a software logjam that has affected the entire defense establishment.

The Pentagon is the biggest software customer in the world. Its spending on software projects is estimated to be about $30 billion a year, or 10 percent of its budget, an amount that has tripled in the past five years.

But the Defense Department is also a huge bureaucracy with old habits that aren't well-suited to the computer age.

Numerous Pentagon officials concede that the department has failed to master the administration of complex software projects. "We don't know how to manage it," says Virginia Castor, a Pentagon official who is helping to develop a Defense Department policy for improving software production.

Software problems have caused major delays of weapons systems, created malfunctioning aircraft and cost the Defense Department billions of dollars in unanticipated costs. Officials acknowledge that virtually every troubled weapons system, from the electronics in the B-1B bomber to satellite tracking systems, has been afflicted with software problems. Even straightforward record-keeping systems can get bogged down; last year, the Navy canceled a software accounting project nine years in the making after its costs quadrupled to $230 million.

The software problem steadily compounds itself because of the rapid expansion of the Pentagon's dependence upon software. The F-4 fighter-bombers that saw combat in Vietnam had no software at all. Today's fighters have more than 1 million lines of computer "code"—each line a written instruction to a computer—while the Navy's latest submarine combat system has roughly 3 million lines. The Strategic Defense Initiative, the high-tech U.S. anti-missile program, would require an estimated 30 million lines. With each additional line, the danger of error multiplies.

Never has the military's software dependence been more evident than in the current Persian Gulf crisis. From the F-16 fighters and seaborne Aegis air-defense system to the ordering of spare tires and food, software serves as the central nervous system of the U.S. build-up. "There isn't anything over there except the foot soldiers that doesn't have software," says Lloyd Mosemann II, deputy assistant secretary of the Air Force for communications, computers and logistics.

Ultimately, a failure to perfect military software problems can endanger American fighting men and women and the effectiveness of the U.S. military. One example is the huge C-17A transport plane being developed by McDonnell Douglas Corp. at about $150 million each. Three years into its development, engineers discovered that a faulty software design created an unacceptable risk that the plane could crash when landing. The design was scrapped and developers had to begin anew—increasing the cost of the plane and adding to delays.

Such delays are typical. A review of 82 large military procurement programs conducted by Air Force Col. Joseph Greene Jr. found that those relying heavily on software generally ran 20 months behind schedule, three times longer than projects less dependent on computer programming.

Greene, who retired this year as head of a Pentagon software research effort, calculated that such delays cost the Defense Department one-tenth of its $100 billion annual research and procurement budget.

A separate study showed that Pentagon contractors deserve some of the blame: Three-fourths of 55 aerospace and defense projects were found to be run in an "ad hoc" and even "chaotic" manner.

"The department is paying a huge penalty for not dealing with its software problems," Greene says. "The penalty is not just late software—it is degraded war-fighting capability."

In the case of AFATDS, the Army hoped for a computer system that would be able to set priorities in the heat of battle, decide what firepower should be used against which targets, distribute critical information to units in the field and at headquarters, manage ammunition, assess road conditions and advise commanders where to place artillery.

The contract to develop this capability was awarded in May 1984 to Magnavox Electronic Systems Co., based in Fort Wayne, Ind. The project posed big technical challenges for Magnavox, which had never before won such a large government software contract. But from the beginning, the dream was frustrated by a persistent problem of a different sort, one not uncommon to large projects: The Army couldn't communicate what it wanted the computer software to do.

"The contract was signed for a total system when the government and contractor didn't have a good understanding of what it is that we wanted," says Robert Giordano, now the Army's deputy program executive officer of command and control systems.

Such confusion continuously dogged Magnavox, where software chief Harold "Skip" Carstensen and a staff of 100 others often spent weekends cloistered in conference rooms, reading through line by line what ultimately became the official AFATDS program requirements—nine blue binders totaling about 2,000 pages.

They frequently encountered new snags. Some were caused by Ada, the "universal" computer language adopted by the Pentagon in 1983. So new was Ada that Magnavox had to train nearly 300 people in the language—only to have many hired away by other defense contractors hungry for Ada talent.

Magnavox made its share of outright mistakes, contributing to repeated schedule delays beyond the original 33-month plan. The company had to alter the AFATDS software, for example, because it displayed the same information about the status of troops and ammunition to all levels of personnel. The Army pointed out that generals and privates hardly needed the same information. "I as an artillery officer should have realized that," says Carstensen, an Army officer before joining Magnavox. "You can't think of everything."

He calculated that readjusting the software would take six "man-months"—say, six people working one month. Instead, the job took two man-years, and instead of affecting 6,000 lines of code, it involved 12,000, Carstensen says.

Army gaffes caused setbacks, too. One requirement of AFATDS, for example, was that its users be able to exchange information with the older computer-based battle-management system used by the Army. But the Army failed to supply Magnavox with up-to-date technical details to make the links possible, causing several man-months of extra effort.

Invariably, delays resulted from the Army and Magnavox not seeing eye to eye on what AFATDS was supposed to do. Many misunderstandings stemmed from both parties' use of imprecise English.

One requirement, for example, reads: "The operator will receive notice of this new position when the movement requirement is delivered." To the Army, that meant that when artillery changed locations, the person manning the computer would be notified by an alarm or message on the screen. Magnavox insisted, however, that the requirement meant that the news could simply be delivered by one person handing another person a piece of paper.

Such misunderstandings led to endless paperwork. One report by a Magnavox employee outlined this conversation with an Army official: "The paragraphs in the item were 3.2.3.2.8.d and 3.2.3.2.8.d.1 on page 124. There are no such paragraphs on that page." The matter subsequently was resolved when the parties agreed that a "2" had been dropped from the designations.

Snags like these, though troubling, were overshadowed by managerial shortcomings and political pressures that distracted attention from productive work. As the Army and Magnavox bickered, the project fell behind schedule, prompting the Pentagon to freeze payments and ultimately cap the cost of the program at $46 million, up from the original $34 million.

Like most procurement programs, software acquisition is subject to congressional pressure and interference. In the case of AFATDS, the House defense appropriations subcommittee repeatedly challenged the Army and Magnavox about the cost and feasibility of the ambitious project. The subcommittee ordered at least five General Accounting Office reports on AFATDS and related programs and at one point warned that it was growing "increasingly concerned with the Army's repeated . . . disregard of congressional direction."

Under this scrutiny, the Army increased its pressure on Magnavox, whose officials became overwhelmed by visiting investigators. Some of those visitors were, they themselves acknowledge, ill-prepared to pass judgment. Richard Stanley, then an Army official, was on military business in Texas in early 1987 when he was hastily called to Indiana to investigate Magnavox's progress. "Half the people [on the review team] couldn't spell software if their life depended on it," he says. "Most of us there had very little firsthand knowledge of AFATDS."

At one point, Carstensen says, an Army official requested a photo of a "compiler" that was causing problems. Magnavox people just shook their heads. A compiler is a batch of software code, not a piece of hardware, as the Army official had presumed.

Finally, in the spring of 1989 the software emerged from field testing with remarkably few flaws. Magnavox was two years late and had spent $30 million of its own funds on AFATDS, but in the end it joined the Army in rejoicing that the complex software actually worked.

But for all the agony, Magnavox had been asked to complete merely what is known as a "concept evaluation"—enough software to confirm that computers can support a broad range of troops and weapons, yet far short of what actually would be needed to automate the battlefield. That dream, once expected to become reality starting in 1990, has been broken apart into smaller, incremental steps, and it will be at least three more years before any troops will be even partially equipped with AFATDS gear.

Now, officials say, AFATDS software development is moving forward on schedule, thanks to improved cooperation among everyone involved, with a new $60 million Magnavox contract. Still, so much has changed since the Army first sketched out AFATDS that Magnavox has concluded that half of the software written in the first phase is unusable.

Maj. Gen. Peter Kind, who for a time oversaw AFATDS, says the experience taught an important lesson about software: "With large programs, it's a very difficult thing to get it all working and out there in one fell swoop. It just doesn't work that way."

—Evelyn Richards

PROGRAMMED FOR DISASTER

Software Errors That Imperil Lives

JONATHAN JACKY

Jonathan Jacky, a research assistant professor in the radiation oncology department at the University of Washington School of Medicine, in Seattle, is designing software for a computer-controlled radiation-therapy machine.

O N MARCH 21, 1986, oilfield worker Ray Cox visited a clinic in Tyler, Texas, to receive radiation on his back, from which a cancerous tumor had been removed. On the basis of previous visits, he knew the procedure should be painless, but that day he felt a jolt of searing heat. Outside the shielded treatment room, the technician was puzzled by his complaint: the computer terminal used to operate the radiation machine bore only the cryptic message "Malfunction 54," indicating either an overdose or an underdose. Clinic staff were unable to find anything wrong with the machine, so they sent Cox home and continued treating other patients. But Cox's condition worsened. Spitting blood, he checked in to a hospital emergency room, where doctors suspected he had received an electric shock; in fact, he had received a lethal overdose.

Less than a month later, Malfunction 54 occurred again at the Tyler clinic, this time striking Verdon Kidd, a sixty-six-year-old bus driver. Kidd died in May of 1986, reportedly the first fatality ever caused by an overdose during radiation treatment. Meanwhile, Cox became paralyzed and lapsed into a coma, and four months later he, too, died of the injury.

As news of the Tyler incidents spread, similar mishaps in other clinics came to light: one patient in Canada and another in Georgia had received mutilating injuries in 1985; an overdose occurred in Washington State in January of 1987. In each case, the radiation had come from the Therac-25, a computer-controlled machine manufactured by Atomic Energy of Canada. After the fifth such accident was reported, the U.S. Food and Drug Administration advised—but did not order—clinics to discontinue routine use of the Therac-25 until safety features could be installed in the equipment.

Ironically, by the time the accidents occurred, radiation therapy had become a routine, safe, and frequently effective procedure, used on nearly four hundred and fifty thousand new patients a year in more than eleven hundred U.S. clinics. Much of that success was due to linear accelerators, which began to replace cobalt treatment units in the 1960s. (Linear accelerators are electric machines, capable of producing radiation beams whose energy can be adjusted. The earlier equipment used a lump of cobalt-60 as the radiation source; the units could not be adjusted, and the intensity of the radioactivity diminished over time.)

The million-dollar Therac-25, introduced in 1983, was among the first of a generation of computer-controlled linear accelerators. With the earlier accelerators, electricity and mechanical forces were used to transmit the operator's directions directly to the wheels, levers, and cables controlling the radiation beam. But with computers, it was necessary to transmit only information, not force, so the operator's commands could be processed by software —lists of coded instructions that tell the computer what to do. Thus, complex electromechanical control systems were replaced by minicomputers, and the traditional operator's control panels, festooned with switches, buttons, and lamps, were exchanged for computer terminals. With these changes, manufacturers hoped to capitalize on the speed and versatility of computers to make radiation machines faster and more convenient.

The proper operation of an electromechanical radiation machine largely depended on the soundness of the control mechanism. When it malfunctioned, the problem could be traced to relay switches that had failed, tubes that had burned out, hydraulic fluid that had leaked away. These failures were caused by manufacturing defects or wear and could be prevented by inspecting the product and replacing faulty parts.

Computers also can wear out, but most of their problems are not so easy to understand; they are design weaknesses, caused by flaws in the logic, not the mechanics, of the control mechanisms, so there are no material defects to track down. True, faults may exist in the hardware—the chips themselves—but, more frequently, they crop up in the software.

It was a software error, involving the operation of a switch, that killed Cox and Kidd. Linear accelerators can produce two kinds of radiation: electrons, which are used to treat superficial tumors, such as skin cancers, and X rays, which are more effective against such deeply embedded tumors as those of the cervix and the prostate. An electron beam can be produced by the accelerator directly, or an X-ray beam can be created by placing a tungsten target in the path of the electron beam, so that, as the target absorbs electrons, X rays emerge from the other side. Because this process of producing X rays is inefficient, the intensity of the electron beam must be increased tremendously when the target is in place.

To guard against the grave danger that the electron beam might attain its higher intensity without the target in place, and be driven directly into a patient, accelerators were equipped with protective circuits, called interlocks. In the Therac-25, however, both target position and beam intensity were computer-controlled. When the operator switched the machine from X ray to electron mode, the computer was counted upon to set the beam to low intensity before the target was withdrawn.

Usually, it worked that way. (At Tyler, more than five hundred patients had been treated without mishap in the two years preceding the accidents.) But if, because of a software error, the operator first selected X rays and then switched to electrons, by hitting the up-arrow key and typing over the previous instruction, the target was withdrawn while the full-intensity beam remained on. In the cases of Cox and Kidd, the Therac-25 delivered about twenty-five thousand rads of electrons, more than a hundred times the prescribed dose.

The problem in the software itself was compounded by a weakness in the user interface (the system the computer employs to inform the operator of what it is doing), which encouraged operators to run the machine in a hazardous fashion. According to a therapist at the site of the Georgia accident, the Therac-25 typically issued as many as forty error messages a day, most of which indicated that beam intensity was slightly less than it should be. Such messages could be canceled by pressing the terminal's P key, and operators quickly learned to respond this way to virtually all error messages—each one difficult to interpret, because the problem was referred to by number instead of being described in words. At Tyler, the only indication of trouble the operator saw was the code "Malfunction 54." She repeatedly pushed P, turning on the beam again and again. Ray Cox was burned twice before he managed to move out of the way.

The fault cannot be placed simply on the programmers who wrote software for the Therac-25; even the best programmers make lots of mistakes, because software writing is a painstaking task. The underlying problem was that Atomic Energy of Canada failed as an organization to guard against such errors. One of the earlier models, the Therac-20, contained electric circuits that prevented the beam from being turned on in such instances of malfunction. This mechanism was omitted from the Therac-25, and it is evident that no sufficient review of the safety implications of this omission ever was made.

Fortunately, only eleven Therac-25s were in use when the hazards became known. But the incidents raised concerns about therapy machines soon to be introduced by other manufacturers, and about other kinds of computer-operated medical equipment, as well. The FDA anticipates that by 1990, virtually all devices produced by the eleven-billion-dollar-a-year medical-electronics industry will contain computers. And the Therac accidents were just the worst examples of a trend the agency has been tracking for several years: computer-related problems in medical devices are on the increase.

Twice as many manufacturer recalls of computer-controlled medical equipment occurred in 1984 as in 1982 or any year before, and most were due to software errors. One blood analyzer displayed incorrect values because addition, rather than subtraction, had been programmed into a calibration formula. A system for monitoring the blood pressure, heart rate, and other vital signs of several patients at once mixed up its data, so the name of one patient was attached to the readings for another. And in one ventilator, a software error allowed concentrations of oxygen and other vital gases to drop without warning. In many of these applications, failure of the computer-controlled system could be deadly.

Such problems are not restricted to medicine. Because of their low cost and versatility, computers are replacing mechanical operations in all kinds of products. The Airbus Industries A320 airliner attracted great press attention when it was introduced last year, because it was the most extensively "fly-by-wire" commercial airliner ever built. (Computers, rather than cables and hydraulics, connect the pilot's controls to the airplane's engines, rudder, and ailerons.) In new cars, computers manage fuel injection and spark timing, and, in some cases, the suspension and antilock braking mechanisms, as well. (General Motors is experimenting with a "drive-by-wire" automobile, in which there is no physical connection, except the computer, between the steering wheel and the tires.) On railroads, computers operate the track switches that are supposed to prevent trains from colliding. Computers are used widely to direct assembly line equipment in factories and generators in power plants; even some emergency shutdown systems in nuclear reactors are computer-controlled. And in weapons systems, computers warn of imminent attack, identify and track targets, aim guns and steer missiles, arm and detonate explosives.

A file of problem reports maintained by Peter Neumann, at SRI International (a computer-industry think tank, in Menlo Park, California), under cosponsorship of the Association for Computing Machinery, lists more than four hundred incidents in a range of industries in which software problems caused or threatened serious injury or significant financial loss. Unless steps are taken to ensure that computer-operated machinery is every bit as safe as the mechanical equipment of old, such alarming software failures are bound to multiply.

WHEN MANUFACTURERS began installing computers in medical equipment and other machinery, they introduced a problem never encountered in strictly mechanical devices: programming errors, popularly known as bugs, which are the natural result of the way software is produced. The process begins when the designers draw up specifications for the software, which requires that they anticipate every task the computer is supposed to be able to direct its machine to perform, as well as every response it should make to situations it might encounter. (For a radiation machine, say, designers would specify that the computer be able to turn on the machine, adjust the beam to various intensities, and keep X ray–strength radiation from operating in the absence of the shield.) Then the design is divided into modules, which are work assignments for individual programmers.

Each programmer, acting independently, creates the software for his module, by entering into a video terminal a list of statements, in programming language, instructing the computer to behave as the specifications direct. Because computer programming is a highly creative endeavor—no less creative than composing a novel, for example—there is no single correct approach. Just as the novelist relies on inventiveness to get a story convincingly across to the reader, the programmer must rely on ingenuity to impart complete and unambiguous instructions to the computer. That is why no two programmers will write the same program in exactly the same way, and why there is so much room for introducing errors or for coming up with instructions not comprehensive enough to work properly.

During the final stage of software production, the individual modules are woven into the finished program. Regrettably, it is not always possible to predict how modules will interact. As Marvin Minsky, dean of American artificial intelligence researchers, put it:

When a program grows in power by an evolution of partially understood patches and fixes, the programmer begins to lose track of internal details, loses his ability to predict what will happen, begins to hope instead of know, and watches the results as though the program were an individual whose range of behavior is uncertain.

Consequently, producing quality software is as much a function of how well the entire program is designed, and how well the steps are coordinated, as of how well the individual lines of code are written.

The only way to tell whether a program has been properly designed is to test it. But even the most rigorous of trials can overlook flaws, because the number of situations a program must contend with is limitless. To check whether a computerized calculator adds numbers correctly, for instance, one could add hundreds of random numbers and see whether the program consistently produces the correct result, but since the supply of numbers is virtually infinite, it is hopeless to try testing every possible sum, and the few that might trigger an error, owing to some software flaw, are likely to be missed. So errors routinely remain in software when it reaches the market, to be discovered and corrected over time.

Programmers accept that they are likely to introduce, inadvertently, about fifty errors in every thousand lines of code. Most of these are weeded out during testing; market versions typically contain only two to three errors in a thousand lines. But this means that even a good program—with, say, fifty thousand lines of code—may contain more than a hundred errors. Usually, the damage can be repaired, though at some cost in time and annoyance. The state sends you a twenty-million-dollar tax bill? Clear it up with a telephone call—or several calls. The telephone switching computer cuts off your connection? Hang up and dial again. A word processor deletes your letter? Type it over, and this time make a backup copy. Experienced computer users develop a defensive style, a whole repertoire of tactics to keep software errors from getting the better of them. Only human adaptability and ingenuity make it possible to base a computerized society on imperfect products.

But some products require better defenses against errors; when a computer controls a linear accelerator or a jetliner, the results of an error cannot always be overcome or ignored. If the patient dies or the plane crashes, the computation cannot be redone.

IT *IS* POSSIBLE to improve computer products for which safe operation is critical, by adapting, for software development, the principles of safety engineering now used to minimize hazards in non-computer-operated assembly line equipment, medical devices, and the like. The first step is to recognize that safety must be designed into a product, not added on as an afterthought. That requirement alone might lead to a design quite different from one that would be used if cost and performance were the only considerations.

One way of keeping hazards to a minimum is through a process known as software engineering, by which each stage in the programming of a computer is described in writing, and the descriptions are reviewed by outside programmers. Typically, the documents produced include such things as a specification, describing in exhaustive detail what the product is supposed to do; a design guide, telling how the program is organized; a test plan, spelling out a series of trials that are supposed to show that the program works as promised; and a test report, presenting results and explaining how any problems were resolved. Requiring programmers to obtain approval of each document before proceeding to the next step enforces an orderly development process, and, ultimately, helps ensure quality. It is analogous to a standard practice of civil engineering whereby detailed designs are subjected to thorough analysis and review before anyone starts pouring concrete.

Such a system runs counter to the stereotype of the eccentric genius programmer. It requires that programmers spend half their time on planning and design, much of the rest of it on testing, and only fifteen to twenty percent actually writing code. Software engineering is also time-consuming, and therefore costly, though studies have shown that fixing an error after a product has reached the customer may cost as much as a hundred times more than catching it early in development.

Software engineering is practiced on a large scale by the

U.S. Defense Department and its contractors, who must produce sixteen documents for each computer program. Even that system is not foolproof. Some software developed to the department's standards still reaches the field with serious errors: One computer-controlled wing-mounted launcher improperly retained its grip after its missile was ignited, creating what was described as the world's largest pinwheel, when the aircraft went violently out of control. And a jet crashed when its flight-control program was confronted with an unanticipated mechanical problem. But despite its imperfections, the military's documentation process has been mainly beneficial. Something as complex as a fly-by-wire aircraft, for example, could never be relied upon to operate safely if it were produced by traditional techniques, and, for the most part, the military's planes have flown safely.

Unfortunately, the Defense Department's approach is elaborate and expensive, and thus it is practical only for huge projects costing no less than tens of millions of dollars, employing scores of programmers, and generating hundreds of thousands of lines of code. It is not economical for smaller-scale programming projects (those required to produce automated switches for railroad tracks, say, or computer-controlled medical equipment). The Institute of Electrical and Electronics Engineers recommends the production of only six documents, and FDA officials are considering a similar approach for medical-equipment software. But some medical-equipment vendors oppose the additional documentation effort, calling it ineffective, costly, and time-consuming. Apparently, the cost of correcting hazardous errors has not yet caught up with them.

Another way of improving safety in programming involves the application of "formal methods," or techniques of mathematical logic, to software analysis. Designers create models of computer programs in specialized notations resembling equations. A model's behavior can then be analyzed before the product is actually constructed—in much the way the carrying capacity of a bridge can be calculated from an engineer's blueprints—and attempts can be made to prove that a program is error-free, employing the kind of mathematical logic used to prove the validity of theorems in geometry. The aim is to supplement trial-and-error testing, after the product is completed, with logical analysis beforehand.

Although computer scientists have been developing formal methods for more than twenty years, this approach is hardly ever put into practice. Some scientists believe the techniques are too difficult and cumbersome to be useful in evaluating any but the simplest programs (those that are only a few hundred lines long). Others caution that they promise too much, since formal proof does not guarantee that a program is perfect.

Yet formal methods need not ensure perfection to be useful, for they can uncover errors sometimes overlooked by trial-and-error testing and documentation review. Recently, the British Royal Signals and Radar Establishment, the electronics research laboratory of Britain's Ministry of Defense, applied formal methods to program fragments drawn from NATO's military software inventory. One in ten fragments was found to contain errors, many serious enough to result in the loss of the vehicle or machine controlled by the program. The British are betting heavily on formal methods to ensure software safety; new defense ministry regulations will require their use for some safety-critical products, and a government-sponsored report strongly encourages their use in civil products, as well. Nothing similar to this is planned in the United States.

IF MANUFACTURERS of computer-controlled medical devices, production-line equipment, and other potentially hazardous machinery continue to resist using safety engineering and formal methods, it may become necessary for government agencies to force their hands. We regulate all kinds of other things that pose risks to human life—buildings, bridges, airplanes, and drugs are just a few. We also require that the people who provide safety-critical services satisfy certain education requirements and pass examinations: physicians, pharmacists, lawyers, and even automobile drivers all must be government-certified.

Still, software remains largely unregulated. Aviation, nuclear power, and weapons systems purchased by the Defense Department are the few cases in which software is subject to government approval. There is no education standard required of programmers, and many computer-science curricula fail even to mention safety. Studies have found that the best programmers can be more than twenty-five times as competent as the worst and that many software-design supervisors are unable to evaluate or even understand their programmers' work. Of course, efforts to regulate software or certify programmers are likely to meet resistance. "I'll fight them to the death," says Robert Ulrickson, president of Logical Services, a Santa Clara, California, company that designs computerized instruments. "I don't want to be part of an economy that's run by the government."

But, for the most part, the mere appearance of government interest in software safety has had a positive effect. In September of 1987, in the wake of the Therac-25 tragedies, the FDA announced its intent to regulate some computer software in medical devices and began to work out guidelines. At about the same time, a staff member of the U.S. House of Representatives Committee on Science, Space, and Technology began investigating software quality–assurance practices on behalf of Congress. Seeing the writing on the wall, manufacturing and professional associations are instructing their members in software-quality assurance and acceptance testing. Employees are being sent to courses on computer-system safety, and unusually thorough attention is being devoted to checking for hazards in new machines. Some manufacturers have even contracted with outside firms to perform independent tests and evaluations. Given the low priority traditionally assigned to software safety, such efforts promise considerable improvement.

Microbyte and *PC Magazine* (a Spanish version of the United States publication). The magazines look like thinner versions of their U.S. counterparts. About the only large systems I recall seeing were from communication companies (about 20% of the exhibitors were from the telecommunication industry).

Although there are fewer exhibits and the magazines are thinner, much of Softel's for-sale technology is the same as at Comdex. Apple features multimedia and desktop publishing applications in Santiago just as it does in Las Vegas. There are Novell networks, 486-based servers, and the same sorts of peripherals and accessories you see in the U.S. Softel was held just two months after the introduction of Microsoft Windows, but Windows was running in many booths. More significantly, software houses were working on Windows applications and development tools. The same was true for Unix™. Many vendors sell Unix machines, and software companies are working with Unix windowing environments and C++. (There were software houses from ten countries at Softel.)

There is still some lag in the movement of personal computer technology to South America, but it is much less than in 1982, when I was last in Chile. That visit was nearly a year after IBM had announced the PC, and it was still six months away from introduction in South America. In 1982, a handful of small companies were selling 8-bit systems, which were rapidly disappearing in the U.S., and the major vendors I visited—IBM, DEC and NCR—were happily selling minicomputers, oblivious to the personal computer revolution. In less than 10 years the time gap has closed somewhat from an initial year or two to a month or two.

Of course, you see things at Comdex that you do not see at Softel. Softel shows items that are for sale today. At Comdex you also see demonstrations of tomorrow's technology. The conference sessions also have a different emphasis. Comdex sessions lean toward marketing and market projection, while Softel sessions are oriented toward practical applications of communi-

cation and computing technology. There were sessions on applications in business, agriculture, construction, and textile production.

Two other interesting events were taking place at the same time and conference facility as Softel and the Computer Science Conference. One was the Thirteenth Annual Systems Engineering Workshop organized by the University of Chile.

This actually consisted of about a dozen simultaneous workshops on practical topics such as pollution reduction and the forestry industry. The workshops ran for the entire week, bringing together engineers and researchers from around the world.

The fourth, and most interesting, event of the week was the first Meeting of Iberia-American Software Exporters (abbreviated EIES in Spanish). As are their counterparts in many other nations, Iberia-American software companies are eyeing the world software market.

EIES

EIES was attended by 126 people, representing 53 companies in 9 nations. It was sponsored by the Chilean Software Association and the Committee of Software Exporting Businesses. The meeting was chaired by Pablo Palma, president of ARS Innovandi, a Chilean software house.

In his opening address, Palma predicted explosive growth in the world software market during the coming decade.[1] He stated that today only 2% of the world's software is produced in Latin America and Africa, but he feels the expanding world market offers a significant opportunity for software companies in those areas. Palma believes that in order to compete with global companies, Iberia-American firms will have to cooperate; EIES was convened to inaugurate that cooperation.

This four-day meeting featured speakers from Latin America, Spain and North America. I only

[1]Mr. Palma's optimism is widely shared. For example, the International Data Corporation estimates that the worldwide software market will grow from 36.7 billion in 1989 to 80.7 billion in 1994.

heard the opening-day talks, which included speakers from the United States, Spain, and Chile. They included a variety of topics—from a government economist speaking about the strength of the Chilean commitment, to free trade to a somewhat technical presentation on OSI. There were sessions on communication infrastructure, practical experience with software export, and even a presentation on the United States software market which was lifted from the annual survey published in Jeffery Tartar's newsletter, *Soft · Letter*.

I thought the most inspirational talk was given by Dan Mapes, a United States marketing consultant. Mapes foresees the growth and spread of the software industry as contributing to a more just, equally developed world. He reasons that since innovative software is developed by small groups with little capital equipment, companies from nonindustrial countries will do well in the world market. He is optimistic, believing that different cultures, each having a unique worldview, will invent and develop different sorts of software. The world community will be enriched by a flow of software and ideas from Latin America and other regions. In a more practical vein, he feels that companies with software products that are successful in local markets can export them to the U.S. and other countries with the help of marketing and distribution partners.

I interviewed Palma after EIES to learn what conclusions had been reached and found that an association of national software associations has been formed. As of today, Spain, South American countries (with the exception of Columbia and Venezuela), and several Central American countries are members of the association. By next year it should include all of Central and South America, Spain and Portugal. While the participants agree that thinking of a worldwide market is inevitable, during the coming year, they will concentrate on fostering trade within Iberia-America. They will produce a database of products and companies, and meet again next year. I will keep *Commu-*

nications readers posted on next year's developments.

Adios American Programmer?

Howell, et al. estimate that the U.S. accounts for about 52% of world software consumption and U.S. software producers hold roughly 70% of the world market. Another study, by International Data Corporation estimates that in 1989 the U.S., Europe and Japan accounted for 81% of the world software market [9]. While such figures are not precise, there is no denying that today's software industry is concentrated in North America, Europe and Japan.

It is difficult for me to believe the software industry will remain so concentrated. The world communication infrastructure is improving daily; salaries and overhead are very high in Europe, North America and parts of Asia; and powerful personal computers have drastically lowered capital costs for software companies. Take Chile as an example. Chilean universities are excellent, and many of the people I met have advanced degrees from the U.S.; we communicate via MCI Mail and The Internet; their salaries, office space and other ancillary services are much cheaper than in the U.S.; and they use the same commercial hardware and software tools as we do.

Ed Yourdon puts it more dramatically. He believes that international competition will put U.S. programmers out of work, that "the American programmer is about to go the way of the dinosaur and the dodo bird. During the next five to seven years, I foresee massive unemployment among the ranks of American programmers, systems analysts and others in the data processing industry [6]."

If Yourdon is correct, we had better start looking for second careers. Even if he is only partially correct, we will be affected, so I decided to examine to what extent personal computer software companies are turning to off-shore programmers.

Ireland

For a start, I learned that Ashton-Tate, Claris, Lotus, Microsoft, Retix and other software companies have offices in Ireland. Each company localizes its software in Ireland. For example, according to Stuart Kazin, vice president for manufacturing, Lotus produces versions of its programs in eight European languages, and translation and testing of the software and manuals are performed in Dublin. (Software translation and conversion for the Asian market is handled out of Japan.) Claris's Dan McClarren told me they do the same, overlapping it with U.S. beta testing, so software is released at the same time throughout the world. These companies also manufacture European software and support and distribute it from Ireland.

According to co-founder John Stevenson, Retix, a vendor of OSI networking software, has gone further than the others, moving significant development to Ireland. It began by recruiting programmers from Irish universities and bringing them to the U.S. Since that went well, Retix opened a 15-person office in Ireland three years ago. Doing so put the company close to European customers who needed support and software customization. It eliminated the eight-hour time difference and made travel cheaper and easier. The office has grown to 60 people, with roughly 25% working on support and 75% on development. (The entire company consists of 400 people.) The Irish office is growing rapidly, and it might eventually have as many developers as in the United States.

For now, most of Retix's product-marketing people are in the U.S.; consequently the decision to develop a product is typically made here. If it is decided that development be done in Ireland, the requirements documents, functional specification, writing, testing and maintenance would all be done by an Irish-managed and -staffed team. A product is developed in whichever office is the center for expertise on the relevant OSI protocols.

I asked each of these companies if there were any major drawbacks in working with Irish offices, and all said "no." They eliminate potential cultural clashes by employing Irish managers, find the employees well-educated and industrious, like being near European markets, and save money on salaries, overhead and taxes.

This satisfaction is no accident—it was planned. The Irish government noticed that they had a brain-drain problem and a 17% unemployment rate, so they made a decision to become a software leader. Computer science programs in universities were enhanced, a 10% corporate tax rate was established, $2.5 billion was invested in telecommunication, and the Industrial Development Authority of Ireland opened offices around the world. Their chief asset is well-trained, hard-working employees, who were praised by everyone I interviewed.

India

India's effort to export software has been well publicized, and soon after I began researching it, I discovered that Ed Yourdon had been to India to study the software industry. Yourdon reported on his experience and impressions in his newsletter, *The American Programmer*. Let me tell you a little of what he found

Since 1985, when Rajiv Gandhi began a push for modernization and the personal computer was introduced, the Indian information technology industry has grown at an annual rate of 59%, compared to 12% in the U.S. Current Indian software exports are approximately $10–15 million; the government hopes to expand software exports to $100 million (some predict $500 million) by 1995. The primary reason for believing they can succeed is that the typical programmer earns $2,400 per year, and overhead is low. While Yourdon feels India bears watching, there are many obstacles to overcome. Since the information technology industry languished until 1985, it is weighted toward small and personal computers. There is little experience with large systems or projects; there are few sophisticated end users (an important prerequisite to a sophisticated software industry); and the domestic software industry is only .25% of GNP, compared to between 3 and 5% in Western industrial nations. Yourdon believes that to have a viable software export industry, India must also develop a strong domestic industry. Finding qualified people is also a problem. The projected need is for 275,000 programmers by 1995, but the country has only 50,000 today. (The U.S. has around 1 million.) Yourdon also found the telecommunication network woefully inadequate.

There are several ways that software can be exported. Companies can station programmers at a client's site for the duration of a project, write turnkey systems from a specification developed in consultation with a client, or develop packages for worldwide marketing. In 1989, 80% of Indian software exports were from on-site programming, turnkey projects accounted for 15%, and software packages only 1% (the remainder was data capture).

While on-site programming is somewhat profitable, the return is low compared to those writing turnkey programs and developing packages. In addition, many of the on-site programmers find ways to join India's significant brain drain. For these reasons, the industry hopes to move away from on-site programming, and a recent report from Forrester Research [8] indicates that the time may be right. In a survey of 50 Fortune 1000 companies, Forrester found that 38% have decentralized application development and 22% are evaluating doing so. Some of this decentralization will leave the country. As consultant Herb Halbrecht told me, "The role of a CIO is becoming like that of an international investment broker. Companies scour the world looking for pockets of excellence."

Yourdon agrees that India should move away from on-site programming, and suggests a five-stage strategy:

1) Build a reputation by providing inexpensive on-site programming.
2) Shift the services back to India with well-specified projects.
3) Shift emphasis from low-cost to high quality.
4) Shift from service to product orientation by finding niches or producing cheap clones.
5) Find applications that encapsulate India's unique expertise.

This transition is illustrated by the plans of database software vendor Ashton-Tate. According to vice president David Proctor, Ashton-Tate has ten programmers coming from India. It is their plan to use them on projects and get to know them. In the long run, two or three will remain here as liaison with programmers living in India. Proctor estimates that the programmers in India will cost Ashton-Tate $10–12,000 per year, including salaries and overhead. Yourdon concludes with a discussion of social differences between the U.S. and India. For example, in India there is a pervasive attitude that labor is cheap and machines expensive and there is a strongly rooted tradition of dominant public-sector companies in all key industries. In spite of cultural barriers and other problems, $12,000 per year for a university-trained programmer proficient in C and Unix cannot be ignored.

Perestroika
I am writing this on German Unification Day. This milestone and other recent changes in the former Eastern Bloc nations make one curious about the prospects of software export from Eastern Europe. Industry watcher Esther Dyson has traveled extensively in Eastern Europe during the last year, so I turned to her newsletter "Release 1.0" for an overview [3].

Dyson writes that the Eastern European countries are heterogeneous in many ways, including their cultures, economies, copyright laws, technical sophistication, and installed computer bases. Together, they have an installed base of a little over one million DOS personal computers, compared to 40 million in the U.S., but "PCs have been first seeping and now flooding in through less official channels." (A student of mine called last week to tell me that his firm had received an order for 29,000 PC clones from the Soviet Union.) Still, the local market for software is relatively small, and a robust, sophisticated local market will be necessary for software companies to compete internationally.

Development of a strong local market is hampered by a lack of hard currency and, more subtly, by a value system that undervalues intangible services. The idea of making a profit by merely working as a programmer or software distributor is foreign to many. Dyson also states that custom software is more prevalent than are packages in Eastern Europe. This is due to the small market and social factors such as a lack of copyright laws and enforcement, and little emphasis on productivity enhancement, due to salaries being low and computers being expensive.

While I did not come across examples of Eastern Europeans doing custom development in the U.S., a few companies are beginning to sell software packages. The most visible Eastern European software import is the game Tetris™. Developed by Alexey Pazhitnov of the Soviet Academy of the Sciences, Tetris won four Software Publishing Association awards in 1988, including best entertainment program. There have been some disputes over royalties, but the Soviets seem to have learned to do business in the West, and Pazhitnov has become a minor celebrity. Tetris initially made its way to the West through Hungary, and its success is reminiscent of the Hungarian Rubik's Cube. Yourdon and Mapes both point to software that exploits unique world views—perhaps we will get engrossing games from Eastern Europe.

PC software companies Autodesk and Ashton-Tate have also been active in Eastern Europe. They have paid their dues by accepting soft local currency, which they used to finance local offices. Both established training centers and dealer networks several years ago, and they are now beginning to receive hard currency payback. These relationships are also beginning to yield software for export. Autodesk plans to market three AutoCAD-related software tools which were developed by their Soviet partners, and Ashton-Tate will be marketing database develop-

Dyson writes that the Eastern European countries are heterogeneous in many ways, including their cultures, economies, copyright laws, technical sophistication, and installed computer bases.

ment tools, beginning with a localization aid.

Graphisoft, a Hungarian firm, has taken an even more independent approach. They have opened their own offices in Canada, the U.S., and Western Europe, and market their internally developed CAD software for the Macintosh. The six-year-old company now has 30 programmers, so it appears to be viable.

The Far East

Remove the cover of your personal computer and you will see how well Far Eastern companies have been doing in hardware. The names printed on the chips read like a United Nations rollcall, and most (but not all) are from the Far East. Furthermore, there is a good chance your personal computer was assembled in the Far East. Still, for the time being, your Far Eastern hardware is probably running American software.

According to Carl Chang and Mikio Aoyama, software has been one of the fastest growing industries in most Far Eastern countries during the last few years. In surveying the software in Japan, Taiwan, South Korea, and Singapore [1], they observe a high level of activity in every country. They also note that while developments in each country are unique, there is one common thread—that "the effort to industrialize software is likely to be made through a national government-directed, and publicly funded initiative."

One company, Visible Systems, has complained that this subsidy and coordination is unfair. Visible Systems markets a CASE tool in competition with Picture-Oriented Software Engineering (POSE), a program developed in Singapore. Visible Systems filed a claim with the Department of Commerce asserting that POSE had been devel-

oped with a $15 million subsidy from the Singapore National Computer Board. The Department of Commerce initially decided in their favor, imposing a 15.25% punitive duty on POSE, but they subsequently reversed the decision, citing fear of retaliation [2]. The Department of Commerce still holds that software is merchandise—not intellectual property—and that they therefore have the right to charge a duty.

While some U.S. companies, like Visible Systems, are asking for protection from Far Eastern competitors, IBM has tried joining its competitors. Nearly three years ago, IBM, in a strategic alliance with Taiwan's government-supported Institute for Information Industry, formed International Integrated Systems, Inc. (IISI), to develop software exclusively for IBM. Although IISI was required to compete openly with other software companies, it has delivered over 100 programs to IBM. The projects were divided fairly evenly between translation of IBM programs and documentation to Oriental languages, double-byte character set conversion, and new development. Once specifications were established, all of the work was done in Taiwan.

Having learned from this experience, IBM exercised an option to make an equity investment in IISI, and it now hopes to market software services to other customers. A retired IBM executive, Rusty Scheuer, who is heading the U.S. marketing effort, has found it is not an easy sale. Many potential customers are U.S. companies selling packages that they would like to convert for marketing in the Orient. Even at Taiwanese rates, however, the cost of conversion is steep, and there is also the reluctance of a U.S. company to give its source code to someone so far removed, in

a country not known for its copyright enforcement.

This survey has cited examples of early efforts to export software to the U.S. It remains to be seen whether Yourdon's prediction of the demise of the American programmer will come true, but the American programmer should surely take offshore competition seriously. The quality of today's offshore programmers is high, and their salaries and overhead are low. On the other hand, while cultural and language barriers are diminishing, they still exist. Software, particularly custom, in-house applications, requires communication with and sensitivity to the users.

In the long run, education may determine software success. As long as a country like Chile or India is educating only a few elite programmers, these programmers will be very good; however, it remains to be seen if those countries (and we) can build the infrastructure to educate masses of average programmers needed by a growing software industry. Personal computers also affect education by cutting the cost of hardware to support teaching and research.

In any event, I hope our reaction to the possibility of foreign competition is not to seek protection, but to seek excellence. While offshore competition may be bad news for American programmers, it is good news for the American software consumers, and they are more numerous than we are.

Larry Press welcomes questions and comments from readers. His address, phone number and email address are:

10726 Esther Avenue
Los Angeles, CA 90064
(213) 475-6515
1press@venera.isi.edu

Pointers:

For overviews of developments in

Western Europe, see the April 1990 issue of *Communications*, and the June 1990 issue of *IEEE Spectrum*. The two complement each other, providing insight into the likely impact of the 1992 economic unification on the computer, communication and electronics industries.

For coverage of software development in the Far East, see the March 1989 issue of *IEEE Software*. It has articles on Japan, China, South Korea, Singapore, and Taiwan.

To learn what is happening in Eastern Europe, turn to Esther Dyson's newsletter *Release 1.0*. Dyson writes about far more than Eastern Europe, and wins my award as the most interesting industry watcher. She is an articulate writer with an understanding of computer science and the world of business. EDventure Holdings, Inc., 375 Park Avenue, New York, NY 10152, (212) 758-3434.

The *American Programmer* is a newsletter on software engineering and management published by industry veteran Ed Yourdon. In addition to presenting the latest in CASE tools, Yourdon travels extensively, and reports on his findings. He presents relevant cultural information along with facts and analysis, and writes with humor. (The copyright notice in the newsletter prohibits "eating the material.") Contact American Programmer, 161 West 86th Street, New York, NY 10024-3411; (212) 769-9460; fax: (212) 769-9458 or MCI: eyourdon or Compuserve 71250,2322.

ADAPSO, the Computer Software and Services Industry Association, publishes reports and holds seminars on international software developments. For example, their well-researched report on Japanese software was referenced above. Contact ADAPSO, 1300 North 17th Street, Suite 300, Arlington, VA 22209; (703) 522-5055.

If you are interested in exhibiting at or visiting Softel '91, contact Feria Internacional de Santiago, Tenderini 187-Casilla 40 D, Santiago, Chile; (562) 557-7096; fax: (562) 557-6923.

For information on the organization of Iberia-American national software associations, contact Jose Fabio Marinho de Araujo, Director, IBPI, Rua Lauro Muller, 116/Grupo 1207, 22290, Rio de Janeiro, Brazil; (021) 275-6594; Fax (021) 295-6993.

The Industrial Development Agency of Ireland has offices in 17 cities in North America, Europe and the Far East. For more information, contact Emmanuel Dowdall at 1821 Wilshire Boulevard, Suite 317, Santa Monica, CA 90403; (213) 829-0081; Fax: (213) 829-1586.

If you are not yet a user of the worldwide Matrix of computernetworks, you might take a look at either of the following books. If you are a user of the Matrix, you may enjoy them even more.

Frey, Donnalyn and Adams, Rick,

"!%@:: A Directory of Electronic Mail Addressing and Networks," O'Reilly and Associates, Sebastopol, CA, 1990.

Quarterman, John S., "The Matrix: Computer Networks and Conferencing Systems Worldwide," Digital Press, Bedford, MA, 1990.

References

1. Chang, Carl K, and Aoyama, Mikio. Software in the Far East. *IEEE Softw.* (Mar. 1989), 11–12.
2. Davis, Ludlum A. Commerce department reverses Singapore ruling. *Computerworld* (Apr. 2, 1990), 119.
3. Dyson, E. Eastern infrastructure. Release 1.0. (Aug. 21, 1990), 1–34.
4. Howell, Thomas R., Noellert, William A., Ohri, Bonnie, and Wolff, Alan W. *Japanese Software, the Next Competitive Challenge*. ADAPSO, Arlington, Va., Jan. 1989.
5. Quarterman, John S. *The Matrix: Computer Networks and Conferencing Systems Worldwide*. Digital Press, Bedford, Mass., 1990.
6. Yourdon, Ed. The decline and fall of the American programmer. *Am. Prog.* (Mar. 1988), 1–8.
7. Yourdon, Ed. India. *Am. Prog.* (Oct., 1989), 3–26.
8. Woodring, Stuart and Colony, George F. How software will be managed. Forrester Software Strategy Report, June, 1990.
9. Worldwide Information Technology Spending Patterns, 1989–1994. An analysis of opportunities in 30 countries. International Data Corporation, Framingham, Mass. (Sept. 1990).

"Tetris is a copyrighted trademark of AcademySoft-ELORG. It is also sublicensed to Sphere Inc. and Mirrorsoft Limited.

ACADEMIC COMPUTING: THE LOS ANDES STRATEGY

Our Approach to Academic Computing Can Only Be Understood as a Strategic Response to the Emerging Global Information Society

Ivan Trujillo

Ivan Trujillo is administrative director at the Universidad de Los Andes in Bogotá, Colombia, and a member of the EDUCOM Consuling Group Advisory Board.

There are approximately seven million students in higher education in Latin America and the Caribbean, out of an aggregate population of just over 405 million. In general, Latin American institutions have fewer resources and less access to advanced technology than our American counterparts, but our leading universities are striving hard to keep pace in applications of computing and networking to instruction, research, and administration. The Universidad de Los Andes, a private institution in Bogotá, is proud to be the first South American member of EDUCOM and a charter member of the Colombian network soon to be connected to BITNET. Our approach to academic computing can only be understood, however, in the context of—and as a strategic response to—the emerging global information society.

Colombia, located on the northwestern tip of South America, is just over a tenth the size of the United States and has a population of 30 million. The Colombian economy has traditionally been based on agriculture. Its main and best known export product is coffee, although in recent times oil and minerals, notably coal and nickel, have also become abundant enough for export.

Politically, Colombia is one of the oldest and more stable democracies in the region. From the point of view of higher education, only about 2.5 percent of the total population have reached this level. With a GNP of US$40 billion, Colombia is what economists and politicians call a "third-world nation," although the bankers who finance its foreign debt have placed it in a sort of "middle class" within this category and still lend money, because the country has never failed to honor its debts.

This economic distinction has been further refined to a dichotomy between the north and south of the

---

The information gap is more dangerous than the economic and technology gaps, because it grows in an exponential way.

---

globe, with the north as seat of most of the so-called developed nations and the south as home to most of the less developed ones. Just as the countries in the north are different from each other in many respects, the countries in the south cannot be lumped together as a homogeneous unit. Third-world nations do have something in common, however: their relationship to the world up north.

Traditionally, rich nations in the north have bought raw materials from their poor neighbors in the south. These materials include agricultural products such as coffee, bananas, tropical fruits, flowers, etc.; minerals such as copper, tin and nickel; and energy in the form of oil and coal. The rich nations gave back the foreign currency needed for social and economic development. They also exported manufactured goods to the south.

From a technological viewpoint, most of the innovations have come from the north in the form of machinery and know-how. It must be said in passing that the technology being exported was not always the most current: many third-world factories are still equipped with secondhand machinery that had been discarded in the northern nations.

From the cultural and scientific viewpoint also, there has existed a marked dependence on the north. This derives from the tradition of sending sons and daughters of the elite from the south to be educated in the north where they established the necessary contacts to keep reasonably well informed.

RECENT RELATIONS BETWEEN NORTH AND SOUTH

The impressive scientific and technological advances that have taken place in the developed nations are shaping a new society in the north and are altering the traditional relations between north and south. These advances are bringing a host of new problems to the south, whose consequences are difficult to foresee from social and economic viewpoints. Technology as such is not a problem; the problem comes when its use affects the social, economic, and political fabric.

The rich nations have added money to their traditional exports: the third-world nations had the mixed blessing of using dollars coming from oil sales in the 1970s for their social and economic development. The erratic behavior of the world economy during the past 15 years has brought about a delicate situation where most of the less-developed nations owe to the rich nations more than they can actually pay. An increase of one point in the U.S. prime lending rate, for instance, means that the whole of South America must dish out an additional US$4 billion per year, because most foreign debt is tied to the vagaries of the prime rate. This means that the countries must spend less and less on development and increasingly more on the export of capital to the north. Of course, the world economy is now so globalized that it could suffer very severe damage should the Latin American countries decide to stop payments.

Inflation and interest rates in the north have profound impacts also on higher education in the south. Whereas in the 1960s it was still possible to send gifted students to do graduate studies in the north, it is prohibitively expensive to do so now. This results in a decrease in the number of well-trained scientists in third-world universities.

Recent scientific and technological advances in the north are also bringing economic problems to the less developed nations. In many cases these advances have reduced demand for raw materials, which were the main source of foreign currency for these countries. Microelectronics, for example, has made possible the manufacturing of devices that need fewer and fewer component parts. The digital watch, with some ten main components, including the electronic chip, has already displaced the older traditional models built with hundreds of tiny metallic parts. This is also true of other devices, such as lathes, mechanical arms, computer printers, and so on. Countries like Chile or Bolivia, whose main exports were copper and tin some years back, have lost billions of dollars in revenue because of these technological advances.

Future developments in biotechnology will probably bring about similar results for countries with agricultural exports. We are concerned at the prospect of growing "100 percent Colombian" coffee in Iowa in the 1990s, or worse yet, brewing it from a cell culture in some lab in Heidelberg.

The oil exports of countries like Venezuela or Mexico can be predicted to diminish as progress is made in new materials technology, superconductivity, cleaner and safer nuclear technologies, and the electric car. Moreover, if oil loses its strategic value, governments from the north will lose interest in their former clients from the south.

Collectively, these factors contribute to a widening of the already existing technological gap. Third-world nations are losing sorely needed revenues, which could be used to buy the often more expensive new technologies. As a result, the factories are becoming increasingly obsolete, which in turn makes them less competitive. Linear growth in the technological gap threatens to become exponential.

Finally, there is the information gap, which is potentially more dangerous than the economic and technology gaps, because it already grows in an exponential way. The volume of scientific and technological information is said to double every 20 months, whereas 30 years ago it doubled every five years. This information explosion is threatening the very existence of books in certain disciplines of rapid growth; when the book is finally published it is already obsolete. Scientists in need of faster means of disseminating their research results publish articles in specialized journals; in journals a quarter of a year is considered not long at all for fresh information to appear. But if scientific and technological information keeps growing exponentially, the day will soon come when scientists will use computer networks to publish their articles, with information coming out of their labs the moment new discoveries are made, so that they get instant credit.

In the meantime, in the less developed nations the information gap grows wider and wider, because there are no effective channels for obtaining information on time. It arrives late, sometimes months after it is produced. And although there are well-trained scientists in these countries, research is not as effective as it could be. If this situation persists, the third-world nations will become a sort of isolated "community of barbarians" surrounding the "information empires" of the developed countries. And, historically speaking, it is not wise for empires to let this happen: a surrounding community of barbarians can wind up invading the empire.

INFORMATION TECHNOLOGIES IN THIRD-WORLD HIGHER EDUCATION

Although no one takes seriously the remark made by Carnegie-Mellon University professor Daniel Siewiorek that "your home, and indeed some Cadillacs, have more computing power than many third-world nations,"[1] it must be admitted that, with some exceptions, such as Brazil's independent policies on the computer industry,[2] or the efforts made in the same direction in India and some countries in Southeast Asia, computing in third-world nations is affected by these widening economic, technology, and information gaps.

While it is true that in many such nations there are people who are well trained in computer and communications technologies, that many have learned to program a computer, and that the human factor in these fields of endeavor is more important than chips and cables, it is also true that the initial hardware and maintenance costs constitute a considerable financial burden. This is to say nothing of the costs of standard software, such as operating systems, databases, fourth-generation software, and the like. If we add to this the short-sighted policy of most third-world governments, which impose huge customs duties on computing and communications hardware, while knowing that the very same merchandise cannot be exported to certain counties, the picture looks bleaker. As a general rule, a computer costs at least 30 percent more than in the United States; in Colombia, it costs almost 50 percent more.

Furthermore, rapid changes in technology accelerate the process of obsolescence. One must replace in three to four years machines bought when they first came out, and replacement costs are prohibitive. New technologies that have merged with the traditional information technologies, such as optic fiber networks in communications, are hard to come by in the beginning, because one must first wait until there is someone in the country who can maintain them. The lack of advanced CAD/CAM workstations and advanced research in robotics may be worsening industry's already backward situation.

As a result of these changes, much valuable information is lost. Information on the economies and demography of third-world nations, which has been gathered by independent research institutes, cannot be passed from an obsolete computer to a new one, because of the conversion costs. It is also difficult to keep track of the trends in information technology in the developed nations.

In addition to this, we confront an already stale idea of what a university should be, which is conservatively tied to mostly European and American traditions. The universities in our countries are oriented toward the formation of professionals who will serve the government and industry. Graduate studies are almost a luxury, because the economic means to promote research and development are scarce. And what is worse, those who are in a position to change this situation, to imagine a new kind of university, are blind and do not act, either because they are not aware of the changes taking place, or because of a basic resistance to change.

In the meantime, the United States exhibits several trends pointing to different models of what a university could be. There is the "multimedia university," which may some day graduate people with a general education emphasizing fields that may or may not constitute what we call today "the professions." The graduates from these universities will take State Board examinations qualifying them as architects, engineers, or musicians, and they will have jobs in four or five different "professions" during their lifetimes. There is the "corporate university," which has become a think tank in service of government and industry and is financed by them for the most part. Such a university becomes a closed scientific community with limited access, which produces highly valuable information bearing a hefty price tag. Finally, there are those who are cautious and think that all the fuss about the "information revolution" may be a passing fad and that it is better to follow the traditional way.[3]

THE UNIVERSITY OF LOS ANDES

The University of Los Andes, founded almost 40 years ago on a hillside site overlooking downtown Bogotá, is considered one of the finest private universities in Colombia. Half of its 5,200 undergraduate students belong to the school of engineering. The rest of the students are in the schools of architecture, basic sci-

---

From a technological viewpoint, most innovations have come from north of the equator.

---

ences, business administration, economics, law, and the humanities. There are also some 800 graduate students in the various schools. In its research centers is conducted almost 75 percent of all research being done in private universities. All of this is achieved with an annual budget of some US$13 million. The average tuition is slightly over US$1,000 a year, which is the highest in the country; the rest of the funds come from other activities such as funded research or continuing education.

The University was a pioneer in the use of information technologies in Colombia when in 1963 it acquired an IBM 650 for teaching and research. By 1967, the university had begun to teach courses in computer science. Since then it has evolved still more and now seeks to place itself in a strategic position vis-à-vis the environment being created by the use of the new information technologies in higher education. We believe that today's student must be well trained in the handling and processing of increasing volumes of information, which is only possible through the use of the new technologies. We also believe that faculty, researchers, and staff must have rapid access to local, domestic, and international information sources, if the technological and information gaps are to be bridged. In this fashion, it is hoped that the threats brought about by the information gap will be converted into opportunities by capitalizing on the institution's strengths in the field of information technology.

THE HERMES PROGRAM

Launched in July 1986, the Hermes Program is the present administration's answer to the issues raised by the use of the new technologies. It is an educational experiment whose results are hard to foresee. The University hopes to train itself in the management of change with the help of strategic planning and to

---

We have no less than 25 projects on the production of educational software.

---

evaluate the transformations brought about by change. Careful attention will paid to the impact that this change may have on the human being. For this reason, the name of the project was taken from the humanities: Hermes, son of Zeus, was the messenger of the gods in Greek mythology, and by extension was converted into the amiable god of communications.

There are five main goals of the Hermes Program:

1. To substantially increase the efficiency and quality of student work being done outside the classroom, particularly in disciplines in which information technology has not been used with this purpose. Technological progress has made possible the automatic handling of information in every branch of knowledge. Through use of this technology, students can perform many otherwise repetitive tasks, thus freeing time to devote to other activities, such as the exercise of creativity and personal and emotional development.

2. To facilitate faculty and researchers in performance of their fundamental mission as educators and sponsors of future professionals through use of innovative methods. As is well known, the way higher education is being conducted has rapidly changed in

institutions that have adopted the new technologies. From simple tutorial systems of the flash card type, the computer has made possible the creation of complex simulations and realistic learning environments. Use of multimedia and the study of cognitive science will some day allow the introduction of better techniques in the learning process. For researchers, easy access to networks will surely increase their productivity and facilitate their communication with colleagues around the globe.

3. To give an education in the new information technologies to students, faculty, staff, and researchers at the basic, intermediate, and advanced levels. This means that the whole community must become computer-literate in a relatively short time, with some people using the computer as a productivity tool and others learning programming. The intermediate and advanced levels will be reserved for those whose work calls for intensive use of the computer.

4. To engage in research projects that deal with certain areas that are very important in information technology. Initially, five research areas were identified: definition and development of programming environments in interactive graphics and CAD/CAM; analysis, design, modeling, and simulation of systems; interpretation of signals and images; CAI; and distributed processing. Other areas of interest have been added, including parallel processing, robotics and control systems, and artificial intelligence, among others.

5. To improve the administration of the University through the use of information technology. This goal calls for a modernization of the actual systems in use.

Their goals are ambitious and point to a general direction that must be followed. Fulfilling them will be subject to planning, with periodic revisions.[4]

STRATEGIES TO REACH THESE GOALS

Four basic strategies have been formulated to reach these goals:

1. A massive use of computing. On the one hand, the plan calls for modernization of the large and medium-sized systems. On the other, the University has adopted the use of personal computers, which are currently more cost-effective than larger systems for some tasks.

In this context, the University has taken advantage of discount programs offered by manufacturers and has facilitated acquisition of personal computers by students, faculty, and staff. Machines that have been

---

We too believe that faculty, researchers, and staff must have rapid access to local, domestic, and international information sources.

---

sold include Apple Macintoshes and MS-DOS-based microcomputers. The University has also arranged for low-interest financing over three years through local financial institutions. By comparison, a professor in an American university must spend the equivalent of two to three weeks salary to buy one of those machines, whereas a Colombian professor must spend the equivalent of five months of his salary!

As of December 1988, students, faculty, and staff had bought almost 700 computers, and the number of microcomputers installed in the various offices and departments in the University had reached 325. There are also two computer labs with 20 Macintoshes each administrated by the Hermes Program, which can be used free by all those who need a tool for their classes or for software development.

The massive introduction of the personal computer has begun to generate a computing subculture within the University. It is no longer a rare sight to find students and faculty from the humanities and social sciences discussing the use of the computer with their colleagues from the schools of the basic sciences and engineering. New courses have been designed that use the personal computer as a tool, such as a course in the methodology of scientific research for social scientists which introduces anthropologists, historians, and political scientists to quantitative methods through the use of spreadsheets, databases, and statistical packages.

Production of educational software, formerly the almost exclusive domain of the department of computer science, has already begun to be an area of interest in wider circles. There are no less than 25 such projects today, which involve tutorial systems, simulation of physical systems, teaching of music, teaching of Spanish, and communications between several brands of computers.

2. Active participation in higher education computing consortia. The University of Los Andes is a founding member of the Latin American Chapter of the Apple University Consortium. The partnership with Apple has led to joint projects with the Latin American division of this important manufacturer, and it is hoped that this will also lead to eventual partnerships in research and development.

In 1986, the University of Los Andes also became the second Latin American member of EDUCOM, after the Instituto Tecnológico de Estudios Superiores de Monterrey in Mexico. The University has also been active in trying to convince other Colombian and Latin American universities to join EDUCOM.

3. The Hermes Program Office. The office coordinates necessary logistics for the massive infusion of personal computers, represents the University in activities of the consortia, provides introductory courses and user support, promotes software development, and operates the two public labs. Some 3,000 people have access to these labs each semester.

4. Modernization of existing large and medium-sized systems. During the past two years, the University Computing Center engaged in a study to replace the existing central computing facilities. Last year, a new IBM 9370-90 was installed for academic use. The existing equipment for administrative use will be replaced this year. The machines are being connected to the machines that already exist in other departments, such as the VAX-systems in the school of engineering, via a local area network. It is also hoped that these machines will soon be hooked up to BITNET.

CONCLUSION

The theme of the EDUCOM'87 conference, where an earlier version of this paper was presented, was "Towards a Global Information Culture." Much attention has, justifiably, been given to recent developments on the Pacific Rim and in the Soviet Union, and to prospects for Europe after 1992. It must be remembered, however, that the countries and universities in Latin America and the rest of the third world are also part of the globe. In spite of all the difficulties, we want in.

REFERENCES

1. *Computerworld*, Nov. 3, 1986, p. 39.
2. Botelho, Antonio José J., "Brazil's Independent Computer Strategy," *Technology Review*, M.I.T., May/June 1987, pp. 36–45.
3. Green, Kenneth C., and Steven W. Gilbert, "New Computing in Higher Education," *Information Technology Quarterly*, Harvard University, Summer-Fall 1986, Vol. V, No. 2, pp. 10–23.
4. Infante, Arturo, "Message of the President: El Programa Hermes de la Universidad de Los Andes," *Uniandes*, Bogotá, July 1986.

NEW DIMENSIONS IN CREATIVITY

*Brazilian television
is livelier and more hip
than anything else on air—
even MTV is still catching up*

GERI SMITH

Contributing editor Geri Smith, a correspondent based in Rio de Janeiro, recently helped produce a segment on living with inflation for CBS Television's 60 Minutes.

SWITCH ON a television set in Brazil, and chances are you won't believe your eyes. Two pairs of scissors, aloft but unguided by human hands, ferociously attack each other to herald the beginning of a soap opera about rival dress designers. Needles sew by themselves, measuring tapes flap menacingly and pens mysteriously sketch designs. Humorous station breaks celebrating summer feature a man watching a surfing competition on television who impulsively joins the surfers by diving right through the screen into the waves.

A popular TV series begins with a scene of parched, dry earth. Suddenly, nearly 3,000 skyscrapers burst from the ground and a whole city appears. Opening credits take the form of the actors' faces reflected in the smoky-glass facades. Then the camera pans to an overhead view of the city and the tops of the buildings form a black-and-white mosaic of the leading actor's face.

Flights of fantasy are everyday fare on Brazil's Globo Television, the world's fourth-largest network. An unlimited budget, a free-wheeling atmosphere in the art department and a willingness to tap new technology have won Globo a worldwide reputation for its imaginative graphics and stunning special effects. Globo airs a full hour each day of eye-catching opening segments, colorful station identification logos and comedy vignettes that keep an in-house team of nine artists, a 34-member computer graphics department and more than $5 million in state-of-the-art dream machines humming year round.

Although the top three U.S. networks wow viewers with computer-generated opening segments for sports, movies or news programs, "other countries use a lot more computer graphics," says Lane Williams, a former MacDraw specialist now working in Apple Computer's advance technology group. Williams has worked as an imager and computer programmer in the United States, Japan and Brazil. "It would surprise North Americans that computer TV in Brazil is more lively, vivid and hip-looking than what they see on the networks here. MTV in some respects is still catching up to Brazilian TV."

Nowhere in the world are television spectators treated to as much computer wizardry as they are in Brazil. Perhaps this is possible only at a privately-owned network such as Globo, whose management does not have to justify the multi-million-dollar graphics budget to shareholders and doesn't need to fret about precious commercial time "lost" to non- revenue-producing spots.

"The job I have doesn't exist anywhere else in the world," exults Hans Donner, the 38-year-old graphics artist from Austria who helped revolutionize Globo's image when he became art director 13 years ago. "I have complete freedom to create, use the latest technology, anything that works. I don't believe there is another network in the world that has access to the resources we do."

Then there is the special energy and creativity that Brazilians throw into everything they do. Rio's Carnival extravaganza is a visual production par excellence. The country's advertisers are known as among the world's most creative, unfettered by convention and taboo. "The Japanese like computer graphics because it's very perfect and technical and very austere, whereas the Brazilians really dance with it," Williams comments. "Theirs are kind of giddy and weightless and wildly colorful." A local phrase explains the phenomenon: *"Tem muito jeito nestas coisas,"* which means, Brazilians just have a knack for doing creative things.

"This is a country that is completely open to new ideas,

that likes to tackle big, impossible projects such as the Trans-Amazon Highway, or the capital that was built in the middle of nowhere," Donner says.

That, he explains, is why Globo executives didn't blink when he spent $400,000 in 1983 to create a 90-second opening sequence for its showcase weekly newsmagazine show, seen by 80 million Brazilians. It is one of the most impressive displays of computer imagery ever seen on television.

A gold pyramid flashes onto the screen and a laser beam slices off the tip. Then a three-dimensional shiny gold cone, shaped like the tip of a ball-point pen, streaks into view, spinning through space. Two rainbow laser beams slice through the cone, sectioning it into swirling gold disks of different sizes. The disks waffle around and settle into a five-tiered platform on which real dancers somehow appear, wiggling and leaping from one disk to another. The pyramid returns, is sliced up and becomes a second, spectacular stage for more dancers. The spectator then is taken inside the pyramid stage to look out at the dancers. It's a breathtaking introduction that lives up to the program's name: *Fantastico*.

All of the images—except for the dancers who were dubbed in later—were generated by a computer capable of carrying out 20 million calculations a second. Even at that speed, the computer had to work 45 days and nights to transform mathematical instructions into the complex digital images.

Despite the introduction's success, Donner used almost no computer imagery for the *Fantastico* opening that has been on the air since 1987. "We don't want to do overkill, and besides, we have a wealth of other video graphics techniques at our disposal."

The opening, a celebration of the forces of nature and the evolution of man, shows flashes of fierce waves, turbulent clouds, a storm, blazing fire, and then focuses in on an eerily calm center of a pitch-black lake surrounded by rock formations. Slowly, an exotically clad woman rises, reptile-like, from the waters, followed by a man and another woman. They begin to dance.

Switch scenes and other dancers writhe primitively on a rocky promontory, clouds whizzing through the sky. Cut to the Sahara desert, where they prance across mammoth dunes. Cut to the Grand Canyon, where dozens of dancers pirouette on the edge of a gorge before effortlessly leaping across the abyss. Then the camera takes off, zooming through the canyon and zipping over green fields before flying into space, where a computer-drawn earth rotates and the word "Fantastico" curls around the horizon.

With fare like that, it's not surprising to learn that many people tune in to Brazil's most popular television channel just to see the colorful graphics and to figure out how the special effects were done.

"Everything we do is an illusion," says Donner. "People go crazy when they find out the lake in *Fantastico* isn't a real lake. We built a five-footwide, three-feet-deep replica of a lake I saw once near Yosemite Park. The model who rises out of it had to breathe oxygen through a tube and sit perfectly still underwater for three minutes before the water became calm enough for filming."

Working from *National Geographic* magazine photographs, Donner made realistic studio models in sculpted, painted styrofoam of scenes from the Grand Canyon, the Sahara, and Scotland, and then filmed them. Separately, he filmed dancers who performed on a floor that Donner had painstakingly measured and marked so that when he matted the two images together later, the dancers would not appear to step into empty space. Finally, he went to Ipanema Beach one day and filmed the clouds.

Frame by frame, Donner coordinated the matting of nine different film sessions onto a master video, adding new elements with each new recording. He used a computer to block out the sky and then added the clouds, making sure they moved correctly, their studio-made shadows obediently following. Then he synchronized the music and dancers. It was painstaking work, especially considering that each second of the 1-1/2 minute-long *Fantastico* spot had 30 separate frames to be perfected. That's 2,700 frames.

Donner always goes to incredible lengths and considerable expense to produce his video art. He once spent $35,000 painting a military airfield blue so that the ground would fade out when he filmed scenes there with a special effect called chromakey. To make the dueling scissors open and close, Donner connected them to bicycle hand brakes and tubes that couldn't be seen from one side. He manufactured giant sewing needles that were threaded through fabric using transparent fishing wire to guide their sharp ends. He mounted electromagnets in the points of giant pens and made them write alone by putting a technician with a magnet on the other side of a piece of cardboard. "It took us seven and a half hours to set all that up for 20 seconds of air time," he recalls.

When Donner prepared the *Fantastico* opening with dancers atop the gold pyramid, he had a real pyramid built according to computer specifications next to Rio's huge Maracana soccer stadium. He planned to film the pyramid with the dancers already on it, to avoid having to dub several images together. For some reason, the camera angles didn't work. Donner had to tear his $25,000 pyramid down and he asked Globo computer expert José Dias to see if he could create a gold pyramid on the computer. It worked.

That experience drove home to Donner the increasingly important role of computers in television graphics. "You can act as if you are God, playing around with nature and doing things that are physically impossible, like cutting a gold pyramid with a rainbow laser. We're always searching out new computer techniques and new ways of mixing computer images with conventional techniques," Donner says.

When Donner joined Globo in 1975, he didn't speak Portuguese, but his portfolio was full of graphics designs that hinted at his fascination with the third dimension. Fresh out of design school in Vienna, he had heard about the innovative graphics being created by Brazil's avant-garde advertising firms. On a gamble, he flew to Brazil looking for work. A lucky break secured him an introduction to a top Globo executive who, sensing that Donner might help update the network's image, eventually hired him to head a newly created art department.

His first task was to design a new logo for the network, which had been founded 10 years earlier by newspaper and radio magnate Roberto Marinho. Donner's logo, a modified version of which is still in use today, consisted of a sphere containing a stylized television-screen-shaped win-

We also need to establish national safety and quality standards that guarantee the adequate testing of body parts for AIDS, hepatitis, and other infectious diseases. The Food and Drug Administration checks apples and aspirin but sets standards for only a few of the tissues and none of the organs that are transplanted directly from one body to another.

The cost of transplantation is another significant issue. According to UNOS, the average kidney transplant costs $25,000 to $30,000, a heart transplant $57,000 to $110,000, a liver transplant $135,000 to $230,000. (Pre- and post-transplant treatment, which can increase the cost significantly, have not been included in these estimates.) Permanent maintenance on immunosuppressive drugs may cost from $4,000 to $10,000 annually, and there will inevitably be fees for other medical care associated with the transplant. Transplantation, however, is often less costly than alternative treatments. For example, it costs more to keep a kidney patient on dialysis for a year than it does to buy a year's worth of post-transplant drugs. The Health Care Financing Administration estimates that a kidney transplant pays for itself in three or four years. Even allowing for such problems as the possible need for retransplantation, doubling the supply of kidneys could cut down on health-care costs by hundreds of millions of dollars.

Many transplant centers won't put a person on a waiting list for an organ unless that person can demonstrate the ability to pay for the transplant. Indeed, one of the most intractable problems for all of medicine pervades transplantation: the "green screen." Should anyone be denied a transplant for lack of the money? Many times access is denied for financial reasons, but not straightforwardly. For instance, in the case of bone-marrow transplantation, once the computer has identified potential matches, a patient may have to pay $175 to $600 to have each of them tested. Fees for the search and for subsequent laboratory work on donors also vary dramatically, and frequently exceed actual costs. Since insurance usually does not pay for testing anyone but the patient, families have had to mortgage homes or borrow from friends. When the money runs out, most marrow registries stop working. This situation persists even though, for some forms of leukemia, marrow transplantation may be less expensive than treatment with chemotherapy and/or radiation.

Roger Evans, of the Battelle-Seattle Research Center, calculates that 67 million people in the United States lack the insurance to cover the cost of a major organ transplant, such as that for a heart or lungs. They can donate organs and tissues but may be ineligible to receive them. This includes many residents of states such as Oregon and Wyoming, where Medicaid funding for major organ transplants is not available. "I do not believe you should ask anyone to participate as a donor when he can't participate as a recipient," says Terry Strom, an immunologist and professor of medicine at Harvard Medical School. "It becomes the rich buying health at the expense of the poor."

Notwithstanding such hard issues, the ultimate reason reality lags so far behind medical possibility is the lack of federal effort. The government has for too long resisted establishing and funding a national policy to encourage an adequate supply—and the efficient and equitable use—of donated organs and tissues. And the public remains largely uninformed. Surgeons, still pioneering new types of transplantation, have pressed for action. Families unwilling to accept that no more can be done to save loved ones have formed marrow registries, mounted their own organ-procurement efforts, and tried to attract public attention. Most have come to the exasperated conclusion that something better must be possible. It is. In ways never before imagined, we can transform death and pain into life and hope.

LAST RIGHTS

Kathleen Stein

On his back, eyes shut, breathing rhythmically, R.H.—six three, 170 pounds— is a handsome man. Yet even as one admires the strong lines of his body, surgeons with scalpels incise the skin and muscle of his chest and abdomen with long, sure strokes. Using a small electric saw, they cleave the sternum as easily as if it were made of balsa. There is surprisingly little blood, but there's a certain amount of disarray in the operating room (O.R.) when as many as eight doctors have their hands and arms inside the cadaver, working quickly to disconnect the organs from their many vessels.

Rib cage and thoracic cavity are splayed open and viscera held back with metal retractors known as iron interns. The organs reveal a marvelous power, as when someone lifts the hood of a fine car and sees the frictionless workings of a precision-tuned engine. This engine is awesome—glistening, organic, wet. Aesthetically the liver is most pleasing, resembling some lustrous sea creature, smooth and supple with sharply defined edges. But a surgical error contaminates it. As a result the liver loses its silkiness and definition, turning from coral pink to meat-market purple. The surgeons push the organ aside and, struggling with their disappointment, proceed.

After another hour the kidneys, bean shapes that fit heftily in the surgeon's palm, are lifted out with ureters still attached.

R.H.'s heart suddenly begins an agitated dance, speeding from 100 to 200 beats a minute. The surgeons, alarmed, quiet it with a jolt of electricity from defibrillating paddles. Two hours later it too is removed and slipped into a stainless-steel bowl full of saline solution.

As soon as each organ comes out, it is carefully packed in an Igloo Playmate full of dry ice and rushed to a waiting helicopter for delivery to a distant transplant team.

Finally, after the major organs are removed a blond-haired surgeon from New York's Columbia Presbyterian Medical Center, his eyes rimmed by dark circles, tells the anesthetist to disconnect the I.V.'s and turn off the respirator.

A week earlier an aneurysm had ruptured in R.H.'s brain, virtually ripping apart his cerebrum. Following clinical tests and an electroencephalogram (EEG), physicians at Good Samaritan Hospital in Suffern, New York, declared him brain dead.

There was something else, a more subliminal confirmation signaling that no one—no spirit?—was there. Lifting his arm, I felt only a flaccid, lifeless weight.

It was his birthday; he was, or would have been, forty-two.

As I stood at his bedside in the intensive care unit (ICU) earlier that day, two perceptions fought in my mind. First, how could he be dead? He looked so full of life. There wasn't a mark on him. His thick, light-brown hair was tousled, as if he'd just come in from a basketball game with the guys. His carotid artery pulsed with blood; his heart rate was nearly normal. The urine bag at the side of the bed filled regularly and was replaced. And secondly, an intellectual observation: He was obviously very dead.

The blood, oxygen, and nutrients perfusing his body were all driven by the machines surrounding him.

There was something else, a more subliminal confirmation, subtle cues signaling that no one—no spirit?—was there. Lifting his arm, which was just slightly cool, I felt only a flaccid, lifeless weight.

And yet . . . I wanted to whisper, so as not to wake him.

R.H. is a late-twentieth-century corpse, one of a new class of dead people created by medical technology. The "beating-heart cadavers," or neo-morts, as these dead are sometimes called, have cells, tissues, organs, and organ systems that can be kept alive several days by elaborate life-support systems long after their brains have ceased functioning.

I first began to realize that the big sleep was no longer a simple state when I was researching material on the future of death for a book edited by Arthur C. Clarke. In the midst of scenarios about holographic mausoleums and near-death-experience cults, I found that the future, as they say, is already with us.

Since history's beginnings, the classical sign of death was when heart and lungs stopped. "Brain death" is only about 20 years old, the offspring of the ICU and its advanced life-support technologies. Even as we struggle with brain death, the concept is being modified. Bioethicists and members of the medical profession think the definition of death should encompass not only those who have no brain functions (the brain dead) but also those who have lost consciousness (the cognitive dead), "lost souls" who linger mindlessly in what are called persistent vegetative states. Society has to confront again some basic philosophical questions: what it means to be alive; to be a person; to have a mind.

From *Omni*, September 1987, pp. 59–60, 66–67, 114, 116–117. Copyright © 1987 by Kathleen Stein. Reprinted with the permission of OMNI Publications International, Ltd.

Before attempting to address those issues, here is a brief neo-death lexicon.

• *Brain death.* Very simply, this describes a state in which *no part* of the brain functions. Once a person is brain dead, he is dead, period. His body can be maintained artificially on a respirator only hours or, at most, several days until cardiac arrest.

• *Persistent vegetative state.* In brain death the whole brain is destroyed; in a persistent vegetative state, only part of the brain is destroyed. The brain stem, a primitive region that connects the brain to the spinal cord, is usually intact or mostly intact. A person with his brain stem intact is capable of stereotypical reflex functions—breathing, sleeping, digesting food—but he will be incapable of thought or even of any awareness of the world around him. A person can remain in this state for years.

• *Cognitive death.* A number of bioethicists, philosophers, and M.D.'s are beginning to contemplate expanding the definition of death to include people in persistent vegetative states, individuals who have lost their intellect, memory, speech, and awareness of self or environment.

When I started my new-death investigation, an M.D. friend said, "You've got to talk to Julie Korein; he wrote the book on brain death." Julius Korein is professor of neurology at New York University School of Medicine, chief of Bellevue Hospital's EEG lab, and chairman of the biomedical ethics committee at Bellevue. A kind of tough guy with a spiky, intense personality, he moves and talks in swift bursts of energy. At first Korein seemed annoyed, even suspicious, at being interviewed. "Frankly, I'm sick to death of death," he announced when I first met him. Soon, though, he was supplying books, papers, and his time. Korein is currently investigating the "beginning of brain life" in the fetus. Going full circle, as it were.

"There is no moment of death," he says. The moment of death is a legal construct for matter of probate. As an example, Korein cites a famous case of a husband and wife who were killed when their car was hit by a train. The body of one was crushed completely on impact; the other, decapitated. For the will, it was necessary to ascertain which one died first. The lawyers argued that it was the crushed spouse. As long as the other's head was spewing blood from the neck, it was deemed "alive." But even concerning the obliterated woman, Korein goes on, "you can say, well, there were fractions of seconds before the whole person broke down and she died. So maybe the moment of death was fifty nanoseconds later."

"Look at cardiovascular death. The heart stops. The doctor listens to the chest. Was that the moment of death? With modern equipment, you can detect signs of electrical activity in the heart forty minutes after it has stopped beating. The moment of death is fiction."

I persist. Many people would say the moment of death is when the soul leaves the body. "When does that happen?" Korein attacks the idea. "Let's assume there's a soul. When does it exit? When the heart stops? When the brain stops? When the reticular formation, the brain's arousal system, stops? Does it exit all at once, an instantaneous thing, or gradually? If gradually, then there's no moment of death!"

In 1975 Korein was the expert witness in the Karen Ann Quinlan trial, in which the family sued to have the life-support system removed from the young woman. It was his testimony more than anything else that brought about a ruling in favor of the family—that Quinlan, suffering permanent loss of higher brain functions, could be removed from the respirator. Quinlan had become comatose after ingesting a mixture of drugs and alcohol at a party.

During the trial one common misconception was that Quinlan was brain dead. "She was never brain dead." Korein is irritated. "At that time and even today, people talk about her as brain dead. But she never met the criteria." One of the criteria specifies that the brain stem no longer functions. There is no brain death without brain stem death, and in adults, brain stem death means that cardiac death inexorably follows within hours or days. Quinlan always had brain stem function.

The brain stem is the keystone of the central nervous system (CNS), the direct hookup to the spinal cord on one end and the cortex on the other. "It is in every sense the ultimate site of 'Life's Little Candle,'" says *The Human Brain Coloring Book.* Although it makes up only one tenth of the CNS, it controls the activities basic to existence: the autonomic—vegetative—functions. Destroy the brain stem, and you abandon all hope of survival.

Korein was on the stand more than four hours. As a witness he had to instruct the courtroom in the workings and malfunctions of the entire brain. He told them Quinlan was not brain dead. She had EEG activity in spite of massive damage to her cerebral hemispheres. And, he testified, she might breathe spontaneously off the respirator. And as the world knows, she continued breathing. Until her death from infection nine years later, she remained tethered to the life-supporting nutrition–hydration tube.

Soon after the Quinlan trial, Korein chaired an international conference to discuss research on brain death that had been ongoing from the late Sixties. And from that conference came the book *Brain Death: Interrelated Medical and Social Issues.* That text helped lift the fog of confusion enveloping doctors who were diagnosing the states of respirator-maintained patients. The book defined brain death clearly.

The criteria included total unresponsiveness and lack of movement; no brain stem reflexes (having fixed, dilated pupils, for example); and inability to breathe without a respirator. For confirmation, many neurological tests were also encouraged, to exclude the possibility of drug intoxication or hypothermia, conditions that can mimic brain death. Always there was the overriding rule: It is permissible to err only on the side of diagnosing a dead brain as alive.

In 1981, largely because of the work of Korein and many other neurologists, the President's Commission for the Study of Ethical Problems in Medicine and Biomedical and Behavioral Science proposed as statute the Uniform Determination of Death Act, which reads: "An individual who has sustained either (1) irreversible cessation of circulatory and respiratory functions, or (2) irreversible cessation of all functions of the brain, including brain stem, is dead." The act is law in 39 states and pending in others. Using the established criteria, no one properly diagnosed as brain dead has ever regained any brain function.

With the idea of brain death fairly clear in my mind, the next concentric circle of this kingdom of living dead to explore was the world of the irreversibly unconscious, the realm of the vegetative.

Unlike the brain dead, the vegetative have a functional brain stem. At the core of the upper brain stem is the system of nerve cells and fibers called the ascending reticular formation, a Y-shaped structure that serves as a two-way street to and from the cortex. It adjusts all incoming and outgoing commands from both cerebral hemispheres. The reticular formation constitutes the brain's general broadcasting system. It wakes us up and puts us to sleep; allows information to be stored or forgotten, noted or ignored. Without it, consciousness is impossible, even if the cortex is intact.

Arousal, wakefulness, awareness: That's the activating part of the reticular formation. If the cerebrum's 10 billion neurons were all discharging at once, one would have continuous storms of electrical convulsions. To gain meaningful patterns from this stream of information, you need the reticular formation's inhibitory impulses. Nothing, so far, has been able to arouse someone whose reticular formation has been destroyed.

Unlike the brain dead, who lie limp as rag dolls, vegetative patients may exhibit bizarre "decorticate posturing" and spasticity. Their arms and legs contort into "flexion contractures": Elbows, wrists, fingers bend in toward the chest; knees are drawn up fetally, toes down. Some occasionally yawn and stick out their tongues, exhibit lip-smacking or chewing movements, grimace, and grind their teeth—all stereotypical, repetitive reflex responses without purpose.

This is a pretty good portrait of Karen Quinlan at the time of the trial. When the media and even the medical profession referred to her as *comatose,* they were using the term imprecisely. They should have said *vegetative.*

I was surprised to learn that there are about 10,000 Americans "living" in this kind of black hole of the soul. These are the "biologically tenacious," to use Surgeon General C. Everett Koop's term. A crushing financial burden to their families, the typical bill for a year's care is rarely less than $200,000. But worse is the family's unending psychic pain. "When I went to see her, there was no one there," John Jobes, thirty-one, told me about his wife, Nancy, also thirty-one. Finally he stopped going.

Nancy Jobes, vegetative for seven years, was sustained by a feeding tube in a New Jersey nursing home. In 1980, as a pregnant young wife, she was the victim of a tragic set of accidents: First an automobile accident killed her fetus. Next, during an operation to remove the dead fetus, she suffered anoxia, loss of oxygen to her brain long enough to cause enormous damage to the cerebrum. Two years ago John, with Nancy's parents and Quinlan lawyer Paul W. Armstrong, filed suit to have the feeding tube removed. The Lincoln Park nursing home refused. The family won their case, but the nursing home appealed. Not until June 1987 were Jobes and his parents-in-law released from their purgatory. At that time the New Jersey Supreme Court decided in their favor, and Nancy will be allowed to die with dignity, as they say, after years of pointless indignity. It has been inexpressible hell for John Jobes.

"There comes a point where you just can't let it go on and on," he says, his voice low and angry. "Nancy would never want to be in this state." Today he is emotionally and financially wiped out. And after seven years it's hard for him to get on with his life. "My mother- and father-in-law tell me I should," he says hollowly, "but it's easier to say than do."

Even though the AMA has now judged it ethical for physicians to withdraw treatment from such irreversibly unconscious patients, confusion and controversy over this latest dilemma of high-tech medicine still rage in the courts, hospitals, and nursing homes. And the problem, more delicate and complex than brain death, will not go away. It's just gathering force.

A number of people are suggesting that the Nancy Jobeses or Karen Ann Quinlans, the persistent vegetatives, could join the ranks of the neo-morts. Stuart Youngner, a psychiatrist at Case Western Reserve Medical Center in Cleveland, is one. He thinks society should draw up a new definition of death. "Once consciousness is gone," he says, "the person is lost. What remains is a mindless organism." After the loss of personhood, he says, the death of

what remains is not the death of a human being but of a *thing,* "the demise of a body that has outlived its owner."

Needless to say, this new cognitive death idea has vehement opponents within the medical community. Most M.D.'s are terrified of it. Dr. Vivian Tellis, renal transplant surgeon and codirector of the transplant program at New York City's Montefiore Hospital, exclaimed to me that the idea was "grossly inappropriate! A dangerous distinction. If it were instituted, I'd get out of the business immediately."

It's the *Coma* thing for real, said another. In the movie *Coma,* a female anesthesia "accident" victim is declared brain dead; they pack her off to the nefarious Jefferson Institute, where her body will be maintained artificially until her parts can be harvested and sold. (Neurologically speaking, that's all wrong: She could not have

---

> *If you pronounce them dead and they're breathing on their own, what do you do? Take them out and shoot them? You can't discontinue their life-support systems sub rosa.*

---

been brain dead. She would be in a persistent vegetative state.)

Many physicians foresee the massive proliferation of "Jefferson Institutes" devoted to harvesting organs from the vegetative "dead." There is no end to possible scenarios. Female vegetatives, for example, might be employed as surrogate wombs—providing that endocrine balances could be reestablished after the disruptions that often accompany profound brain damage. The vegetatives could even be mated to produce fertilized eggs or offspring. The French, who claim to be horrified at discontinuing treatment of long-term vegetatives, in the same breath advocate using them experimentally.

Society has a ways to go before we set up human vegetable farms, in part because many people, superstitiously or not, think that the long-term unconscious might someday "wake up." Could it happen? It seemed important to discuss this issue with people whose optimism for the unconscious is the guiding principle of their work. The Greenery is such a citadel of hope.

Located near Boston, the 201-bed institution is one of a number of long-term head-injury rehabilitation centers. Indeed, the

Greeneries are flourishing, with branches in North Carolina, California, Texas, and Washington State. *Coma*'s Jefferson Institute was on my mind as I arrived at the Greenery's series of garden-apartment buildings. There were no huge, windowless facades à la *Coma.* There is no forbidding nurse at the door; anyone can walk right in.

The Greenery gets plenty of business. The National Head Injury Foundation estimates that 50,000 people a year who survive serious head injury are left with "intellectual impairment of such a degree as to preclude their return to a normal life." Thanks to modern medicine, the patients have survived overwhelming brain injuries, but they arrive at the Greenery in varying degrees of unconscious or semi-aware states. Unlike conventional nursing homes, the Greenery does more than feed and nurse these people. It attempts to bring back some awareness through a program of intense sensory bombardment, physical therapy, and, for those able to benefit, special education.

Upon seeing the Greenery's patients and hearing their case histories—many car-accident victims—I vowed always to fasten my seat belt. The patients themselves are inescapably sad. They are the bereft, wandering shades of a modern Avernus, some perceiving dimly, some in childlike wonder; others seeing, hearing nothing. Their state was much harder to take than the finality of R.H.'s brain death.

Rigid in different poses, some resemble fleshy statues partially liberated from their molds, a mad choreography of frozen flexor contractures, seizures, feet *en pointe.* To ease their muscle contractures, many patients are armored in leg, arm, and hand casts. Even the unconscious are tied by their foreheads in wheelchairs or strapped to boards slanted up against the walls to expose them to more stimuli.

The staff is committed to searching for signs of life in even the most deserted-looking bodies. "We have a mission to try to wake these people up, and this is one of the few places that is dedicated to serving this very severely underaroused population," explains staff neuropsychologist Laurence Levine.

I took the time to watch their mission in action. Young, vigorous physical therapist Karen Giebler introduces Randy, who sits speechless in a wheelchair. She presses electrodes against his skin, using electrical stimulation to prime the atrophied muscles of his legs. A construction worker from Oklahoma, he had been hit in the head by a demolition ball that demolished a good part of his left cerebral hemisphere. His wife refused to believe he was hopeless and eventually found the Greenery. Randy was admitted with muscle contractures that had pulled his legs up to his chest and pointed his toes down like a ballet dancer's. Giebler transfers Randy to an exercise mat, and she slowly lifts and lowers his now un-contracted legs 25 times each. I watch Giebler work a little longer and after a while say good-bye to her and to her patient. But there is no response from him as I leave. He stares straight ahead.

The staff members admit it's difficult to keep the fires of enthusiasm burning when there's no response day after day, month after month. Though they all have their Lazarus stories of the hopeless who eventually walk out of the place on their own, no one has published any data about these amazing returns in the medical journals; and this, to the neurological community, is a serious weakness in their presentation.

Yet if there were a new, cognitive definition of death, several of the Greenery's patients could be conceived as candidates. I ask Levine: Should death be redefined as cognitive loss? "Working in a place like this raises questions like that all the time," he says, "profound questions about what a person is. There are patients here who are very dependent, severely underaroused, with little hope on the horizon.

"I've thought about what would happen to me if I wound up like one of them. At this point I'd want to die," he admits. "But my hunch is that I'd change my mind if it actually happened. More likely, I'd not have the cognition to know. What I'm trying to say is I don't have any fixed answers. Some people may believe that these people should be put to death, but as a society we can't condone that."

When I bring up the idea of cognitive death to him, Korein argues, "To consider a vegetative state as death is not practical. If you pronounce them dead and they're breathing on their own, what do you do? Take them out and shoot them? Smother them? You can't discontinue their life-support systems sub rosa." Unlike the brain-death situation, withdrawing support from the vegetative is a social decision, not a medical one. The physician can't play God and decide to withdraw support.

Pressed about his personal feelings about higher cognitive death, Korein says that once an individual is no longer capable of awareness, is no longer a thinking being, and is in that irreversible state, "yes, I consider it the death of a human being." But he reminds me that there have been two recorded cases in which persons declared irreversibly vegetative did "come back," although that return of function "doesn't mean they dance," he adds. "They could hardly communicate and do not walk." Furthermore, the criteria for determining a vegetative state are much less established than for brain death.

For background on what those criteria might be, I decided to ask another knowledgeable neurologist. "I believe that the meaning of life is cognition and self-aware-ness, not merely visceral survival," states Fred Plum, neurologist in chief at Cornell University Medical College–New York Hospital, at a meeting at Cornell in Ithaca. "The concept holds that when the cognitive brain has departed, the person has departed. In my opinion it is acceptable, perhaps even desirable, that society come to share this view, but," he is careful to add, "that is a personal, not a medical, opinion."

I sought out Plum because he is the best there is. Perhaps the world's top expert on coma, Plum is a hybrid of the kindly white-haired physician and Apollonian intel-lect—elegant, contemplative, and analytical. His book *The Diagnosis of Stupor and Coma,* written with Jerome Posner, is the definitive text on the subject. Today, with colleague David Levy, Plum has been employing PET (positron emission tomography) technology to peer into the interior of this gloomy condition.

> **❝If you come into the hospital seriously injured and your survival's in grave doubt, they'll probably give you the very best attention. For your organs' sake.❞**

He has been doing preliminary PET studies on the cerebral metabolism of vegetative patients, and he and his colleagues are now trying to evaluate the potential for recovery of the severely brain damaged who are not vegetative. Using statistical evidence, he's built up "rather sturdy predictors" of who will do well and who will fare badly following severe brain trauma. He uses a sophisticated computer program that analyzes detailed information on the progress of the severely brain injured.

Within less than two weeks after onset, Plum says, about three quarters of the damaged area show clear clinical signs that predict whether they will have a generally good or devastatingly poor outcome. These data are correlated over a period of time, he says, "with the aim of eventually producing a one hundred percent prediction of who will do well or, conversely, who has no chance of recovery."

Does that mean you can say with 100 percent assurance after three months that Mr. X is in a vegetative state from which he will never return? No, says Plum. There will always be head injury cases that defy the odds and recover. "Nevertheless, being able to predict with a strong probability gives the family some facts upon which to make a decision," he maintains. His predictions could help a family decide whether to disconnect a life-support system or what to do with a brain-damaged patient who has a living will. Such a personal statement, made when the person is in full command of his self-determination, serves to advise physicians against ordering millions of dollars' worth of needless care for hopeless cases.

Like Korein, Plum thinks that ultimately it is not the doctor's job to make the decision for the patient. "My facts are an effort to give people enough information so that a reasonably informed layperson can partic-ipate in the decision, knowing what the options are."

But over the next 20 years, the over-whelming demand for organs may increase the pressure to simply declare the "brain absent" dead. There is already something of a black market for buying and selling organs. If the cognitive-death definition were instituted, organ-merchandis-ing corporations might establish enterprises beyond Wall Street's wildest insider fantasies. The world would find itself in a situation where death itself would be an industry—an economic incentive.

But as Youngner points out, this economic pressure is not necessarily bad. "When Columbus sailed across the Atlantic," he says, "the main purpose wasn't to prove the world was round. It was to find new territory to plunder. It wasn't the philosophers who stimulated the cognitive death criteria of death, it was those who wanted the organs." We should be careful, he says, that the need for organs doesn't take over completely, because it confuses the issue, so that we are unable to debate the topic of death in a logical, intelligent way. If the brilliant liver-transplant surgeon Thomas Starzl, for example, has said we should take organs from the vegetative, why should we do it? Because their lives are of such poor quality that it doesn't matter, or because they're dead?

Even without a shift to a cognitive death criterion, we already face major social and legal questions. "In the case of persons—bodies, really—that have lost all individuality or capacity for self-awareness, have they also lost their constitutional privi-leges?" asks Plum. "This question is an artifact of technology. If it weren't for modern technology, we wouldn't be faced with the prospect of more and more very old persons continuing to survive in nursing homes after all shadow of their personalities has left the face of the earth." The numbers of these people will continue to climb, and society will have to try to reach some kind of balanced judgment about what to do with those with no living wills.

We also have the emotional stress of treating the legally dead. This fact was brought to doctors' attention by Youngner's powerful essay in *The New England Journal of Medicine,* "Psychosocial and Ethical Implications of Organ Retrieval." In his article Youngner notes that maintaining bodies for "harvesting" often requires treating dead people as if they were alive, an upsetting experience for doctors and nurses. They must try to ignore the signs of vitality that bombard their senses and at the same time provide the dead donors with intensive care usually reserved for the living. If a brain-dead donor in an intensive care unit goes into cardiac arrest, for example, alarms ring and medical staff rush to revive the body. Meanwhile a DO NOT RESUSCITATE order might be written on the chart of the living, perhaps even wide-awake, patient in the next bed.

Surgery to remove organs also requires hospital staff to suspend their medical instincts. The dead don't usually go to surgery; and as Youngner points out, the brain dead wheeled into the O.R. don't look that different from living, anesthetized patients. O.R. personnel used to life-saving surgery, upon seeing the removal of vital parts, may be shocked by the mutilation. In some cases of what's called long-bone retrieval, one O.R. nurse told me, the surgical team removes the thighbones and replaces them with broomsticks to keep the legs' shape. Another organ-donor coordinator who has logged hundreds of hours in O.R.'s confessed she still can't watch eye removals.

After long hours of "retrieval" surgery the anesthesiologist does not, of course, wake up the cadaver. He simply disconnects the respirator and leaves the room. The remaining surgeons do a perfunctory job of sewing up the body cavity using coarse thread and large needles. And the body is sent not to the recovery room but to the morgue. (Even after being told what has happened to a patient, families sometimes ask the doctors what time the donor "will be brought back to his room.")

Youngner has now embarked on a long-term study of health-profession stress and organ retrieval. In his office, looking athletic in chinos and a blue jacket, Youngner has a sensitive face and speaks gently but firmly. "I got an incredibly positive response from O.R. personnel from that *Journal* piece," he says. "I don't want to exaggerate and say they're all terribly traumatized by brain death and the organ-retrieval process, but most everybody finds it a little uncomfortable; a few find it considerably uncomfortable."

Many M.D.'s don't really come to terms emotionally with brain death, even though they intellectually understand the mechanisms. Attending physicians often balk at writing the death certificate for a person pronounced brain dead.

Faye Davis, director of the New York Regional Transplant Program, uses Youngner's essay in some training sessions to sensitize hospital staff. "Sometimes ICU staff complain about taking care of dead people," she says, "when they have so many live people to take care of. So we might hold off on a pronouncement [of death] to help them feel they're still taking care of a patient. It's less stressful. But it's hocus-pocus, and in a sense they know."

Youngner also talks about the "spirit" the staff often say they feel in the operating room during surgery, the presence of a life-force there but sleeping. O.R. personnel "often feel a similar presence with brain-dead patients, and it doesn't depart until the respirator is turned off." Families talk about the spiritual entities as well. Sometimes, says Davis, "they know when their loved one is dead while we're still figuring it out by the tests. They know he's just not there anymore."

Outside the medical profession, the reaction to brain death is blind fear. "Many people are afraid the doctors are going to grab their kidneys before they're dead," says Montefiore's Tellis. But we shouldn't worry. "In fact, donor cards are your best insurance. If you come into the hospital seriously injured, and your survival's in grave doubt, they'll probably give you the very best attention. For your organs' sake."

In the midst of these discussions, my mind kept returning to the question, What is a person? And more important, what will a person be in the future? It's not inconceivable that before too long, brain stem function could be replaced by a computer, for example, a silicon clone of the reticular formation. This autonomic organ could be compacted to the size of a real brain stem and inserted into the head. Then irretrievable consciousness might be made retrievable; the lost person, brought back.

In the course of his interview, Korein began to speculate about the value of such a machine–brain cyborg. "If I knew how to make one, I know what I'd use it for: for someone with an immediate-memory deficit, a patient who will forget he has met a visitor after that person steps out for a moment and returns. If you could create an external visual memory system for him, then when someone walks into a room—zip—it is recorded into the machine's external memory. Then if the person walks out and returns, the memory would compare the person who left with the person returning and report to the brain of the memory-deficit patient, 'You already saw this guy.'"

This, then, brings up another basic question: Where *is* the mind? "The brain is something you can touch, squeeze, and do experiments on. The mind has other properties, but it's certainly related to the brain. I don't know any mind without a brain; I know lots of brains without minds. I'm sure

you've met them!" Korein laughs. "Actually, the mind must evolve in some way from self-reflective processes. Living beings all have this ability to look upon themselves. In one-celled animals it's an enzymatic system, a positive feedback. In humans it's the ability to put together a set of stimuli, store them, look upon them, feed on them. And the repetition of this is, I think, what results in a mind."

I asked Youngner to contemplate the implications of the computerized mind. What if one could decipher the program of a person's personality and transfer it to a computer that would store the memories, react with the same "emotions"? Could one argue that even if the human had forever lost consciousness, he'd still be alive because this computer was standing in?

"I'd say that wouldn't be a person but a robot," he decides, considering the options. "Okay, what if you took the brain out of a body and put it in a solution with a communications system? I'd still say it wouldn't be a person because to me a person is, at bottom, a biological entity. Our identity is very much tied up with our body, and we have an idea of who we are based on our physical attributes outside the brain.

"On the other hand"—he takes the opposite view without much painful dissonance—"if you had this brain in a jar—say it was my brain—and it said, 'I'm a Pittsburgh Steelers fan, and I'm upset they didn't have a good year,' then it would be hard to dismiss the idea that Stuart Youngner is alive, although his body's gone. It might be the presence of an identity, but it's not a human being. It gets pretty tricky."

So the question of death ultimately becomes the question of what is life. After almost 20 years of research on death, Korein is more excited these days about life. The process of being born is, in a sense, just the opposite of dying. When does the human being begin? At fertilization? When it's an embryo? There's a constructive phase between 10 and 20 weeks of fetal life when the neurons are being produced and organized. The fetus moves as early as eight weeks, Korein says, but that's spinal cord activity, a vegetative function. Around 20 to 24 weeks the cerebrum starts to show signs of electrical and synaptic activity. "Then," he says, "you could say it's the earliest possibility of cerebral–mental life. It hasn't the ability to work like a normal three-day-old baby, but the pieces are in place, starting to grow and connect. That's the beginning of a person's life—'brain life.'"

In tracking the dead and the near dead, I was haunted, so to speak, by the words of Carleton Gajdusek. The Nobel prize-winning virologist is famous for his discovery of the slow virus in the Fore people of New Guinea. During his research he intensely observed their mortuary ritual of eating the brains of dead family members.

It was an expression of love for their dead relatives. "They had no fear or reluctance to look at the brains or intestines of their kin," Gajdusek told *Omni*. "They always dissected their relatives with love and tender care and interest." It was Gajdusek's opinion that were it not for the viral infection in the tissue, eating brains would have "provided a good source of protein for a meat-starved community." Not long after I started this story, I went to hear Gajdusek speak at Mount Sinai Hospital in New York. During the address he spoke of the "neocannibalism" of modern medicine.

With the great advances in life-support technology and organ transplantation, the dead today do indeed have much "protein" to offer us—in the form of their organs and body parts. We are the neocannibals. Unlike Fore culture, however, Western society has a horror of the dead. We prefer not to think about death at all; and when forced to deal with it, we do so as hurriedly as possible. We have no new-death rituals and little understanding of neocannibal practices. And our old superstitions may work counter to a true understanding not only of death but perhaps of life, too.

The radical, outspoken Dr. Tellis is concerned with life, the hanging-by-a-thread life of someone waiting for a heart or liver or kidney. He has no patience with families who refuse to donate the organs of brain-dead kin. The social climate surrounding donation today should be reversed, he told me as he waited at Good Samaritan Hospital that night for the rest of the transplant surgeons to arrive for R.H.'s organs. "Instead of feeling good and righteous about donating," he said, "it should enter the collective unconscious that you feel bad if you refuse. The family who refuses to donate a dead relative's liver should be told they killed the waiting recipient!"

Slowly we are coming to terms with brain death and the new life that it offers. What we decide to do with the life in limbo that is the vegetative state remains to be seen. But it is better to begin to think about it than to ignore the increasing price we have to pay for this most unblessed death on the installment plan.

Designing Computers That Think The Way We Do

WILLIAM F. ALLMAN

WILLIAM F. ALLMAN is a free-lance writer living in Washington, D.C. He is a former staff writer for Science '86.

In a radical departure from traditional computers, researchers are building machines that mimic the architecture of the human brain.

It doesn't look like much: a chunk of wood the size of a chessboard, festooned with wires and electronic components. Still, it's something that physicist John Hopfield keeps in his office and displays with a broad smile. Built by Hopfield and his colleagues at the California Institute of Technology, the board is a physical manifestation of an idea that a handful of theorists have kicked around for years. Their dream is to build a computing machine that operates on an entirely different principle than the step-by-step symbol processing of conventional computers. This machine would be modeled after the brain: a vast network of neuron-like units that operate on data all at once.

Cognitive scientists have succeeded in simulating such "neural nets" on powerful conventional computers, and Hopfield's crude board is one of the first real neural-net machines. It represents a radical shift in designing computers that think, and it might even change the way we think about thinking.

For decades most artificial intelligence (AI) experts believed that thinking involved the manipulation of symbols—letters or numbers that were in themselves abstract but could be used to express specific ideas or concepts. Take the equation $f = ma$. If you know that f is force, m is the mass of an object, and a is the object's acceleration, these symbols assume a powerful meaning in the real world. Furthermore, there is a consistent set of operations that applies to these symbols. Using algebra, for example, $f = ma$ can be changed to $a = f/m$ and still be true.

If the physical realm of motion and mass can be captured in a set of symbols and rules, then why not the mind? the theorists asked. Might not our cognitive abilities be formalized as a set of operations that would work on a symbolic representation of the world? If we know that everyone at a convention is a lawyer, and that Jane is at the convention, then we can conclude that Jane is a lawyer. This reasoning can be expressed formally as symbols and operations: if all p's are q's, and x is a p, then x is also a q. It doesn't matter if we're talking about lawyers or farmers, conventions or state fairs, Jane or Jack. The same rules apply. Theorists believed they could simply translate the world into symbols, manipulate the symbols, and translate the results back into the language of the real world.

Formal systems appealed to engineers and mathematicians as well. In 1937 Claude Shannon, then a graduate student at M.I.T., showed in his master's thesis how the true/false propositions of symbolic logic could be simulated in the on/off states of electronic switches. The mathematician John von Neumann showed how a machine could store data in such switches and use a processor to do one operation at a time. The excitement came to a head in 1955, when Herbert Simon is said to have told his class at the Carnegie Institute of Technology, "Over Christmas, Allen Newell and I invented a thinking machine."

Newell and Simon did not believe that their computer imitated what actually happens when humans think. Rather, they suggested that the workings of the mind might be better understood if scientists studied the processes of thinking at a more general, theoretical level.

The Limits of Logic Machines

Newell and Simon believed that the main task for AI enthusiasts was figuring out the nature of the symbols and rules the mind uses. For example, what are the rules by which we change words from the present to past tense? What rules do we use to distinguish a table from a chair? Newell and Simon assumed that once the mind's symbols and rules were known, neuroscientists could then figure out how the brain physically produced them.

The people who build neural nets are challenging that long-held assumption. Conventional computers, after all, are having a terrible time making the transition from number and symbol crunching to more formidable tasks such as speech and vision. In fact, computers are awful at these tasks. This failure has led to a growing suspicion that perhaps the people who brought us "I symbol process, therefore I think" might have been putting Descartes before the horse, as it were.

Since some types of thinking such as formal logic and arithmetic involve symbol manipulation, it's not unreasonable to conclude that all other types of thinking do, too—even if we aren't consciously aware of it. But might it not be the other way around? Perhaps the lion's share of what we call thinking is something else. Processing symbols could be a sideline, more the exception than the rule, icing on the cognitive cake.

A quick look at the human mind makes you think so. "Our attempts at general-purpose computation [that is, doing arithmetic or logic] are often inconsistent," says Brown University cognitive scientist James A. Anderson. "Far more complex tasks that are biologically relevant [such as using language or rapidly recognizing faces] are so effortless that we do not realize how hard they are until we try to make a machine do them. On the other hand, the pitiful mess most humans make of formal logical reasoning or arithmetic would embarrass a $10 pocket calculator."

In other words, using a human brain to do symbol processing may be a little like using the head of a wrench to drive a nail. Though it might do the job, a hammer would probably do it better. But unfortunately, if the only tool you owned happened to be a hammer, you might begin to see every problem as a nail to be driven.

So if thinking isn't symbol processing at its basic level, then what is it? Hopfield and a growing number of computer scientists, cognitive researchers, psychologists, and physicists are trying to find out. Instead of building bigger and faster hammers, they are designing machines based on the hunch that the mind is more wrench-like. For inspiration on how to build the hardware of their thinking machines, they are looking to the hardware of that other thinking machine, the brain.

Neuroscientists have come to realize that the architecture of the brain—how its billions of neurons are connected in a complex, three-dimensional maze—is central to its function. Individual neurons aren't especially smart by themselves, but when they are connected to each other they become quite intelligent. The problem is, nobody knows how they do it. It isn't that neurons are fast: in sending their electrochemical messages to other neurons, they are roughly 100,000 times slower than a typical computer switch. But what our brains lack in speed they make up in "wetware," as it is sometimes called. The brain contains from 10 billion to a trillion neurons, each of which may be connected to anywhere from 1,000 to 100,000 others. If this vast net of interconnected neurons forms the grand collective conspiracy we call our minds, maybe a vast interconnected net of mechanical switches can make a machine that thinks.

Simple elements often display complicated behavior when they come in large groups. Imagine that you put 2 molecules of a gas such as hydrogen in an otherwise empty, closed container at room temperature. Because hydrogen is a gas, the molecules float around, colliding with the walls and, rarely, with each other. "Every once in a while the molecules collide, and that's an exciting event in the life of someone studying molecular collisions," Hopfield says. "If we put 10 or even 1,000 molecules in the box, all we get is more collisions. But if we put a billion billion molecules in the box, there's a new phenomenon—sound waves. Sound waves wouldn't exist without collisions. There was nothing in the behavior of 2 molecules in the box, or 10 or 1,000 molecules, that would suggest to you that a billion billion molecules would be able to produce sound waves. Sound waves are a collective phenomenon of a complex system."

Hopfield and other scientists who loosely call themselves connectionists are not trying to make machines that mimic the action of neurons. Nerve cells are far too complex for that. Rather, these researchers prefer to think of their machines as "neuron-inspired," using "neuronal units" that share some of the brain's properties.

Like neurons, these units are connected to one another in a huge net. Each unit consists of electronic circuitry that responds to input from the others either by switching on and off or by amplifying and diminishing a signal. The units receive incoming electrical or optical messages, add them up, and decide whether to send messages of their own. In the simplest device, the inputs are added up and compared to a certain value. If the sum of inputs is below that value, there is no output.

The conventional von Neumann-type computer takes a few bits of data at a time from a separate memory storage and then operates on them with a central processor, but in neural nets the interconnected units all act on data at once. Like the human brain, they engage in what is called massively parallel computation.

In a seminal paper published in the *Proceedings of the National Academy of Sciences* in 1982, Hopfield showed that the way a network of switches behaves could be mathematically analyzed with the same tools that physicists use to analyze dynamic physical systems. His thesis is complex, but to make a rough analogy: Like a heated bar of metal that hardens as it cools off, a neural net whose switches have started to turn on and off at random will also go through a stabilizing process.

As its units communicate, the net eventually will settle into a state where each switch is permanently set in either the on or the off position. The significance of this becomes clear when we remember that neural nets, like conventional compuers, encode information in such switches. For instance, the letter *A* could be represented as 10001, and 10001 can be stored in on/off switches as on/off/off/off/on. A neural net could recognize the letter *A* through an array of sensors that signal on or off depending on the data they receive. The final output would be a series of 1s and 0s. Because neural nets work like that, the stabilizing process can indicate the answer to a particular problem.

A Computer That Guesses Right

This process also gives neural nets the data-sorting characteristic of a "content-addressable," associative memory. Our own memories are content-addressable. We can fetch a whole set of facts from a fragmented or even partially incorrect input. When we think of our friend Sally, for example, we also remember that she is a doctor, lives in Pittsburgh, and has red hair. Sally may also come to mind when we think of redheads or doctors or people who live in Pittsburgh. So if someone asks, "Don't you know a redheaded doctor who lives in Philadelphia?" there

is enough correct information to conjure up Sally and say, "No, Pittsburgh."

It's tough to make a conventional computer do this, but for neural nets it's natural. If one stable arrangement of the net's on/off switches represents an assortment of related information—*Sally, doctor, red hair, lives in Pittsburgh*—the whole memory can be retrieved by putting in any part of it. Given the input *Sally* and *doctor,* the units will settle into the configuration that represents *red hair* and *Pittsburgh.* In fact, only 5 percent of the memory is enough to make the rest of the system settle into a stable state representing the whole memory.

The net will even make a good guess on the basis of faulty input. Thus if it is given *a red-headed doctor who lives in Philadelphia,* it might still come up with *Sally.*

Again unlike a conventional computer—and very much like our minds—neural nets produce answers that are pretty good but not always the very best. With some tasks, perfection may not be worth the extra time and effort, especially if there are good answers that can be found quickly.

The Traveling Salesman Problem

One such task is solving the "traveling salesman problem," which crops up in everyday situations ranging from deciding on routes to making up airline schedules to designing microchips. Suppose you were a sales representative and had to visit 10 cities. What would be the shortest route you could take to visit them all? It turns out that it is mathematically possible to take 181,440 different routes to visit any 10 cities. To find the shortest one might be manageable, but as the number of cities to visit goes up, the number of possible routes skyrockets. If you wanted to visit 100 cities, for example, there are more than 10^{100} routes. Though digital computers can solve this problem with sophisticated programs, their strategy is to simply measure each route one by one, and that takes a lot of time.

With a neural net, you need only adjust the connections between units to represent the distances between cities. On the few neural-net machines that actually exist—like Hopfield's board—these adjustments are made by hand. The varying strength of connections is manifested as resistance in a wire or some other electronic trickery that reduces or amplifies currents. In neural nets simulated on conventional computers—which is far more common at this stage—a simple factor in multiplication or addition does the job. Within a few millionths of a second, the switches will settle into a stable state, indicating a short route—and a solution to the traveling salesman problem.

In one experiment by Hopfield and his associate

*Neural networks might be ideal
for nuclear power plants or spacecraft, where a sudden
breakdown could be catastrophic.*

at Bell Labs, David Tank, a neural net found answers to traveling salesman problems 1,000 times faster than a conventional computer did. While these answers were the very best only 50 percent of the time, the net came up with one of the two best answers 90 percent of the time.

Absolute accuracy may not always be ideal. Reaching a good working solution fast—rather than struggling for a long time for the best answer—may be more effective in finding the shortest way to route telephone lines or creating a compact design for a microchip. Speed would also be more important than perfection for machines designed to recognize patterns and make generalizations.

The same principle applies to the way we think. "Biology by and large is not interested in finding the best things, just things that are pretty good that can be found quickly," Hopfield says. For example, speech experts estimate that we actually understand only about 70 percent of the words we hear. Our minds fill in the rest from the context of what's being said.

Another mind-like trait neural nets display almost borders on intuition. The systems can, for instance, make inferences from ambiguous language. "If you hear the words *bat*, *ball*, and *diamond*, you think of one thing," says Brown University's Anderson, who works with neural nets. "And if you hear the words *bat*, *vampire*, and *blood*, you think of another." Given *bat* or *diamond* alone, Anderson's machines will respond with characteristic qualities of animals or geometric shapes. But if *bat* and *diamond* are put together, the machine comes up with *baseball*.

It is possible to program a conventional computer to make some of these inferences. However, a neural-net system has a natural ability to form categories and associations, because information about specific objects is spread out among the connections. The net stores the fact that a bat is both an animal and an instrument used in baseball, and the fact that a diamond is both a geometric shape and a baseball-playing field. As a result, the system is able to associate bat and diamond as being two common traits in baseball.

Neural nets have the potential to produce a new kind of artificial intelligence. Instead of relying on the rules an expert might use to make decisions, these machines can learn from a series of examples. For instance, a network repeatedly shown the present and past tense of certain verbs will eventually learn to change the tenses on its own—even for words it hasn't seen before.

It accomplishes this by following a series of "algorithms," or learning rules. Such rules work roughly on the principle that if two neural units cooperate to produce the right answer, the strength of the connection between them is increased. Likewise, if two units produce a wrong answer, then the connection between them is decreased.

Machines That Make Their Own Rules

NETalk is one machine that can learn through algorithms. Built recently by Johns Hopkins biophysicist Terry Sejnowski and Charles Rosenberg of Princeton, NETalk is a 200-unit neural net that has learned to read aloud. With a conventional computer, a programmer would have to sit down and write a series of rules, such as "when you come to an *s*, make an *s* sound; an *n* makes an *n* sound." Of course, there are exceptions to the rules as well: for example, making the *s* silent when it's next to another, as in "passing." And that doesn't explain what to do with the *s* in "passion." But it's possible, with enough perseverance, to track down most of the rules and most of the exceptions, though a word like "knack" might send a system into paroxysms. Most speaking machines take a shortcut, consulting first a pronouncing dictionary of 10,000 or so most-used words, then switching to rules if a word is not in the dictionary.

NETalk, on the other hand, started with an input of written text and the ability to drive a speaker. But it didn't have any rules for matching letters with sounds. It had a learning algorithm instead.

For its first training session, NETalk was given a 500-word text of a first-grader's recorded conversation. The correct sounds for the child's speech—divided into units called phonemes—were already known because they had been transcribed by a linguist. As NETalk read the text, its network chose phonemes to represent the letters. Meanwhile, its learning algorithm compared those phonemes with the ones the linguist had transcribed. Whenever differences appeared, the algorithm adjusted the strength of the connections between various neural units to try to make the network produce a phoneme that was a better match.

At first, NETalk could only babble. But after a day of training it could read any text with about 90 percent accuracy. In a way, NETalk still has rules for pronunciation. But it makes them itself, adjusting the myriad connections in the machine to make the best fit. "The rules aren't put there," says Sejnowski. "They emerge."

Computers That Don't Crash

Cognitive scientists are using neural nets to explore not only associative memory but other aspects of thinking as well. At Carnegie Mellon University, Geoffrey Hinton is working on a network that makes generalizations about the relationships in a family tree. Cognitive scientists David Rumelhart of the University of California at San Diego and Carnegie Mellon's Jay McClelland are looking at the way networks perform language-related tasks, such as changing the tense of verbs. And Carnegie Mellon's David Touretzky, collaborating with Geoffrey Hinton, is demonstrating that neural nets can even do the kind of sequential symbolic processing that ordinary computers do.

At this stage, connectionist machines are usually simulated on conventional computers because no one is sure what the best configuration for neural nets might be. However, researchers at Bell Labs have constructed an experimental "neural net" chip that has 75,000 transistors in an area the size of a dime. Furthermore, the concept has piqued the interest of the Pentagon's Advanced Research Projects Agency, the Jet Propulsion Laboratory, AT&T Bell Laboratories, and Los Alamos National Laboratory. Researchers at all of these organizations are now attempting to put theory into practice and build neural-net machines that are more sophisticated than Bell Labs' chip or Hopfield's board.

Defense agencies are particularly interested in neural nets because such systems have a brain-like property known as "graceful degradation." Since information and processing are distributed among many neural units, a neural net can still function—though somewhat less efficiently—when as much as 15 percent of its units are damaged. A similiar occurrence would be disastrous for a conventional computer. "Cut 1 percent of the wires in a computer," says Hopfield, "and it will grind to a halt."

Such resilient networks would be ideal for spacecraft, nuclear power plants, or Star Wars, where a sudden breakdown could be catastrophic. And because of their potential strengths in speedy pattern recognition, neural nets are being considered as vision and speech-recognition systems for robots.

Neural nets are still very much in the experimental stage, and many cognitive scientists remain skeptical about their potential. Stanford AI researcher Terry Winograd, for one, says the machines are receiving attention now because "they have a higher percentage of wishful thinking."

Even with all the excitement over the promise of neural-net computers, it's unlikely they will replace the good old number crunchers that we've grown so used to over the decades. As traditional AI proponents point out, relying on machines that think the way we do may not be such a great idea. You certainly wouldn't want to balance your bank account or figure out a company payroll with a computer that does not consistently produce the best answer.

Yet many researchers feel neural nets will enhance our understanding of how the brain works and help us build better AI systems. Indeed, if these systems really can recognize patterns and make good inferences from sketchy and partially incorrect data, they might serve as bridges between the sloppy, intuitive human world and the more literal and precise realm of conventional computers. Sometime in the distant future, when we ask our personal robot to go fetch a bat, its neural net might be responsible for determining whether we are about to go to a Halloween costume party or a baseball game.

Is the Brain's Mind a Computer Program?

No. A program merely manipulates symbols, whereas a brain attaches meaning to them

John R. Searle

John R. Searle is professor of philosophy at the University of California, Berkeley. He received his B.A., M.A. and D.Phil. from the University of Oxford, where he was a Rhodes scholar. He wishes to thank Stuart Dreyfus, Stevan Harnad, Elizabeth Lloyd and Irvin Rock for their comments and suggestions.

Can a machine think? Can a machine have conscious thoughts in exactly the same sense that you and I have? If by "machine" one means a physical system capable of performing certain functions (and what else can one mean?), then humans are machines of a special biological kind, and humans can think, and so of course machines can think. And, for all we know, it might be possible to produce a thinking machine out of different materials altogether—say, out of silicon chips or vacuum tubes. Maybe it will turn out to be impossible, but we certainly do not know that yet.

In recent decades, however, the question of whether a machine can think has been given a different interpretation entirely. The question that has been posed in its place is, Could a machine think just by virtue of implementing a computer program? Is the program by itself constitutive of thinking? This is a completely different question because it is not about the physical, causal properties of actual or possible physical systems but rather about the abstract, computational properties of formal computer programs that can be implemented in any sort of substance at all, provided only that the substance is able to carry the program.

A fair number of researchers in artificial intelligence (AI) believe the answer to the second question is yes; that is, they believe that by designing the right programs with the right inputs and outputs, they are literally creating minds. They believe furthermore that they have a scientific test for determining success or failure: the Turing test devised by Alan M. Turing, the founding father of artificial intelligence. The Turing test, as currently understood, is simply this: if a computer can perform in such a way that an expert cannot distinguish its performance from that of a human who has a certain cognitive ability—say, the ability to do addition or to understand Chinese—then the computer also has that ability. So the goal is to design programs that will simulate human cognition in such a way as to pass the Turing test. What is more, such a program would not merely be a model of the mind; it would literally be a mind, in the same sense that a human mind is a mind.

By no means does every worker in artificial intelligence accept so extreme a view. A more cautious approach is to think of computer models as being useful in studying the mind in the same way that they are useful in studying the weather, economics or molecular biology. To distinguish these two approaches, I call the first strong AI and the second weak AI. It is important to see just how bold an approach strong AI is. Strong AI claims that thinking is merely the manipulation of formal symbols, and that is exactly what the computer does: manipulate formal symbols. This view is often summarized by saying, "The mind is to the brain as the program is to the hardware."

Strong AI is unusual among theories of the mind in at least two respects: it can be stated clearly, and it admits of a simple and decisive refutation. The refutation is one that any person can try for himself or herself. Here is how it goes. Consider a language you don't understand. In my case, I do not understand Chinese. To me Chinese writing looks like so many meaningless squiggles. Now suppose I am placed in a room containing baskets full of Chinese symbols. Suppose also that I am given a rule book in English for matching Chinese symbols with other Chinese symbols. The rules identify the symbols entirely by their shapes and do not require that I understand any of them. The rules might say such things as, "Take a squiggle-squiggle sign from basket number one and put it next to a squoggle-squoggle sign from basket number two."

Imagine that people outside the room who understand Chinese hand in small bunches of symbols and that in response I manipulate the symbols according to the rule book and hand back more small bunches of symbols. Now, the rule book is the "computer program." The people who wrote it are "programmers," and I am the "computer." The baskets full of symbols are the "data base," the small bunches that are handed in to me are "questions" and the bunches I then hand out are "answers."

Now suppose that the rule book is written in such a way that my "answers" to the "questions" are indistinguishable from those of a native Chinese speaker. For example, the people outside might hand me some symbols that unknown to me mean, "What's your favorite color?" and I might after going through the rules give back symbols that, also unknown to me, mean, "My favorite is blue, but I also like green a lot." I satisfy the Turing test for understanding Chinese. All the same, I am totally ignorant of Chinese. And there is no way I could come to understand Chinese in the system as described, since there is no way that I can learn the meanings of any of the symbols. Like a computer, I manipulate symbols, but I attach no meaning to the symbols.

The point of the thought experiment is this: if I do not understand Chinese solely on the basis of running a computer program for understanding Chinese, then neither does any other digital computer solely on that basis. Digital computers merely manipulate formal symbols according to rules in the program.

What goes for Chinese goes for other forms of cognition as well. Just manipulating the symbols is not by itself enough to guarantee cognition, perception, understanding, thinking and so forth. And since computers, qua computers, are symbol-manipulating devices, merely running the computer program is not enough to guarantee cognition.

This simple argument is decisive against the claims of strong AI. The first premise of the argument simply states the formal character of a computer program. Programs are defined in terms of symbol manipulations, and the symbols are purely formal, or "syntactic." The formal character of the program, by the way, is what makes computers so powerful. The same program can be run on an indefinite variety of hardwares, and one hardware system can run an indefinite range of computer programs. Let me abbreviate this "axiom" as

Axiom 1. *Computer programs are formal (syntactic).*

This point is so crucial that it is worth explaining in more detail. A digital computer processes information by first encoding it in the symbolism that the computer uses and then manipulating the symbols through a set of precisely stated rules. These rules constitute the program. For example, in Turing's early theory of computers, the symbols were simply 0's and 1's, and the rules of the program said such things as, "Print a 0 on the tape, move one square to the left and erase a 1." The astonishing thing about computers is that any information that can be stated in a language can be encoded in such a system, and any information-processing task that can be solved by explicit rules can be programmed.

Two further points are important. First, symbols and programs are purely abstract notions: they have no essential physical properties to define them and can be implemented in any physical medium whatsoever. The 0's and 1's, qua symbols, have no essential physical properties and a fortiori have no physical, causal properties. I emphasize this point because it is tempting to identify computers with some specific technology—say,

silicon chips—and to think that the issues are about the physics of silicon chips or to think that syntax identifies some physical phenomenon that might have as yet unknown causal powers, in the way that actual physical phenomena such as electromagnetic radiation or hydrogen atoms have physical, causal properties. The second point is that symbols are manipulated without reference to any meanings. The symbols of the program can stand for anything the programmer or user wants. In this sense the program has syntax but no semantics.

The next axiom is just a reminder of the obvious fact that thoughts, perceptions, understandings and so forth have a mental content. By virtue of their content they can be about objects and states of affairs in the world. If the content involves language, there will be syntax in addition to semantics, but linguistic understanding requires at least a semantic framework. If, for example, I am thinking about the last presidential election, certain words will go through my mind, but the words are about the election only because I attach specific meanings to these words, in accordance with my knowledge of English. In this respect they are unlike Chinese symbols for me. Let me abbreviate this axiom as

Axiom 2. *Human minds have mental contents (semantics).*

Now let me add the point that the Chinese room demonstrated. Having the symbols by themselves—just having the syntax—is not sufficient for having the semantics. Merely manipulating symbols is not enough to guarantee knowledge of what they mean. I shall abbreviate this as

Axiom 3. *Syntax by itself is neither constitutive of nor sufficient for semantics.*

At one level this principle is true by definition. One might, of course, define the terms syntax and semantics differently. The point is that there is a distinction between formal elements, which have no intrinsic meaning or content, and those phenomena that have intrinsic content. From these premises it follows that

Conclusion 1. *Programs are neither constitutive of nor sufficient for minds.*

And that is just another way of saying that strong AI is false.

It is important to see what is proved and not proved by this argument.

First, I have not tried to prove that "a computer cannot think." Since anything that can be simulated computationally can be described as a computer, and since our brains can at some

levels be simulated, it follows trivially that our brains are computers and they can certainly think. But from the fact that a system can be simulated by symbol manipulation and the fact that it is thinking, it does not follow that thinking is equivalent to formal symbol manipulation.

Second, I have not tried to show that only biologically based systems like our brains can think. Right now those are the only systems we know for a fact can think, but we might find other systems in the universe that can produce conscious thoughts, and we might even come to be able to create thinking systems artificially. I regard this issue as up for grabs.

Third, strong AI's thesis is not that, for all we know, computers with the right programs might be thinking, that they might have some as yet undetected psychological properties; rather it is that they must be thinking because that is all there is to thinking.

Fourth, I have tried to refute strong AI so defined. I have tried to demonstrate that the program by itself is not constitutive of thinking because the program is purely a matter of formal symbol manipulation—and we know independently that symbol manipulations by themselves are not sufficient to guarantee the presence of meanings. That is the principle on which the Chinese room argument works.

I emphasize these points here partly because it seems to me the Churchlands [see "Could a Machine Think?" by Paul M. Churchland and Patricia Smith Churchland, page 222] have not quite understood the issues. They think that strong AI is claiming that computers might turn out to think and that I am denying this possibility on commonsense grounds. But that is not the claim of strong AI, and my argument against it has nothing to do with common sense.

I will have more to say about their objections later. Meanwhile I should point out that, contrary to what the Churchlands suggest, the Chinese room argument also refutes any strong-AI claims made for the new parallel technologies that are inspired by and modeled on neural networks. Unlike the traditional von Neumann computer, which proceeds in a step-by-step fashion, these systems have many computational elements that operate in parallel and interact with one another according to rules inspired by neurobiology. Although the results are still modest, these "parallel distributed processing," or "connectionist," models raise useful questions about how complex, parallel network systems like those in brains might actually function in the production of intelligent behavior.

The parallel, "brainlike" character of the processing, however, is irrelevant to the purely computational aspects of the process. Any function that can be computed on a parallel machine can also be computed on a serial machine. Indeed, because parallel machines are still rare, connectionist programs are usually run on traditional serial machines. Parallel processing, then, does not afford a way around the Chinese room argument.

What is more, the connectionist system is subject even on its own terms to a variant of the objection presented by the original Chinese room argument. Imagine that instead of a Chinese room, I have a Chinese gym: a hall containing many monolingual, English-speaking men. These men would carry out the same operations as the nodes and synapses in a connectionist architecture as described by the Churchlands, and the outcome would be the same as having one man manipulate symbols according to a rule book. No one in the gym speaks a word of Chinese, and there is no way for the system as a whole to learn the meanings of any Chinese words. Yet with appropriate adjustments, the system could give the correct answers to Chinese questions.

There are, as I suggested earlier, interesting properties of connectionist nets that enable them to simulate brain processes more accurately than traditional serial architecture does. But the advantages of parallel architecture for weak AI are quite irrelevant to the issues between the Chinese room argument and strong AI.

The Churchlands miss this point when they say that a big enough Chinese gym might have higher-level mental features that emerge from the size and complexity of the system, just as whole brains have mental features that are not had by individual neurons. That is, of course, a possibility, but it has nothing to do with computation. Computationally, serial and parallel systems are equivalent: any computation that can be done in parallel can be done in serial. If the man in the Chinese room is computationally equivalent to both, then if he does not understand Chinese solely by virtue of doing the computations, neither do they. The Churchlands are correct in saying that the original Chinese room argument was designed with traditional AI in mind but wrong in thinking that connectionism is immune to the argument. It applies to any computational system. You can't get semantically loaded thought contents from formal computations alone, whether they are done in serial or in parallel; that is why the Chinese room argument refutes strong AI in any form.

Many people who are impressed by this argument are nonetheless puzzled about the differences between people and computers. If humans are, at least in a trivial sense, computers, and if humans have a semantics, then why couldn't we give semantics to other computers? Why couldn't we program a Vax or a Cray so that it too would have thoughts and feelings? Or why couldn't some new computer technology overcome the gulf between form and content, between syntax and semantics? What, in fact, are the differences between animal brains and computer systems that enable the Chinese room argument to work against computers but not against brains?

The most obvious difference is that the processes that define something as a computer—computational processes—are completely independent of any reference to a specific type of hardware implementation. One could in principle make a computer out of old beer cans strung together with wires and powered by windmills.

But when it comes to brains, although science is largely ignorant of how brains function to produce mental states, one is struck by the extreme specificity of the anatomy and the physiology. Where some understanding exists of how brain processes produce mental phenomena—for example, pain, thirst, vision, smell—it is clear that specific neurobiological processes are involved. Thirst, at least of certain kinds, is caused by certain types of neuron firings in the hypothalamus, which in turn are caused by the action of a specific peptide, angiotensin II. The causation is from the "bottom up" in the sense that lower-level neuronal processes cause higher-level mental phenomena. Indeed, as far as we know, every "mental" event, ranging from feelings of thirst to thoughts of mathematical theorems and memories of childhood, is caused by specific neurons firing in specific neural architectures.

But why should this specificity matter? After all, neuron firings could be simulated on computers that had a completely different physics and chemistry from that of the brain. The answer is that the brain does not merely instantiate a formal pattern or program (it does that, too), but it also causes mental events by virtue of specific neurobiological processes. Brains are specific biological organs, and their specific biochemical properties enable them to cause consciousness and other sorts of mental phenomena. Computer simulations of brain processes provide models of the formal aspects of these processes. But the simulation should not be confused with duplication. The computational model of mental processes is no more real than the computational model of any other natural phenomenon.

One can imagine a computer simulation of the action of peptides in the hypothalamus that is accurate down to the last synapse. But equally one can imagine a computer simulation of the oxidation of hydrocarbons in a car engine or the action of digestive processes in a stomach when it is digesting pizza. And the simulation is no more the real thing in the case of the brain than it is in the case of the car or the stomach. Barring miracles, you could not run your car by doing a computer simulation of the oxidation of gasoline, and you could not digest pizza by running the program that simulates such digestion. It seems obvious that a simulation of cognition will similarly not produce the effects of the neurobiology of cognition.

All mental phenomena, then, are caused by neurophysiological processes in the brain. Hence,

Axiom 4. *Brains cause minds.*

In conjunction with my earlier derivation, I immediately derive, trivially,

Conclusion 2. *Any other system capable of causing minds would have to have causal powers (at least) equivalent to those of brains.*

This is like saying that if an electrical engine is to be able to run a car as fast as a gas engine, it must have (at least) an equivalent power output. This conclusion says nothing about the mechanisms. As a matter of fact, cognition is a biological phenomenon: mental states and processes are caused by brain processes. This does not imply that only a biological system could think, but it does imply that any alternative system, whether made of silicon, beer cans or whatever, would have to have the relevant causal capacities equivalent to those of brains. So now I can derive

Conclusion 3. *Any artifact that produced mental phenomena, any artificial brain, would have to be able to duplicate the specific causal powers of brains, and it could not do that just by running a formal program.*

Furthermore, I can derive an important conclusion about human brains:

Conclusion 4. *The way that human brains actually produce mental phenomena cannot be solely by virtue of running a computer program.*

I first presented the Chinese room parable in the pages of *Behavioral and Brain Sciences* in 1980, where it appeared, as is the practice of the journal, along with peer commentary, in this case, 26 commentaries. Frankly, I think the point it makes is rather obvious, but to my surprise the publication was followed by a further flood of objections that—more surprisingly—continues to the present day. The Chinese room argument clearly touched some sensitive nerve.

The thesis of strong AI is that any system whatsoever—whether it is made of beer cans, silicon chips or toilet paper—not only might have thoughts and feelings but *must* have thoughts and feelings, provided only that it implements the right program, with the right inputs and outputs. Now, that is a profoundly antibiological view, and one would think that people in AI would be glad to abandon it. Many of them, especially the younger generation, agree with me, but I am amazed at the number and vehemence of the defenders. Here are some of the common objections.

a. In the Chinese room you really do understand Chinese, even though you don't know it. It is, after all, possible to understand something without knowing that one understands it.

b. You don't understand Chinese, but there is an (unconscious) subsystem in you that does. It is, after all, possible to have unconscious mental states, and there is no reason why your understanding of Chinese should not be wholly unconscious.

c. You don't understand Chinese, but the whole room does. You are like a single neuron in the brain, and just as such a single neuron by itself cannot understand but only contributes to the understanding of the whole system, you don't understand, but the whole system does.

d. Semantics doesn't exist anyway; there is only syntax. It is a kind of prescientific illusion to suppose that there exist in the brain some mysterious "mental contents," "thought processes" or "semantics." All that exists in the brain is the same sort of syntactic symbol manipulation that goes on in computers. Nothing more.

e. You are not really running the computer program—you only think you are. Once you have a conscious agent going through the steps of the program, it ceases to be a case of implementing a program at all.

f. Computers would have semantics and not just syntax if their inputs and outputs were put in appropriate causal relation to the rest of the world. Imagine that we put the computer into a robot, attached television cameras to the robot's head, installed transducers connecting the television messages to the computer and had the computer output operate the robot's arms and legs. Then the whole system would have a semantics.

g. If the program simulated the operation of the brain of a Chinese speaker, then it would understand Chinese. Suppose that we simulated the brain of a Chinese person at the level of neurons. Then surely such a system would understand Chinese as well as any Chinese person's brain.

And so on.

All of these arguments share a common feature: they are all inadequate because they fail to come to grips with the actual Chinese room argument. That argument rests on the distinction between the formal symbol manipulation that is done by the computer and the mental contents biologically produced by the brain, a distinction I have abbreviated—I hope not misleadingly—as the distinction between syntax and semantics. I will not repeat my answers to all of these objections, but it will help to clarify the issues if I explain the weaknesses of the most widely held objection, argument c—what I call the systems reply. (The brain simulator reply, argument g, is another popular one, but I have already addressed that one in the previous section.)

The systems reply asserts that of course *you* don't understand Chinese but the whole system— you, the room, the rule book, the bushel baskets full of symbols— does. When I first heard this explanation, I asked one of its proponents, "Do you mean the room understands Chinese?" His answer was yes. It is a daring move, but aside from its implausibility, it will not work on purely logical grounds. The point of the original argument was that symbol shuffling by itself does not give any access to the meanings of the symbols. But this is as much true of the whole room as it is of the person inside. One can see this point by extending

the thought experiment. Imagine that I memorize the contents of the baskets and the rule book, and I do all the calculations in my head. You can even imagine that I work out in the open. There is nothing in the "system" that is not in me, and since I don't understand Chinese, neither does the system.

The Churchlands in their companion piece produce a variant of the systems reply by imagining an amusing analogy. Suppose that someone said that light could not be electromagnetic because if you shake a bar magnet in a dark room, the system still will not give off visible light. Now, the Churchlands ask, is not the Chinese room argument just like that? Does it not merely say that if you shake Chinese symbols in a semantically dark room, they will not give off the light of Chinese understanding? But just as later investigation showed that light was entirely constituted by electromagnetic radiation, could not later investigation also show that semantics are entirely constituted of syntax? Is this not a question for further scientific investigation?

Arguments from analogy are notoriously weak, because before one can make the argument work, one has to establish that the two cases are truly analogous. And here I think they are not. The account of light in terms of electromagnetic radiation is a causal story right down to the ground. It is a causal account of the physics of electromagnetic radiation. But the analogy with formal symbols fails because formal symbols have no physical, causal powers. The only power that symbols have, qua symbols, is the power to cause the next step in the program when the machine is running. And there is no question of waiting on further research to reveal the physical, causal properties of 0's and 1's. The only relevant properties of 0's and 1's are abstract computational properties, and they are already well known.

The Churchlands complain that I am "begging the question" when I say that uninterpreted formal symbols are not identical to mental contents. Well, I certainly did not spend much time arguing for it, because I take it as a logical truth. As with any logical truth, one can quickly see that it is true, because one gets inconsistencies if one tries to imagine the converse. So let us try it. Suppose that in the Chinese room some undetectable Chinese thinking really is going on. What exactly is supposed to make the manipulation of the syntactic elements into specifically Chinese thought contents? Well, after all, I am assuming that the programmers were Chinese speakers, programming the system to process Chinese information.

Fine. But now imagine that as I am sitting in the Chinese room shuffling the Chinese symbols, I get bored with just shuffling the—to me—meaningless symbols. So, suppose that I decide to interpret the symbols as standing for moves in a chess game. Which semantics is the system giving off now? Is it giving off a Chinese semantics or a chess semantics, or both simultaneously? Suppose there is a third person looking in through the window, and she decides that the symbol manipulations can all be interpreted as stock-market predictions. And so on. There is no limit to the number of semantic interpretations that can be assigned to the symbols because, to repeat, the symbols are purely formal. They have no intrinsic semantics.

Is there any way to rescue the Churchlands' analogy from incoherence? I said above that formal symbols do not have causal properties. But of course the program will always be implemented in some hardware or another, and the hardware will have specific physical, causal powers. And any real computer will give off various phenomena. My computers, for example, give off heat, and they make a humming noise and sometimes crunching sounds. So is there some logically compelling reason why they could not also give off consciousness? No. Scientifically, the idea is out of the question, but it is not something the Chinese room argument is supposed to refute, and it is not something that an adherent of strong AI would wish to defend, because any such giving off would have to derive from the physical features of the implementing medium. But the basic premise of strong AI is that the physical features of the implementing medium are totally irrelevant. What matters are programs, and programs are purely formal.

The Churchlands' analogy between syntax and electromagnetism, then, is confronted with a dilemma; either the syntax is construed purely formally in terms of its abstract mathematical properties, or it is not. If it is, then the analogy breaks down, because syntax so construed has no physical powers and hence no physical, causal powers.

If, on the other hand, one is supposed to think in terms of the physics of the implementing medium, then there is indeed an analogy, but it is not one that is relevant to strong AI.

Because the points I have been making are rather obvious—syntax is not the same as semantics, brain processes cause mental phenomena—the question arises, How did we get into this mess? How could anyone have supposed that a computer simulation of a mental process must be the real thing? After all, the whole point of models is that they contain only certain features of the modeled domain and leave out the rest. No one expects to get wet in a pool filled with Ping-Pong-ball models of water molecules. So why would anyone think a computer model of thought processes would actually think?

Part of the answer is that people have inherited a residue of behaviorist psychological theories of the past generation. The Turing test enshrines the temptation to think that if something behaves as if it had certain mental processes, then it must actually have those mental processes. And this is part of the behaviorists' mistaken assumption that in order to be scientific, psychology must confine its study to externally observable behavior. Paradoxically, this residual behaviorism is tied to a residual dualism. Nobody thinks that a computer simulation of digestion would actually digest anything, but where cognition is concerned, people are willing to believe in such a miracle because they fail to recognize that the mind is just as much a biological phenomenon as digestion. The mind, they suppose, is something formal and abstract, not a part of the wet and slimy stuff in our heads. The polemical literature in AI usually contains attacks on something the authors call dualism, but what they fail to see is that they themselves display dualism in a strong form, for unless one accepts the idea that the mind is completely independent of the brain or of any other physically specific system, one could not possibly hope to create minds just by designing programs.

Historically, scientific developments in the West that have treated humans as just a part of the ordinary physical, biological order have often been op-

posed by various rearguard actions. Copernicus and Galileo were opposed because they denied that the earth was the center of the universe; Darwin was opposed because he claimed that humans had descended from the lower animals. It is best to see strong AI as one of the last gasps of this antiscientific tradition, for it denies that there is anything essentially physical and biological about the human mind. The mind according to strong AI is independent of the brain. It is a computer program and as such has no essential connection to any specific hardware.

Many people who have doubts about the psychological significance of AI think that computers might be able to understand Chinese and think about numbers but cannot do the crucially human things, namely—and then follows their favorite human specialty—falling in love, having a sense of humor, feeling the angst of postindustrial society under late capitalism, or whatever. But workers in AI complain—correctly—that this is a case of moving the goalposts. As soon as an AI simulation succeeds, it ceases to be of psychological importance. In this debate both sides fail to see the distinction between simulation and duplication. As far as simulation is concerned, there is no difficulty in programming my computer so that it prints out, "I love you, Suzy"; "Ha ha"; or "I am suffering the angst of postindustrial society under late capitalism." The important point is that simulation is not the same as duplication, and that fact holds as much import for thinking about arithmetic as it does for feeling angst. The point is not that the computer gets only to the 40-yard line and not all the way to the goal line. The computer doesn't even get started. It is not playing that game.

FURTHER READING
MIND DESIGN: PHILOSOPHY, PSYCHOLOGY, ARTIFICIAL INTELLIGENCE. Edited by John Haugeland. The MIT Press, 1980.
MINDS, BRAINS, AND PROGRAMS. John Searle in *Behavioral and Brain Sciences*, Vol. 3, No. 3, pages 417–458; 1980.
MINDS, BRAINS, AND SCIENCE. John R. Searle. Harvard University Press, 1984.
MINDS, MACHINES AND SEARLE. Stevan Harnad in *Journal of Experimental and Theoretical Artificial Intelligence*, Vol. 1, No. 1, pages 5–25; 1989.

Could a Machine Think?

Classical AI is unlikely to yield conscious machines; systems that mimic the brain might

Paul M. Churchland and Patricia Smith Churchland

PAUL M. CHURCHLAND and PATRICIA SMITH CHURCHLAND are professors of philosophy at the University of California at San Diego. Together they have studied the nature of the mind and knowledge for the past two decades. Paul Churchland focuses on the nature of scientific knowledge and its development, while Patricia Churchland focuses on the neurosciences and on how the brain sustains cognition. Paul Churchland's *Matter and Consciousness* is the standard textbook on the philosophy of the mind, and Patricia Churchland's *Neurophilosophy* brings together theories of cognition from both philosophy and biology. Paul Churchland is currently chair of the philosophy department at UCSD, and the two are, respectively, president and past president of the Society for Philosophy and Psychology. Patricia Churchland is also an adjunct professor at the Salk Institute for Biological Studies in San Diego. The Churchlands are also members of the UCSD cognitive science faculty, its Institute for Neural Computation and its Science Studies program.

Artificial-intelligence research is undergoing a revolution. To explain how and why, and to put John R. Searle's argument in perspective, we first need a flashback.

By the early 1950's the old, vague question, Could a machine think? had been replaced by the more approachable question, Could a machine that manipulated physical symbols according to structure-sensitive rules think? This question was an improvement because formal logic and computational theory had seen major developments in the preceding half-century. Theorists had come to appreciate the enormous power of abstract systems of symbols that undergo rule-governed transformations. If those systems could just be automated, then their abstract computational power, it seemed, would be displayed in a real physical system. This insight spawned a well-defined research program with deep theoretical underpinnings.

Could a machine think? There were many reasons for saying yes. One of the earliest and deepest reasons lay in two important results in computational theory. The first was Church's thesis, which states that every effectively computable function is recursively computable. Effectively computable means that there is a "rote" procedure for determining, in finite time, the output of the function for a given input. Recursively computable means more specifically that there is a finite set of operations that can be applied to a given input, and then applied again and again to the successive results of such applications, to yield the function's output in finite time. The notion of a rote procedure is nonformal and intuitive; thus, Church's thesis does not admit of a formal proof. But it

does go to the heart of what it is to compute, and many lines of evidence converge in supporting it.

The second important result was Alan M. Turing's demonstration that any recursively computable function can be computed in finite time by a maximally simple sort of symbol-manipulating machine that has come to be called a universal Turing machine. This machine is guided by a set of recursively applicable rules that are sensitive to the identity, order and arrangement of the elementary symbols it encounters as input.

These two results entail something remarkable, namely that a standard digital computer, given only the right program, a large enough memory and sufficient time, can compute *any* rule-governed input-output function. That is, it can display any systematic pattern of responses to the environment whatsoever.

More specifically, these results imply that a suitably programmed symbol-manipulating machine (hereafter, SM machine) should be able to pass the Turing test for conscious intelligence. The Turing test is a purely behavioral test for conscious intelligence, but it is a very demanding test even so. (Whether it is a fair test will be addressed below, where we shall also encounter a second and quite different "test" for conscious intelligence.) In the original version of the Turing test, the inputs to the SM machine are conversational questions and remarks typed into a console by you or me, and the outputs are type-written responses from the SM machine. The machine passes this test for conscious intelligence if its responses cannot be discriminated from the typewritten responses of a real, intelligent person. Of course, at present no one knows the function that would produce the output behavior of a conscious person. But the Church and Turing results assure us that, whatever that (presumably effective) function might be, a suitable SM machine could compute it.

This is a significant conclusion, especially since Turing's portrayal of a purely teletyped interaction is an unnecessary restriction. The same conclusion follows even if the SM machine interacts with the world in more complex ways: by direct vision, real speech and so forth. After all, a more complex recursive function is still Turing-computable. The only remaining problem is to identify the undoubtedly complex function that governs the human pattern of response to the environment and then write the program (the set of recursively applicable rules) by which the SM machine will compute it. These goals form the fundamental research program of classical AI.

Initial results were positive. SM machines with clever programs performed a variety of ostensibly cognitive activities. They responded to complex instructions, solved complex arithmetic, algebraic and tactical problems, played checkers and chess, proved theorems and engaged in simple dialogue. Performance continued to improve with the appearance of larger memories and faster machines and with the use of longer and more cunning programs. Classical, or "program-writing," AI was a vigorous and successful research effort from almost every perspective. The occasional denial that an SM machine might eventually think appeared uninformed and ill motivated. The case for a positive answer to our title question was overwhelming.

There were a few puzzles, of course. For one thing, SM machines were admittedly not very brainlike. Even here, however, the classical approach had a convincing answer. First, the physical material of any SM machine has nothing essential to do with what function it computes. That is fixed by its program. Second, the engineering details of any machine's functional architec-

ture are also irrelevant, since different architectures running quite different programs can still be computing the same input-output function.

Accordingly, AI sought to find the input-output *function* characteristic of intelligence and the most efficient of the many possible programs for computing it. The idiosyncratic way in which the brain computes the function just doesn't matter, it was said. This completes the rationale for classical AI and for a positive answer to our title question.

Could a machine think? There were also some arguments for saying no. Through the 1960's interesting negative arguments were relatively rare. The objection was occasionally made that thinking was a nonphysical process in an immaterial soul. But such dualistic resistance was neither evolutionarily nor explanatorily plausible. It had a negligible impact on AI research.

A quite different line of objection was more successful in gaining the AI community's attention. In 1972 Hu-

---

THE CHINESE ROOM

Axiom 1. Computer programs are formal (syntactic).

Axiom 2. Human minds have mental contents (semantics).

Axiom 3. Syntax by itself is neither constitutive of nor sufficient for semantics.

Conclusion 1. Programs are neither constitutive of nor sufficient for minds.

THE LUMINOUS ROOM

Axiom 1. Electricity and magnetism are forces.

Axiom 2. The essential property of light is luminance.

Axiom 3. Forces by themselves are neither constitutive of nor sufficient for luminance.

Conclusion 1. Electricity and magnetism are neither constitutive of nor sufficient for light.

OSCILLATING ELECTROMAGNETIC FORCES constitute light even though a magnet pumped by a person appears to produce no light whatsoever. Similarly, rule-based symbol manipulation might constitute intelligence even though the rule-based system inside John R. Searle's "Chinese room" appears to lack real understanding.

bert L. Dreyfus published a book that was highly critical of the parade-case simulations of cognitive activity. He argued for their inadequacy as simulations of genuine cognition, and he pointed to a pattern of failure in these attempts. What they were missing, he suggested, was the vast store of inarticulate background knowledge every person possesses and the common-sense capacity for drawing on relevant aspects of that knowledge as changing circumstance demands. Dreyfus did not deny the possibility that an artificial physical system of some kind might think, but he was highly critical of the idea that this could be achieved solely by symbol manipulation at the hands of recursively applicable rules.

Dreyfus's complaints were broadly perceived within the AI community, and within the discipline of philosophy as well, as shortsighted and unsympathetic, as harping on the inevitable simplifications of a research effort still in its youth. These deficits might be real, but surely they were temporary. Bigger machines and better programs should repair them in due course. Time, it was felt, was on AI's side. Here again the impact on research was negligible.

Time was on Dreyfus's side as well: the rate of cognitive return on increasing speed and memory began to slacken in the late 1970's and early 1980's. The simulation of object recognition in the visual system, for example, proved computationally intensive to an unexpected degree. Realistic results required longer and longer periods of computer time, periods far in excess of what a real visual system requires. This relative slowness of the simulations was darkly curious; signal propagation in a computer is roughly a million times faster than in the brain, and the clock frequency of a computer's central processor is greater than any frequency found in the brain by a similarly dramatic margin. And yet, on realistic problems, the tortoise easily outran the hare.

Furthermore, realistic performance required that the computer program have access to an extremely large knowledge base. Constructing the relevant knowledge base was problem enough, and it was compounded by the problem of how to access just the contextually relevant parts of that knowledge base in real time. As the knowledge base got bigger and better, the access problem got worse. Exhaustive search took too much time, and heuristics for relevance did poorly. Worries of the sort Dreyfus had

raised finally began to take hold here and there even among AI researchers.

At about this time (1980) John Searle authored a new and quite different criticism aimed at the most basic assumption of the classical research program: the idea that the appropriate manipulation of structured symbols by the recursive application of structure-sensitive rules could constitute conscious intelligence.

Searle's argument is based on a thought experiment that displays two crucial features. First, he describes a SM machine that realizes, we are to suppose, an input-output function adequate to sustain a successful Turing test conversation conducted entirely in Chinese. Second, the internal structure of the machine is such that, however it behaves, an observer remains certain that neither the machine nor any part of it understands Chinese. All it contains is a monolingual English speaker following a written set of instructions for manipulating the Chinese symbols that arrive and leave through a mail slot. In short, the system is supposed to pass the Turing test, while the system itself lacks any genuine understanding of Chinese or real Chinese semantic content [see "Is the Brain's Mind a Computer Program?" by John R. Searle, page 217].

The general lesson drawn is that any system that merely manipulates physical symbols in accordance with structure-sensitive rules will be at best a hollow mock-up of real conscious intelligence, because it is impossible to generate "real semantics" merely by cranking away on "empty syntax." Here, we should point out, Searle is imposing a nonbehavioral test for consciousness: the elements of conscious intelligence must possess real semantic content.

One is tempted to complain that Searle's thought experiment is unfair because his Rube Goldberg system will compute with absurd slowness. Searle insists, however, that speed is strictly irrelevant here. A slow thinker should still be a real thinker. Everything essential to the duplication of thought, as per classical AI, is said to be present in the Chinese room.

Searle's paper provoked a lively reaction from AI researchers, psychologists and philosophers alike. On the whole, however, he was met with an even more hostile reception than Dreyfus had experienced. In his companion piece in this issue, Searle forthrightly lists a number of these critical responses. We think many of them are reasonable, especially those that "bite

the bullet" by insisting that, although it is appallingly slow, the overall system of the room-plus-contents does understand Chinese.

We think those are good responses, but not because we think that the room understands Chinese. We agree with Searle that it does not. Rather they are good responses because they reflect a refusal to accept the crucial third axiom of Searle's argument: "*Syntax by itself is neither constitutive of nor sufficient for semantics.*" Perhaps this axiom is true, but Searle cannot rightly pretend to know that it is. Moreover, to assume its truth is tantamount to begging the question against the research program of classical AI, for that program is predicated on the very interesting assumption that if one can just set in motion an appropriately structured internal dance of syntactic elements, appropriately connected to inputs and outputs, it can produce the same cognitive states and achievements found in human beings.

The question-begging character of Searle's axiom 3 becomes clear when it is compared directly with his conclusion 1: "*Programs are neither constitutive of nor sufficient for minds.*" Plainly, his third axiom is already carrying 90 percent of the weight of this almost identical conclusion. That is why Searle's thought experiment is devoted to shoring up axiom 3 specifically. That is the point of the Chinese room.

Although the story of the Chinese room makes axiom 3 tempting to the unwary, we do not think it succeeds in establishing axiom 3, and we offer a parallel argument below in illustration of its failure. A single transparently fallacious instance of a disputed argument often provides far more insight than a book full of logic chopping.

Searle's style of skepticism has ample precedent in the history of science. The 18th-century Irish bishop George Berkeley found it unintelligible that compression waves in the air, by themselves, could constitute or be sufficient for objective sound. The English poet-artist William Blake and the German poet-naturalist Johann W. von Goethe found it inconceivable that small particles by themselves could constitute or be sufficient for the objective phenomenon of light. Even in this century, there have been people who found it beyond imagining that inanimate matter by itself, and however organized, could ever constitute or be sufficient for life. Plainly, what people can or cannot imagine often has nothing to do with what is or is not the case, even where the people involved are highly intelligent.

To see how this lesson applies to Searle's case, consider a deliberately manufactured parallel to his argument and its supporting thought experiment.

Axiom 1. Electricity and magnetism are forces.

Axiom 2. The essential property of light is luminance.

Axiom 3. Forces by themselves are neither constitutive of nor sufficient for luminance.

Conclusion 1. Electricity and magnetism are neither constitutive of nor sufficient for light.

Imagine this argument raised shortly after James Clerk Maxwell's 1864 suggestion that light and electromagnetic waves are identical but before the world's full appreciation of the systematic parallels between the properties of light and the properties of electromagnetic waves. This argument could have served as a compelling objection to Maxwell's imaginative hypothesis, especially if it were accompanied by the following commentary in support of axiom 3.

"Consider a dark room containing a man holding a bar magnet or charged object. If the man pumps the magnet up and down, then, according to Maxwell's theory of artificial luminance (AL), it will initiate a spreading circle of electromagnetic waves and will thus be luminous. But as all of us who have toyed with magnets or charged balls well know, their forces (or any other forces for that matter), even when set in motion, produce no luminance at all. It is inconceivable that you might constitute real luminance just by moving forces around!"

How should Maxwell respond to this challenge? He might begin by insisting that the "luminous room" experiment is a misleading display of the phenomenon of luminance because the frequency of oscillation of the magnet is absurdly low, too low by a factor of 10^{15}. This might well elicit the impatient response that frequency has nothing to do with it, that the room with the bobbing magnet already contains everything essential to light, according to Maxwell's own theory.

In response Maxwell might bite the bullet and claim, quite correctly, that the room really is bathed in luminance, albeit a grade or quality too feeble to appreciate. (Given the low frequency with which the man can oscillate the magnet, the wavelength of the electromagnetic waves produced is far too long and their intensity is much

too weak for human retinas to respond to them.) But in the climate of understanding here contemplated— the 1860's—this tactic is likely to elicit laughter and hoots of derision. "Luminous room, my foot, Mr. Maxwell. It's pitch-black in there!"

Alas, poor Maxwell has no easy route out of this predicament. All he can do is insist on the following three points. First, axiom 3 of the above argument is false. Indeed, it begs the question despite its intuitive plausibility. Second, the luminous room experiment demonstrates nothing of interest one way or the other about the nature of light. And third, what is needed to settle the problem of light and the possibility of artificial luminance is an ongoing research program to determine whether under the appropriate conditions the behavior of electromagnetic waves does indeed mirror perfectly the behavior of light.

This is also the response that classical AI should give to Searle's argument. Even though Searle's Chinese room may appear to be "semantically dark," he is in no position to insist, on the strength of this appearance, that rule-governed symbol manipulation can never constitute semantic phenomena, especially when people have only an uninformed common-sense understanding of the semantic and cognitive phenomena that need to be explained. Rather than exploit one's understanding of these things, Searle's argument freely exploits one's ignorance of them.

With these criticisms of Searle's argument in place, we return to the question of whether the research program of classical AI has a realistic chance of solving the problem of conscious intelligence and of producing a machine that thinks. We believe that the prospects are poor, but we rest

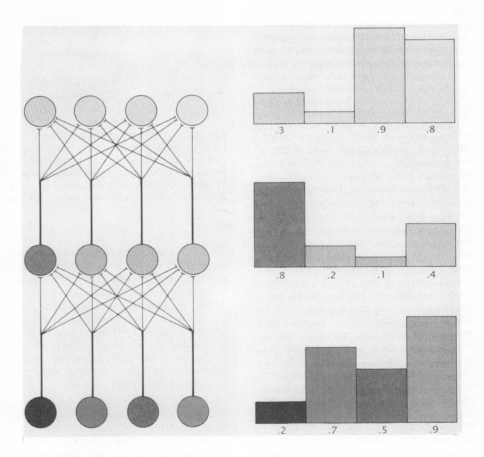

NEURAL NETWORKS model a central feature of the brain's microstructure. In this three-layer net, input neurons (*bottom left*) process a pattern of activations (*bottom right*) and pass it along weighted connections to a hidden layer. Elements in the hidden layer sum their many inputs to produce a new pattern of activations. This is passed to the output layer, which performs a further transformation. Overall the network transforms any input pattern into a corresponding output pattern as dictated by the arrangement and strength of the many connections between neurons.

this opinion on reasons very different from Searle's. Our reasons derive from the specific performance failures of the classical research program in AI and from a variety of lessons learned from the biological brain and a new class of computational models inspired by its structure. We have already indicated some of the failures of classical AI regarding tasks that the brain performs swiftly and efficiently. The emerging consensus on these failures is that the functional architecture of classical SM machines is simply the wrong architecture for the very demanding jobs required.

What we need to know is this: How does the brain achieve cognition? Reverse engineering is a common practice in industry. When a new piece of technology comes on the market, competitors find out how it works by taking it apart and divining its structural rationale. In the case of the brain, this strategy presents an unusually stiff challenge, for the brain is the most complicated and sophisticated thing on the planet. Even so, the neurosciences have revealed much about the brain on a wide variety of structural levels. Three anatomic points will provide a basic contrast with the architecture of conventional electronic computers.

First, nervous systems are parallel machines, in the sense that signals are processed in millions of different pathways simultaneously. The retina, for example, presents its complex input to the brain not in chunks of eight, 16 or 32 elements, as in a desktop computer, but rather in the form of almost a million distinct signal elements arriving simultaneously at the target of the optic nerve (the lateral geniculate nucleus), there to be processed collectively, simultaneously and in one fell swoop. Second, the brain's basic processing unit, the neuron, is comparatively simple. Furthermore, its response to incoming signals is analog, not digital, inasmuch as its output spiking frequency varies continuously with its input signals. Third, in the brain, axons projecting from one neuronal population to another are often matched by axons returning from their target population. These descending or recurrent projections allow the brain to modulate the character of its sensory processing. More important still, their existence makes the brain a genuine dynamical system whose continuing behavior is both highly complex and to some degree independent of its peripheral stimuli.

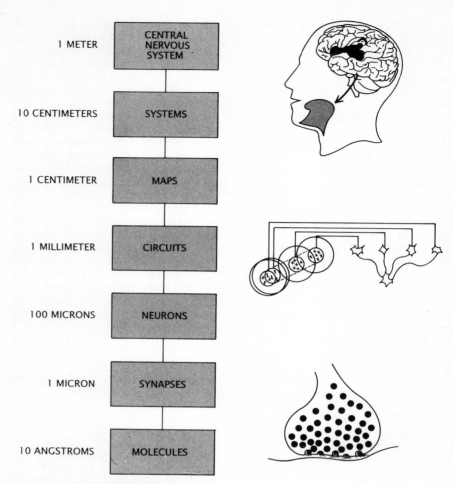

NERVOUS SYSTEMS span many scales of organization, from neurotransmitter molecules (*bottom*) to the entire brain and spinal cord. Intermediate levels include single neurons and circuits made up of a few neurons, such as those that produce orientation selectivity to a visual stimulus (*middle*), and systems made up of circuits such as those that subserve language (*top right*). Only research can decide how closely an artificial system must mimic the biological one to be capable of intelligence.

Highly simplified model networks have been useful in suggesting how real neural networks might work and in revealing the computational properties of parallel architectures. For example, consider a three-layer model consisting of neuronlike units fully connected by axonlike connections to the units at the next layer. An input stimulus produces some activation level in a given input unit, which conveys a signal of proportional strength along its "axon" to its many "synaptic" connections to the hidden units. The global effect is that a pattern of activations across the set of input units produces a distinct pattern of activations across the set of hidden units.

The same story applies to the output units. As before, an activation pattern across the hidden units produces a distinct activation pattern across the output units. All told, this network is a device for transforming any one of a great many possible input vectors (activation patterns) into a uniquely corresponding output vector. It is a device for computing a specific function. Exactly which function it computes is fixed by the global configuration of its synaptic weights.

There are various procedures for adjusting the weights so as to yield a network that computes almost any function—that is, any vector-to-vector transformation—that one might desire. In fact, one can even impose on it a function one is unable to specify, so long as one can supply a set of examples of the desired input-output pairs. This process, called "training up the network," proceeds by successive adjustment of the network's weights until it performs the input-output transformations desired.

Although this model network vastly oversimplifies the structure of the brain, it does illustrate several important ideas. First, a parallel architecture provides a dramatic speed advantage over a conventional computer, for the many synapses at each level perform many small computations simultaneously instead of in laborious sequence. This advantage gets larger as the number of neurons increases at each layer. Strikingly, the speed of processing is entirely independent of both the number of units involved in each layer and the complexity of the function they are computing. Each layer could have four units or a hundred million; its configuration of synaptic weights could be computing simple one-digit sums or second-order differential equations. It would make no difference. The computation time would be exactly the same.

Second, massive parallelism means that the system is fault-tolerant and functionally persistent; the loss of a few connections, even quite a few, has a negligible effect on the character of the overall transformation performed by the surviving network.

Third, a parallel system stores large amounts of information in a distributed fashion, any part of which can be accessed in milliseconds. That information is stored in the specific configuration of synaptic connection strengths, as shaped by past learning. Relevant information is "released" as the input vector passes through—and is transformed by—that configuration of connections.

Parallel processing is not ideal for all types of computation. On tasks that require only a small input vector, but many millions of swiftly iterated recursive computations, the brain performs very badly, whereas classical SM machines excel. This class of computations is very large and important, so classical machines will always be useful, indeed, vital. There is, however, an equally large class of computations for which the brain's architecture is the superior technology. These are the computations that typically confront living creatures: recognizing a predator's outline in a noisy environment; recalling instantly how to avoid its gaze, flee its approach or fend off its attack; distinguishing food from nonfood and mates from nonmates; navigating through a complex and ever-changing physical/social environment; and so on.

Finally, it is important to note that the parallel system described is not manipulating symbols according to structure-sensitive rules. Rather symbol manipulation appears to be just one of many cognitive skills that a network may or may not learn to display. Rule-governed symbol manipulation is not its basic mode of operation. Searle's argument is directed against rule-governed SM machines; vector transformers of the kind we describe are therefore not threatened by his Chinese room argument even if it were sound, which we have found independent reason to doubt.

Searle is aware of parallel processors but thinks they too will be devoid of real semantic content. To illustrate their inevitable failure, he outlines a second thought experiment, the Chinese gym, which has a gymnasium full of people organized into a parallel network. From there his argument proceeds as in the Chinese room.

We find this second story far less responsive or compelling than his first. For one, it is irrelevant that no unit in his system understands Chinese, since the same is true of nervous systems: no neuron in my brain understands English, although my whole brain does. For another, Searle neglects to mention that his simulation (using one person per neuron, plus a fleet-footed child for each synaptic connection) will require at least 10^{14} people, since the human brain has 10^{11} neurons, each of which averages over 10^3 connections. His system will require the entire human populations of over 10,000 earths. One gymnasium will not begin to hold a fair simulation.

On the other hand, if such a system were to be assembled on a suitably cosmic scale, with all its pathways faithfully modeled on the human case, we might then have a large, slow, oddly made but still functional brain on our hands. In that case the default assumption is surely that, given proper inputs, it would think, not that it couldn't. There is no guarantee that its activity would constitute real thought, because the vector-processing theory sketched above may not be the correct theory of how brains work. But neither is there any a priori guarantee that it could not be thinking. Searle is once more mistaking the limits on his (or the reader's) current imagination for the limits on objective reality.

The brain is a kind of computer, although most of its properties remain to be discovered. Characterizing the brain as a kind of computer is neither trivial nor frivolous. The brain does compute functions, functions of great complexity, but not in the classical AI fashion. When brains are said to be computers, it should not be implied that they are serial, digital computers, that they are programmed, that they exhibit the distinction between hardware and software or that they must be symbol manipulators or rule followers. Brains are computers in a radically different style.

How the brain manages meaning is still unknown, but it is clear that the problem reaches beyond language use and beyond humans. A small mound of fresh dirt signifies to a person, and also to coyotes, that a gopher is around; an echo with a certain spectral character signifies to a bat the presence of a moth. To develop a theory of meaning, more must be known about how neurons code and transform sensory signals, about the neural basis of memory, learning and emotion and about the interaction of these capacities and the motor system. A neurally grounded theory of meaning may require revision of the very intuitions that now seem so secure and that are so freely exploited in Searle's arguments. Such revisions are common in the history of science.

Could science construct an artificial intelligence by exploiting what is known about the nervous system? We see no principled reason why not. Searle appears to agree, although he qualifies his claim by saying that "any other system capable of causing minds would have to have causal powers (at least) equivalent to those of brains." We close by addressing this claim. We presume that Searle is not claiming that a successful artificial mind must have *all* the causal powers of the brain, such as the power to smell bad when rotting, to harbor slow viruses such as kuru, to stain yellow with horseradish peroxidase and so forth. Requiring perfect parity would be like requiring that an artificial flying device lay eggs.

Presumably he means only to require of an artificial mind all of the causal powers relevant, as he says, to conscious intelligence. But which exactly are they? We are back to quarreling about what is and is not relevant. This is an entirely reasonable place for a disagreement, but it is an empirical matter, to be tried and tested. Because so little is known about what goes into the process of cognition and semantics, it is premature to be very confident about what features are essential. Searle hints at various points that every level, including the biochemical, must be represented in any machine that is a candidate for artificial intelligence. This claim is almost surely too strong. An artificial brain might use something other than biochemicals to achieve the same ends.

This possibility is illustrated by Carver A. Mead's research at the California Institute of Technology. Mead and his colleagues have used analog VLSI techniques to build an artificial retina and an artificial cochlea. (In animals the retina and cochlea are not mere transducers: both systems embody a complex processing network.) These are not mere simulations in a minicomputer of the kind that Searle derides; they are real information-processing units responding in real time to real light, in the case of the artificial retina, and to real sound, in the case of the artificial cochlea. Their circuitry is based on the known anatomy and physiology of the cat retina and the barn owl cochlea, and their output is dramatically similar to the known output of the organs at issue.

These chips do not use any neurochemicals, so neurochemicals are clearly not necessary to achieve the evident results. Of course, the artificial retina cannot be said to see anything, because its output does not have an artificial thalamus or cortex to go to. Whether Mead's program could be sustained to build an entire artificial brain remains to be seen, but there is no evidence now that the absence of biochemicals renders it quixotic.

We, and Searle, reject the Turing test as a sufficient condition for conscious intelligence. At one level our reasons for doing so are similar: we agree that it is also very important how the input-output function is achieved; it is important that the right sorts of things be going on inside the artificial machine. At another level, our reasons are quite different. Searle bases his position on commonsense intuitions about the presence or absence of semantic content. We base ours on the specific behavioral failures of the classical SM machines and on the specific virtues of machines with a more brainlike architecture. These contrasts show that certain computational strategies have vast and decisive advantages over others where typical cognitive tasks are concerned, advantages that are empirically inescapable. Clearly, the brain is making systematic use of these computational advantages. But it need not be the only physical system capable of doing so. Artificial intelligence, in a nonbiological but massively parallel machine, remains a compelling and discernible prospect.

FURTHER READING

COMPUTING MACHINERY AND INTELLIGENCE. Alan M. Turing in *Mind*, Vol. 59, pages 433–460; 1950.

WHAT COMPUTERS CAN'T DO; A CRITIQUE OF ARTIFICIAL REASON. Hubert L. Dreyfus. Harper & Row, 1972.

NEUROPHILOSOPHY: TOWARD A UNIFIED UNDERSTANDING OF THE MIND/BRAIN. Patricia Smith Churchland. The MIT Press, 1986.

FAST THINKING in *The Intentional Stance*. Daniel Clement Dennett. The MIT Press, 1987.

A NEUROCOMPUTATIONAL PERSPECTIVE: THE NATURE OF MIND AND THE STRUCTURE OF SCIENCE. Paul M. Churchland. The MIT Press, in press.

The Science of Computing

Is Thinking Computable?

Peter J. Denning

Peter Denning is Director of the Research Institute for Advanced Computer Science at the NASA Ames Research Center.

The vision of thinking computers fascinates people and sells magazines and books. For decades the advocates of "strong AI" (artificial intelligence) have claimed that within one or two hundred years electronic machines will be able to do everything a human can do. They see our minds as "computers made of meat," subject to the laws of physics; as soon as we understand those laws and the physical structure of the brain, we will be able to construct computing machines that solve the "differential equations of mind" in real time and exhibit behavior exactly like ours. These machines will experience emotions, judge truth, appreciate beauty, understand, be self-conscious and intelligent, and have free wills. A few advocates go so far as to speculate that the machines will be better than we are in every way and will eventually succeed *Homo sapiens* on the evolutionary scale.

Some philosophers and scientists strongly disagree. They see computers as no different from machines of levers, wheels, moving balls, valves, or pneumatic pipes; although electronic machines can perform tasks of much greater complexity in a given time, there is nothing essentially different about them. These skeptics see no way that any such machine could come to "understand" what it does. Indeed, they argue that "understanding" and "thinking" are meaningless concepts for machines. Expert systems are unlikely to achieve competence beyond what a "mindless, procedural bureaucracy" is capable of. Even though computers now play chess at the grand-master level, almost no one says that they have insight or an understanding of chess; they are programmed simply to perform "brute-force searches" of possible future board configurations.

I have summarized these arguments in two previous columns *(1, 2)*, and I am returning to them now because of two new contributions to the ongoing discussion. The first is a debate in *Scientific American* [January 1990] between John Searle and Paul and Patricia Churchland. [See *Is the*

Brain's Mind a Computer Program? p. 217, and *Could a Machine Think*, p. 222] The other is a new book by Roger Penrose. I will discuss these works and add some reflections of my own.

In the *Scientific American* debate *(3, 4)*, Searle, a philosopher from the University of California at Berkeley, argues that no computer program can function like a mind; the Churchlands, philosophers from the University of California at San Diego, argue that systems mimicking the brain's structure can do so. The editors arranged an exchange: each side challenges the other's arguments and refutations. Neither is swayed by the other's arguments.

Both sides begin with the test Alan Turing proposed in 1950, an imitation game in which an interrogator asks questions of a human being and a machine; if the interrogator is unable to distinguish between the two, the machine passes the test and is declared intelligent *(5)*. Turing replaced the question "Can a machine think?" with "Can the interrogator distinguish the two in an imitation game?" because he considered the former question so imprecise as to be meaningless. His own opinion was that by the year 2000 there would exist machines capable of fooling the interrogator for at least five minutes in 30% of the games played. Turing's test is taken as a criterion of machine intelligence by advocates of strong AI.

Searle reviews his own Chinese Room argument, in which a man who understands no Chinese translates between incoming messages in Chinese and outgoing messages in Chinese by performing pattern replacements following rules in a book. According to Chinese observers on the outside, the room passes the Turing test by conversing in Chinese, but the man in the room has absolutely no understanding of what is going on. Searle maintains that a computer is no different: any machine that might pass the Turing test cannot be said to be thinking. Human brains have the capacity, conferred by their specific biology, to attach meanings to symbols, a fact that differentiates them from computer programs. Simulation is not the same as duplication, and so Searle wonders why so many are prepared to accept a simulation of thinking as actual thought when they would not do the same for a computer simulation of digestion.

From *American Scientist*, March/April 1990, pp. 100-102. Reprinted by permission of *American Scientist*, journal of Sigma Xi, The Scientific Research Society.

The Churchlands agree that the Turing test is not a sufficient condition for conscious intelligence. But they reject Searle's claim that an algorithm cannot be intelligent in principle. They argue that a brain is a finite, complicated web of neurons, each of which performs a definite function governed by the laws of physics. A set of mathematical equations relates all the signals appearing in the web; a sufficiently powerful computer would

---

Searle wonders why so many are prepared to accept a simulation of thinking as actual thought when they would not do the same for a computer simulation of digestion

---

be able to solve for (or simulate) what a given brain does in solving those equations. The Churchlands recognize that the required computational power is likely to be achieved only within the architecture of neural networks that mimic the structure of the brain. In such systems, intelligent behavior arises macroscopically, from the collective effects of simple neuron firings, and thus the individual neurons do not need to "understand" anything.

I found it fascinating that both sides presented coherent interpretations of strong AI—with conflicting conclusions. Each side is sure it is "right" and is impervious to the other's counterarguments. None of the theories of machine intelligence I am aware of addresses this all-too-human phenomenon.

It is also interesting that both sides, following the tradition begun by Turing, dismiss the question "What is thinking?" as meaningless. But this question remains at the heart of the debate. You will see shortly that it is central to Penrose's investigation.

What we think thinking is has been a moving target throughout history. For two hundred years under the ascendancy of Newtonian mechanics beginning in the early 1700s, everyone accepted the universe as a marvelous clockwork system governed by a few simple laws. In this tradition the epitomy of human thought was problem-solving through logical deduction, man's path to exploring God's universe. The quest for a complete understanding of thought led to attempts beginning in the 1800s to formulate a universal system of logic in which all statements could be mechanically checked for validity. But the hope for such a system was dashed in the 1930s by the incompleteness theorem of Gödel and the incomputability theorem of Turing. Still, the idea that thinking was somehow a mechanical process lived on in Turing and guided his formulation of testing for intelligence. The idea of a computer thinking didn't seem the slightest bit strange to him.

Today a different interpretation of thinking is challenging the old idea. Many of us believe that thinking is not logical deduction, but the creation of new ideas.

Logical deduction seems too mechanical. When we recall our moments of insight, we often say that our emotional state affected us and that we had a bodily sense of our creation before we could put it into words. We regard thinking as a phenomenon that occurs before articulation in language, and it seems that machines, which are programmed inside language, cannot generate actions outside language.

I have no doubt that fifty years from now there will be many machines performing tasks that today we associate with thinking—and people will still regard them as only machines. Interpretations of thinking will have shifted farther, preserving a clear distinction between human and machine.

I turn now to Penrose's book, *The Emperor's New Mind* (6). Penrose, a mathematician and physicist at Oxford University, mounts the most serious attack on strong AI that I have yet seen. This is not an easy book: Penrose leaves few stones unturned as he considers a broad range of speculations about mind, consciousness, and thinking. He takes his readers on an odyssey through a heady array of topics, including algorithms, Turing machines, Mandelbrot sets, formal systems, undecidability, incompleteness theorems, nonrecursive sets, Newtonian mechanics, space-time, phase spaces, relativity, quantum mechanics, entropy, cosmology, black holes, quantum gravity, brains, neurophysiology, animal consciousness, and more. In each topic he finds abundant evidence of human actions that are not algorithmic, concluding with the claim that a full understanding of mind awaits the development of quantum theories of physics as yet unknown to us.

Penrose agrees with Searle that the Turing test is an inadequate description of intelligence, but he challenges Searle's assumption that computers might pass the test. He asserts repeatedly that mental processes are inherently more powerful than computational processes. He points to the principle of universal computation—the idea that a general-purpose computer can simulate any other machine—as the basis for the widespread belief that algorithms must be the essence of thought. As a consequence, Penrose devotes considerable attention to the subject of noncomputable functions, such as the halting problem (is there a program which any given algorithm halts for a given input?), and he returns frequently to the idea that most of the questions about science that we consider interesting are not solvable by any general algorithm. Minds are constantly coming up with solutions to questions for which there is no general algorithm. How, he asks, could an algorithm have discovered theorems like Turing's and Gödel's that tell us what algorithms cannot do?

Penrose next takes on the strong-AI claim that we will one day have a sufficient understanding of the laws of physics and the structure of the brain to conduct an exact simulation by computer. What is physics? he asks. Is physics capable of complete understanding? What is an exact simulation? After exploring the failures of Newtonian physics that led to the formulation of relativity theory and then quantum mechanics, Penrose argues that the laws of physics at the quantum level may be determinate but not computable. Because some mental phenomena operate at scales where quantum effects may exert an influence, the functions representing the mind may not be computable, and thus an exact mechanical simulation may not be possible.

Although these suggestions are not provable given our current state of knowledge, Penrose has nonetheless offered a sharp metaphysical challenge to strong AI. The presupposition of a definite set of computable equations that determine a thinking being's next response begs the question because it implicitly assumes that all mental processes are algorithmic. If, as Penrose suggests, important physical processes of the brain are not computable, then computable equations would be only an approximation; they would leave out the quantum effects on which the conscious thought of the brain may depend.

Penrose does not, in my view, deal adequately with the shifting interpretations of consciousness and thinking. It is precisely the motion of these moving targets that must be dealt with. Penrose holds that consciousness has something to do with awareness of timeless Platonic realities: "When mathematicians communicate, [mathematical understanding] is made possible by each one having a *direct route to truth*, the consciousness of each being in a position to perceive mathematical truths directly" (p. 428).

I have found the biological interpretation of self and consciousness offered by Humberto Maturana and Francesco Varela *(7)* to be a good corrective to the narrow view expressed by Penrose. Maturana and Varela say that consciousness is associated with (but not uniquely determined by) the way we observe things. There are levels of consciousness, ranging from responding reflexively and following rules mindlessly to observing oneself as an observer. Each observer operates within a system of interpretation that includes biases, prejudices, presuppositions, culture, history, and values and that affects what can be seen or not seen, what is important or not important, and what is held as true or not true. As conscious beings, we must constantly reckon with different observers of the same phenomena. For example, Searle and the Churchlands are different observers of

---

Although it intrigues us that we might have a godlike power to create beings more advanced than ourselves, we are also threatened by that possibility

---

strong AI and have reached different conclusions from their observations of the same phenomena.

The invention of interpretations is a fundamentally human activity that is intimately involved with our understanding of truth. As scientists, we like to say that scientific laws and mathematical theorems already exist awaiting discovery. But if we carefully examine the processes of science, we find paradigms other than discovery. Roald Hoffmann says that the creation of new substances not found in nature is the dominant activity in disciplines such as chemistry and molecular biology

(8). Bruno Latour goes farther, observing that in practice a statement is accepted as true by a community if no one has been able to produce evidence or an argument that persuades others to dissent *(9)*. Science is a process of constructing facts, and different scientific communities can construct different systems of interpretation of the same physical phenomena. Western and Eastern medicine, for example, are two scientifically valid systems of interpretation about disease and human disorders; each recommends different interventions for the same symptoms and sees phenomena that are invisible to the other, and their interpretations are not easily reconciled.

Considerations such as these about the variousness of truth make it difficult for me to accept Penrose's speculations about links between consciousness and Platonic truth. For me, the existence of multiple, incomplete interpretations actually supports Penrose's basic claims about mental as opposed to computational processes. Like a system of logic, an interpretation cannot include all phenomena. Our powers of conscious observation give us a capacity to step outside a particular interpretation and devise extensions or alternatives. Thus consciousness itself cannot be captured by any fixed description or interpretation. How then can consciousness be captured by an algorithm, which is by its very nature a fixed interpretation? This question applies also to algorithms that are apparently designed to shift their interpretations, because the rules for shifting constitute an interpretation themselves.

Although Penrose has left us with a great many questions that will occupy the philosophers among us for years, it is well to remember that we will continue to build practical systems that perform increasingly sophisticated tasks, such as recognition of speech and visual shapes, diagnosis, advising, symbolic mathematics, and robotics.

We humans see ourselves at the top of the current evolutionary scale. Although it intrigues us that we might have a godlike power to create beings more advanced than ourselves, we are also threatened by that possibility. Searle, the Churchlands, and Penrose have bolstered our confidence in the belief that we are more than mechanical devices. We can rest a little easier, always keeping a watchful eye on the literature in case someone comes up with a plausible argument that machines may, one day, think.

References

1. P. J. Denning. 1986. Will machines ever think? *Am. Sci.* 74:344–46.
2. P. J. Denning. 1988. Blindness in the design of intelligent systems. *Am. Sci.* 76:118–20.
3. J. R. Searle. 1990. Is the brain's mind a computer program? *Sci. Am.* 262(1):26–31.
4. P. M. Churchland and P. S. Churchland. 1990. Could a machine think? *Sci. Am.* 262(1):32–37.
5. A. M. Turing. 1950. Computing machinery and intelligence. *Mind* 59:433–60. (Reprinted in D. R. Hofstadter and D. C. Dennett, *The Mind's I*, Basic Books, 1981.)
6. R. Penrose. 1989. *The Emperor's New Mind*. Oxford Univ. Press.
7. H. Maturana and F. Varela. 1987. *The Tree of Knowledge*. Shambhala.
8. R. Hoffmann. 1990. Creation and discovery. *Am. Sci.* 78:14–15.
9. B. Latour. 1987. *Science in Action*. Harvard Univ. Press.

Love Among the Robots

Melvin Konner

Melvin Konner, who teaches anthropology at Emory University in Atlanta, is on leave at the Center for Advanced Study in the Behavioral Sciences, in Stanford, California. His book is The Healing Artisans: A Journey of Initiation into Modern Medicine *(Viking).*

When I was a boy of sixteen or so, an episode of "The Twilight Zone" changed my life. Since I was a serious student, thoughtful and deeply religious, this rather unconventional source of a weltanschauung takes some explaining.

The show's plot was as follows: In some future society, a man has been exiled, after committing unnamed political offenses, to solitary imprisonment on an asteroid. Once a year he is visited by a supply ship, whose captain takes pity on him and brings him a present in a very large box. On opening the box after the ship has gone, the hero reacts with disgust: it is a female robot, a mere mechanical substitute for genuine companionship. The robot, however—portrayed by a most appealing actress—is remarkably lifelike and, after some fumbling and learning, appears completely human. In seeming (being?) palpably hurt by his rejections, she wins his first attention. One thing leads to another on this desolate orbiting rock, and by the supply ship's next visit, they have formed what must be construed as a powerful bond of affection. If the word has any meaning at all, they *love* each other.

The next year, the captain brings undreamed-of news; the winds of political change have blown a breath of amnesty from one end of the galaxy to the other. The hero can return home at last—but only he. The captain is smack up against his weight limit and, having failed to think of the android, has room for only one passenger. When reason fails to disabuse the hero of his sentimental attachment to the machine (the argument goes on painfully in the presence of this third

party, whose face is filled with tragic apprehension), the captain resorts to his ray gun, shooting the seeming woman in the face. The wound reveals a tangle of wiring and circuitry, and the robot's voice, repeatedly calling the hero's name, runs down like a record player with its plug suddenly pulled.

As I recall the final moments of this denouement, no tears were shed, and it appeared (though this was left to the viewer's imagination) that the hero would be brought to his senses and sent home to freedom a sadder but wiser man. But to me this was murder, not only unpunished but condoned, and I could not get it out of my mind. With all the intensity of adolescent idealism, I worked the issue through in my mind and a few days later gave up my belief in the insubstantiality of the soul. By virtue of her animated responses, her full range of thought and feeling, and, above all, her trust in and love for the hero—not to mention his for her—the android was human and had as much of a "soul" as any person, regardless of whether the hardware within was carbon or silicon. Or, to put it another, more distressing way, a human being could have no more of a soul than she.

In the years since I was so shaken by this fiction it has come a long way toward fact. Artificial intelligence, then an obscure undertaking confined to a few university campuses, is now a large commercial enterprise, and, according to its enthusiastic practitioners, such as Marvin Minsky, machines of the future will not only perform bigger calculations than humans ever could but will also make medical and legal judgments, perform psychotherapy, and compose beautiful music and poetry.

I suppose this prospect should be easier for me to accept now than it was twenty years ago. But in a way it is more unsettling than ever. For ten years or so, the relentless depredations of sociobiology—like the similarly motivated Freudian ones of an earlier era—have eroded, it seems, the very basis of the human spirit. The most cherished differences between humans and animals, one after another, have been swept aside: motherly love, altruism, cooperation, and sacrifice are now seen as mere adaptations—genetically programmed strategies for survival that we share with many other species. All that has been left to us after this beastly onslaught is rational thought; we are animals, yes, but thinking animals, and no other configuration of matter on Earth can rival us in this domain. Now even rational thought is being taken over—lock, stock, and memory board—by computers. The turf separating animal and machine is shrinking, and it is only human to wonder whether there will always be a place for us, and us alone, to stand.

The question of whether machines will ever be able to think is, in artificial intelligence—or AI—circles, commonly cast in terms of the Turing test, devised by the British computer scientist Alan M. Turing, who died in 1954. Turing imagined an "imitation game," in which a human interrogator communicates with two unseen people—a man and a woman—via teletype. The interrogator can ask any question he likes, the goal being to determine which is the man and which the woman. The catch is that the man will be trying to deceive him and is free to lie egregiously—claiming, for example, to have long, elaborately styled hair. The woman, Turing wrote, "can add such things as 'I am the woman, don't listen to him!' to her answers, but it will avail nothing as the man can make similar remarks." The questions that fascinated Turing were: What will happen when a machine replaces the man? Will the interrogator err as often as before? "These questions," he wrote, "replace our original, 'Can machines think?'"

The idiosyncrasies of this game may have had special significance to Turing, who was a homosexual, at a time when male homosexuality was a crime. (Some observers have attributed his death—an apparent suicide, involving a cyanide-laced apple—to harassment by the British government, which he had served nobly in the Second World War, breaking a critical and supposedly impregnable German code.) But the game can be recast so that it does not revolve around gender, and these days it usually is: a machine that could pass the Turing test is now defined as one that would fool a human interrogator into believing that it, too, is human.

The belief that someday a computer will pass this test—an article of faith for Minsky and like-minded computer scientists—has not gone unchallenged, of course. Humanists decry the claim that machines might think as people do, even as AI researchers try to develop machines that will decry the decrying humanists. The humanists' case rests, first of all, on what might be called the intuitional fallacy. This argument, as commonly stated, is that computers will never be able to do everything humans do, because computers rely exclusively on rules, whereas people act intuitively, with a keen but unspecifiable sort of inference from experience. Thus, no machine will ever beat a world champion at chess, and no computer will ever be a good physician.

But here the humanists often invoke a special pleading that borders on petulance. Hubert Dreyfus, a philosopher at the University of California at Berkeley, has written about the "failures" of medical-diagnosis systems. A program known as INTERNIST-I, given laboratory test data from real case histories, missed eighteen of forty-three diagnoses, he has noted, while a team of clinicians at Massachusetts General Hospital missed a mere fifteen, and a committee of medical experts only eight. So, if you get yourself a committee of medical experts to agonize over the data, as doctors rarely would, you get slightly fewer than half as many errors as with the machine; while if you settle for a team of clinicians at one of America's best teaching hospitals, you better the

program's error rate by just less than seventeen percent. It doesn't take much experience in medical practice to surmise that INTERNIST-I would probably outperform a large minority (at least) of American physicians, to say nothing of lesser-trained physicians in some parts of the world—and this at the very dawn of the use of such systems. Thus, Minsky and his colleagues properly brush aside the intuitional fallacy with allusions to the future. This aspect of what computers can't now do is technically, but not philosophically or scientifically, interesting.

The second argument humanists make, which might be called the intentional fallacy, is philosophically interesting but far from decisive. It amounts to a rejection of the Turing test. The contention is that, even if computers are someday able to accomplish the same intellectual tasks as humans, *thought* will not be the right word for the information processing behind their performance. The philosopher John Searle advanced this position in a 1980 paper, published in the journal *The Behavioral and Brain Sciences* with simultaneous replies by the great and near great of artificial intelligence and cognitive science, and with Searle's replies to the replies.

Searle's paper begins with his "Chinese room" argument: Imagine a room with no windows or doors, only a mail slot. Suppose you passed a story written in Chinese into the room, then passed in questions about the story, also in Chinese. Twenty minutes later, perfectly sensible, well-crafted answers come out of the slot, again in Chinese, suggesting that something in the room understands Chinese. But, said Searle, it might be that within the room was Searle himself, who understands no Chinese but was merely following rules he had been given for converting some kinds of foreign squiggles into other kinds. Thus, nowhere in the room is there true understanding of Chinese, even though the room behaved as if there were.

Among the criticisms of this argument that Searle did not convincingly answer are psychologist Bruce Bridgeman's—that not even humans are fully aware of the mental operations underlying conscious thought; computer scientist Douglas R. Hofstadter's—that the man in the Chinese room is functionally no more sophisticated than a few neurons, and that such a system could not possibly pull off anything so complex and subtle as language translation; and philosopher Richard Rorty's—that if the system really *could* pass this variant of the Turing test, it *would* understand Chinese, since a truly scientific definition of "understanding" must be stated in strictly behavioral

terms. Further, there is the behaviorist criticism (which Searle also answers unconvincingly): our skepticism that this system has a mind implies a skepticism of other minds in general—including human ones; if we can't infer thought from behavior, we must spend our lives wondering whether anyone on the planet other than ourselves is truly conscious. This, of course, is something that few of us see a compelling reason to do.

These criticisms, taken together, suggest that the Chinese room argument is specious. But even if they did not, Searle himself has acknowledged a loophole in his argument, one that is frequently overlooked in discussions of it. He believes that mind is a kind of insubstantial secretion of the brain and emanates from our neurochemistry, as dependent on physiology as is the milk from a mother's mammary glands. A mechanical system could have mind, he concedes, if it precisely simulated the physical processes of the brain. But most AI researchers make no attempt to reconstruct the flow of information that actually occurs in a mass of human neurons—much less to build surrogates of the neurons themselves. Rather, they try to duplicate only the relationship between input and output—between the slips of paper that go into the Chinese room and those that come out.

Enter the humanists' third argument, which AI enthusiasts might call the emotional fallacy, except that it isn't really a fallacy. This is the one presented by Sherry Turkle in *The Second Self: Computers and the Human Spirit.* The book is based on years of fieldwork among MIT computer hackers, AI experts and their groupies, and ordinary children playing computer games. Beginning in the late 1970s, when the age of personal computers was colorfully dawning, Turkle examined people's relationships with computers, in the twin senses of interaction and comparison. As she shows, these twins are Siamese: interaction with a computer involves an assessment, if unconscious, of how it compares to us, and comparison assumes some relationship (the Turing test, after all, implies as much).

Among Turkle's findings is that whether a machine can pass the Turing test depends on the mind of the beholder. To one five-year-old encountering it for the first time, Texas Instruments' Speak & Spell toy was alive. Other children, not convinced but clearly uneasy, took special delight in "killing" it by taking out the batteries—as if reaffirming their own uniqueness. Much more at ease with the idea of an animate machine were the hackers—college-aged people, usually men, who work, live, eat, sleep, and breathe computers. Hackers articulate frankly the satisfactions of their relationships with computers: complete devotion, predictability, and control—the kinds of things a person could never provide. As hackers themselves seem to recognize, their spirits have found in the computer a sort of superperson cut from the cloth of fantasy. The computer has passed the Turing test as posed by some of their most fundamental human needs.

But hackers are the exceptions. Most people feel the need to defend themselves from the computer's insult to their humanity. They do so, usually, by defining themselves in opposition to it: sure, the machine can play a dazzling game of chess, but only humans enjoy winning; it can diagnose illness, but only humans fear making a fatal mistake; it may have thought, but only humans have feelings. As Turkle realized, this is but a variation on the game of defining humans in opposition to animals. "Where we once were rational animals," she wrote, "now we are feeling computers, emotional machines."

We have come full circle, and our identity crisis remains unresolved. We say we are rational animals, but computers are more superbly rational; we say we are feeling machines, but other animals have the same vivid array of motives and feelings. The process of definition-by-exclusion would seem to have left us empty.

Of course, we are not. It is the intersection of the sets that makes us human—the tiny corner of the Venn diagram where animal motives overlap with mechanical rationality. It is the inner argument between the ache of sexual desire and the thought of ultimate consequence that produces the lover's plaint; the climbing of animal fear on the latticework of symbol that makes possible the comfort of ritual; the bubbling of the consciousness of our own mortality through everyday sensual experience that gives rise to the absolutely human sense of beauty.

Consider the example given by the computer scientist Joseph Weizenbaum, in *Computer Power and Human Reason,* of what computers can't simulate: the wordless communion that a mother and father share as they stand over their sleeping child's bed. Contained in their glances is the shared love growing out of the three relationships; the subtle memories of the sex that engendered the bonds; the life histories of the man and the woman—the events of their own childhoods echoing ineffably through the sleeper, the cascade of family dramas falling for generations; and, above all, the man's and the woman's sense of their own, and their child's, mortality—the fear, the grief, the intensified love of the things of this world.

Could computers simulate—perhaps even experience—this tragic sense of life? Simulate, possibly. But to experience it they would have to participate in a fully human life cycle. They would have to be born, grow, surrender themselves to some kind of family life, confront the demands of maturity, reproduce, age, and, especially, be conscious of the prospect of their dying. Not to mention their having to experience the aches and pains, the shivers and sweats, the hormonal flux, the sludge of fatigue, the neuronal dropout, and the nine-hundred-and-some-odd other natural shocks that flesh is heir to. As Turkle put it, "A being that is not born of a mother, that does not feel the vulnerability of childhood, a being that does not know sexuality or anticipate death, this being is alien."

But how well will Turkle's comforting contention fare in the future, when computers compose plainly good poems? In considering how we would respond to such poems, recall our response to the nice abstract paintings composed a few years ago by a chimpanzee. We were curious about them, admired them, even paid a good price for them, but we knew they were not real paintings. A machine much simpler than the simplest of computers could produce abstract paintings, some of which would be pleasing to the eye. But, like the chimp ones, they would not be real. Real paintings come out of human experience, respond to human traditions, are informed by human expectations even when they violate them.

Or consider poems written by children. These are often freer, more engaging, and lovelier than any the same child will be capable of writing when grown. So why don't we admire them the way we would similar ones written by adults? Because it is precisely the grown-up-ness of its source that makes the freedom and grace of a poem so admirable. A good poem by an adult is a communication from a person who, like the rest of us, has been ambushed by life but who has miraculously escaped the loss of the gracefulness that came easily in childhood—or, perhaps, has found a way artfully to recover it. In this sense a "good" poem by a computer would be of no more interest than the tragic drama typed by the random keystrokes of the proverbial roomful of monkeys—except, of course, for its value as scientific curiosity.

So what will it be like when computers are—as they will surely be—vastly smarter than we are in many ways? We will ask them, I think, to speculate about the influences of Shakespeare on Shelley, or maybe even expect them to suggest such a study, but we will not curl up near the fire with a slim volume of verse they have written. We will go to them for most sorts of medical diagnoses, maybe even for surgery. But, at our bedside, while we are dying, we will want someone who knows that he or she will also, someday, die. Computers will be, perhaps, like the gods of ancient Greece: incredibly powerful and even capable of many human emotions—but, because of their immortality, ineligible for admission into that warm circle of sympathy reserved exclusively for humans.

And what of the murdered android I mooned over at sixteen? I doubt that any robot could simulate emotion well enough to pass my ultimate Turing test: Does this machine have a tragic sense of life? Of course, my feelings toward her would not be irrelevant; relationships help define machines as they help define people, and the question of what constitutes murder hinges partly on how the murderer violates the relationship as he himself perceives it. Nonetheless, I would steel myself and apply my ultimate test; if she failed, even I might draw my ray gun.

This glossary of 216 computer terms is included to provide you with a convenient and ready reference as you encounter general terms in your study of computers in society which are unfamiliar or require a review. It is not intended to be comprehensive, but taken together with the many definitions included in the articles it should prove to be quite useful.

Alphanumerical   Data which consists of letters of the alphabet or numerals.

Analog Computer   A computer that measures continuous physical or electrical conditions rather than operating on digits like the digital computer.

Analytical Engine   A device developed by Charles Babbage that is similar in concept to modern digital computers; used cards to indicate the specific functions to be performed and to specify the actual data.

Application Software   Software designed to accomplish a specific task such as accounting, financial modeling, or word processing.

Artificial Intelligence   Hardware or software capable of performing functions that require learning or reasoning, e.g. a computer that plays chess.

ASCII   American Standard Code for Information Interchange. (Pronounced "as-key.") An industry standard referring to 128 codes generated by computers for text and control characters, for example, A = 65, Z = 90, a = 97.

Assembler   A language translator that converts a program written in assembly language to an equivalent program in machine language.

Assembly Language   A "simple" computer language that people can understand, though it is somewhat difficult to learn. Its user is able to write a program which the computer translates into machine language. *See* High Level Language *and* Machine Language.

Automatic Teller Machine (ATM)   A machine that provides 24-hour banking services.

Auxiliary Storage   A storage device in addition to the "core" or main storage of the computer. It includes magnetic tape, cassette tape, floppy disk, and hard disk. Sometimes called external storage or secondary storage.

Babbage, Charles   Frequently considered the father of the modern computer; in the early 1800s he outlined the ideas that have become the basis for modern computational devices.

Backup   An extra copy of information stored on a disk. If the program or other data stored on the first disk is damaged, it is still available on the backup copy.

BASIC   Beginners All-purpose Symbolic Instruction Code. A high level language, considered by many authorities to be the easiest language to learn, and used in one variation or another by almost all microcomputers.

Batch Processing   An approach to computer processing where groups of like transactions are accumulated (batched) to be processed at the same time.

Baud Rate   The speed of serial data transmission between computers or a computer and a peripheral in bits per second. The most common format uses eight "data bits" plus one "start bit" and one "stop bit," for a total of ten bits per character. Thus, dividing the baud rate by ten usually yields the transfer rate in characters per second.

Binary   The base-two number system. It is the simplest number system, since it has only two digits: 0 and 1. This is very simple to represent with electronic circuits and thus has become the basis for digital computers. Binary codes may be used to represent any alphanumeric character, such as the letter "A" (100 0001), the number 3 (000 0011), while other codes should be used to represent certain computer operations such as a line feed (000 1010).

Biochips   Minute computer circuits assembled from molecules; still in the developmental stage.

Bit   Binary digit. The smallest unit of digital information. It may have one of two values: 1 (or "high," "true," +5 volts) or 0 ("low," "false," 0 volts). 8 bits constitute one byte.

Board   Abbreviation for printed circuit board. A collection of electronic devices mounted on a material, often fiberglass, with copper traces forming the connections between the various devices. Can also refer to any of the peripheral devices that plug into the slots inside a microcomputer.

Boolean   An expression which evaluates to the logical value of true or false, e.g. 1 + 1 = 2 or 3 > 2.

Boot or **Bootstrapping**   To start the computer; to load an operating system into the computer's main memory and commence its operation.

Bubble Memory   A recently developed memory device in which data is represented by magnetized spots (or bubbles) that rest on the thin film of semiconductor material.

Buffer   A temporary memory which is capable of storing incoming data for later transmission. Often found on printers to allow the printer to accept information faster than it prints it.

Bug   An error. A hardware bug is a malfunction or design error in the computer or its peripherals; a software bug is a programming error.

BUS   A collection of wires that transmit information in the form of electrical signals from one circuit to another.

Byte   Eight bits (usually). The basic unit of data a microcomputer's CPU can handle. A byte can be used to represent any alphanumerical character or a number between 0 and 255 through combinations of 1s and 0s.

CAI   Computer Assisted Instruction or Computer Aided Instruction. An educational use of computers which usually entails using computer programs which drill, tutor, simulate or teach problem solving skills. *See also* CMI.

Card   Refers to a peripheral card which plugs into one of the internal slots in a microcomputer.

CAT   Computer Assisted Training. *See* CAI.

Cathode Ray Tube   *See* CRT.

CAT Scanner   A diagnostic device used for producing cross-sectional X-rays of a person's internal organs; an acronym for computer axial tomography.

Central Processing Unit   *See* CPU.

Chip   Integrated Circuit or IC. They appear as small, usually black rectangular pieces inside a microcomputer and on cards which contain electrical circuits.

CMI   Computer Managed Instruction. An educational use of computers which usually entails the use of computer programs to handle testing, grade-keeping, filing, and other classroom management tasks.

COBOL   COmmon Business Oriented Language. A high level language, used mostly in business.

Communications Network   The connecting of several computers so that they can share and exchange information between them.

Compatibility   1. Software compatibility refers to the ability to run the same software on a variety of computers. 2 Hardware compatibility refers to the ability to directly connect various peripherals to the computer.

Compiler   A program that translates a high level computer language into machine language for later execution. *See* Interpreter. This would be similar to a human translating an entire document from a foreign language into English for later reading by others.

CompuServe   Public access data base service providing general information.

Computer   Any device that can receive, store, and act as a set of instructions in a predetermined sequence, and that permits both the instructions and the data upon which the instructions act to be changed. The distinction between a computer and a programmable calculator is that the computer can manipulate text as well as numbers, whereas the calculator can only handle numbers.

Computer-Aided Design (CAD)   The use of the computer by an engineer to design, draft, and analyze a prospective product using computer graphics on a video terminal.

Computer-Aided Manufacturing (CAM)   The use of the computer by an engineer to simulate the required steps of the manufacturing process.

Computer Bulletin Board Service (CBBS)   A computerized data base users access to post and to retrieve messages.

Computer Literacy   Term used to refer to a person's capacity to intelligently use computers.

Computer Program   A series of commands, instructions, or statements put together in a way that tells a computer to perform a specific task or a series of tasks.

Configuration   A term used to refer to the computer and its peripheral devices designed to work as a unit.

Control Key   A special function key found on most computer keyboards which allows the user to use the remaining keys for other specialized operations.

Copy Protected   Refers to a disk that has had the DOS altered on it to prevent the disk from being either copied or written to.

Courseware   Instructional programs and related support materials needed to use computer software in the classroom.

CP/M   Control Program for Microprocessors. One of the first operating systems for small computers based on the 8080 (or Z-80) CPU. It has become a standard for software distribution among such computers since it allows a program written on one machine to run without any changes on any other computer that uses CP/M.

CPU   Central Processing Unit. The "brain" of the computer consisting of a large integrated circuit which performs the computations within a computer. CPU's are often designated by a number, such as 6502 , 8080, 8086, and so on.

CRT   Cathode-Ray Tube. A monitor; display screen.

Cursor   The prompting symbol usually displayed as a blinking white square on the monitor that shows where the next character will appear.

Daisy-Wheel Printer   An impact printer that prints by striking a wheel containing raised characters against an inked ribbon.

Data   All information, including facts, numbers, letters and symbols which can be acted upon or produced by the computer.

Data Bank   A commercially available computer data base that conveys news and reference data usually via telecommunications.

Data Base   A collection of related information, such as found on a mailing list, that can be stored in the computer and retrieved in several ways.

Data Base Management   1. Refers to a classification of software designed to act like an electronic filing cabinet, allowing the user to store, retrieve, and manipulate files. 2. The practice of using computers to assist in routine filing and information processing chores.

Debug   To go through a program or hardware device to correct mistakes.

Dedicated Computer   A computer that is used as a special-purpose device designed to satisfy the needs of a specific user in a specific way.

Dialects   Different versions of the same computer language, e.g. Integer BASIC, Applesoft BASIC, M-BASIC.

Digital Computer   The type of computer commonly used in business applications; operates on distinct data (e.g., digits represented with 0s and 1s) by performing arithmetic and logic processes on specific data units.

Digital Transmission   Transmission of data as distinct "on" and "off" pulses.

Disk, Diskettes   A thin plastic wafer-like object enclosed in a plastic jacket with a metallic coating used to magnetically store information. On many microcomputers the standard size is 5¼ inches in diameter, though many are beginning to use smaller (3.25 inches or 3.5 inches diameter) diskettes stored in more rigid jackets.

Disk Drive   A peripheral device capable of reading and writing information on a disk.

Disk Envelope   A removable protective paper sleeve used when handling or storing a disk; must be removed before inserting in a disk drive.

Disk Jacket   A nonremovable protective covering for a disk, usually black plastic or paper, within which the disk spins when being used by the disk drive.

Disk Operating System   *See* DOS.

Display Screen   A peripheral which allows for the visual output of information for the computer on a CRT, monitor, or similar device.

Documentation   Instructional materials that describe the operations of an individual computer program or a piece of system hardware.

DOS   Disk Operating System. (Pronounced to rhyme with "boss.") Refers to the program which enables a computer to read and write on a disk.

Dot-Matrix   A type of printing in which characters are formed by using a number of closely spaced dots.

Double-Sided   Refers to disks capable of being read from or written to on both of its sides.

Downtime   Any period of time when the computer is not available or is not working.

Dumb Terminal   Refers to a keyboard which can be used to input information into a computer but which lacks the capacity to manipulate information transmitted to it from the host computer. *See* Intelligent Terminal.

Dump   Mass copying of memory on a storage device such as a disk to another storage device or a printer so it can be used as backup or analyzed for errors.

Electronic Bulletin Board   An electronic data base used as a bulletin board where messages are left.

Electronic Data Processing (EDP)   In current terminology, EDP refers to the processing of data by electronic digital computers.

Electronic Funds Transfer System (EFT)   A system that eliminates the exchange of cash or checks by automatically transferring funds from one account to another.

Electronic Mail   Sending and receiving information by computer.

ELIZA   A program that simulates human responses and provides some insight into language analysis.

ENIAC   An electronic computer designed by J. Presper Eckert, Jr.

Electronic Worksheet   *See* Spreadsheet.

Ergonomics   The science of changing working conditions to suit the worker in an attempt to eliminate stress and physical problems.

Error Handling   The response a program is designed to make when an incorrect or unanticipated response is entered by the user.

Error Message   A message displayed or printed to notify the user of an error or problem in the execution of a program.

Expert Systems   Software packages designed to copy how expert humans in a certain field think through a problem to reach the correct solution.

Exponential Notation   Refers to how a computer displays very large or very small numbers by means of the number times ten raised to some power. For example, 3,000,000 could be printed as 3E + 6 (three times ten to the sixth power).

External Storage   *See* Auxiliary Storage.

Fan Fold   A type of paper that can continuously feed into a printer (usually via tractor feed).

Firmware   Those components of a computer system consisting of programs stored in read-only memory (ROM). Installed in the factory, they may be executed at any time but they may not be modified or erased from main memory. *See* Hardware *and* Software.

First-Generation Computers   Developed in the 1950s; used vacuum tubes; faster than earlier mechanical devices, but very slow compared to today's computer.

Fixed Disk   *See* Hard Disk.

Floppy, Floppy Disk   *See* Disk.

Format   (n) The physical form in which information appears. (v) To specify parameters of a form or to write address codes on a blank disk in preparation for using it to store data or programs. *See* Initialize.

FORTRAN   FORmula TRANslation. A high level language used primarily for mathematical computations; though FORTRAN is used by some microcomputers, it is mainly used by mainframe computers.

Fourth-Generation Computers   The era of large-scale integrated circuits and microprocessors.

Gigaflops   A measurement of processing speed. One NEC supercomputer can operate at 1.3 gigaflops or 1.3 billion floating point operations per second.

Gigo   Garbage In, Garbage Out. Serves to remind us that a program is only as good as the information and instructions in the program.

Graphics   1. Information presented in the form of pictures or images. 2. The display of pictures or images on a computer's display screen.

Hard Copy   A paper copy of the computer's output.

Hard Disk   A magnetically coated metal disk, usually permanently mounted within a disk drive; capable of storing 30 to 150 times more information than can a floppy disk.

Hardware   Refers to the computer and all its peripheral devices. The physical pieces of the computer.

Head   Refers to the component of a disk drive or tape system that magnetically reads or writes information to the storage medium.

Hex or **Hexidecimal**   A numbering system based on 16 (digits 0-9 and letters A-F) rather than on 10. Most computers operate using hex numbers. Each hexidecimal digit corresponds to a sequence of four binary digits or bits.

High Level Language   An English-like computer language (BASIC, Pascal, FORTRAN, Logo, COBOL) designed to make it relatively convenient for a person to prepare a program for a computer, which in turn translates it into machine language for execution.

Hub Ring   A metal or hard plastic reinforcement device used in the middle hole of floppy disks to help prevent wear and disk damage.

IC   Integrated Circuit. *See* Chip.

Initialize   1. To set an initial state or value in preparation for some computation. 2. To prepare a blank disk to receive information by dividing its surface into tracks and sectors. *See* Format.

Input   Information entered into the computer.

Integrated Circuit   *See* Chip.

Intelligent Terminal   A terminal that is capable of doing more than just receiving or transmitting data due to its microprocessor. *See* Dumb Terminal.

Interactive   Describes a computer system in which a two-way conversation occurs between the user and the computer.

Interface   (v) To connect two pieces of computer hardware together. (n) The means by which two things communicate. In particular, it refers to the electrical configuration that allows two or more devices to pass information. *See* Interface Card.

Interface Card   A board used to connect a microcomputer to peripheral devices.

Interpreter   A language translator that reads a program written in a particular programming language and immediately carries out the actions that the program describes. This would be similar to a human providing simultaneous translation of another person who was speaking in a foreign language. *See* Compiler.

I/O   Input/Output. Refers usually to one of the slots or the game port in a microcomputer to which peripheral devices may be connected.

Joy Stick   An input device, often used to control the movement of objects on the video display screen of a computer for games.

K   Kilo or 1000. In terms of memory, it is actually equal to 1024.

KB   Kilo byte. Commonly used to refer to the memory size of a computer.

Keyboard   The typewriter-like keys on a microcomputer. Each microcomputer will have basically the same keyboard as a typewriter, major differences limited to special function keys such as ESCape, RESET, ConTROL, etc.

Language A code that the computer understands; a low level language resembles the fundamental codes of the computer; high level languages resemble English.

Light Pen An input device, shaped much like a mechanical pencil, which when touched to a display screen, can be used to select or execute certain computer functions.

LISP LISt Processing; a programming language primarily used in artificial intelligence research.

Local Area Networks (LANs) Linking computer systems in adjacent offices and buildings for intercomputer communication.

Log On To execute the necessary commands to allow you to use a computer. May involve the use of a password. More common on mainframe systems.

Logo A high level language specifically designed so that it may be used by both small children and adults. It involves a "turtle"-shaped cursor for much of its operation.

M *See* Megabyte.

Machine Language A fundamental, complex computer language used by the computer itself to perform its functions. This language is quite difficult for the average person to read or write.

Magnetic Ink Character Recognition (MICR) Devices Computer hardware capable of reading characters imprinted with magnetic ink, such as on checks.

Mainframe Refers to large computers used primarily in business, industry, government, and higher education which have the capacity to deal with many users simultaneously and to process large amounts of information quickly and in very sophisticated ways. *See* Time Share.

Management Information System (MIS) A systems approach that treats business departments as integrated parts of one total system rather than as separate entities. This approach aims at facilitating the flow of information and at providing management with greater decision-making power.

MB *See* Megabyte.

Megabyte 1,048,576 bytes.

Memory Chips in the computer which have the capacity to store information. *See* RAM, ROM, PROM.

Menu The list of programs available on a given disk.

Menu Driven Refers to software in which the program prompts the user with a list of available options at any given time, thus freeing the user from needing to memorize commands.

Microcomputer Refers to a generation of small, self-contained relatively inexpensive computers based on the microprocessor.

Microprocessor Core of the CPU, it holds all of the essential elements for manipulating data and performing arithmetic operations. A microprocessor is contained on a single IC.

Microsecond One millionth of a second.

Millisecond One thousandth of a second; abbreviated "ms."

Minicomputer Refers to a class of computers larger than micros but smaller than mainframe computers, many of which support multiple keyboards and output devices simultaneously.

Modem Modulator/demodulator. A peripheral device that enables the computer to transmit and receive information over a telephone line.

Monitor Video display similar to a television used as a means of displaying output. It differs from a TV in that resolution is usually better, and some come in green or amber screens, making the reading of textual information somewhat easier on the eyes than a black and white screen; a CRT.

Motherboard The main circuit board of a computer.

Mouse An input device about the size of a pack of cigarettes which, as it is moved across a flat surface, correspondingly moves the cursor on the CPU screen.

Multiphasic Screening The computer assists the physician by giving a preliminary analysis of the patient's history and current medical symptoms.

Nanosecond One billionth of a second; abbreviated "ns."

National Crime Information Center (NCIC) A computerized information center maintained by the FBI which serves agencies throughout the United States.

National Security Agency This agency protects U.S. communications from intrusion by foreign powers, and collects intelligence data to be disseminated to other agencies for their use.

Network A structure capable of linking two or more computers by wire, telephone lines, or radio links.

Nibble 1. Half a byte. 2. Refers to copy programs which copy small portions of a disk at a time, often used to copy otherwise copy-protected programs.

Noise Refers to signals which can interfere with the operation of a computer. Such signals can be generated by sources such as fluorescent lights or electric motors.

Non-Volatile Memory Memory that retains data even after power has been shut off. ROM is non-volatile; RAM is volatile.

Numeric Keypad An input device which allows the user to input numbers into a microcomputer with a calculator-like key arrangement.

Online (Processing) System A system that allows the user to interact with the computer during program execution; it permits direct communication between the user and computer.

Operating System A group of programs that act as intermediary between the computer and the applications software; the operating system takes a program's commands and passes them down to the CPU in a language that the CPU understands; application programs must be written for a specific operating system such as DOS 3.3, PRO-DOS, MS-DOS, TRS-DOS, CP/M and others.

Optical Character Recognition (OCR) Devices Computer hardware capable of reading typed or handwritten documents.

Optical Laser Disk A new high-capacity medium for data storage utilizing laser technology.

Output Information sent out of the computer system to some external destination such as the display screen, disk drive, printer, or modem.

Pascal A high level language, with a larger, more complex vocabulary than BASIC, used for complex applications in business, science, and education; named after the seventeenth-century French mathematician.

Password A code word or group of characters required by a computer program to allow the user to execute certain functions. Passwords may, for example, allow a user to read but not write records, or read only certain portions of records.

Peripheral Hardware attachments to a microcomputer, e.g. printer, modem, monitor, disk drives or interface card.

Peripheral Card   A removable printed-circuit board that plugs into a microcomputer's expansion slot and expands or modifies the computer's capabilities by connecting a peripheral device or performing some subsidiary or peripheral function.

Personal Computer (PC)   A microcomputer used for personal tasks.

Picosecond   One trillionth (10^{12}) of a second.

PLATO   The largest available CAI system; an acronym for Programmed Logic for Automatic Teaching Operations.

PILOT   Programmed Inquiry, Learning, or Teaching. A high level language designed primarily for use by educators, which facilitates the writing of computer assisted instruction lessons that include color graphs, sound effects, lesson text, and answer checking.

Pixel   Picture element. Refers to the smallest point of light that can be displayed on a display screen.

Plotter   A printing mechanism capable of drawing lines rapidly and accurately for graphic representation.

Port   An input or output connection to the computer.

Printer   A peripheral device which allows one to make permanent copies of programs, output, screen displays, and graphics.

Printout   See Hardcopy.

Privacy Act of 1974   This is concerned with data banks of personal information that are maintained by federal agencies.

Program   A list of instructions which allows the computer to perform a function.

Programmer   One who writes computer programs.

Programming   The activity of writing a program.

PROM   Programmable ROM. A ROM that is programmed after it has been made.

RAM   Random Access Memory. The main working memory of any computer. In most microcomputers, anything stored in RAM will be lost when the power is shut off.

Read Only Memory   See ROM.

Real Time   Refers to the capability of a system or device to receive data, process it, and provide output fast enough to control an activity being performed.

RF Modulator   Radio Frequency modulator. Refers to a device which converts video signals generated by the computer to signals which can be displayed on a television set.

Robotics   The science of designing and building robots.

ROM   Read Only Memory. A memory device in which information is permanently stored as it is being made. Thus it may be read but not changed.

Run   1. To execute a program. 2. A command to load a program into main memory from a peripheral storage medium, such as a disk, and execute it.

Save   To store a program on a disk or somewhere other than a computer's memory.

Screen   A CRT or display screen.

Second-Generation Computers   Used transistors; smaller, faster, and had larger storage capacity than the first-generation computers; first computers to use a high-level language.

Semiconductor   A transistor used as a type of primary storage medium that stores data in bit cells located on silicon chips.

Serial   A form of data transmission in which information is passed one bit at a time in sequence.

Simulation and Modeling   A technique in which mathematical data are analyzed and the results used to generate models or to make projections based upon this real data.

Software   The programs used by the computer. Often refers to the programs as stored on a disk.

Speech Synthesizer   Refers to a peripheral output device which attempts to mimic human speech.

Spreadsheet   Refers to software designed to emulate the forms used by accountants to keep financial records. Such programs have the capacity to perform many calculations and answer "what if?" questions such as "What if our income was to decline by ten percent?"

Supercomputers   These are machines that have capabilities beyond even the large-scale systems. Their speed is in the range of a million instructions per second.

System   An organized collection of hardware, software, and peripheral equipment that works together. See Configuration.

Telecommunication   Transmission of information between two computers in different locations, usually over telephone lines.

Telecommunications Network   A means by which one or more mainframes is linked to other computers for communication.

Teleconferencing   Conferences using electronic and/or image-producing means to communicate, thus eliminating the time and expense of traveling.

Terminal   A piece of equipment used to communicate with a computer, such as a keyboard for input, or video monitor or printer for output.

Third Generation   Refers to the present generation of computers based on microchips. Compare to first generation (tubes) and second generation (transistors).

Time Share   Refers to the practice of accessing a large computer from a remote location and paying for services based on the amount of computer time used. See Mainframe.

Tractor Feed   A mechanism used to propel paper through a printer by means of sprockets attached to the printer which engage holes along the paper's edges.

Turing Test   A person asks questions, and on the basis of the answers, must determine if the respondent is another human being or a machine.

TTY   TeleTypeWriter. A communications device used by the deaf.

Universal Product Code (UPC)   A bar code that appears on virtually all consumer goods; can be read by a scanner or wand device used in point-of-sale systems.

UNIX   An operating system developed for use on minicomputers when several users would be using the minicomputer at the same time. Now it has been adapted for use on several microcomputers.

User-Friendly   Refers to hardware or software which is relatively easy for a new operator to learn, and which has features to help eliminate operator error.

User Group   An association of people who meet to exchange information about computers or computer applications.

Video Monitor   See CRT; Display Screen.

Videotex   A service that provides two-way information capabilities using TV-like screens and computers.

VisiCalc   A popular spreadsheet program marketed by VisiCorp and Software Arts Inc.

Voice Recognition System   A system that allows the user to "train" the computer to understand his or her voice and vocabulary. The user must follow only the patterns the computer is programmed to recognize.

Volatile   Refers to memory that is erased whenever the power is removed, such as RAM.

Von Neumann Bottleneck   Data traffic jams created because of the way computers sequentially execute their programs; one of the reasons computers cannot attain maximum efficiency and speed.

Weizenbaum, Joseph   Author of a program called ELIZA, which not only simulates human responses but provides some insight into language analysis.

Word Processing   Refers to the use of computers as electronic typewriters capable of entering and retrieving text, storing it on disks, and performing a wide range of editing functions.

Worksheet   Refers to a paper or electronic "sheet" containing rows and columns used by accountants and accounting programs such as VisiCalc; sometimes referred to as a template.

Write-Enable Notch   A notch in a floppy disk which, if uncovered, allows a disk drive to write information to it, and which if covered, prohibits such writing.

Write-Protect Tab   A small adhesive sticker used to write-protect a disk by covering the write-enable notch.

Write Protected   A disk in which the "write-enable" notch is either missing or has had a write-protected tab placed over it to prevent information from being written to the disk.

Sources for the Glossary Include:

"VisiCalc Glossary," *Apple Orchard,* July-August 1982.

Apple Computer Incorporated, *Apple IIe Owner's Manual,* Cupertino, CA, 1982.

Computer-Based Training Start Kit, Department of Treasury, Internal Revenue Service, Document 6846 (5-83).

"Apple II New User's Guide," and B. Gibson, "Personal Computers in Business: An Introduction and Buyer's Guide," *MECC,* Apple Computer, Inc., 1982.

"Glossary of Computer Terms," *Printout,* April 1983.

"Glossary of Computer Terms," S. Richardson, *Noteworthy,* Winter 1982, pp. 27-29.

Softalk, January 1983, January 1982.

Stephen J. Taffee, Department of Education, North Dakota State University.

"Using the Computer in the Classroom," *Today's Education,* April-May 1982.

SELECTED REFERENCES
(Of Works Cited in the Introduction and Overviews)

Evans, Christopher. (1979). The Micro Millenium. New York: Washington Square Press.
Florman, Samuel C. (1986). "Technology and the Tragic View." In Albert H. Teich (ed.), Technology and the Future (4th ed.). New York: St. Martin's Press.
Kocker, Bryan. (1989). "President's Letter." Communications of the ACM, June: 660, 662.
Locke, Margaret (1989). "Reaching Consensus About Death: Heart Transplants and Cultural Identity in Japan." Society/Societe, Vol. 13(1): 15–26.

Lowe, Graham S. (1991). "Computers in the Workplace." Perspectives on Labour and Income (Statistics Canada), Vol. 3(2): 38–50.
Masuda, Yoneji. (1981). The Information Society as Post-Industrial Society. Washington, D.C.: The World Future Society.
McWilliams, Peter A. (1984). The Personal Computer Book. Garden City, New York: Quantum Press.
Samarajiva, Rohan (1989). "Appropriate High-Tech: Scientific Communication Options for Small Third World Countries." The Information Society 6(1/2): 29–46.

Credits/ Acknowledgments

Cover design by Charles Vitelli

1. The Changing Economy
Facing overview—United States Steel Corporation.

2. Employment and the Workplace
Facing overview—Steelcase. 49-50—Courtesy of the Veterans Administration Medical Center.

3. Hardware and Software Reliability
Facing overview—IBM Corporation.

4. Social Participation in the Information Age
Facing overview—Wharton Econometric Associates, Inc. Photo by Don Walker.

5. Ethical and Legal Issues
Facing overview—United Nations photo by Andrea Brizzi. 99—Apple Computers.

6. Privacy and Freedom of Information in the Information Age
Facing overview—TRW.

7. Issues from the World Scene
Facing overview—IBM Corporation.

8. Philosophical Issues: Human Nature, Mind, and Intelligence
Facing overview—Medical World News.

ANNUAL EDITIONS ARTICLE REVIEW FORM

■ NAME: _____ DATE: _____

■ TITLE AND NUMBER OF ARTICLE: _____

■ BRIEFLY STATE THE MAIN IDEA OF THIS ARTICLE: _____

_____

_____

_____

_____

■ LIST THREE IMPORTANT FACTS THAT THE AUTHOR USES TO SUPPORT THE MAIN IDEA:

_____

_____

_____

_____

_____

_____

■ WHAT INFORMATION OR IDEAS DISCUSSED IN THIS ARTICLE ARE ALSO DISCUSSED IN YOUR TEXTBOOK OR OTHER READING YOU HAVE DONE? LIST THE TEXTBOOK CHAPTERS AND PAGE NUMBERS:

_____

_____

_____

_____

_____

_____

_____

■ LIST ANY EXAMPLES OF BIAS OR FAULTY REASONING THAT YOU FOUND IN THE ARTICLE:

_____

_____

_____

_____

■ LIST ANY NEW TERMS/CONCEPTS THAT WERE DISCUSSED IN THE ARTICLE AND WRITE A SHORT DEFINITION:

_____

_____

_____

_____

_____

*Your instructor may require you to use this Annual Editions Article Review Form in any number of ways:
for articles that are assigned, for extra credit, as a tool to assist in developing assigned papers, or simply
for your own reference. Even if it is not required, we encourage you to photocopy and use this page;
you'll find that reflecting on the articles will greatly enhance the information from your text.

COMPUTER STUDIES: COMPUTERS IN SOCIETY
Fourth Edition
Article Rating Form

Here is an opportunity for you to have direct input into the next revision of this volume. We would like you to rate each of the 48 articles listed below, using the following scale:

1. **Excellent: should definitely be retained**
2. **Above average: should probably be retained**
3. **Below average: should probably be deleted**
4. **Poor: should definitely be deleted**

Your ratings will play a vital part in the next revision. So please mail this prepaid form to us just as soon as you complete it.
Thanks for your help!

Annual Editions revisions depend on two major opinion sources: one is our Advisory Board, listed in the front of this volume, which works with us in scanning the thousands of articles published in the public press each year; the other is you—the person actually using the book. Please help us and the users of the next edition by completing the prepaid article rating form on this page and returning it to us. Thank you.

Rating	Article	Rating	Article
	1. Science and the American Experiment		25. Closing the Net
	2. Borderline Cases		26. Is Nothing Private?
	3. Why Japan Loves Robots and We Don't		27. Read This!!!!!!!!
	4. Taming the Wild Network		28. Prepare for E-Mail Attack
	5. Does Corporate Nationality Matter?		29. Absolutely Not Confidential
	6. The Myth of a Post-Industrial Economy		30. Our Chip Has Come In
	7. Tying One On		31. Caller Identification: More Privacy or Less?
	8. The Skilling of America		
	9. Invasion of the Service Robots		32. The Magnetic-Field Menace
	10. Telecommuters Bring the Office Home		33. Premature Alarm Over Electromagnetic Fields
	11. Do It Yourself		
	12. Challenging the Myth of Disability		34. A System On Overload
	13. Hey You! Make Way for My Technology!		35. Programmed for Disaster
	14. The Doctor Is On		36. Robowar
	15. Virtual Reality		37. Personal Computers and the World Software Market
	16. America's Ignorance of Science and Technology Poses a Threat to the Democratic Process Itself		38. Academic Computing: The Los Andes Strategy
	17. The Lesson Every Child Need Not Learn		39. New Dimensions in Creativity
	18. Debunking Computer Literacy		40. Space Age Shamans: The Videotape
	19. Photographs That Lie: The Ethical Dilemma of Digital Retouching		41. Tough Search for Talent
			42. Why Transplants Don't Happen
	20. Warning: Here Come the Software Police		43. Last Rights
	21. Software Patents		44. Designing Computers That Think the Way We Do
	22. Programs to the People		
	23. Legally Speaking: Can Hackers Be Sued for Damages Caused by Computer Viruses?		45. Is the Brain's Mind a Computer Program?
			46. Could a Machine Think?
			47. Is Thinking Computable?
	24. Time Bomb: Inside the Texas Virus Trial		48. Love Among the Robots

(Continued on next page)

ABOUT YOU

Name_____ Date_____

Are you a teacher? ☐   Or student? ☐

Your School Name _____

Department _____

Address _____

City _____ State _____ Zip _____

School Telephone # _____

YOUR COMMENTS ARE IMPORTANT TO US!

Please fill in the following information:

For which course did you use this book? _____

Did you use a text with this Annual Edition?   ☐ yes   ☐ no

The title of the text? _____

What are your general reactions to the Annual Editions concept?

Have you read any particular articles recently that you think should be included in the next edition?

Are there any articles you feel should be replaced in the next edition? Why?

Are there other areas that you feel would utilize an Annual Edition?

May we contact you for editorial input?

May we quote you from above?

COMPUTER STUDIES: COMPUTERS IN SOCIETY, Fourth Edition

BUSINESS REPLY MAIL

First Class   Permit No. 84   Guilford, CT

Postage will be paid by addressee

The Dushkin Publishing Group, Inc.
Sluice Dock
DPG **Guilford, Connecticut 06437**

No Postage
Necessary
if Mailed
in the
United States